Confessions of a Dedicated Englishman

Also by David English

Bunbury Tails

Bunnybados

Bunbury's Play Ball

Rajbun's Story

Tale of Two Kitties

A Winter's Tail

Bunburys Down Under

Bunchester United

Bun Noel

The Bumper Bunbury Album

Bee Gees: The Legend

Mad Dogs and the Englishman

DAVID ENGLISH

Confessions of a
Dedicated Englishman

The hilarious, heartwarming and
heady world of the actor, music producer and
'Godfather of English cricket'

MACMILLAN

First published 2006 by Macmillan
an imprint of Pan Macmillan Ltd
Pan Macmillan, 20 New Wharf Road, London N1 9RR
Basingstoke and Oxford
Associated companies throughout the world
www.panmacmillan.com

ISBN-13: 978-1-4050-5361-7
ISBN-10: 1-4050-5361-5

1 3 5 7 9 8 6 4 2

A CIP catalogue record for this book is available from
the British Library.

Typeset by SetSystems Ltd, Saffron Walden, Essex
Printed and bound in Great Britain by
Mackays of Chatham plc, Chatham, Kent

'Rare, Precious and Beautiful'

This book is dedicated to Amy Rose, David, Chloe Avalon, Annie, Robyn English, Barry and Linda Gibb, Eric Clapton, Ian Botham, Sir Viv Richards, 'Miami' Johnny Cousins, Naynesh Desai and to all the Bunburys throughout the world.

CONTENTS

Special thanks to:

Soulmate Lady Jane Cruder and my niece Medha Laud.

'K.C.' Keith Curtis and David Betteridge for their dazzling photography.

Rt Hon Richard Caborn, Lady Leonie Phillips, David Morgan,
David Collier and Hugh Morris at the ECB, Ken Lake and ESCA, Colin
Graves, Nick Ivil, Ray Merridew, Paul Thwaites, Joe Cuby, Dame Lisa
Robson, Louise Agran, Frankie MacGregor, Neil Eckert, Phil Toms,
Michelle Shaya, Sarah Pritchard, Paul and Rachel Beck, John Hurst,
Hugh Williams, Robin Ford, Bobby Baker, Peter Danks, Toby Davidson,
Nigel Wray, Andrew Varley, Stephanie Thorburn, Andrew Peters, Julian
Stansfield, Lynn Wilson, John Morgan, John Goldsmith, Lord Liverpool,
Dr 'Willi' Harris, Andy Jacobs, Paul Hawksbee, Liam Fisher, Keith
Perry, Robert Philip, Gareth Davies, Lord MacLaurin, Kirti Patel, Simon
Dyson, Rod Marsh, Troy Cooley, Peter Moores, Peter Wright, Karen
Mogilner, Diana Haddesley, Romel and the boys at 'The Day of the Raj'
(Britain's finest restaurant), Johnny Shine, Chris Durand, Edward Ben-
tall, Chris Laing, Holly Bellingham, Simon Turner, Lord Richard Atten-
borough, Robert Stigwood, Stephen Fry, Piers Morgan, Paul McGee,
Dave Pett, Michael Wilson and Edgegrove School, Mike Milton and
Finchley CC, Dilys Clarke, Peter Mellor, Whitefields School, Stephanie
Thorburn, Steve Lovell, Alan Coates, Steve, Ashley, Travis, Mickey and
Ali Gibb, Dick Ashby, Ron and Marina Hobson, Debbie Frost, Billy and
the gang at Mill Hill PO, Bobby the Milk, Dave Chapman . . . and extra
special thanks to Esther from Bordeaux, Brigitte Bardot from St Tropez,
Robert Graves in his chair and the magnificent Richard Milner and the
brilliant team at Pan Macmillan.

FOREWORD BY STEPHEN FRY

'What you really are is a Bunburyist. I was quite right in saying you were a Bunburyist. You are one of the most advanced Bunburyists I know.'

OSCAR WILDE *The Importance of Being Earnest*

Those of us who paid careful attention to the glorious triumphs of the England Test side last summer may have noticed, amongst the unparalleled hoopla and hullabaloo of the press, mention made from time to time of David English and the Bunbury Cricket Club. Headlines like 'The Godfather of English Cricket', 'England's Secret Weapon', 'English and England' and 'Where the Ashes Were Really Won' may have puzzled some of the hundreds of thousands of new converts to the summer game.

If England were ever going to beat Australia, surely it would be through professionalism, supreme physical fitness, modern sports psychology, the killer instinct, wanting it more? What part could possibly be played by a cricket club founded on principles of fun, friendship and frolic? How could the brainchild of an eccentric (to the point of sectionable derangement) music-industry guru have anything to do with what will be for all time known as The Greatest Ashes Season Ever?

No one could deny that the England squad responsible for the monumental Test rubber of 2005 displayed all the virtues demanded of modern sportsmen. Athleticism, tactical and strategic brilliance, pitiless finishing and technical superiority were at last on display for all to see. But were those the qualities that got us talking about cricket as never before in pubs, clubs, shops, offices, schools and sitting rooms around the nation? Wasn't there something else? The images that first come to mind are those of Michael Vaughan holding Freddie Flintoff by the ears, a smile on his face as broad as the Vale of York and, above all, Flintoff's arm around the shoulder of a forlorn Brett Lee at the end of that imponderably great second Test match. Respect for the enemy, comradeship and delight in each other's company, pleasure in the achievements of fellow players and genuine sympathy and help offered when things went wrong – these old-fashioned virtues of sportsmanship, warmth and passion were surely the defining memories? For all their admirable and necessary professionalism, this was an England side that knew that cricket is not a sport, but a game. A game to be played hard, certainly, but a game that responds badly to sulking, meanness and cold-hearted calculation, a game that cannot be won by a fighting unit alone, no matter how tough, but can be won, and won gloriously, by a team.

Would Ashley Giles have come back to make the crucial break-throughs he made had the side been no more than a ruthless fighting machine? Would each of the players have been able to ride out their inevitable moments of disappointment and failure if this were a squad of individuals? Of course there were technical reasons behind the great win: superiority with reverse swing, ingenious planning and so forth, but let us not overlook the importance of that hoary old quality team spirit. I wouldn't want to overstate it and get all mawkish, but nor would I want it to be ignored. I believe that the spirit in which the series was played explains not just the triumph but the nation's delirious response to it. We were all as proud of the manner of the victory as of the fact of it.

The part played by David English and the Bunbury Cricket Club cannot be overlooked. When Flintoff, Vaughan, Trescothick, Harmison, Hoggard, Bell, Collingwood and Giles were young teenagers they found a mentor and father-figure in David and a vital part of their completion as cricketers in the absorption of the Bunbury spirit. It was here they learned the truth that for success at the highest level sportsmanship and professionalism are far from incompatible: they are essential. One without the other is useless. Sportsmanship is not a sentimental extra bolted on to please old fools like me; it is a vital ingredient in forging a team that guarantees to get the most out of each individual. Golfers may have to pay psychologists to investigate the darkest inner recesses of their egos and identities, but cricketers thrive when they play for each other, not for themselves.

There are other cricket clubs of course: grand outfits like I Zingari and the Free Foresters, the MCC itself and many more, but the Bunbury Cricket Club has become the institution where talented youngsters thrive in an atmosphere not of terrifying competition (they'll get plenty of that at school and county level) but of comradeship, banter and encouragement. It is not a training ground for technique, it is no kind of replacement for a national academy, but rather something much rarer, a place where the young are allowed to take pleasure in their talents, to glory in the idea of cricket. The mighty grin on the face of Flintoff was a Bunbury grin. With respect to Wilde, the true Bunburyist understands the importance of not being earnest . . .

Another season beckons. More youngsters will learn those lessons, more of us broken-down old cricket lovers will get a chance to parade in our yellowing whites, more money will be raised for the Bunbury charities and, most of all, more friendships will be forged in a spirit of laughter and the shared love of cricket.

FOREWORD BY PIERS MORGAN

I think it was when I dropped a catch while standing ten rows into the stunning new OCS stand at the Oval that I realized what it was to be a Bunbury cricketer.

Or perhaps it was when the former boxer Lloyd Honeyghan took two sensational one-handed catches at cover while speaking on his mobile phone.

Actually, having given it more thought, I think the pivotal Bunbury moment for me came when Sir Viv Richards was run out first ball that day, batting in his own charity game, and refused all desperate pleas from players on both sides to bat on.

It was the most extraordinary day's cricket I have ever been involved in, but no less than I expected from an event organized by the Loon, David English.

'Piers mate, journalistic legend, TV superstar, you must come and play for the Bunburys, you'll love it!' he shrieked excitedly down the phone.

Flattery always works with me, mainly because I get so little of it.

'It's at the Oval, next Friday, and you'll be playing against a Sir Viv Richards eleven.'

WHAT? I was going to step onto that hallowed Test match turf to pit my wits against the most ferocious and brilliant batsman I have ever seen?

Cancel all engagements. I'm there.

When the great day arrived I was shockingly nervous and

ludicrously early – having made the fatal error of asking English what time I should get there.

'11 a.m. start, maestro; don't be late.'

Late? I was so early they literally had to open the gates for me. English himself ambled in at midday, Sir Viv around 1 p.m., and the rest of our stars seemingly whenever they felt like it. But no matter; I was in the Surrey dressing room, had picked Mark Butcher's locker (well let's face it, it wasn't getting much use last season) and was swapping very bad jokes with Frank Skinner.

Word came that Sir Trevor McDonald had pulled out sick at the last minute, but the good news was that his replacement as main ITN news anchorman Mark Austin was playing instead and was a much better cricketer.

Suddenly English called me over and said, rather ominously, that it was time for my 'induction ceremony'. I braced myself for the worst but all it consisted of was him holding my shoulders and chanting:

> *A Bunbury stands for freedom,*
> *Stands for fun,*
> *Stands for ever being young;*
> *So do a good turn unto others,*
> *Never turn from your quest,*
> *For you are a Bunbury*
> *And a Bunbury does his best.*

He then presented me with my Bunbury sweater. It was all strangely moving. I suddenly felt part of a rather special club, one built on foundations of integrity, charitable purpose and, above all, fun.

Sir Viv came into the dressing room to issue some last minute warnings. 'Morgan, I'm after you,' he growled menacingly. 'You're my target man today.' I didn't know whether to laugh, feel flattered, or cry in fear.

'Yeah right Viv, we'll see,' I muttered lamely. This was like pitting a Pekinese against a Rottweiler – it was going to be short and horrible.

The Bunburys fielded first, all twenty-three of us. English explained that he always overbooked his team because 'it helps keep the runs down if you have twice as many fielders'. There was no arguing with the logic.

After an over of the twenty–twenty match, six of us were ordered off. It was proving literally impossible to score a run. The opposition smashed fours and sixes galore after that, but we were all waiting for the big moment and eventually it came – Sir Vivian swaggered to the crease in that instantly recognizable intimidatory style.

We wished the bowler, Frank Skinner, good luck and took our places in the various stands waiting for the inevitable onslaught. Frank bowled a well-pitched medium-paced delivery, Sir Viv cracked it to the extra cover boundary and set off for the compulsory lazy single to get off the mark. An eighteen-year-old young man lurking by the boards had other ideas though, charging to the ball, picking it up and hurling down the stumps in a flash of action that would have put Gary Pratt to shame.

Sir Viv was yards out. But we all pretended it hadn't happened. Sir Viv didn't, though; he just put his bat under his arm and walked off.

English ran after him: 'Vivvy, Vivvy, they've come to watch you bat, not us piss about. Please come back . . .'

But the great man was having none of it. 'I play by the rules man,' he said simply, and majestically. We all groaned, and then collectively asked the jubilant young fielder what the **** he thought he was doing.

An hour later, it was my turn to bat. I walked out to see Sir Viv taking off his jumper. 'This boy's MINE,' he said.

I blocked his first off-break (he's taken thirty-two Test match wickets). 'You're boring me, man,' he smirked. The second ball was tossed up a little higher. I charged down the track, caught it on the half volley, and saw it sail for six over square leg. Sir Viv collapsed in agony. I nearly collapsed in ecstasy. 'Hey Viv, hope that's more exciting for you, mate.'

I hit the next ball one bounce for four, to his disgust. Then he tossed another one up, I charged down the track again, smashed it right off the middle, and stood back to celebrate another boundary when to my horror I saw this fifty-two-year-old man leap three feet in the air, and the ball end up in his left hand high over his head. 'Thank you and goodnight,' laughed Sir Viv.

Later he explained to me: 'Man, that was one of my best ever catches, I had to get you or I would never have heard the end of it.' And I am almost sure he meant it. I can't remember the result, and I can't remember much of the cricket. But I will never, ever forget the over I faced from Sir Viv at the Oval.

'Bunbury cricket is fantasy cricket, Piers,' said English over a drink later. 'Dreams come true.'

And he is so right. But it's more than that. Bunbury cricket reminds even the best players why they started playing the game. If you want to know the influence David English MBE has had on the English game then go to a Test match with him and watch from a hospitality box as he chats to the entire England team *while they play*.

'Hey Freddie boy, how are you, mate? . . . Hi Jonesy lad . . . Hey Harmy, spice it up a bit son, this is boring.' They all look shocked at first, then spy the Loon's cheeky smiling face, and they start laughing. He has brought most of our Ashes-winning heroes through his other cricket hobby, the English Schools Cricket Association.

The Bunburys raise a fortune for charity, and they allow cricket fans like me to enjoy moments we will never forget. But the Bunburys also give even the greatest players in the world what we all need most: a good laugh. As the saying goes: 'When the great scorer in heaven comes to write your name, it matters not if you won or lost but how you played the game.'

Happy Birthday, and long may the Bunburys play the game.

PART ONE

Living the Dream

Bunburys – the Epitome of Life

'Life is not the breaths you take. It's the magic moments that take your breath away.'

It's 6.30 a.m., 30 October 2005. I'm driving high above the Yorkshire Moors. The Silver Lady cuts through the autumn winds. Deep below in the valley, the lights of Cleckheaton flicker in a neon mosaic as the Wallace and Gromits turn in their beds desperate for an extra half-hour's sleep. In the distance, the crimson dawn is breaking over Brighouse and for just one moment I feel on top of the world. Last night I attended the marvellous annual dinner of the English Schools Cricket Association. Handsome Harold from Huddersfield was elected chairman for the next year.

'Yer can always tell a Yorkshire man. But you can't tell him much.' Harold Galley, a larger than life Gilbert and Sullivan character was in his element entertaining the room with stories of ESCA's glorious past. The English Schools Cricket Association: a brotherhood of schoolmasters under the guidance of general secretary Ken Lake. The greatest band of unpaid volunteers who are the first to discover a young Flintoff, Vaughan or Trescothick contesting their skills in the playground at the age of six or seven. Twenty years ago I joined the Association to form the Bunbury ESCA Festival.

I love each and every one of them. They are my adopted family. Dressed in sports jackets, club ties, cavalry twills and an array of scuffed suede shoes, they are the disciplinarians with a true passion for the game who have devoted hours of their time in nurturing and motivating the young boys and girls, giving them the opportunity to play, have fun and thrive.

In 1987 Cyril Cooper, the general secretary of ESCA, arranged a meeting with me. Cyril was long in wisdom and short on words, with a remarkable capacity to prick the bubble of the pretentious and pompous. With his quick mind he was a brilliant negotiator, whose command of the ESCA executive was a revelation. His dry sense of humour and wicked observations were legendary. He admired and respected young people and they him. He was a real night owl, working tirelessly for the Association that had discovered the likes of Botham, Gooch, Gower, Gatting, Hussain and Stewart. He travelled the length and the breadth of the UK, instilling the importance of cricket into the schools. He journeyed thousands of miles by train. Cyril must have been through Crewe more times than Dario Gradi.

'David, we need your expertise. We are struggling to find sponsorship for the England U15 Festival. Can you help? Without funding, the jewel in our ESCA crown will fade and die.'

It was the quickest decision I would have to make in my life. To help find our future stars. To take them from the playground to the Test arena. What an honour. It fulfilled my ambition. Although I had played a good standard of cricket via the Lords ground staff, Finchley CC, the Cross Arrows, MCC and Middlesex CCC, I did not possess the class and staying power of a David Gower or Ian Botham. But this chance would fill that void. I could help the really talented to maximize their potential. A true labour of love.

I shook Cyril's hand. The tea was poured and my love affair with ESCA had been born. I became Cyril's prodigal son. For the past twenty years I have raised the finance through sponsorship for the festival, the first ever schoolboy 'Test series' against South Africa and two U15 Junior World Cups.

Why Bunbury? From the mythical character in the *Importance of Being Earnest?* The village in Cheshire, or the town South of Perth, Australia?

None of these. Bunbury is derived from my collection of children's books featuring cricket-playing rabbits. The adventures of Ian Buntham, Viv Radish from Bunny Bados, Dennis Lettuce and Rodney Munch from Hare's Rock, Golden Hare Gower and little Raj Bun from Bungalore. Playing in the Bunson and Hedges, Catwest Final, against the Crafty Cats from Whiskertown, managed by Chairman Miaow and captained by Mike Catting.

So how do you become a Bunbury boy or girl?

Well, each year, 100,000 boys and girls aged fourteen and a half, whether they attend a state or private school, will first have to play for their school team. Then their county and finally after another trial, represent their region. The four regions, north, south, west and midlands will then converge on a different county each year, where they will play against each other in a 'Round Robin' tournament. From these forty-four players the selectors will then pick the best eleven who will represent England. The Bunbury ESCA Festival is now unquestionably the most important Schools Cricket week for under-fifteens in this country. In the England and Wales Cricket Board's Development of Excellence programme it represents the pinnacle of a young cricketer's career and the start of the golden brick road to full England honours.

Bunbury, England U19's, National Academy, England A, England. Ninety-five per cent of all our Test cricketers have been discovered at this festival, including eight out of the eleven England players who beat Australia in the recent Ashes series.

To me, Bunbury is the very epitome of what life is all about. It has passion, devotion, excitement and tension, skill, determination, friendship, successes and disappointments, toughness, kindness and a commitment to a challenge. Under-fifteen captures the moment between childhood and manhood; the players are faintly worldly-wise but with the refreshing outlook of children. They are adolescent, perhaps having experienced their first shave, but still peeking over the Coca-Cola cans and dreaming of playing for England. They play with a free spirit, without fear of failure and oblivious to the demons they'll have to tackle in later years.

Last summer Michael Vaughan and his band of Bunbury brothers who had grown together from the flower of their youth, beat Australia. Freddy Flintoff, Marcus Trescothick, Steve Harmison and Matthew Hoggard had retained their Bunbury etiquette and sporting behaviour to beat the old foe for the first time in twenty years. To them, sport is not about abusing referees, telling your captain to eff off, diving in the penalty area, consuming performance-enhancing drugs, taking bribes to throw matches, or pocketing bungs. It's about playing hard for each other, especially when under the greatest pressure. The musketeer spirit. One for all and all for eleven. As Bunbury boys they had so much character, so much belief, so much ability and confidence in each other that there was no way Australia could win in spite of all the talent and endeavour in their side.

England's Bunbury eleven under the expert eye of coach Duncan Fletcher had reached another audience. What a transformation in the parks and down the side roads. Football disappeared. Wheelie bins for wickets replaced sweaters for goal posts. Had to be instant cricket. All the kids wanted to be Freddy or Pietersen. They were bursting to mimic what they'd seen on television. Replica Rooney shirts were swapped for Harmison and Hoggard. Maidens were bowled over from Cleckheaton to Penzance, Brighouse to Aberdeen. Ladies in hairdressers and supermarkets talked passionately about the 'Race Horse' Simon Jones and 'George Clooney' Ashley Giles.

'Aren't they lovely!' cooed Jackie the bank teller.

'Can you bring that Freddy into the bank, Dave? Me and the girls would love to meet him!'

'Tell me, Dave, what are they really like?'

'Jackie, they haven't changed since they were fifteen. Must be that Bunbury charm!'

Another ambition was to help the sick and needy, the disadvantaged and disabled. It breaks my heart to see people suffering, especially the very old and little children.

In 1969 whilst I was working for the London *Evening News*, Princess Anne had asked me to help her raise money for the Save The Children fund. I loved to help the kids. Using my contacts, I managed to raise big sums for such a worthy cause. So why not combine both my passions, fundraising and cricket?

It was the summer of 1987. My pal 'Miami John' Cousins and I went to visit Eric Clapton in his Surrey retreat. When we arrived Eric was watching England playing Test cricket on television. He was fascinated by one I.T. Botham. 'Look at his style. What a great heart he has playing for his country.'

'Tell you what, El, do you fancy a game?' I enquired.

'Sure, why not,' said Slow Hand.

So the three of us retired into the magic garden (you can see six counties on a clear day) and proceeded to play.

'Why don't we take it a step further?' I suggested. 'Let's form the Eric Clapton XI, play at Ripley and make a few bob for charity.'

So on 5 July 1987 the Eric Clapton XI took on the might of the Ripley Nomads at the Ripley Court School, by kind permission of the headmaster. Admission by programme, adults one pound – children free. Bar courtesy of the Half Moon and Seven Stars 1.30 p.m.– 7 p.m. As Eric led us onto the pitch the heavens opened and the rain fell in torrents. I had phoned up my special pals to play. Phil Collins kept wicket. Bill Wyman and Eric stood in the slips puffing on fags, both wearing plastic macs and sou'westers, looking the wrong way through the entire match. Dennis Waterman entertained the troops before disappearing into the beer marquee, David Essex charmed the ladies at long off, Gary Mason roared with laughter continuously at square leg, Spandau Ballet's John Keeble chased every ball like a terrier and Norman Cowans opened the bowling. There was Ringo Starr and Oliver Tobias, Geoff Howarth and Peter Scudamore.

4,500 people watched, soaked to the skin, mesmerized by the antics of E.C.'s motley crew and a tidy sum was raised for the Royal Marsden and St Luke's Hospital, Guildford, for cancer research. My celebrity cricket idea had worked.

The stars had enjoyed the Sunday afternoon delight – a welcome distraction from their normal lives. The punters loved to watch the antics of these famous fish out of water and the proceeds of our endeavours had gone to a good cause. Surely the ethos of life. Work hard, play hard, have fun, everybody wins. The E.C. xi became the Bunbury xi a few years later because of Eric's work commitments. But he still continued to support us even when he broke his finger whilst fielding in the slips and to crown it all as he was leaving the pitch a big bumblebee stung him on the other hand.

Over the years the Bunburys have assembled some wonderful teams, often taking the field with twenty-five players. E.C., Sir Viv Richards, Ian Botham, Elton John, George Harrison, Audley Harrison, Sam Fox, Ian Wright, Gary Lineker, Shane Warne, Brian Lara, Lawrence Dallaglio, Matt Dawson, Mike Catt, Rory Bremner, Graham Gooch, Frank Skinner, the Bee Gees, Andy Flintoff, Dennis Lillee and hundreds of other magnificent mavericks have distinguished themselves in the Bunbury colours of gold and green.

We have played on Test grounds, village greens, at schools and on the beach, in front of kings and queens, group captains and lords. We are the only cricket team to have played at Wembley Stadium and in front of the Sky TV cameras to commemorate the fiftieth Anniversary of VE Day at the Oval. On this occasion I fielded twelve players in the slips all drinking red wine and smoking large Cuban cigars. At the end of the over, nobody moved; Sam Fox, David Gower, Trevor McDonald, Gary Lineker and co. just continued partying, resulting in twelve players standing at mid-on. Our fun-filled days for all the family have now raised over nine million pounds for different charities ranging from the NSPCC, Leukaemia Research, When You Wish Upon A Star, Mencap, Childline, Cancer Research and the Guide Dogs for the Blind Association. On their inauguration and presentation of Bunbury kit, I remind all my players of the Bunbury Code of Honour.

> *A Bunbury stands for freedom*
> *Stands for fun,*
> *Stands for ever being young;*
> *So do a good turn unto others,*
> *Never turn from your quest,*
> *For you are a Bunbury*
> *And a Bunbury does his best.*

After my speech there is an enormous roar of approval in the dressing room welcoming our new recruits to the Bunbury band of brothers – a respect that cannot be bought but has to be earned.

Once a Bunbury, you're in for life.

Another Lonely Night in Doncaster

So I'm sitting in this chateau, Le Maison Talbooth, deep in the English countryside. Sprawling about the Wordsworth Suite, I pluck grapes from a Wedgwood bowl and fling open the shutters.

I'm here to conduct the auction at Graham Gooch's scholarship dinner, but that's in six hours' time and I can just sit and absorb the magic of Dedham Vale, immortalized in the paintings by John Constable. Surrounded by unchanged landscapes and Wordsworth's wonderful poems, this must be the closest thing to heaven.

Earlier I had swung up the A12 in my Windsor Blue Rolls Royce Corniche accompanied by two ladies. One is winged and silver, perched at the end of my bonnet, impatient as the wind, my pathfinder sailing along a tarmac sea.

The other is a Transylvanian topless go-go dancer slouched over my back seat. Twelve hours ago she was exciting and enticing, dancing on the tables in skyscraper heels. Now her face is a crumbling mass of eyeliner and lipstick slumped on the exquisite beige hide with blue piping. I look in my mirror; two blue eyes peer out from the residue of last night. There is a cough and a splutter.

'Darlink, how much further to the 'otel? I need a Te Quila.'

It was not always this luxurious. After-dinner speaking has taken me to every part of Britain, to every nook and cranny, along B roads and motorways to far-flung destinations. Be it the Mansfield Working Man's Club or the hallowed halls of Eton College.

Twenty years ago I sat on a train and watched the kestrels soar high over the slag heaps of Alfreton. The journey from King's Cross lasted just two hours. The trick was always to buy a second-class ticket and plonk yourself in the first-class dining room. If you ate slowly your meal could last the full two hours of the trip. Mind you, it took two hours to engage a plate of British Railways roast beef, a formidable task. On one occasion there was cause for celebration. One of their pork pies was twenty-one!

The waitress, a young Jock with chipped fingernails, walks the aisle clutching jugs of tea and coffee. Valiantly she tries to stay on her feet as the intercity 125 rocks and rolls through the heart of England. Some of the hot beverages land in your cup, the rest down your strides. Advice: always wear corduroys; they drain easier. A couple of Guinnesses help ease the nerves that tear through your belly. You never know if they're going to like you. I'm not that famous, so they don't know what they're getting. You have to make 750 piss artists laugh or you're fucked. The train trundles through Grantham. The platform is windswept and deserted except for a couple of spotty-faced spotters in anoraks. I wish I were with them. The guard's voice breaks my reverie, blurting through the loud-speaker: 'Chesterfield'.

Alight, off through the car park clutching my suit bag and check into the Station Hotel. The solitary confinement of my room, just me and the trouser press. Hang my suit in the plywood wardrobe, go to the window and through the condensation see the bright neon of the Trebor factory. It's five o'clock and the workers wend their way through the driving rain to catch the bus, thrilled to go home, change and paint the town red. It's Friday night and Chesterfield is alive with possibility. Now the same pre-performance ritual. Empty your pockets, two teddy bears, a watch and rings on the bedside table, into bed for a kip. Up at six, subconsciously stringing together likely stories for the speech, watch the TV news, cup of tea, custard cream biscuits. Never felt so lonely. Earlier I had a quick 'butchers' at the dining room: an armada of empty chairs and tables sit with menus and serviettes placed on white starched tablecloths like sails of a ship. Check if there is a mike stand. I like to keep my hands free to gesticulate and animate my stories.

Seven for seven thirty, you're met by the hon. sec. who takes you to a VIP bar to meet the first eleven captain, local mayor and dignitaries. They buzz around you and buy you drinks, desperately hoping you are as funny as your pre-publicity; what a charade, what a fucking pain in the arse. If possible find the man with the money, get it up front, go to the disabled toilet and count it – is it all there?

I learnt that from working with Chuck Berry and Little Richard back in 1971. For years the black artists from the USA had been ripped off – luckily 'the cheque's in the post' scenario was long gone. I had taken Chuck to TV Centre to appear in a Stanley Dorfmann in Concert programme for BBC 2. On his dressing-room door it said 'Mr Charles Berry', but five minutes to showtime our Chuck had no particular place to go.

'No pay, no play,' said Chuck to the frazzled BBC producer nervously pacing the room in his roll-neck pullover and sensible Clarks Shoes.

'But Mr Berry this is the BBC,' pleaded the producer.

'Fuck the BBC,' said Johnny B, not so good.

Somehow £2,000 in readies was found from the staff canteen. Carefully, Chuck counted each note and satisfied, strapped on his faithful red Gibson, did the famous duck walk down the corridor into the studio and gave it 'Roll Over Beethoven' at full volume. I would have loved to have been Chuck Berry. And to have spent more time with some of his iconic rock 'n' roll contemporaries.

One evening in St Louis, I sat round a piano with Jerry Lee Lewis, Little Richard and Bo Diddley. They told me, 'We were so angry at getting ripped off by promoters, Chuck went in there and changed the business for us. He couldn't understand that if fifty-eight cents were earned from each record sold and the artist got one cent, well, who got the other fifty-seven?'

He decided to go out on his own. He'd pack his briefcase containing a toothbrush and change of pants, pack his guitar into his Cadillac and drive to one hundred gigs a year. His contract stipulated that the promoter had to supply a local rock 'n' roll band at each venue and the only requirement was that they had to know Chuck Berry's greatest hits.

I spent some time with Bruce Springsteen in Asbury Park, New

Jersey. The great thing about Bruce is that on meeting him he's exactly the genuine guy you expect him to be. I asked him if he knew Chuck. 'Sure, I was twenty-three years old and I was opening the bill with Jerry Lee Lewis. Chuck Berry was heading the show. My first album was just out. We drove down to Maryland overnight from the previous gig. The promoter said they'd get a local band to back him. We told him, 'No way, we'll back him. It would be an honour to back the great Chuck Berry.'

'So we did a thirty-minute set that went down well. Jerry Lee then followed us, standing on his piano; the crowd were having a great time. But there was no Chuck Berry. It was getting close to the time to go on. Chuck hadn't arrived and the promoter was getting real nervous. "Go back on there," he told us. "No way, I'm not going out there." They're howling for Chuck, five minutes to show time. Chuck arrived, pulled up in his Cadillac, took out his guitar case and went straight into the promoter's office. Chuck said he wanted $11,000. He'd keep $10,000 and the other $1,000 was to go to the backing band, if they played OK and the equipment worked. He then walked into the band room. I asked him, "What songs are we going to do?" and he said, "We're going to do some Chuck Berry Songs!"

'We go on stage. The crowd are going insane. He opens up his guitar case, tunes his guitar and the lights go up. I asked him, "What are we going to start with?" The band is in total panic. What song? What key? Chuck pays no attention. He bangs his foot down and goes into his duck walk. Now Chuck plays in a lot of strange keys: E flat, B flat. Our bass player is the historian in the band. So we all look at him. He picks the key. The crowd are going nuts. Chuck runs back to us and says, "Play for that money, boys!" And we're thinking, what money, we're doing this for nothing. But of course we didn't tell him. The night ends up with a brawl in front of the stage. His amp blows up whilst we're playing "Johnny B. Goode". He walks off the stage straight into his car and he's gone.

'He probably doesn't remember us. But what a story! When I'm sixty-five or seventy I can tell my grandchildren. If they ask me, did

I ever meet Chuck Berry, I'll tell them yeah, as a matter of fact I backed him one night!'

The auction is a real worry. How many more Alec Stewart England caps or Steve Waugh One Day International shirts can I buy? My garage is full of memorabilia, dare I say hundreds of thousands of pounds, accrued over the years at benefit functions and charity bashes. There must be 500 proud owners of Alec Stewart's England cap out there, not bad considering he only played for his country on 135 occasions!

The reason I have my hand up continually at these auctions is because apart from the cash going to a good cause I can't bear those pregnant silences when people are just too fucking mean to enter into the spirit of the evening. Even when acting as the auctioneer, I've very often ended up driving home with a car full of Beckham shirts, Tiger Woods gloves and a limited edition (probably one million in circulation) of a Bradman signed print.

I nearly came a cropper with the Don. It was at one of Duncan Fearnley's pre-season lunches held at the wonderful County Ground, New Road, Worcester. I use the term 'lunch' very loosely, as we invariably had pre-drinks from twelve until four, sat down for soup at five and were still tackling our pudding at nine. It was during the days of the mighty Carphone Warehouse sponsorship of Worcestershire CCC that Ian Botham and Graham Dilley had come to New Road to revitalize the county into winning all the one-day competitions. Worcester was now, quite simply, the Manchester United of cricket. The cherished final item of the auction was a rare signed framed print of Donald Bradman. Two Carphone Warehouse directors were jousting for the item, bidding neck and neck for £9,000. Whether it was the white wine or the heady mix of the adrenalin and the rush of audience participation that prompted me to put my hand up and shout '£10,000' I don't know, but I was up there with the big boys, transfixed, and would have probably gone on to mortgage my house.

We had reached £15,000 when I was aware of a movement under the table and a hand pulling on my trouser leg.

It was Duncan, red faced and sweating profusely.

'Shut up, you stupid bastard. I've got a free one for you in the car!'

In Tune with the Loon

It was Ian Botham who christened me the Loon, a title I carry with great affection and pride. I personally don't consider myself mad, more a visionary. I think people who lead so-called 'normal' lives are crazy because they don't chase their dreams.

Push yourself to the limits, extend yourself to the full. There is no point looking out of the window and staring at the mountain. Go and climb it. Give it your best shot. Never go to bed and wonder what might have happened. Never rely on luck. Luck doesn't just happen: luck is when opportunity meets preparation. It's better to light one candle than to curse the darkness.

The notes in life are right underneath our fingers. We've just got to take the time to find the right ones for us. Then make your music, unplugged, keeping in harmony with others less fortunate, giving them love, charity, compassion and encouragement.

For our children, it is vital to demonstrate that the simple acts of giving and coming together can give you unpursued happiness and improve you as a human being, but also to teach them that it is those ineffable moments of happiness that become the memories we cherish and transform mere existence. Above all, do it with a smile and a generous heart, keeping up, even on the down days. Remember, laughter is the shortest distance between two people.

Now, go out and live the dream. And remember to love the game more than the prize, because without the game there is no prize.

I am an impressionist writer. I live in a kaleidoscope and see life as a succession of colourful moving images. Artists are tortured souls. Take Van Morrison's wonderful songs. His dreams are sweet, but he finds the reality bitter. As a Piscean I am hounded and bounded by the two fish, one pulling me to sweet dreams, the other dealing with the demons of the day. Look at Van Gogh. How could a man with such a psychological illness create such devastating art, canvasses of intense heartfelt drama fired up by the anguished desire for affection? But it is the extremes that bring out the best in an artist. To wallow in alcohol with prostitutes, to hold your hand over the candle burning yourself till you pass out, to be consumed by angst, full of guilt and remorse and then to lift yourself by the notion of wispy, lazy brushstrokes depicting sunlit gardens, straw hats and quiet days by the river. I have worked with many musicians who have to plunge to the depths before they can soar to an exquisite beauty.

Country music is about harmony and reality. It can be plain everyday poetry on real issues recorded in your living room with a front-porch mentality. I went to Nashville with Barry Gibb when he recorded 'Indian Summer' with the Gatlin Brothers and Roy Orbison. To hear them sing in harmony as naturally as breathing, using their voices as shimmering instruments, painting pictures with words . . . 'The Desert That Beckons . . .', 'Sweethearts Of The Rodeo', 'Crazy'. Beautiful but working class. Where do songs come from? It's a mystery. Different rails, different trails: 'Teenage Lover To Unwed Mother', 'Don't Come Home A Drinkin' (with Lovin' on Your Mind)', 'You Ain't Woman Enough To Take My Man' – a bit of mountain, a bit of country, a bit of blue grass . . . Somewhere else bound on a nighttime Greyhound. I met Bob Dylan, the voice of the college students, down by the railroad track, and Willie Nelson, who brought the hippies and the rednecks, the cowboys and the longhairs together.

Writing is a very private thing. Even your nearest and dearest cannot take part in it, but the beauty and youthful innocence of an Emmylou Harris sitting quietly in the corner can engender comfort and great inspiration. As president of RSO Records, I always tried to protect the artists from the commercial edge. Great talent will always rise to the top. All the guys in business suits and the lawyers will never eclipse the artist's spirit. It's about the beautiful landscapes and the lost highway. They say that beauty is only skin deep, but that's deep enough for most of us. Who cares what your pancreas looks like as long as on the face of things you look sensational?

So it was the essence of Van Gogh's art to take the simple and unregarded things of the world and show just how extraordinary they are – a realist who painted the world as he saw it. Things like railways and chimneys, as well as the pale orange setting sun and pretty women lost in conversation on the corner of boulevards.

We all dream of infinite love and beauty. One day I'll live in Montmartre, writing thoughts on the back of napkins and kissing girls in dark cafes.

It was close to Montmartre where the horror of the haemorrhoid first reared its ugly head.

Pain by the Seine

The George V Hotel stood impressively on the left bank, unlike the opera house, which was under siege.

It was 1974 and I had brought West, Bruce and Laing to Paris to play the first ever pop concert at the capital's heart of culture.

An elegant night at the opera had turned into a riot as the tumultuous trio had rocked the chandeliered house to its knees. As the riot police burst into the velvet auditorium, I rounded up the lads and legged it stage left into the cobbled street, back to the safe haven of the opulent George V, leaving behind an atmosphere of excited frenzy.

The fabled hotel, which encourages you 'not to nick their famous bathrobe but will turn a blind eye if you do, penalty the guillotine' boasted a twenty-four-hour room service rich in culinary delights. While me and the boys tucked into our gourmet beggars' banquet, lead guitarist and mountain of soul Leslie West, already twenty stone, visibly increased in size as plates of snails and frog's legs were washed down by gallons of champagne. It was early doors as we made our fond farewells and stumbled to our rooms.

It must have been six a.m. when things took a turn for the worse. I was propelled on a wave of gastronomic delight somewhat *très vite* to la salle de bain. As I sat on the throne trying to see a couple of friends off to the coast, my powers to push down came to no avail. I was constipated in situ. After an enormous effort combined with a blood-curdling 'Aaagh' my bottom finally exploded, followed by a large *objet d'art*, which appeared between my splayed buttocks. It was agony. I waddled to the phone and called reception.

'*Un médecin, s'il vous plaît, à chambre numéro 164, très vite.*'

'What eees wrong, monsieur?' came the voice of concern.

'J'ai un grand champignon dans – ma derrière,' came my somewhat strained response.

Monsieur le médecin, Vincent Fouchette, arrived clutching his Gladstone bag flanked by two medical students who were doing work experience.

'Lie on your back, monsieur,' ordered the doc. Spreadeagled on my ornate four-poster, Monsieur Fouchette inspected 'the mushroom in my behind'. His eyes watered at the sight of my anal apparition.

'Quelle horreur, monsieur! Quelle haemorrhoid!'

The medical students nodded and took notes as I almost passed out in pain. To make matters worse I had agreed to visit an old '*ami*' of mine, Jean Pierre Cottereau, who lived in Le Mans. I dragged my disabled derrière to the Gare du Nord and steamed out of the station. I was the only passenger standing all the way. I stared out of the window and absorbed the French countryside. The heady optimism of spring had vanished on the summer breeze. I felt as though I was travelling through the full joyous luminosity of a Monet painting, pastel light filtering through the dense foliage of a wood, or the poses of figures fleetingly as we whizzed through a village. I saw a graveyard full of white crosses from the First World War, which conjured up a nostalgia for pretty girls and cornfields left behind for the horror of the western front. Meanwhile my eastern back was giving me some serious jip.

Jean Pierre, a wonderful host, had organized a surprise party in my honour. So there I stood with all these super smooth frogs, individualists en masse. In other words they liked to do things on their own, so long as everyone else did the same. And the French girls? Well, they were a different class. Not as physically stunning as the Nordic nubiles or as sultry as the Italians or spirited as the Brazilians. But les mademoiselles 'know how to make the best of themselves'. For example, if her legs were on the large side she'd never wear a mini skirt, but a midi with a slit up the side revealing a flash of thigh. Super feminine, classy with a dab of Guerlain behind the ears; just think of Catherine Deneuve or Brigitte Bardot. This, plus the fact they spoke the most beautiful language on God's earth.

Dream as though you are going to live for ever, live as though you are going to die tomorrow; the pain in my bum was agony but I got stuck in, drank the wine, made the girls laugh and danced to Johnny Hallyday. Great pain can be an irresistible force for dancing. I cuddled and embraced the moment encapsulated by the all-encompassing power of the mademoiselles. The secrets of Le Style Français. It is not simply about the clothes. It is about attitude. The French girl is sure of herself. She knows that being chic is not about being perfect, but about making an impression. She has the confidence to mix things – the fur wrap with the chiffon slip, the velvet coat with jeans. It is about flair, pardon mon afflair! It is about her intelligence, the attention she pays to gestures, the way she walks, and it is about her soul. Her overwhelming sense of being ran through my soul. Soul is the wind beneath your wings; it lifts you up and digs within.

The next day I hugged Jean Pierre and left with a head full of scent and a pocket full of numbers.

Le Mans station stood deserted in the half-light of a summer evening. The platform lay empty except for a porter who swept without thinking, clenching a Boyard's Maize cigarette in a brown-toothed smile. Then I spotted the blonde in a trenchcoat, tightly belted and high heeled, two leather suitcases either side of her black-stockinged legs. As the eight forty p.m. SNCF to Paris trundled in, I moved towards her and asked if I could help her with her luggage.

'Allow me, mademoiselle.'

She looked at me through blue eyes, her golden hair swept back, a complexion like porcelain, high cheekbones, bright red lips pouting provocatively, and smiled. 'Merci, monsieur. Tenez les valises.' She glided up the vertical steps of the train revealing an exquisite flash of ankle.

I staggered in her wake, manfully trying not to show the extreme discomfort of my Parisian pile whilst tackling the steepness of the situation.

It was a typical French train. All the compartments were full, mainly of soldiers smoking and Algerians who seemed to move from one provincial town to another. I wanted to avoid sitting at all costs.

'Mademoiselle, come and stand in the corridor.' We chugged out of Le Mans wedged in opposite each other. The conversation was polite. I just looked at her beautiful face and exercised my O-level French. We exchanged names: 'Je m'appelle Davide.' 'Vivienne,' she purred. My knee entered her V through the folds of her raincoat. I'd never felt so turned on. There was an instant attraction. I undid the belt of her coat. My hand went downwards and felt her moistness. She in turn took my hand and pulled it into the enchanted land. We were now dovetailed south of the border, jogging in and out to the rhythm of the rail. It was a jigsaw made in heaven. The magic tingle up front compensated for the anal horror in my nether regions.

I occasionally looked over my shoulder, but the Algerians were oblivious, too busy staring out of the window of their compartment. Then as we entered the Gare du Nord, the paradise stroke beckoned and I exploded inside her. Suddenly there was uproar from within the carriage as the soldiers stood and applauded. Unbeknown to us they had watched our vertical jogging in the reflection of the window. What a performance! Vivienne and I unplugged. I held her head in the fold of my arms to hide her blushes. As the train came to a halt, we bowed to our audience and I lifted her onto the platform.

'Davide, I must go; my fiancé is waiting.' Through the blur of the passengers walking to the gate, I could see a young man peering towards us clutching a bunch of flowers.

As we approached the gate I patted Vivienne on her bottom, taking one last look at her beautiful face, then peeled off to the left.

Our brief encounter was over. Sex with a stranger on a train. Exciting, dangerous ... As the euphoria started to subside I felt deserted and empty, lost to the world hobbling into the hubbub of the Parisian night.

EC Was Here

It was 2001. So I went back to find Eric Clapton. Off the main drag through Shere and Peaslake past Winterfold and Albury until the double yellow brick road tapers off to the single track where only one car can pass at a time. Somewhere, from the back of my mind, memories came to the fore. I was overwhelmed by nostalgia. Thirty years had passed and yet I was slipping back as though it was yesterday. His music rang in my ears and acted as a soundtrack to my journey.

Two lovers were frolicking in the beer garden oblivious to time and the day rushing by. The valley drenched in colours of varying greens lay still and the land was at peace, except for the call of the wood pigeon and the landlord taking delivery of a barrel or two. Thirty years ago we straddled the bar and laughed until we were hoarse. The old saloon was thick with banter and flirting wildly for the moment, gorging ourselves with fun and nonsense. Guinness and vodka were consumed in reservoirs, fuelling the imagination and firing us up for love and wanton pleasure. Sometimes he would play and the music soared above the uproar, taking us to another plane. Guy Pullen, Peter the prison warder, the mighty Sid Perrin, and old Scratcher from the village would hang on to their glasses and every note that touched a nerve and took us to another land.

The Windmill, run by a marvellous old military man called Dutch, stood at the top of Eric's drive. OK, so we could enjoy a few beakers at home, but it didn't beat the social feeling of being in the pub. We would hit the Windmill at 10.30 in the morning. It was a great centre for pleasure. On one occasion I got the train to Guildford where Eric met me in a full-blown armoured car, guns, the lot. We never walked from his house. We always drove the 300 yards to the Windmill in one of his Ferraris. To be honest, El often risked his life by driving his car in various degrees of dangerous states after he'd had a few. There was the time he'd come back from Australia and got off the plane drunk and jet-lagged. He came home, got into his Ferrari, drove it down the hill and hit a laundry van head on. It was a bad crash. El had to be cut out of his car. He was taken to hospital suffering from concussion and stayed in for a couple of days with a broken nose. He could be reckless. He had a love of danger. The danger is what made it electric. Playing the blues made him live on the edge. I think that in order to play in the way some of the great ghetto blues players had performed, he really had to experience life on that level. I think El kept pushing his body to the limit of its endurance.

One thing for certain: he was a brilliant actor with a ruthless streak who loved a bird. One day this bloke walked into the bar, rugged, Celtic, with a head of tight curls, wearing a diamond stud in his ear, a long brown coat and stout brown boots tied down with laces. He had the look of a journeyman, a carouser with sparkling eyes, High Plains Drifter meets Hard Nose the Highway. On his arm was a willowy blonde with stars on her cheeks and golden hair tied back by a rainbow ribbon. El's eyes lit up, so did mine. The Irish rover approached Eric and asked him if he could sing for him. Fleetingly, El's reverie of the beautiful blonde was broken.

'Of course you can, man.'

'Curly' stood in the middle of the bar and sang like a dream. As soon as he had finished he disappeared into the toilet. El was in like a flash, getting the telephone number of the blonde. 'Curly' returned. El was moved. 'Incredible, man. Take this.'

El took off his Rolex watch and gave it to the singer, moved by the performance, but buoyed by the thought of the beautiful girl's number safe in his pocket.

When we left the pub it was snowing. The moon was out and the dogs were barking.

'I'll walk to the house, El.'

El was fired up. 'Fuck off Arf,' (he always calls me Arf) 'you poofter, get in the vehicle!'

As I disappeared down the drive, El roared after me, swerving from side to side in his Ferrari. I dived in the hedge to avoid certain death. Back in the house he was rampant. He took a samurai sword off the wall and turned on me. 'Right, Arf, meet your doom!' Down came the sword with an ominous crash. It was like a scene out of the Pink Panther as he chased me round the house swishing the sword and crying like a banshee.

'Keep going, Dave, I thought to myself. Inspector Clouseau will tire at about 1 a.m. He always does.'

Sure enough when the clock struck one, the warrior lay down his sword and gave me a hug. 'I'm tired, Arf,' he said yawning. 'I'm off to bed.'

I was awoken in the morning by E.C. standing over me and demanding to know 'Where's my fucking watch?'

'El, you're an old artful dodger. You gave it to that geezer so you could pull his bird.'

E.C. gave me one of his mischievous laughs and declared, 'And you, Arfur, can go straight to your hamper for the rest of the day!'

This I duly did and in the confines of the four small walls (my hamper was actually Willow, El's dog's kennel) I wrote the following verse based on the mysterious troubadour from the previous night.

The Ballad of Riff McCoy and Panama Jack

Riff McCoy and Panama Jack went to Bolivia and never
    came back.
Something they saw or something they found
Something they tried that grew in the ground
There's gossip and stories nothing is clear
But they still talk about them as though they were here.
The women they left
The seeds that were sown
The places they travelled
Their faces were known

They're heroes and villains in everyone's eyes
Their like's gone for ever but no one denies
There's a place in our hearts if they ever come back.
For Riff McCoy and Panama Jack – so empty your glasses
    and fill 'em again!
And drink up a toast to these gentlemen.
They fought – to the end in the face of attack – Here's to
    Riff McCoy & Panama Jack!

I have never thought of myself as subservient. But in the presence of the high and mighty, I have enjoyed being a prisoner of their excessive behaviour and 'everything in the world is possible' mentality. To experience the great pressure of enormous pleasure in self-inflicted solitary confinement whilst planning the Great Escape has for me been the ultimate prize.

To be honest I enjoyed being in Eric's hamper, where I could sit and plan the next mind game to topple my master, who in truth was to combine our desire for social pursuit and how to achieve the maximum act of skulduggery.

Likewise, for thirty years I have been happy to be in the custody of Mr. I.T. Botham. In the mid eighties, whilst playing for Somerset, Captain 'Beefy' would give me the call, probably from the comfort of the physio's table stretched out preparing for another earth-shattering innings of mass destruction.

'Loon, get your arse down here; I've got a couple of days off and we can have some fun!'

Summoned by the High Priest of Mischief I'd board the bone-rattler at Paddington and steam westwards to Taunton. Staring out of the window at the wonders of the White Horse chalked up on the Wiltshire hills and further down the line the hustle and bustle of the market town of Westbury, I thought about the adventure ahead. Somerset County Cricket Ground stood just a stone's throw from the station. The Somerset lads were a fantastically friendly bunch. On arrival Roy Kerslake, Peter Hill and Dennis Breakwell made me very welcome. 'Whato Loony, what's the latest gag?' Through the packed crowds deeply knowledgeable about the game and the best drop of cider, up the steps to the pavilion patrolled by Andy Withers and Peter 'Jock' McCoombe, Beefy and Viv's minders and into the hallowed sanctuary of the dressing room 'admission by permission of the captain only'.

In the engine room lay the greatest cross section of society imaginable. From left to right Roebuck and Marks, the Cambridge academics, pored over the Times crossword. Next was 'Dasher' Denning, Colin Dredge and Trevor Gard, the homegrown heroes, Nigel Popplewell, brilliant and dishevelled son of a judge, the tall, imposing Brian Rose, who drove beautifully off the front foot in spite of rapidly declining eyesight, Phil Slocombe, a panther at cover point who married an American and now sells antiques, young Gary Palmer. 'Ere, Beefy, I've got this invite for a dinner and dance this Friday, black tie seven for seven thirty, ten pounds. Ten pounds for half an hour is a bit steep, isn't it?'

There at the far end was a legendary trio: Joel 'Big Bird' Garner, who had been known to come off the field end of play Thursday, drive three hundred miles to Manchester to support a friend's function and be back the next morning for eleven a.m. start; the mighty Viv 'washing and brushing up' for hours, preparing for a night out on the town; and Beefy sitting bare-chested in his flannels, farting and burping and wondering which teammate to headlock next.

After a few pints in the bar Beefy and Viv rounded up the lads and off we went to the Kings Club to enjoy a riotous night before returning to the Wolfman's lair at three a.m. Set as an Alcatraz in leafy suburbia, number eight Pikes Avenue was Beefy's 'Apocalypse Now'. Vultures flew overhead, the grass was overgrown, barbed wire surrounded the compound patrolled by Ian's loyal henchman, Andy Withers, and the entire contents of the fridge consisted of thirty tins of Stella Artois, a green loaf and a piece of cheddar cheese, sell-by date August 1928. The TV, white hot, groaned under the continuous twenty-four-hour showings of *Rambo*, *Conan the Barbarian* and *Hawkslayer*, etc.

I have been known to be incarcerated in Cell Block H for weeks at a time. Occasionally I'd be joined by Beefy's 'new best friend' whom he had arm-wrestled to the floor the previous evening fuelled by a vat of red wine, or the occasional unsuspecting journalist from American *Time Life* who had been sent to study the legend. There would be a trail of sycophants to the gates of number eight, come to pay homage to their master. From time to time I'd be summoned to accompany his lordship on a daring raid on humanity, but I spent most of my sentence trying to steal Beefy's kit. For a long time Ian suspected that most of his England blazers, sweaters and caps hung in my wardrobe at number twenty-six Kingdon Road, West Hampstead. I'd hastily shove as much of his equipment as I could in a black bin liner and endeavour to tunnel out of the lair. I'd escape to the 'Swiss border' that stood in the shape of Taunton station, only to be arrested by a Beefy henchman who apprehended me on platform one to London. So near but so far.

'Loony, we're playing India at Lords next week. We'll nip round your house first for my kit then on to NW8. I want to bowl them out twice quickly cos there is a race meeting on the Monday evening at Windsor and my pal Tony Ives is riding a sure-fire winner.' So confident in his own ability, Beefy could win England a Test match almost single-handed.

Day four of the Test match and England were well on course for a victory. I was standing at the Nursery End watching with Don Wilson's young professionals and Mickey Hunt's gang of mowers. Beefy standing at second slip spotted me and with a breathtaking moment of method acting seemed 'to go in the leg'. A few words were exchanged with captain Mike Brearley and the old boy hobbled down to me at third man. 'Right, Loon, I'm going to knock over these last Indians, so bring the Saab round at six and we're off to the Windsor races.'

This audacious act was performed in front of a packed crowd of 30,000 plus millions on TV. To say Beefy's prognostications fell short of the mark was indeed an understatement. He ran in and bowled flat out at India's number three, but Dilip Vengsarkar had decided to capitalize on his own Indian summer, smashing the ball to all parts for a dazzling 174. The faster Beefy bowled, the further Dilip sloshed it. It was an amazing spectacle to behold. At five past six we roared through the Grace Gates to Windsor. 'So the bloke can bat. I'll have him tomorrow,' grumbled Beefy.

Tony Ives, Beefy's jockey pal, indeed won. We returned to the West End and spent all his winnings on a slap-up meal. Lots to drink and tap dancing on the tables. Next day India continued to bat and the match was drawn. Another quiet night followed in the company of 'Mad' Mickey Chick, landlord of the King and Queen at Wheatley near Oxford. Beefy, the barman, insisted that one pound from every pint served went to Leukaemia Research. There was singing, arm-wrestling and a full-blown punch up just to end another spectacular night. Covered in sawdust after rolling on the floor with two Hells Angels from the Oxford chapter, I managed to escape with the 'Beef' battered, bruised but reasonably happy. You can push the parameters and sometimes you feel lost to the world, out of control.

By now I had been a prisoner of Mr Indestructible for fourteen days. I'd grown a beard; I had suitcases under the eyes and resembled something from Papillon.

On day fifteen we went to Thruxton where Beefy was to race for Saab.

Beefy recalls: 'A year later when I went racing at Thruxton for them, I managed to write off two of their machines in the same day at a cost of around £24,000. I'd fancied giving it a real blast; here was a chance to pin back my ears and go as fast as I could. I went out there with a rally driver, who talked me through the course and all was going well until we approached what looked like a reasonably comfortable corner: At the Apex there was a hump, but the technique for getting round was simple, or so I thought. What I was supposed to do was put my foot down and just drive through it. We built our speed up nicely. I did as I had been told and came through the corner flat out. The problem was that once we were past the hump I over-compensated, with the result that we slid into the grass and through the barriers and bails of straw totally out of control.

'It was amazing that no one was hurt because the impact shunted the chassis to such an extent that the car was wrecked. The only damage (at least to myself) had been to my pride and I was determined to get back out there as soon as possible. Within an hour Saab had fitted me out with another car and this time we put in three or four good laps and managed to clock up some impressive times. On the fifth circuit I felt I had the speed just right, around 110 miles an hour, when the wheels slid and caught the drainage ditch on the far side of the same corner. The car slipped up in the air, the nearside wheel snapped off and we found ourselves rolling down the hill. The car went over four or five times and it felt like being on the inside of a spin dryer. I was dead lucky again to walk off unscathed, although my co-driver, Mike Binnion, cut his head on the driver's mirror. As for the car, this time there was no doubt whatsoever that it was a complete write-off. Apart from the missing wheels, the bonnet, boot and roof had caved in. The only things that worked were the doors. At least I proved that Saab's cars did the job when it came to safety! I showed the world that you could crash Saabs at over 100 miles an hour and still walk away smiling! Saab was not slow at spotting the opportunity and proceeded to tour the car around for the next six months letting people know just that.'

At the end of the day we managed to engage the entire band of the Coldstream Guards into a big drinking spree. As they piped their way down the track I signalled them off to the right, straight into the Johnny Walker whisky tent, a highly popular diversion, which led to the guards taking off their Busbys, laying down their instruments and getting stuck into the whisky. It was a wonderful end to the day. I stood on a table and boomed out my gags, Beefy was a phenomenal host and like the battered Saabs we left Thruxton at two thirty in the morning happy but totally wrecked. Perfect preparation for Somerset's Benson and Hedges game versus Warwickshire at Edgbaston on the same day.

Warwickshire posted a good score. Beefy typically made things happen, rather than wilt under the pressure. He's always had the ability to come back even when the team seems down and out, and an enormous pride in his performance, built on a staggering foundation of self-belief. 127 not out and five for thirty-one under his belt, the old boy decided a celebration was in order. That's a change!

Day seventeen and I could hardly stand up. After visiting five or six of Ansells' finest with former Warwickshire fast bowlers Bob

Willis and David Brown, I managed to escape through a pub toilet window on a council estate just outside Balsall Heath. As I clambered to freedom I noticed a scrawled message just above the bog roll. 'Have a safe trip Loon, love Beefy xxx.' He'd known I was going and the sod even knew my escape route! I missed him already as I legged it over the emotional wasteland to Birmingham's New Street station, just in time to catch the one-thirty a.m. milk train to London Euston.

For over thirty years we have tripped the light fantastic – and the burgling of his kit? Well, the measure of the man who repays loyalty with great generosity of spirit can be captured by the following. Beefy was serving some ban or other. These bans made me laugh. When he was hauled up in front of the cricketing beaks, they would sentence him, slap his wrists, then go to the filing cabinet and take out a bottle and two glasses. 'No hard feelings, Ian. Now do you fancy a large gin and tonic?' the chairman of selectors would enquire. And they tell me that no player is bigger than the game!

'Loon, I'll come down to London for your birthday. I want to go low key, avoiding any paparazzi that might be loitering. I'll see you at King's Cross. I'll be on the five past one from Doncaster.'

When I entered the concourse at King's Cross, Beefy was nowhere to be seen.

'Pssssssst!' I couldn't see anything. 'Pssssssst!'

Then I saw a trilby hat peering out from behind the pillar. There he stood wearing a full-length leather coat, looking like someone from the Gestapo. His idea of low key! I went to meet him. Then from under his coat he took a parcel. 'There you are, Loon. Take this. Happy birthday.' It was his England touring blazer, the one he wore on the victorious Ashes tour of 1986–7. Priceless.

As we swept through the maddening crowd to the getaway Saab, he smiled. 'Saves you nicking it later, Loony!'

President of RSO Records

Working for a record company can sometimes be a disheartening experience. Finding yourself upside-down, paralytic in the Balls Pond Coco Rooms, Cleethorpes every other night, looking for the next Beatles, I can assure you, is not the most enviable of tasks and makes you wonder if farming in Argylshire would not be a more soulful experience. Once in a while, however, from the mountains of tapes something original pierces your addled brain and you know that your endeavours have been justified. The answer came to me in the shape of Hugh Nicholson, Ian MacMillan and Timmy Donald, who together formed a band called Blue. Each of their songs are different, but all of them retain a certain distinctive quality that makes you wonder just what to expect next. Just listen to this, their first excellent album and discover Blue for yourselves.

Sleeve Notes for Blue's first Album. RSO. Records March 1973.

David English
New at Ten, Upside-down in Cleethorpes.

Hugh Nicholson: Guitar, keyboards, vocals
Ian MacMillan: Bass, harmonica, vocals
Timmy Donald: Percussion, vocals

Produced by: Hugh Nicholson, Ian MacMillan, Timmy Donald
Engineer: Jerry Boys
Recorded at Sound Techniques & Olympic Studios, March 1973
Remastered at the Mastering Suite, Richmond, London 2002
Photography: Mike Putland
Artwork: Rick Goodale (Blue Logo) Layout : Zuma Graphics

Blue were a smashing band. We gigged up and down the country and nearly always ended up in London's Speakeasy club. In fact all roads led back to this den of iniquity in the Wild West End's Margaret Street. Coq Au Vin, affectionately known by the band as a 'bunk up in the back of a Dormobile' would take us on the long road home from Blighty's in Bolton or the Fiesta in Stockton-on-Tees. Down the M1 stopping at the Blue Boar Cafe and then on past Newport Pagnell and the Toddington Services, all the bands would descend upon the Speakeasy club early in the morning. I used to MC a lot of the proceedings, telling a few gags before introducing the bands. I remember my all-time dream line-up quite clearly. Jimi Hendrix and Jimmy Page on lead guitars, John Lennon on rhythm, Rick Grech from Blind Faith on bass, Billy Preston on keyboards and Keith Moon on drums. What a super group. This plus Screaming Lord Sutch climbing out of a coffin singing lead vocals. It was wildly excessive behaviour. I'm sure INXS and Michael Hutchence would have approved.

Not so, thirty years later in London's Ten Rooms. Early evening I had met England cricketers Michael Vaughan, Andy Flintoff, Rob Key, Min Patel and Aussie Andy Symonds to discuss a Bunbury tour to Brazil. It was shaping up to be a great night. The wine was flowing and the recruitment of lovelies for our South American adventure was going like a house on fire. The tour party proceeded on to the Ten Rooms where the Johnny Altman Band starring Mark Butcher was on top form. Swept along by the euphoria I thought it timely to offer a little table dancing. So I stood on the table and shouted 'Who's Coming To Rio?' dropping my trousers in mid sentence.

My feet failed to touch the ground as three animals in long Nike coats, the type who wore sunglasses indoors, felt my collar and lifted me down the stairs, their walkie-talkies still clacking, before dumping me unceremoniously into the street.

'We don't need rabble like you in this club, so bugger off!'

Freddy Flintoff and Vaughany, somewhat concerned, followed me down. 'Are you OK Dave? Shall we come with you?'

'Bollocks to that! You stay and enjoy yourselves. Tell you what, lads, if they think that's bad you should have seen us thirty years ago!'

Dusting myself down I started a melancholic march through the streets of Soho, threading my way towards Margaret Street like a sixties homing pigeon. As I shambled along flashbacks of the great club nights came to mind. Jeff Beck, Eric Clapton, the Grateful Dead, Keith Richards, Chuck Berry, Jim Morrison . . . But when I arrived at the door it said 'Gowns by Ronnie Simmler'. Once the Speakeasy, it now stood as a Smutter Shop – boy, if only those walls could talk!

As with the players who support my Bunbury Cricket Club, I have always had a deep love, respect and strength of feeling for the artists who recorded for RSO. We were a band of brothers who would sink or swim in the common desire to make great music and have a lot of fun on the way. Looking back, there was very little sinking, but a lot of swimming and dangerous 'touch and go' behaviour every day. It's lilac time here in Mill Hill and the May blossom is blowing in flurries outside my window in hypnotic circles, taking me back on a purple ride to one particularly lively passage in time.

One of our world-famous artists, a seriously lovely person who will remain anonymous, got busted for dope in Nigeria. Phone calls 'to and fro' the Lagos slammer ran red hot from my office in Brook Street. After a little persuasion, my man beat the rap by agreeing to produce the Nigerian police band's official long-playing record. Thirty years later, I'm looking up from my desk and there it is on the wall, the record sleeve with 'my man' sitting, arms crossed, in the middle of the Nigerian Old Bill's official photo.

Released from the trauma of certain imprisonment, languishing in a Nigerian jail, my man came to see me at my RSO offices.

'Many thanks, man.' We embraced. 'Come on, Dave, lunch is on me.'

We roared off to Curzon Street in his bright yellow Jensen Interceptor. 'Mirabelle all right for you, Dave?'

When we arrived there was nowhere to park. Double yellow madness and on top of that an over-officious doorman wearing a long coat and official glossy peaked hat who held out his white gloved hand to intimate it was a good idea for us to 'fuck off'! My man smiled and reversed up. 'Fair enough; hold on Dave!' and with that he shoved the Jensen into first gear and drove straight through two massive glass windows, into the restaurant.

Well, I'd heard of 'drive-in catering', but that one took the biscuit!

I actually got out of my door and asked a passing terrified waiter for a prawn cocktail and 'to see the wine list'.

My man was arrested and banged up in the Saville Row police station. When I visited him, he was sitting grinning in the cell.

'Don't tell me, Dave – they've clamped my car? Anyway, it beats doing porridge in Nigeria, dunnit?'

The Market Gardener

The case of Joey 'Tomato' was a strange one. It was 1979. I was living with Cindy Lee Johnson in Biscayne Park, some twenty miles north of Miami. There we were, nestled amongst the good old boys swigging Budweisers and watching the Dolphins on TV. It was maritime suburbia. Very relaxed. Hunky land cruisers with boats in tow stood in the drives, hammocks swayed gently beneath the palms and the spicy aroma of barbecues hung on the breeze. The temperature never dropped lower than seventy degrees. I had not paid much attention to my neighbours over the road. One day my pal Miami Johnny and I were playing cricket in the drive when suddenly a Cuban cat with curly hair jumped out of the bushes, blazing away with two revolvers.

Johnny and I crossed the road to watch the swarthy Latino empty his two pearl-handled revolvers into what was left of a snake.

The man looked up and with a big smile displaying a diamond inlaid front tooth announced, 'Pleased to meet you. I am Joey D'Amato. Market gardening is my game.'

'Blimey, Joey, I thought you were General Patton, blazing away with those guns!' I joked.

'I like to keep my eye in by knocking off the occasional snake. Now tell me about this cricket,' laughed Joey.

Meeting Joey 'Tomato' certainly left its mark. I started to notice large limousines arriving by day and night. Two-tone Cadillacs slunk up his drive. As I lay in bed with Cindy, I would hear car doors clicking shut and conversations in hushed tones . . . And then one night . . . The noise on our roof! At first I thought it must have been a stray polecat searching for food. There it was again . . . the sound of scraping. I slipped out of the bed and crept through the house out of the back door and into the garden. I was stopped in my tracks as two large figures dressed entirely in black ushered me back inside.

'We are agents Velasquez and Rodrigo, Miami Vice. Do you mind if we ask you some questions?'

In a state of shock I sat down with the officers as Cindy busied about making us cinnamon coffee.

'How well do you know your neighbour?' asked the cop.

'Not well at all,' I said. 'He is Joey "Tomato", a market gardener.'

'Sure,' laughed the officers. 'Maybe magic mushrooms. Joey D'Amato, my friend, is a cocaine dealer, one of the biggest in Miami. He is a member of the Colombian cartel who pushes the highly addictive stuff into the trendy South Beach clubs. Yeah, your man Joey will hook the kids and make them come back for more. We've been watching his movements for weeks and now we're ready to bust him.'

Still numb with shock at the identity of our neighbour, Johnny and I continued our Test match the following morning. It was about midday when Joey surfaced. He stood at his door with that big smile and beckoned.

'Come over here, señors!'

With much trepidation Johnny and I crossed the street and entered Joey's bungalow. Inside there were rows of women packing, sorting and testing fastidiously behind a conveyor belt wearing rubber gloves and hygienic masks. The place had the appearance of a narcotic Sainsbury's. There was even a little laboratory in one of the rooms where two men were processing the white powder.

'Joey, this is crazy,' I spluttered. 'The Feds will get you. They've been watching you from my roof.'

'Hey, lighten up, my friend,' laughed Joey. 'Live for the moment.'

'But you're peddling death,' I continued.

'Don't moralize me, my friend. It's too late for that. They'll never get Joey D'Amato!'

Johnny and I couldn't get out of the place quick enough.

Sure enough, two weeks later all hell let loose. Helicopters circled overhead shining their searchlights on Joey's house and headlamps from the FBI Land Cruisers flashed through our living room. Cindy, Johnny and I watched from behind our curtains as an army of balaclava'd SWAT officers swarmed around his house, blew the door off the hinges and entered. But there was nothing inside. When the mayhem had settled we crossed the street and entered Joey's house. It was empty.

Officer Velasquez approached me. He was holding a business card. 'All he left was this.' On it, it said 'Joey D'Amato, Market Gardener'. The gangster had flown the coup.

It must have been a month later. I was settling into my big brown chair in the front garden when a limo pulled up. Down came the black stained-glass window followed by two pearl-handled revolvers and a curly head with a big smile.

'Hey Señor Dave, I told you they'd never get "The Tomato"! Farewell, my friend.' And with that the limo roared away, gunshots blazing into the azure sky.

Don Key Oaty

Autumn came to Mill Hill like an old rusty overcoat covering the traces of summer and its fading promise of new love and hope.

Hope, that eternal feeling that flickers in your belly and fills the heart with expectation.

The field where children played with a boisterous exultation is now dotted about with different coloured leaves, tears from the trees, orange, green, brown and yellow, crisp under the hooves of the two highland cows and the Spanish donkey who squat and dream of home.

'Donkey', 'Don Quixote', 'Don-Key-Oaty' was getting changed in his dressing room at the back of the Casa Rosso Club, eighteen Canal Strasse, Amsterdam. Shining his hooves and applying his best straw hat, he was ready for the evening's performance.

It was 1975 and 'Jive Talking' was leaping up the charts. I had taken the Bee Gees on a promotional tour of Europe. We had arrived in Amsterdam. Time for a spot of culture. A visit to the Rembrandt Museum? Maybe a bicycle ride to the yellow daffodil fields? No, an evening of sordid delight in the Casa Rosso Live Fucky Fucky Club just edged the collective vote.

Inside the club, the emporium of sin was deliciously decadent, daubed in gilt paint with chipped mirrors. Worn red carpets, holed by cigarette burns, were hidden by the dim light, which outlined the silhouettes of the girls sitting seductively at the bar.

'Look at the ticket,' said Barry. 'It has five sections.'

Floor one: Dodgy Books. Typical story line. Girl in negligée answers knock on door of flat. There is a pig standing there with mud up his legs. After enjoying a bottle of wine they bang away, the cheeky cochon penetrating the peroxide blonde with his corkscrew. They recoil in the afterglow. She has a cigarette; the pig, looking weary, picks up his trotters and leaves.

Under the pictures, this milestone in literature was described in six languages.

'So much for the pig and a poke,' laughed Robin.

Floor two: Porno Films. The cinematic delights of 'Fleshpot' and 'Vice Girls of Rotterdam' were cranking away to a salivating audience consisting mainly of Japanese tourists, macs buttoned up, clutching cameras.

'Nippon up' to the third floor: Strip Tease. Three hot and juicy females in various stages of undress paraded about, sitting on the Bee Gees' laps, exhibiting their assets lasciviously. The show climaxed in Velma, a willowy redhead, bending over backwards protruding her mound of desire, pouting with pleasure and staring directly at Maurice. Then, with an erotic grunt, she flexed her vaginal muscles and let fly. To the amazement of a spellbound audience, a succession of ping-pong balls roared out past the little man in the boat and the John Wayne saddlebags, narrowly missing Maurice's hat.

The power and the passion swept us up to the fourth floor for the live show. There, an MC wearing a pink ruffled shirt and a velvet bow tie announced, 'We do ask the audience not to smoke or laugh as the male performer will find it hard to get an erection.' Out came Sinbad the Sailor who doubled as Rudolf Valentino, proudly displaying his pink trombone. On it was written 'HMS'.

'What's that?' enquired Barry.

'HMS,' piped up Sinbad. 'Oh! When I'm excited it says Hammersmith!'

Hoots of derision from the back. A clutch of Cuban cigars lit up in the front.

'I have made love to women all over the world,' boasted Sinbad whilst giving Marie Antoinette an enormous portion. 'Paraguay, Uruguay, Mexico, Argentina . . .'

'Isn't it time you hung up your balls and called it a day!' cried Robin, posing for the Nikon brigade. We stumbled to the final floor, the Room at the Top.

'What could possibly follow that?' enquired Barry.

Marie Antoinette reappeared and proceeded to dance suggestively to the strains of the Kinks' 'You Really Got Me'. She lay on her back and started to writhe with pleasure. There was a loud 'hee haw' as a donkey was lowered from the ceiling. Still smiling at the audience, Marie Antoinette lifted her hips and directed the Don's appendage, which resembled a baseball bat, inside her. Then as the Don approached the paradise stroke he lifted his tail and let fly. It had been too much for the poor ass. All his bodily functions climaxed at once.

Our Japanese friends who had been snapping away in the front row took the volley full on their chops, changing their complexions from yellow to the Boys in the Brown Stuff.

All hell let loose. The Don was winched up visibly confused,

Marie ran around unfulfilled, screaming like a banshee. The MC reappeared calling for calm. 'No need for panic,' as mayhem drove the punters towards the exits.

The Bee Gees party and I made a hasty departure stage left, legging it down the fire escape that clung perilously to the listed building.

Years later, Barry, Linda and I returned to Amsterdam. We retraced our steps to number eighteen Canal Strasse. But the Casa Rosso had disappeared. Apparently in 1980 it had mysteriously burned down and the owner, a man in a pink ruffled shirt and velvet bow tie, was found floating face down in the canal.

And 'Don Key Oaty'?

He now grazes peacefully in pastures new just outside Mill Hill, London, NW7.

The heart is the fountain of all human feeling. Nobody understood human nature and gave to his fellow beings more generously than Maurice Gibb and yet on 11 January 2003 Mo's heart ceased to beat. Mo threaded the needle between the three brothers, filling the spaces with quick-fire humour and repartee. On stage, his rapport with the audience was second to none. However, he was obsessed with the police.

Before concerts, Mo would make a beeline for the nearest police officer and engage him in friendly chat. The 'Old Bill', often overwhelmed by the presence of fame, would ask Mo if he 'could sign a photo for my wife. Not for me, mind you, but my other half.'

'And her name?' enquired Mo.

'Oh Derek, just sign it to Derek,' stuttered the policeman.

Now for the crunch. Inevitably the policeman would reciprocate with an offer of 'Anything I can do for you?'

Fatal. 'Well, as a matter of fact, I wouldn't mind your hat (or shirt, jacket, badge etc. . . .).'

From the dressing room we would watch the poor unsuspecting lawman disrobe to present Mo with items of his clobber. What he didn't know was that after the show Mo would wear the outfit and go out on the town. Very often he'd come off the stage after entertaining 80,000 punters in, say, Milwaukee, put on his police outfit, get into his vehicle, turn on the red flashing light and sirens and proceed to patrol downtown.

I was actually in Pensacola Florida standing at a bar when Mo came in and arrested a hooker, pressing her up against the counter, splaying her legs for a body search. He emptied the contents of her handbag, where he discovered some marijuana. Handcuffing the girl, who was giving him some serious verbal, Mo marched his 'bust' outside to his car. Minutes later, Mo was stopped by the real cops who, much to the amazement of the hooker, arrested him and took him in for impersonating a police officer.

On another occasion Maurice asked me to fly out to the Isle of Man where he was living. Yvonne had just given birth to his son Adam and he could do with some company. When our plane landed at Douglas Airport there was no sign of Mo. Then suddenly a blue Rolls Royce with a red light flashing roared over the tarmac, stopping at the foot of the plane's stairway. Out jumped this cop wearing full NYPD kit. He ran up the stairs of the plane and demanded to take David English into custody. Handcuffed, I was arrested and bundled into the back of the Rolls, watched by the astonished passengers.

'Great to see you Dave,' smiled Mo, pulling on a cheroot à la Dirty Harry.

We zoomed off to the Liverpool Arms where we met his scouser mates and enjoyed a wild afternoon drinking Guinness, telling gags and playing darts.

Give us Layla

Eric Clapton and Ian Botham had become firm friends ever since I had taken E.C. to Lords where Beefy was playing for England versus Australia in 1986. Eric was not wearing a tie and was refused entry to the pavilion. I got on the blower to Beefy in the England dressing room to explain the dilemma.

'No problem, Loon,' said the Beef. 'I'll be straight down.'

Down came Ian to the pavilion door wearing his pads (he was in next) to confront a massive crowd milling around the entrance.

I introduced him to Eric.

'Beefy, this is E.C.'

'Nice to meet you, man,' smiled Ian. The two legends shook hands. Beefy gave him his England tie. Eric was admitted and their friendship was cemented.

I often took some of my star Bunbury players to Worcester to see Beefy play and enjoy some wild nights afterwards. Eric Clapton, George Harrison, Elton John, Bill Wyman and Jeff Lynne were all regular visitors.

Strangely every time I took Eric to the County Ground Beefy failed to make a big score.

'Tell you what, Beefy. If you score a century on Sunday, I'll play live in a pub of your choice after the game,' challenged Eric.

That's all it took to energize the super-competitive Botham. He clobbered the Essex attack for a mighty 125 off 70 balls.

Job done. Only problem was Eric had not brought a guitar. As E.C, Beefy and the Worcester lads played cards, Ian's PA Andy Withers went to their hideaway home to remove the Fender Stratocaster, which hung on the wall. Eric had presented it to him after the victorious Ashes tour of 1986/87 inscribed 'To Brother Beefy'.

Now they needed an amplifier. Not easy to find in Worcester on a Sunday night. Eric disappeared into the town to find an amp. He finally found a music shop that was open, picked a suitable amplifier and handed the assistant his credit card as he had lost all his cash playing cards. The astonished assistant stared at the card and didn't believe it could be Eric Clapton. It took several calls to the credit card company before Eric could walk out with the goods.

When he descended upon this lovely pub deep in the Worcester-shire countryside, there were two or three people dotted about sipping pints or playing dominoes and darts while a dog yawned by the fireplace with one eye open blearily watching the TV that flickered in the corner. Suddenly, in walked the world's greatest guitarist to ask the landlord if he could plug in his amp and play a few songs. By the time the players from both sides had arrived Eric was in full swing, playing his greatest hits to four people and the old black dog.

A fourteen-year-old boy had excitedly cycled home to tell his dad to bring him his drum kit.

Beefy, Gooch, Pringle, Dilley and Co. enjoyed the night of their lives as Eric's guitar soared into the night.

'"Layla", El, Give Us "Layla"!'

Dreamland

Take us to Dreamland, Dad . . . Down the old A2 in our yellow Ford Consul eating crisps in the back and staring out at Snodland, still asleep, golden slumbers nestled in the valley.

Keep a steady hand on the wheel, Dad, nipping in and out of the lorries lumbering by like elephants on the trunk road to Dover and on to the continent. Over the hills, who's the first to see the sea shimmering like diamonds under a Basildon Bond sky?

Dad, take us to Dreamland, young lovers holding hands, donkeys in twos on the sand. Take us to the helter-skelter, see the faces of the punters screaming in delighted terror, swinging their bodies suspended in space. Then there's the first ride on the magical roundabout with its brightly painted prancing horses and whirling organ. Let's try our luck on the side-shows, throw a hula hoop over the goldfish bowl or pin the Queen of Hearts to the board with a dart, to win a fluffy poodle, a Buckingham Palace in a snowstorm or 'anything off the top shelf'. Didn't you meet Mum in Margate, Dad? Falling in love on the ghost train, blissful innocence and candyfloss kisses beneath 'kiss me quick' hats. The whiff of salt and vinegar is high on the breeze, salt from the sea and vinegar from the fish and chips being scoffed in the bus shelter by Reggie the cabbie from East Ham down for the day with Violet his princess married for forty-two years, 'The only woman I ever loved.'

Here we are holding the towel with one hand while we wrestle off our underpants to replace them with 'go faster' Speedos, hopping about like demented storks with a stiff breeze from the North Sea whipping up our kilts.

At the end of the day it's back on with the T-shirt gingerly over red raw shoulders. Sand is everywhere: in your shoes, in your hair and up the crack of your bum. The tide's coming in; has anyone seen Mum?

Then it's back to the A2 to crawl home in the traffic jam, sore but happy. Back to our road lost in endless green. Far from the sandcastles . . . and the Land of the Dream.

17 November 2003 I return to Margate.

It's Saturday night and I'm sitting on a bench with a lovely girl called Rachel. In the distance dramatic lights flicker above the Isle of Thanet. Margate has a beautiful coastline with sunsets and light, but it is the other side that attracts me, dark and derelict, chipped and faded facades, run-down arcades, tat and dross, seedy and shabby, the heart and soul of a seaside town out of season.

Margate on a Saturday night and the town's tired sheen has a strange allure. A briny whiff bubbles up from the beach. Amusement arcades flicker and wink, pumping demented electronic rhythms into the night.

Cavorting beneath the pulse and glow are throngs of punters down from the East End, out on the lash.

I'm taking Rachel to Frank's Nightclub. Tonight the tribute band Fred Zeppelin are appearing – 'One Night Only, A Must See Show'. Last week The Girls from Flabba entertained the white-stilettoed revellers already queuing ready to flash fake IDs.

With derelict properties dotted around, Margate today seems a far cry from its magnificent artistic heritage. Thackeray, Turner, Rossetti and Dickens were all drawn to the area. T.S. Eliot came to convalesce following a nervous breakdown. But there are no commemorative plaques. Next to Frank's Nightclub there is a grim blockhouse that bears the legend 'Toilets'.

I could write a great seaside thriller here depicting two-bit mobsters from a world of slashed faces and thrills. Beneath the resort's boozing and poverty laps a pale-green sea sucking at the scarred and shabby side of England.

Rachel would play the heroine in my story. She would be pursued by a dollar-chasing arcade owner escaping his own past. They would be Sharon Stone and Robert de Niro in *Casino*. Instead, we'll be cavorting to a ropey version of 'Stairway to Heaven' inside Frank's gilded auditorium with peeling walls and the karaoke bar suffused with drab neglect and peroxide heads of sexually adventurous Traceys and Del Boys – fantastic – wish you were here!

Seaside Love

Music has always acted as the soundtrack of my life. It creates the mood and pulls at the heart-strings, especially when you're driving.

I stare out at the countryside and am inspired by the weathered colours of the natural world; there is a rich melancholy about it. Not in the summer because it's usually very clear, but in the spring and winter when it's very brooding and is conducive to a certain kind of thinking. 'The wind is in from Africa' . . . Joni Mitchell is singing. She paints pictures with her words like a true artist. 'Oh, star bright, star bright, you've got the lovin' that I like, alright, turn this crazy bird around, I shouldn't have got on this flight tonight.'

Her songs are autobiographical, mirroring personal emotions. She seems like a lady who walks on eggs; her music is careful, delicate as though she sails through life frightened of breaking it.

I imagine her staying in my cottage amongst the cricket bats and memorabilia. She is sitting cross-legged on the wooden floor, wearing a pair of jeans, a tiny printed shirt and a plain sweater over the top. Her feet are bare where she's kicked off her clogs, and her fine, fair hair trails across her shoulders almost hiding the silver hoops she wears in her ears. There is a tidy casualness about her appearance, a cleanliness and unrumpled freshness. We'd go out and 'drink wine in some dark cafe'. She'd wear a beret and red lipstick outlining her sensual lips ... 'When I think of her kisses my mind see-saws' ... 'She'd wreck her stockings in some jukebox dive', before I threw her across my shoulder and took her outside to sit on a cliff and stare at the sea under a star-bright sky and the mantle of a Torquay moon.

Sunshine and music always lead me to the sea ... 'You are the sunshine of my life'. Every summer holiday in Torquay, the gem of the English Riviera would beckon. I'd pack up my old VW Beetle 'Sid' with beach tackle and along with my pals Johnny Ashe, Steve Miller and Ray Still we'd make for the south west in search of sea, sun and sexual adventure.

It was the summer of 1972. Down on the promenade love was all around in our Shangri La of Rod Stewart haircuts, 'Maggie May' and George McCrae's 'Rock Me Baby'. Young men from Toxteth having descended the Liverpool mountain, 'Kill a man for his giro', paraded their tanned bodies, hiring out pedaloes, procuring their dates for a night of lingering love in the Casa Marina Club courtesy of their dole money.

Our HQ was the Avondale Guest House, 171 Avenue Road. It was the perfect holiday residence. Herbaceous border, Vauxhall Viva in the drive, three ducks on the wall, run by the wonderful Mrs Doherty and her deaf husband Albert.

'How are you, Albert?' we roared.

'Yes, it looks like rain,' smiled Mr D, extending a friendly hand.

Mrs D loved us like her own sons.

From our 'home from home' cosy retreat we would hit the beach for a day of adventure.

Our routine consisted of a huge English breakfast. Eight thirty on the beach for cricket, football and high jinks. Twelve thirty into the town to drink Stella Artois outside the Castle Tavern, waiting for the Scandinavian students to appear from the E.F. School, all clogs and hot pants, and that was just the boys! Two thirty back to the beach with a coterie of lovelies from Stockholm before attacking the

Grand Hotel for sundowners at six. Our trips to the Grand became a little strained – you can only sign the drinks bill 'Mr E. Presley, Room 142' for so long before the management smell a rat. We changed our location to the magestic Imperial Hotel where we mastered some daring run-outs. Stevie Miller would always be the first off the terrace. Not surprising as he had come a real cropper in the raid on 'The Holi Fook' Chinese restaurant, Heath Street, Hampstead.

It was a balmy summer evening. The four of us had been sitting outside the restaurant drinking Saki and chewing the fat.

'OK lads, time to make our exit. When I give you the nod, Ray, you go up the street. Johnny, you go down and Stevie, you follow me round the back lane. We'll meet in the usual place.' It was crucial to time the Great Escape to a split second. The waiters had gone into the restaurant. 'Go! Go! Go!' I ordered. All seemed to go to plan but when we regrouped on the heath there was no sign of Steve. Apparently on 'Go', the combination of nerves and adrenalin had propelled Steve *into* the restaurant. In a state of panic the unemployed carpenter tore around the restaurant full of number seventeen, fried rice and a large spring roll. Bruce Lee, the head chef, pierced the confusion by pinning Steve's ear to the gents' door with a large fork. To this day, Stevie Miller still wears five earrings in his left ear.

Then there was the Hilton Hotel heist. The same four galloping gourmets settled into the Windows Restaurant with a view to a reasonably relaxed exit, cocksure with recent triumphant departures from 'The Shah Bag' Hampstead, 'The Sitar' Brent Street, Hendon and the 'Day of the Raj' Mill Hill. We agreed that if we were going to get nicked it might as well be on a full stomach.

Well I can confirm that it is not easy to run on a belly full of scampi in the basket, chicken legs and a generous portion of Black Forest cake, washed down by a bottle of Chardonnay and sixteen light ales.

But run we did.

The first inkling that it wasn't going to be 'our night' was when the four of us steamed into four separate glass doors at full speed, opening three, but number four remaining stubbornly closed, splattering Johnny Ashe with a fearful body blow into horizontal submission.

The rest of us hit Park Lane, feet not touching the ground. Momentarily I was in the lead before an athletic waiter brought me down with a crashing rugby tackle. We were marched back meekly to meet the management.

'Fantastic!' cried the waiter. 'It's the best exercise I've had since I won the 100 yards Olympic trials in Jo'burg!' Unbeknown to us our three waiters were all sprint champions from South Africa.

High on the hill lies Harrow School. Silhouetted against an August moon, the midnight runners puffed and panted just below the ancient church of St Mary's overlooking the twinkling lights of Middlesex to London, ten miles away.

The sounds of vomiting after alcoholic indulgence with yours truly in the Spread Eagle pub propelled Messrs Will Haggas, Jeremy Lloyd-Jones and co, dressed in just their running shorts and singlets, through the deserted streets.

The mighty Vic Lewis XI had taken on the Harrow School 1st XI in a charity match in 1978. After the game I had decreed with great gusto, 'Come on lads, the drinks are on me!'

The fact that the boys were not allowed in the pub especially after 'lights out' didn't seem to dampen the ardour of the revellers, who quaffed vast amounts of lager and performed the great drinking songs with enormous zest and fervour.

But alas at closing time the pub was raided by Mr Attenborough the housemaster and his trustee cohorts. Desperate attempts to escape through lavatory windows and the landlord's wine cellar were made but the Wily Attenborough was one step ahead and collared the whole team.

As I drove away I could just make out the outline of future prime ministers, city bankers and the odd dodgy accountant jogging along the summit of the hill.

Years later I reunited with Will Haggas (now a highly successful racehorse trainer) and Jeremy Lloyd-Jones (a De Beers diamond merchant).

'English you bugger, what a night that was. We were under your influence, but tell you what, old Harrovian Winston Churchill would have been proud of us!'

'She was just seventeen, you know what I mean, and the way she looked was way beyond compare . . .'

It was an overcast Torquay Tuesday as me and the boys went on our midday patrol through the town to the Castle Tavern. The sun pierced the clouds like a cigarette burn in a blotting paper sky and a strand of light fell on the white blonde 'barnet' of a smashing little bird holding court surrounded by a gaggle of Nordics, slurping back large vodkas. She wore a yellow top, blue jeans and red clogs. I had found my own Joni Mitchell.

'Here we go lads, that one's for me!'

As I invaded the 'Viking Man's Club' the sing-song Scandinavian turned to pigeon English.

'What is your name?' I enquired.

'Kaisu,' came the reply.

Kaisu Mattila was barely seventeen. She came from Finland, the land of the lakes, and I fell for her bigtime. The thrill of meeting someone special for the first time surged through my body. Standing in that ring of fire in uptown Torquay and staring at her beautiful face, already I was making imaginary plans of things to do together. We exchanged numbers, but would she call? You leave with that sense of not knowing, but if you've hit the mark with the right banter and she does too, if you've made the connection, then everything is possible, opening up the floodgates to stolen weekends in Helsinki.

When we returned to Avondale exhausted, Mrs D was there by the gate to welcome us with a warm smile and a tray of tea and homemade fruit cake.

'And David, Kaisu called for you. She wants you to phone her back.'

At seven thirty I met Kaisu, immediately christened her 'Billy' after my toy Panda and took her for a stroll on the beach. Hand in hand, we came across a straw hat lying on the sand. I gave it an aimless kick and there was a scream. To our amazement beneath the hat was a buried head.

'And what's your name?' I enquired.

'Eddie,' was the reply.

'And what happened to you, Eddie?'

'Well, last night I sank a few pints and sat on the beach to think – it was a beautiful night, the moon was out and the dogs were barking. I must have dozed off. When I awoke the tide had come in and covered me with flotsam and jetsam.'

'Don't move, Eddie,' I said, deeply concerned, 'I'll go and get a shovel.'

'Well, you'd better make it a big one,' yelled Eddie, 'cos I'm sitting on a donkey!'

For the rest of our seaside summer Billy and I were lost on a wave of love. True, she drank large vodkas in the bath and together with her blonde countryfolk created a riotous assembly, but she also possessed the quality of unspeakable gentleness.

We ran through the woods dappled in sunlight, listened to James Taylor and Carole King and when I held her in my arms I felt lost to the world, out of control.

Sad September arrived as the sands of summer passed through our fingers. Billy returned to Helsinki. A month later I visited her, staying at the Alexander Hotel. She met me in the bar and looked fantastic. I wanted to make love to her. For me sexual intercourse had begun in 1963, between the end of the Lady Chatterley ban and the Beatles' first LP.

'No babies, David,' she said, rubbing her tummy.

I went into the toilet and wrestled with the condom machine. I was desperately trying to put in the right money when some Finnish bloke standing at the urinals looked at me quizzically and said, 'No chewing gum . . . It's not chocolate!'

Billy took me on a tour of Helsinki. It was staggeringly beautiful. We stopped outside a large wooden house painted scarlet.

'What is this?' I enquired.

'It's called the Flame Hotel, where people can stay and drink themselves to death,' said Billy.

Fascinated, I watched the folk, happy as Larry, sitting on the wall laughing and chattering, fuelled by pure spirit. Occasionally, the odd character would fall to the ground pissed out of their brains and lay there motionless with a huge grin on their faces. Well, I had heard of a rehab clinic, but in Finland I had discovered my first hab home.

If It Were Not For Hope the Heart Would Break

I finally got to meet Joni Mitchell. It was 1969 at Woodstock – four days of peace and love. 'We are stardust, we are golden, got to get ourselves back to the garden.' I couldn't believe it; what an adventure. I was hitch-hiking down a country road to Woodstock in New York State, a guitar case slung on my back. I stuck out my thumb at a VW Beetle bowling down towards me. It stopped. I got in the back and the driver continued chatting away to the beautiful, cool, long-haired woman in the passenger seat. It was the American Dream, happy, relaxed, handsome, perfect teeth, blue-jeans freedom.

Only slowly did it dawn on me that the people in the front seats were James Taylor and his wife, the utterly and beautifully great Carly Simon. Was I dreaming? No, it was an undeniable reality. Two of the most famous singers in the world had stopped to give me a lift. I wanted to go on for ever. They laughed at my Englishness.

I wish they could have adopted me, but within minutes we had reached the outskirts of Woodstock and they left me on the side of the road to dream of the magical encounter for the rest of my life.

That incident occurred over thirty-five years ago, but doesn't it have an air of Eden-like sweetness compared with anything we might have today? Can you imagine any modern ersatz pop star giving anyone a lift? Those door-locks surely clunk down as soon as the limo leaves the compound. Carly to Kylie: the collapse of civilization.

. . . To sing like James Taylor. Running through woods dappled in sunlight barefoot holding on to my virtue . . . 'You're so vain you probably thought this song was about you.' To push the parameters and find a girl like Carly . . . feeling lost to the world, out of control.

And Woodstock? Half a million crazies having a ball, tearing it up, dancing naked, almost lost my hair, skinny dipping, sliding in the mud, the magnificent self demeanour of the kids.

'One, two, three, four, what are we fighting for?'

'Don't ask me, I don't give a damn, next stop is Vietnam.'

'And it's five, six, seven, open up the pearly gates.'

Jefferson Aeroplane, Canned Heat. There was Janis and Jimi, John Sebastian and Country Joe. Ten Years After and Carlos Santana, Joan Baez and Sly and the Family Stone.

An overwhelming feeling of loving one's brothers and sisters . . . mud is everywhere, Che Guevara T-shirts, the Who. It's a new dawn; the kids are spaced out. Conversations in the open air, sitting around in circles. Far out, man, groovy. Children holding buckets. Love the cat next to you? Psychedelic babies sucking on boobs. Be understanding of the younger generation. LSD, no time for dreams, too busy doing it. Crosby Stills Nash and Young and . . . Joni Mitchell.

I met her backstage with Neil Young. She was really my type. Although she was supremely feminine, she could be one of the boys. She also shared my need to run away and be isolated, to let the ideas percolate from a kaleidoscope of notions into a single colourful vision. Then the need to return to the city and be part of the urban way. To be torn between being on your own and having to be with people. I could see a lot of her in me. Before I met her I had got to understand her through her songs and lyrics. When I met her she was wearing a navy-blue beret over long golden hair which she threw back as she laughed. She was very beautiful and I felt close to her. After hearing her songs I'd expected to see her appear descending from a mountain on the wisps of Wagner in a long chiffon dress with toenails painted scarlet. A magic princess, twinkle, twinkle, little star, court and spark. I felt her sense of passion from the heart, sensuality for the sensation, torn between longing for love and wanting a sense of independence. The need for love and an ongoing search for ambition defines our lives. This conflict produces the art.

I went to the studio with Joni and saw how she worked. Sometimes the adventure slipped away. Other times there would be a million pieces of music in her head and she would be braided together with her musicians producing a wonderful wall of sound. I've always believed in a freedom in approach to music. Looking for different ways to weave the tapestry. A freeform artist exercising freedom. Inclusion not seclusion. Poetry takes a lot of plumbing the depths, whereas cricket takes me out of who I am. It solidifies me and gives me a sense of security. A celebration of our friendship that moves into love. Being in love is very important to me. Come in Joni from the cold and let me warm your heart with love. It's time to get out the pen. It's hard peeling the skin off your own onion . . . you're doing a tightrope walk to keep your heart alive and to love others. 'Doctors' pills give you brand new ills and the gas leaks and the oil spills and sex sells everything and sex kills.' Start off as friends, then look for romantic love. Turbulent times. Joni was so unruly in this business because she didn't want to be a human jukebox. Ask Rory Bremner about being a human jukebox – 'Go on Rory, give us John Major, Nelson Mandela, Gavin Hastings, Geoff Boycott, right now!'

Just have the courage to follow what comes out of you. Can you get through this life with a good heart? In a world full of struggle let the heart rebound back and bloom again. I have found you go through a process of discovery which can only be found by having a child. With a family you feel complete and far less self-important. Caring for others gives you a warm feeling, like living in a feathered canyon. Don't be frightened to let the tears fall. Youth, marriage, fatherhood, the complete journey. I'm still writing my map as I drive, continuing the journey, music, cricket and caring for others. Mirror whoever you are speaking to. Get close up and personal ASAP. Make them laugh and make them feel immediately as though you've known them all their lives. Constantly search those faces for the kind of secrets that they hold.

'It's life's illusion that I recall. I really don't know life at all.'

The One That Got Away

So I'm sitting here in a cafe on the Boulevard St Germain. The cappuccino machine is spluttering as the pretty waitresses shimmy between tables where the young indulge in intense Gauloises – perfumed conversations heightened by the prospect of casual sex. An air of Jean-Paul Sartre prevails. I imagine him mentally entwined with a beautiful blonde, the ultimate philosophical cowboy, an intellectual gunslinger who can outshoot every other thinker in town. But the Elvis or James Dean of philosophy is not here.

It is September 2003. Outside, the Parisians sit preening them-selves with self gratification, terribly chic, peering through designer sunglasses as the last strands of summer shine down on their scented circle and the one empty chair . . . Ah! The one that got away.

July 1970, Rosas, Costa Blanca, Spain. The one empty chair outside Happy John's Snack Bar has been vacated by Jean Pierre Cottereau, my super slim Froggy pal from Le Mans. A kind of Alain Delon lookalike. He was holidaying with our gang of five, Peter 'Bomber' Mellor from the Clitterhouse Estate, Claremont Road, Hendon, Handsome Bazzer, the architect from Chiselhurst, Kent and Johnny Ashe, the Sofa Bed King from Camden Town.

Jean Pierre had left his seat to get the beers in, ice-cold San Miguels, the perfect tonic for a scorching Spanish day.

Earlier that morning we lay on our towels and fried, occasionally looking up to squint at the sun or to clock any tasty birds that wobbled by. We were not alone. Dotted about the beach were the creosote men dripping in gold. Essex lads, so tanned they looked as though they had been painted dark brown.

'Fuckin 'ell, look at that one,' whispered Bomber.

This goddess glided by, very sophisticated, wearing a silk sarong and a beautiful smile. Golden streaked hair sporting a pink flower behind her temple. She resembled a young Catherine Deneuve.

I resembled a tomato. My body was burnt to a shred with just a pair of Speedos separating the northern burns unit from the south. Looking as though I had been hit by napalm on the killing fields of Vietnam, I rose to my feet.

'Watch this, lads.'

The boys laughed. 'You've got no fuckin' chance,' they encouraged. I walked gingerly on the burning sands behind the vision in silk.

Always give it your best shot, I thought; they can only say 'no'. 'Excuse me, sweetheart.'

She whirled around to confront the burnt offering from England and instantly took my breath away.

'So I am your sweetheart?' she enquired with a French accent.

'*Absolument*,' I chortled in my best O-level French. '*Tu es très jolie, mademoiselle.*'

Her eyes had transformed from gently expressive pools of blue to twinkling sapphire lights.

'So you are EEEngleeeesh, monsieur?'

'*Oui, mademoiselle, je m'appelle Davide Anglais.*'

Her coy smile had been replaced in a flash by a joyous laugh.

Fuck me, I thought, keep your nerve Dave boy, you're doing OK here. I felt as though the eyes of the entire beach were watching our liaison. One thing for sure, the gang of four were spellbound. How could Dave the fried tomato get involved with this apparition? Ah! But that's the secret, look them straight in the eyes and make them laugh.

We chatted for a good five minutes, each exercising the language of the other. We were lost to the world. Her name was Karine Mouchelet and she came from Chantilly, just outside Paris.

'*Karine, qu'est ce que tu fais ce soir?*'

'I do not know,' she replied.

'*Ce soir on va dancer.* We will be in Rocky's Nightclub if you can make it.'

She smiled, shook my hand and with a whiff of Chanel No. 5, she had disappeared along the shimmering sands.

I returned to my towel triumphantly to be instantly quizzed by the Spanish inquisition.

'Well, how did you get on?'

'What did she say?'

'Tell you what, lads, we'll have to wait and see.'

I recoiled into semi slumber, the fire in my belly outdoing the glow on the outside. I was consumed by thoughts of the beautiful mademoiselle. The thrill of meeting someone for the first time. I lay on my towel making imaginary plans of our shared experience. Would she come to the club? If she did, well, everything would be possible, opening up that little door in your heart that leads to desire. Desire, such a rare commodity, for once it has gone you are a seed in the wind, blown to infinity. Enjoy the star that twinkles before it goes dull.

Rocky's Nightclub was named after its owner and the fact that the entire disco was hewn out of the rocky cliffs. Rocky hailed from the East End of London, where he had practised as an enforcer. He wore a yellow mohair jacket, a permanent tan and a diamond in his tooth. He had spent some years down south on the Costa Del Crime flourishing in the company of gunmen, mad dogs and mercenaries.

'Evening, lads,' growled our host. 'Where you been, in a microwave? You'll be all right tonight, plenty of birds will be in – it's Friday.'

Our night took on a typical Boys' Own feel: disco dancing, energizing, appetizing, romancing, realizing. Every now and again we regrouped to compare notes on our conquests. Updates on Roman blondes and Transylvanian glamour models – they all looked so sensational. There was a back room, the Las Vegas suite where Rocky encouraged his cronies to gamble. There were murals of Nevada, Las Vegas, 'Lost Wages' – a town plonked down in the desert with no nobler purpose than separating Americans from their wages. Rocky had created his own 'Lost Wages', a mirage, a roulette of immorality.

It was approaching twelve a.m. The time for a dalliance along the beach with the catch of the night beckoned . . . The bewitching hour. I desperately hoped that Karine would appear. I longed to see her lovely face again.

'Dave, you can stop drilling cos it looks as though you've struck oil,' said Bomber.

I turned and there she was.

'Hello, sweetheart,' she smiled.

'*Comment ça va?*'

We danced and I felt helpless, like a child, vulnerable, restless. The power of a woman. From that moment she took control. She told me about her life. She acted and modelled for *Vogue*; she enshrined the melancholic beauty that France craves from its film stars.

In the ensuing days I discovered her grace and her apparent fragility; she was passionate about life. This enabled her to capture lively and communicative emotion with a subtle intelligence. She had a body for modelling and a head for business. But it was her 'elsewhere' that interested me.

The night we made love she had made the decision. She pulled off my shirt in a fluid movement, which was far more expert than if I had done it myself.

Our holiday was drawing to a close. The more I saw Karine the harder it was to say goodbye. I was left to dance on the outside. The soft underbelly of our holiday romance was lost in the warmth of her embrace.

I went back to England. The hopelessness of our love slipped away and I returned to the abstract world. But all the roads in my mind led back to Karine. Within a week I went to visit her in Chantilly. She introduced me to the Cafe Society. It was wonderful to feel solitary in the midst of all those Frogs. A feeling of naughtiness prevailed as we shared the sense of warmth, secure in our anonymity.

She introduced me to Johnny Hallyday, L'idole de Jeunes. Years of chainsmoking Gitanes had given his voice a lacquered splendour. For foreign observers of France, Johnny, along with the whole idea of French rock 'n' roll, had often seemed a joke. The fact that unlike Aznavour, Gainsbourg or Distel he was completely unexportable reinforced his image as a mystifying French obsession like mime or the andoulette sausage.

He was a French phenomenon. In 1973 Johnny told me that he started performing when he was fifteen, doing French versions of American rock 'n' roll songs. He had the same impact in France that

Elvis and the Beatles had in Britain and America. Many years later as Teeny Bop came and went, I noticed that Johnny Hallyday had stuck around.

I was fascinated by Karine's friends, especially the girls . . . the French Connection, Jeanne Moreau types, alluring and cerebral, sadder but wiser girls who loved but tended to lose. Then there were the men: dark, smooth, sultry, aloof frown, finely chiselled features, mysterious and deep.

I flourished amongst the artisans but in my heart I was already missing England. You can only take so much of that smooth sophistication. I secretly longed for football on Hackney Marshes, cricket at Lords and a few pints of Guinness down at the local. Karine sensed the change in my demeanour. Of course I loved her but I simply missed home.

I left her at the Gare du Nord. Earlier we had sat in the Bar Valenciennes, a seductive cafe in the station forecourt with murals depicting toffs alighting from boat trains. My mind wandered. I looked at the departure board and felt the thrill of seeing foreign destinations: Amsterdam, Lucerne, Milan and Warsaw. I could imagine Inspector Maigret pulling on his pipe, waiting for the night trains from Belgium and Germany bringing in the first load of crooks.

'A *bientôt*. I will see you soon.' I kissed and hugged her and boarded the train.

As we steamed out I looked back and waved. She was standing in the pale light inside the station. The delicate green ironwork and the rows of circular lanterns, each one casting the light of a full moon on her beautiful face. Weeks passed by. We kept in touch. She wrote to me:

> *Davide the winds from Paris blow you kisses for ever.*
> *Karine xxx*

Of course I missed her, but the memories began to fade. Perhaps holiday romances should be left on holiday.

Three years later I stared at her photograph. It captured the retina of our Spanish memory. I tried to call her but there was no answer. Love and kindness, understanding and compassion comes from the heart, not the mouth. If the heart is empty the head doesn't matter . . . I decided to go back and find her.

I took the train to the Gare du Nord and then a taxi to where she lived in Chantilly. Chantilly, thirty miles north of Paris, is the home to horseracing in France. It was just after dawn as I walked along the Avenue de Lamorlaye towards her home, having decided to walk the last mile to ponder the forthcoming encounter. Either side of the road, trainers were leading their horses out to the forests for early-morning runs.

I approached numéro 141 with trepidation. My heart was racing as I knocked on the door. After an eternity I heard the turning of a key in the lock. The door opened. Would it be Karine?

'*Bonjour. Monsieur, qu'es que tu veut?*'

A lady, very elegant, in her early sixties, stood before me.

'Madame Mouchelet?' I asked. My throat was dry.

'*Oui*, and you are Davide. You'd better come in,' said the madame.

I entered the room and sat in a very comfy armchair.

'And Karine, madame?'

Madame Mouchelet, sitting on the chair opposite me, leaned forwards and looked me steadily in the eye.

'Davide, Karine was married last Wednesday.'

At first the words didn't sink in. It couldn't be true. Stunned, I recoiled into my chair and listened as Madame Mouchelet unfurled her story.

'She was very heartbroken. She waited and waited for you, Davide. But you did not come and now she has gone.'

If one advances confidently in the direction of one's dreams and endeavours to live the life which he has imagined, one will meet with a success unexpected in common hours . . . The truth is, had she opened the door, would she have taken me back and would we still be married today?

Thirty-four years later, I still wonder where she is and what might have happened.

I never could give up my freedom. Freedom might imply a lot

of loneliness and unfulfilment. It implies the search for fulfilment, which sometimes is more exciting than the fulfilment itself. We are searching for somebody special and one day we think we have found them. Then two weeks later that special feeling has gone. Perhaps we don't allow ourselves enough time to think we've found that special person, because we enjoy the quest so much. We are, in fact, in love with the idea of being in love rather than the reality of the final conquest.

However, it is better to have loved and lost than not to have loved at all. So here I am living in all this space, free to polish my MBE, but very often I think of the one that got away.

Mel, Elv, Big Bus Tour and the Price of Fame

I once spent some considerable time with a world-famous film star. His responses were always illusive, oblique. He leapt from metaphor to metaphor and when he was drinking, the leaps got wider, fuelling his imagination. I would follow him as far as I could and there was always wisdom, deep dark thoughts that touched on our friendship – but beyond a certain level of vodka he sailed out on his own into deeper waters where no mortal could follow.

I have always been drawn to characters with problems. Alcoholics, manic depressives, gamblers, sex addicts, junkies and the violent. I feel their pain and share their troubled minds. I listen and try to allay their demons. During my career in the entertainment business I have had to deal with the deepest emotions and have lost many soulmates to the excesses and terrifying powers of addiction.

For the gifted person there is for ever a search for meaning and an understanding of their place in the world, but an individual like Andy Gibb or Paul Gascoigne, who are blessed with a gift they didn't have to work for, is consumed with the problem. They didn't know what a talent they had and how to protect it. The problem with their gifts is that they didn't know how to acknowledge them. They didn't realize what they had and how to etch it into history.

Since talent is so often the scar tissue over a wound, someone touched with genius will stand out. If you study those you admire for what they've accomplished, you may be able to identify the painful and costly events that made them despair for a time, but in the end they had to thank the fortitude of spirit that made it possible for them to achieve what they did. It makes you realize that everything can be improved. But even the familiar can be looked at in a new light and imagination is more powerful than knowledge. Do you believe in the power of dreams?

Mad Mickey 'the Nutter' from Brighton certainly did, as he hung off the back of Melinda Messenger's DD – her special double-decker bus on day two of 'Mel's Big Bus Tour'. It was the summer of 1997 and I was compering 'The Girl from the Thrillenium's British Tour', visiting the key seaside towns, telling gags, handing out T-shirts signed by the 34DD–25–34 stunner and playing the current hits as loudly as possible through a crackly tannoy.

'I believe I can fly, I believe I can touch the sky . . .' filled the air, not by R. Kelly but by Mad Metal Mickey hanging off our bus.

'I'm sure you can,' I agreed. 'On two bottles of meths, Mickey, you could fly to the moon!'

'Melinder Messenger made a huge splash yesterday as her Big Bus turned Scarborough into S-Cor-Borough,' wrote our sponsor the *Sun* newspaper with banner headlines.

Thousands of cheering fans packed on to the resort's South Bay. 'Come and see our Mel sizzle!' I hollered from the top of the bus. 'She'll sign your shirts, pose for a picture and might even give you a big sunny Scarborough smacker – you never know your luck! But now, ladies and gentlemen, let's have a big welcome for India's number one rock 'n' roll star: please welcome Elvis Patel!'

As well as MCing Mel's shows it was my job to scour the clubs at night for acts to perform on our bus the next day. I had discovered Elvis Patel at Blighty's Club down on the promenade.

'A little less conversation – Elvis Presley lookalike – win a trip for two to Graceland in Memphis, Tennessee.'

I knew the real Elvis quite well. Years before, Barry Gibb and I had gone to see him. Barry had played him some of his tunes and 'The King' went on to record a fantastic rendition of 'Words'.

Most of the folk in Blighty's were 'all shook up' when I arrived. White jumpsuits, black quiffs and curled-up lips were everywhere. I was excited at the prospect of seeing the Elvis performers. I thought of his private life . . . a life that began in the hick town of Tupelo, Mississippi, dazzling hordes of screaming fans, a spell in the army and the most infamous pelvic thrust of all time, before ending up dead on a toilet in Memphis.

First on was a Chinese Elvis (AKA Paul, 'The Wonder of Hyu' or 'the King of Wok 'N' Roll). There was a Dutch Elvis – a clog-hopping shoe salesman from Amsterdam; a gay Mexican Elvis, Elvez, as he was known, who also happened to be a communist; and Elvis Patel, the King Creole of Delhi. But it was Elvis Patel who took my vote with a storming version of 'Return to Sender, the Chapati is in the Blender'.

Next day, atop our bus, the sun burned down on Elvis's turban as he gyrated to 'Heartbreak Hotel'. Mel and I were mingling with the crowds in front of the bus when suddenly the performance took on another direction. It was in the middle of 'Hound Dog', when a high-pitched scream echoed across the beach, immediately unseating a little girl, lost in candyfloss, from her donkey. To our amazement another Indian Elvis had joined our show, much to the displeasure of Mr Patel. Raj Presley, a minicab driver from Hull, had nipped up to the top deck and wrestled the mike from Patel to continue 'Hound Dog' in the key of E. There now followed a full-blown punch-up. As a flurry of rhinestones and Cuban heels kept appearing and disappearing, the crowd roared their approval, thinking it was all part of the act.

Just then there was a figure winging its way across the sky. Was it Batman? No, just Mad Metal Mickey dropping in from Brighton – so much for showbiz!

Worcester Sauce

A lot of my speaking engagements were in the Worcester area. On one occasion, my great pal Duncan Fearnley had invited me to his factory to make me a special bat, along with Eric Loxton at Dunlop Slazenger and Tony Cook at Hunts County Bats. Duncan is without doubt the finest bat-maker in the world. He has hand-made blades for the world's greatest players: Ian Botham, Viv Richards, Graham Gooch, Alan Border and Graeme Hick.

Duncan always started work at six thirty a.m. In the early seventies I was playing for the Vic Lewis Show Biz XI against Swindon Town, a big game and important charity fundraiser.

'Come up early Dave and I'll sort you out,' said Duncan.

I had driven through the mysterious Cotswolds shrouded in early-morning mist, into the Vale of Evesham and arrived at his factory in Sansome Place at six fifteen a.m. Duncan was there to meet me.

'Come inside son and let's get cracking.'

For me, to stand in his factory was like a young boy experiencing the wonder of Toys R Us, for the first time. Duncan set to work using the best willow for the blade and top-quality bamboo for the handle. To watch him work was mesmerizing, a wonderful craftsman lost in his own world of wood, cane, rubber and glue.

Nine thirty a.m. job done.

'There you are, Dave, now go out and score a hundred,' laughed Duncan.

By five twenty-five p.m. I had scored 120 not out against Wiltshire's finest at Swindon Town.

I called Duncan. 'Mission accomplished Dunc, you're a star!' In return for my bats and equipment I would always speak at Duncan's functions. Over the years he's heard and demanded the same gags for Basil D'Oliveira, Jimmy Cumbes and the Worcester lads. 'Joe Jordon, Cuff links, Wire brush and Dettol, Even the bad times are good' have brought the house down all over the county.

Every day Duncan would finish his bat-making at twelve p.m. and retire to the Shakespeare, a well-known hostelry run by a cricket nut, the late Graham Williams. Inside the pub, cricketing memorabilia adorned the walls. As usual we got stuck into Duncan's favourite tipple Blue Nun. Vats of Herr Liebfraumilch's sweetest wine were consumed as the stories flowed at a frenetic pace. Lord Stanley Webb of Chicken Shack fame invariably joined us, along with the rest of the Worcester clan.

'I can't stay too long today, Dunc.' I pleaded, 'I'm speaking tonight at Dursley CC in Gloucestershire.'

Unfazed, the master bat-maker ducked that verbal bouncer. 'Don't worry about that, Dave, now soop up!'

I finally escaped from the Shakespeare at five thirty p.m. and pointed my trusty Saab towards Gloucestershire.

At seven I pulled into a field for a quick kip. At seven forty-five I awoke with a jolt, got out of my car and endeavoured to put on my best DJ. Apart from standing in a large cow pat, the transformation into sartorial elegance was more or less achieved.

I was lost and already an hour late for my speaking engagement. Just then I saw lights coming from a house on the hill. I was strangely drawn to the elegant Victorian mansion, which stood on a wooded slope. I drove up the gravel drive, alighted and knocked on the door. I could hear giggling coming along the hallway and to my amazement, a lady scantily clad in provocative lingerie opened the door. 'Oooh, look who they've sent us girls. It's James Bond!' And with that, the curvy blonde wearing a fishnet catsuit resembling a saucy bank robber pulled me along the passage and into a large room full of gorgeous women.

'You must be Mr Freddy from the agency!' screamed the hostess, wearing just a thong and high heels. I hope what they say about you is true!'

'Yeah that's right, I'm Mr Fred—' Mid sentence I was assaulted by a wave of French knickers, suspenders, stockings and a Teutonic-looking lovely wearing a Nazi uniform and wielding a leather whip.

'Off with his trousers!' cried a sexy milkmaid sitting on my face.

'Let me rip his pants off with my teeth. Go on Mr Freddy, suck on my boobs. They cost my old man five thousand pounds – he calls them my policemen's helmets!'

When the husbands are away the girls will play! I had stumbled onto a full-blown sex party consisting of twenty lovelies and me – Mr Freddy, their stud for the night.

I managed to exit from Caligula through a bathroom window. Staggering to my car I was blinded by the lights of a Porsche speeding up the drive. Inside a blond Adonis wearing a black tie was assembling his bag of tricks. I hammered on his window. Startled, he looked up and opened it. 'You must be Mr Freddy?'

'Yes,' he replied.

'Well, you'd better get in there. They're expecting you!'

It was five to eleven when I finally arrived at Dursley CC and the reception was somewhat frosty, to put it mildly. How could I possibly explain my day? Covered in lipstick and my breath still reeking of Blue Nun, I performed for the second time that night, launching myself into my gags, presented a couple of cups, thanked the local mayor and eventually passed out in the Dursley CC Home Teams Dressing Room at two thirty a.m.

Gnome From Gnome

'Loon, it's got to be this way,' said Rob Bailey, valiantly clutching a map whilst sliding off his seat.

There was loud applause from the back followed by a boisterous chorus of 'Hi ho, hi ho, it's off to work we go!' fuelled by a crate of rapidly disappearing Stella Artois.

Swiftly, I swung the Ford Transit bearing the insignia 'The Irresistible Novelty Company' around the back lanes of deepest, greenest Worcestershire.

We were on our way to a Rob Bailey benefit luncheon at a remote restaurant outside Worcester. I had borrowed the van from a pal of mine who had his own practical jokes / magic shop in

London's Chancery Lane. Apart from 'The Irresistible Novelty Company' emblazoned on the side of the van, there was a giant effigy of Tommy Cooper, complete with fez, on the roof, which lit up every time I applied the brakes. I like to drive incognito to these gigs!

Rob Bailey, legendary Northants CCC and England batsman had rounded up all his pals to come and support his luncheon, which we were led to believe was a sell-out.

'Lots of support from the local businessmen,' promised our host.

Seating arrangements inside the glorified transit with windows was a trifle perilous to say the least. Bailers and I had filled the van with stout wooden chairs. As these were not secured, corners and roundabouts presented a real hazard to the 'Northants Fourteen' – yes, you've heard of the Renault Five 'and' the Birmingham Six, well, welcome to the Northants Fourteen! When we arrived at the location we were told by the host that he had been let down at the last minute and most of the tables had been cancelled. What a fuckin' load of bollocks. The name of the slippery host will remain a secret, but what a wanker. Rob Bailey was a top man and deserved 100 per cent support.

'Never mind,' said Rob. 'The show must go on. Loony, you're in charge.'

Well, I can honestly say it's the first time I've MC'd, spoken and conducted the auction and raffle. Quite surreal. I told my thirteen pals gags for two hours and bought up all the auction items myself. Six of the items were stone statuettes of famous cricketers, some in action mode, others in repose.

It was late when the Northants Fourteen climbed into our van with Tommy Cooper on top. The moon was out and the dogs were barking as we swung our way happily back down the B12413 to Northampton. Just the fourteen of us and our six new friends peering out of the back window, stony faced, 'gnome from gnome'.

You always remember the bad nights. Wakefield Trinity RFC Annual Dinner presented quite a challenge. Firstly, I had fallen into a deep Guinness-induced sleep on the bone-rattler from King's Cross. Awoken suddenly from my reverie by 'This is Wakefield!' screeching through the tannoy, I leapt to my feet and jumped from the train.

Alas, I'd forgotten my suit bag. Panic stricken, I ran to the station manager's office and told him of my plight.

'Don't worry, fella, we'll see what we can do,' smiled the kindly grey-haired custodian.

He phoned ahead to the train, which was by now approaching Doncaster.

'Now son, go and stand on the platform the other side of the tracks.'

A full hour elapsed until I saw the bright light of the express approaching at full speed. I stood back as the 125 rattled through the station. My suit bag was hurled from the guard's van, sliding along the platform, nearly decapitating the station cat.

Wakefield Town Hall, scene of the celebration, was full of sweaty rugby players bursting out of their DJ's, clasping endless pints of Tetleys bitter, reminiscing over the season's high points at fever pitch. The whole scenario reminded me of Richard Harris in *This Sporting Life*.

Engulfed by Yorkshire's crew and brew, I went into my best Prince Charles impersonations. There was a deathly silence followed by muted tones of 'Fookin southern poofter'. 'Steady Dave,' I thought, 'concentrate, keep the mind focused, give them your best repertoire right now . . .' But the ignorant tossers were not interested. They were so pissed they couldn't even see me, let alone hear my best string of one-liners.

Twelve nymphomaniac strippers might have stood a slim chance to entertain. But not Dave English from London town.

Then there was the Hallam and District Tennis Section's Club Supper. The youngsters laughed uproariously at tales of pink trombones and Norwegian hand pumps, but not the old folk. One by one they stood, protested and exited, passing me with stern appraisals of the performance. 'Disgusting, it's bloody disgusting,' and 'What the hell is Fagin the one-eyed assassin?'

Speaking in the hallowed halls of Eton College the headmaster wrapped up the evening's proceedings by declaring, 'Well I can honestly say we've never heard such language here at Eton, but I must say Mr English, you are bloody funny.' All the Rt Hons and their Fiona Foreskin-Jones mums rose to their feet and gave me a rousing round of applause. Same again next year please!

My biggest audience was 500,000 at Blackbush Aerodrome in Hampshire in 1980. I told a few gags and blessed the multitude with my abstract visions of the day. Bob Dylan, who had earlier arrived by helicopter, put his arms around me on stage and looked me in the eye: 'Surreal, man, surreal.'

Eric Clapton and Joan Armatrading were also 'blowin' in the wind'. It was fantastic introducing three artists who embodied the triumphs and lows of their generation. I returned for Bobby Zimmerman's encore. 500,000 of us had absorbed the wonder of his songs which articulated the feelings of the day. As I listened, the naked truth of the lyrics hit home. Years later when I was producing, I dispelled any fancy technical gimmickry and studio tricks – let nothing undermine the strength of the song. Give the artists the freedom to create and express, listen to Bob Dylan, Aretha Franklin and Bruce Springsteen and hear what they have to say.

In 1975 there were 150,000 at Milwaukee's Grand Fair on the shores of Lake Michigan. We were surrounded by love; there were skydivers and warm vibes. 'Embrace the moment ladies and gentlemen, let me hear it for the fabulous brothers Gibb. Barry, Robin and Maurice . . . the Bee Gees!'

Carlos Santana and his 'Black Magic Woman' got twenty minutes of 'The Best of D.E.' at Baltimore's race track in front of 100,000. I've introduced Stevie Ray Vaughan, Buddy Guy, Fleetwood Mac, Michael Jackson, George Harrison's Travelling Wilburys, the Temptations, Crosby Stills Nash and Young but never the Eagles – boy, I'd have loved to check into the Hotel California with those boys. And the smallest audience? Two Sikhs at Edinburgh University watching Viv Richards, Ian Botham and I parading our stories in *The King and I*. Anecdotes, film clips, question and answers. It's the only time the audience was outnumbered by the artists on stage!

'Any Way the Wind Blows...'
Bill Lets the Good Times Roll

It's three p.m. on 12 November 2003. The phone rings. I am awoken from my reverie. 'English, get your arse down to the Albert tonight. I want you to MC the show!' When you get the call from William George Wyman, born in London October 1936, you move! Very much like Eric Clapton, Bill believes in getting straight to the point. Romantically, I get my marching orders every time Bill takes his Rhythm Kings on the road.

'You're our MC, Dave, so get us on and get us off!' said a smiling Bill, puffing on his beloved Silver Kings.

Wherever I am or whatever I'm doing, everything comes to a sudden halt. I am proud to be the MC of this fantastic band for my pal Bill. Top musicians playing real instruments with not a computer in sight!

12 November was extra special. The venue was the Royal Albert Hall. As well as his usual brilliant line-up he had invited some very exceptional guests. Guitarists Mark Knopfler, Peter Frampton and Martin Taylor would be joining resident band members Terry Taylor, Beverley Skeete, Mike Sanchez, Georgie Fame, Frank Mead, Nick Payn, Graham Broad and the marvellous Albert Lee. There would be piano player Dave Hartley, turbo-lunged Sam Brown, daughter of Joe and London's finest, the two and only Chas 'n' Dave, all playing out of respect for Bill.

Arrived at Prince Consort Road, couldn't find a parking spot. Entered door 1, 'Artists', down the stairs and into the backstage bar. A family atmosphere prevailed.

That's the way Bill likes it. Older rock chicks and yesterday's groupies mingle with young kids who run gleefully to their rock mums with sparkle on their cheeks and stars in their eyes. Guitar technicians prepare their master's axes. Chas and Dave stand at the bar, brown brogues, pints of Guinness, tit for tat. I look around the room and watch the roadies nattering with the soundmen; Georgie Fame, a relaxed professor of style is holding court in the corner. Jim Capaldi, master percussionist, laughs uncontrollably while Frank and Nick the horn players eat their meals quietly, their eyes half focused on Sky News flickering in the corner. Some of the faces are caricatures, ravaged by the excesses of the music business, but their shoes are shining. They are survivors and you can't break their spirit. Charlie Watts arrives in his Crombie; so does Bob Geldof wrapped in a Dr Who scarf. Together with their 'old ladies' they sit around Bill's table hunched and laughing, encouraging their pal to do well. To think that for thirty years Bill and Charlie were the best rhythm section in rock with the Rolling Stones.

Eight o'clock. It's show time! The lights are dimmed in the auditorium, as we are led backstage by torchlight through a maze of wires and amps by tour manager Tony Panico. I walk to the centre of the stage and proudly announce the fantastic line-up. Looking out and upwards, the Albert Hall resembles a velvet-tiered cake punctuated by crystal chandeliers. On walk the boys, each one giving me a smile and a 'thank you'. I feel more at home with musicians than any group of people on this planet. The great thing about musicians is they don't expect anything from you, just love and encouragement. They are totally unfazed having experienced life's highs and lows and if you make them laugh they're your friends for ever.

To watch the great guitar players is the best. Knopfler, Frampton, the Taylors, Terry and Martin duelling with the master Albert Lee. I observe them following each other's leads, totally relaxed, lifting us to another level of excellence, each one a treasure of a golden age. Albert's fingers move so quickly they give the songs their first life. People always say to me, 'I met Bill and Mark and they seemed so unaffected, so down to earth.'

Well of course they're not . . . they might appear normal, but at any given time they can turn their hand to their extraordinary genius to entertain. They have nothing else to prove; they have worked hard, done all the striving and they are fulfilled. They have climbed the mountain and having got there can afford to dine out on the summit, each one generously allowing the other to solo and excel, watching and listening very carefully. Even in a crisis, panic is averted on stage.

Georgie Fame is coming to the end of a Ray Charles number when, as he hits the downbeat on his much-travelled Hammond organ, the power goes. All the electrics on stage have gone kaput. The wall of sound dissolves in mid number. In a flash drummer Graham Broad & percussionist Jim Capaldi go into a spontaneous twenty-minute drum solo, whilst the roadies feverishly dash about backstage trying to locate the fault. Amazingly, the audience are none the wiser, thinking the extended drum solo is all part of the show.

At one thirty a.m. I leave the Albert Hall and sit on the steps where the famous have trod. There's just me and the Jamaican fellow across the road securing the Imperial College.

The sound of the six guitars is still ringing in my ears. Tonight I have been reunited with Peter Frampton. Although his long hair has gone he still moves with that youthful exuberance and twinkle in the eye.

Earlier, I had met Mark Knopfler.

'Haven't seen you for ten years, Mark.'

'I remember Dave,' said Mark thoughtfully. 'When you told jokes in the back room of that Chinese restaurant – that's right, man. There was Eric Clapton, Buddy Guy and Robert Cray all there, laughing. Wonderful night.'

'Thirty years I haven't seen Peter and ten years you, Mark.' I wittered on emotionally.

'That's all right, Dave. That's how it goes. The thing is when we meet; we instantly connect as though it was yesterday.'

'Where you been, man?' enquired my new Jamaican cousin.

'What's your name?' I asked.

'Augustine, but friends round here call me Gus. My job is to keep this college secure.'

'Well Gus, I've been to see a great friend of mine.'

'What's his name?' asked Gus.

'Bill Wyman.'

'I know Bill,' laughed Gus. 'He's really good, man!'

'Certainly is,' I agreed. 'He sure can play.'

'Sure can,' said Gus. 'I saw him take a hat trick at the Oval. I've seen him bat against Imran Khan bowling real quick. I've seen him play with Sir Viv and Alec Stewart. He could have been a professional,' he enthused.

'You know what, Gus? I think you're right.'

Just then the wind started to blow down the deserted Prince Consort Road. Gus and I shook hands and left each other with just our respective thoughts of the one and only Bill Wyman.

Nearly Died a Death

A wise man once told me: 'Dave, it's only money and money is only a medium of exchange.

No, playing the game is the thing . . . It's the game that keeps you alive. It's worth everything.'

Well, I'll go along with that train of thought, but when it comes to after-dinner speaking, get your cash and get the fuck out of Doncaster, double quick. I've told you about my largest audience, 500,000 at Blackbush and the smallest, two Sikhs in Edinburgh; now let me tell you about my life and death performance.

I was the guest speaker for Brian Davison, the formidable Leicestershire and Rhodesian all-rounder. 'Davo' had a double identity, playing cricket during the summer, mercenary in the winter. He murdered the bowling from April to September and murdered for money October to February. One of the great characters but, it was fair to say, no one fucked about with 'Davo'.

So there we were, suited and booted at the Grand Hotel Leicester. First on was the West Midlands Commissioner of Police. 'Don't worry, Dave,' he assured me, 'I'll only do ten minutes.' One hour later we were nodding off, having been riveted by tales of parking on double yellow lines outside Sainsbury's and the recovery of some old lady's budgie up a tree.

Next in the firing line was my old pal, Yorkshire and England cricketer Don Wilson. Don did an hour followed by the auction and a raffle. I finally got to my feet at five past one in the morning, surely a Guinness Book of Records entry for the latest speaker? Worse was to follow. Halfway through my repertoire, a bloke had a heart attack on table twenty-seven. As I continued my gags, he was actually carried past me, still on table twenty-seven, dead as a dodo. I left the stage at two thirty. But I had not received my fee from 'Davo'.

'He went that way!' cried the Commissioner. Sprinting through the Leicester night, I finally caught up with the Zimbo on Level Two of the National Car Park.

Tentatively I cornered the mercenary. 'Christ! I thought. I'm a goner now.' 'Davo' reached into his inside pocket. I expected him to draw a Browning with a Carswell silencer. Instead he produced a brown envelope.

'Great speech, Dave!' beamed 'Davo'. 'Lucky you were very funny, otherwise, just think, two of you could have died a death on the same night!'

Rock 'N' Bowl

During the Bunbury games at Brentford FC, South African Test star Richard Snell was performing for the opposition. Out onto the pitch strode the openers for the Bunburys, Chris Broad and Bill Wyman.

'Just a quick word, Richard,' I whispered. 'One of them plays for England, the other for the Rolling Stones.'

To our complete surprise, Snell started to bowl gentle off-breaks to Chris, who then proceeded to dispatch them with great gusto out of the stadium with the utmost style and relish.

Meanwhile, the first ball to Bill shaved his midriff, the next took his 'Benson and Hedges' out of his pursed lips, the third was a 'sandshoe crusher' and the fourth shattered the hopping Billy's wicket.

As an amazed Bill sadly trooped off to the pavilion, the embarrassed fast bowler admitted, 'Cripes, I got them round the wrong way!' Chris Broad, a Rolling Stone? Better get Mick on the phone . . .

Antigua Blues

After a game at Finchley, the incredible Stan Webb's R and B band were playing in a nearby marquee. Unbeknown to Eric Clapton, I had arranged for his guitar to be brought along, just in case the musical mood took him. 'Come on, Eric, it would be a tremendous end to a great Bunbury day,' I pleaded.

Back in the bar, the banter was thick and furious. Suddenly the unmistakable chords of 'Layla' could be heard clearly above the noisy din. I had never seen a bar empty so quickly. There in the tent, Eric the maestro was strutting his stuff with the blues band.

For three hours, 500 enthralled people jogged to the music, punctuated by the occasional punch-up and flying bottle.

'Marvellous,' said Eric, as a horizontal reveller sped past his nose. 'Reminds me of the good old days with the Yard Birds.'

For the next three years, Eric's appearance after the fixture became a legendary event. Blues circles from Chicago to Chingford wondered why the maestro would want to perform in a beer tent in London N3. So did his manager, Roger Forrester. There were even bootleg tapes made – 'Eric Clapton Live with the Bunburys at Finchley'.

Then, in the fourth year, I got a phone call from Eric. 'Arfur,' he said (he always calls me Arfur), 'I've got to call it a day.' Thinking he had played his last Bunbury concert, a relieved Eric went off to Antigua for a well-deserved rest.

But it was too late. Whilst lying on the beach, tanning himself without a care in the world, he overheard the familiar voice of Brian

Johnston on the BBC World Service. 'Don't forget to go to Finchley, where the Bunburys will be performing, followed by the usual wonderful performance by Eric Clapton . . .' Dear old Clappers!

To the astonishment of the assembled bathers on the beach, the usually cool Eric was seen hurling a stranger's radio far out into the Caribbean, followed by a blood-curdling cry. 'English, I'll kill him!'

The Old Brown Chair

It's mid-afternoon as I stretch out in the old brown chair. High up in the hills above Harare the African sun burns down on the gnarled jacaranda. I can barely keep my eyes open as the warmth soothes my melting body and lets me drift away. The leopard stirs in the V of the tree at the sound of my children. A wave of love rushes through the French windows to leap on their old Dad. In the distance above the plains, the sky is darkening. Clouds, pregnant with rain, slide across the landscape, above the flowers, which open their fluted mouths expectantly, eager to quench their thirst.

Inside the house, I wrestle the remote control from my son, who's absorbed by the Cartoon Network, and flick through the channels to Calcutta where the West Indies are playing India in the seething cauldron of Eden Gardens.

Ganguly and his henchmen taking on Hooper and the young West Indians. The Eye of the Tiger versus the Sunshine Boys. It's the tea interval and there, standing in the middle, is the King, Sir Viv Richards, the boss and chairman of the board waxing lyrical about his young blades.

A far cry from Fenners Field with its sedate tranquillity, ringed by academia and students on bicycles where Atherton once stood, and Roger Knight – the chief at Lords, and Dexter of England. It was to Cambridge in 2004 where King Viv came 'to Bunbury' along with his pal Phil Simmons. Together they blazed 130 in 32 minutes against Paul Thwaites' Ashwell Crusaders.

But it is 'The Catch' we will always remember. Baraclough bowled; it was short outside the off-stump, Chris Cowdrey leaned back and pulverized it over cover. Viv had walked in with the stealth of a panther. The ball had passed him. All eyes turned to the boundary but the ball was nowhere to be seen. In a blur, Viv's right arm had snaked to the heavens and caught the thunderbolt in full cry.

So unbelievable was this flash of genius, it took a good five seconds to sink in. The silence of the moment was broken as we smothered the King with congratulations. The whole ground rose to their feet in reverence to acknowledge the master. Another moment of pure magic from the Bunburys, the most incredible bunch of people I have ever met. A team of terriers and mickey takers, show-men, all pure class.

The Bunburys are generously sponsored by Colin Graves of Costcutters, Ray Merridew 'Mr PG Tips', Louise Agran of Nando's, Neil Eckert, Holly Bellingham of Marketform, Andrew Peters and Julian Stansfield of Puma, the *Daily Telegraph*, Kirti Patel of Gold-shield, Lisa Robson of NatWest, Paul Beck at LBM, Paul Thwaites of the Ashwell Group and the irrepressible Joe 'The Hat' Cuby, of EMP plc. In 2003 we welcomed Manjit Chawla, Ronnie Parry, Phil Toms, Michelle Shaya and Sarah Pritchard of Shredded Wheat to put extra heart and energy into our fun-filled days for all the family, and our mission to raise vital funds for the sick and needy, the linking of hands and the touching of hearts.

Dawson's Catch

So I'm sitting here in war-torn Zimbabwe on a rock beneath a flowering jacaranda and I'm thinking of Matt Dawson.

In the V of a jagged tree sits a leopard staring at me with his ear cocked and his tongue swishing left and right, salivating at the prospect of eating this overweight Englishman . . . and I'm thinking of Daws.

Daws the hard man, Daws the belligerent, Daws the 'gee up' merchant. Daws the valiant, the fearless, the patriotic, the consummate entertainer, Daws the Bunbury cricketer.

It was Goughie who told me about the Saint.

'Big un', give old Matt a call; he loves his cricket.'

And so he arrived as we were getting changed. A master of dressing-room parlance, he shook everybody's hand and in our sacred circle of silence was awarded his Bunbury colours.

'Good lad, Matty. Where do you want to field?' I had already heard the whisper of his dodgy shoulder. 'How about cover, Daws?'

'No problem, Skips.'

Ten minutes into the game the 'oppo' opening batsman pulverized a short one outside the off-stump. It screamed over cover. So violent was the stroke I thought it was going to go flat for six. Then in a blur of sweater and arms, cover point jackknifed and backflipped, landing on his shoulder but holding on to the ball, an inch from the ground.

Daws had made the catch of the season. 'Welcome to the Bunburys, my son!'

A big smile from the man. Not a whimper about the already damaged shoulder. Pure class. Since that day, Matt has played regularly for the Bunburys, smashing the ball to all parts, keeping wicket, bowling. Geeing up the 'oppo' and laughing his head off – like fellow Rugby Bunburys Dallaglio, Catt, Liam Botham and Lynagh; these boys are in a different class.

I'm now sitting in the V of the jagged tree staring at the leopard that is sitting on my rock beneath the jacaranda. Unless he moves quickly, it is I who will enjoy spotted leopard and chips followed by spotted dick and balls steamin', helmet gleamin'.

2002 saw our first international tour – the Bunburys went to France! Lazing by the Loire, drinking wine in the cafes before taking on the might of *le coq sportif*. Me, the boys, young Issy, Jacko the Octogenarian, Rob the Badger and Hursty, the last post – sorted! Anoushka, the Polish princess, joined our ranks to open the bowling and send our pulses racing.

It is now evening in Zimbabwe. Ladies from the village come to join me taking tea. See them sashay down the road with their babes in arms, little children with wonderful-sounding names – Memory, Beauty, Love More, Promise and Christmas sit at my feet. They talk and laugh with a radiant smile. There are butterflies and birds in the trees.

The leopard stirs again at the sound of laughter. One eye open, he cocks an ear before snoozing back to dreamland. From my old brown chair I can feel the heartbeat of the nation and its gentle spirit. All is well.

The Postman Only Knocks Twice

It was a Sunday in June 1982 and Ian Botham and Viv Richards had been staying with me. I was down to play for Finchley CC against the might of the Acton and District Royal Mail Sorting Office Third XI. Two o'clock start.

'Come on lads, come up to Finchley and have a quiet day, a couple of pints, stretch out and relax, no pressure.' This notion seemed to appeal to the immortal twin terrors of Somerset.

On arrival, the clubhouse was jumping. Murty, the scorer, was slumped over his pint, still mumbling unintelligibly about the night before, and the paraffin fire was on its last legs. So was Tammy the terrier, stretched out, sound asleep on the darts mat beneath a flickering TV.

Acton were arriving in dribs and drabs, relating horror stories of snarl-ups on the North Circular. Their captain, Augustine, a marvellous Barbadian, wide of girth with a broad smile, welcomed me.

'Hello man, you gotta good side?' he enquired, clasping a large rum.

'Actually, we're two short, Gus,' I confessed.

'Shame, man, dat means me and the boys will give you a good tonking!'

'Well actually, I've just met these two blokes in the pub; one comes from your neck of the woods and the other is some long-haired Herbert from the West Country. They tell me they can play a bit. Do you mind if they join us?'

'No problem, man,' boomed Gus, already savouring the prospect of an easy victory.

'All right lads, you can come in now; Gus says you can play.'

The next moment will stay in my memory for ever.

As two of the greatest cricketers of all time stood silhouetted in the doorway, Gus looked up and seemed to enter into a trance. It was too much to comprehend. His jaw dropped. So did his glass, which instantly woke up Tammy and kick-started the TV into working properly for the first time in twenty years.

That day Viv and Ian scored 326 off 40 overs. The last 10 overs they actually batted left-handed, peppering the rooftops of N3 with an endless barrage of sixes. Viv then kept wicket, while Beefy bowled first-class deliveries to the postmen, right arm, underarm . . .

The boys from Acton batted with supreme West Indian verve and dexterity but just failed to nick a win. But who cared? Still with stars in their eyes, Augustine and his chums together with Viv, Ian and the Finchley lads retired to the bar to drink Captain Morgan rum and tell timeless tales till two in the morning.

Postman Patel

Whilst batting on the beautiful St Lawrence County Ground at Canterbury against Kent CCC, I had moved swiftly into the nineties (ninety for six actually). As I shaped up to face Chris Cowdrey's tenth over, I was suddenly aware of a movement to my right. An Indian gentleman had appeared dressed in grey flannels, white shirt and stout Oxford brogues. Without fuss he took the ball from Cowdrey and proceeded to bowl to me. None of the Kent players looked the least bit shocked as the mysterious Maharaja's third ball span violently, hitting my off stump, bowling me for ninety-seven.

Four of our other batsmen fell to the wizard who finally turned heel and disappeared over the boundary ropes into the hubbub of the Canterbury rush hour. Nothing was said during the remainder of the game. Later in the bar I enquired politely of wicket keeper Steve Marsh, 'Who in the hell was that?'

'Oh that's Mr Patel,' explained Marshy. 'He owns a post office on the corner. He often strolls on to the ground when the mood takes him, has a bowl and returns to his PO contented!'

I've Gotta Get A Message To You

As president of RSO Records I was with the Bee Gees when they wrote 'I've Gotta Get A Message To You'. We recorded it on the same night as we wrote the song. Barry, Robin and Maurice had sung the whole song without three-part harmonies in the chorus. I made them come back and sing the choruses again. They asked me why and I told them they had to sing in three-part harmonies. 'You can't sing it in unison and have no harmonies in the chorus.' So back we drove to IBC studios in Lower Regent Street and sang the choruses in three-part harmonies and that's how the record stands today. It was the group's first ever eight-track recording and on release went to number eight in the American charts, making it their first US Top Ten Hit.

Thirty-five years later I was exploring the Eastern Highlands of Zimbabwe with my family when I came across a post office in the middle of nowhere. It was the Troutbeck PO.

A Trip to the Troutbeck PO

I wrote a letter to Barry Gibb in America.

'I Just Gotta Get a Message to You.'

I knew not where the post office lay; I asked twenty people who looked at me mysteriously and mumbled something about 'crossing the bridge'.

So I took off past the security guard.

'Keep going boss, across the river.'

I looked ahead and saw the ragged clouds and the jagged tree. The asphalt burned through my faithful Nike trainers as I walked up the road, stepping purposefully through the scorching heat. I must have passed thirty or forty fellow travellers who trundled by on the other side of the road. One, a young boy, wore a Manchester United shirt emblazoned with a number six. And there was the pretty young girl, barely sixteen, with a child strapped to her back, smiling and telling me to keep going: 'The post office is on the top of the hill.' Trucks went by carrying the boys from the village, shirts flapping in the wind with smiles as white as piano keys.

'Merry Christmas, boss,' they cried as their breath of gentle endearment dissolved on the breeze.

Old ladies from the village sashayed down the road with baskets perched perfectly on their heads. Displaying talents of balance polished like jewels, they clutched brightly coloured umbrellas, but still took time to shake my hand with soft, leathery palms. With much huff and a large portion of puff I finally reached the old green hut clutching my letter. It was the Troutbeck PO, standing as an Alamo on the crest of the hill.

I peered inside the barred windows to see a calendar, which was opened on October 2001. There were several Zimbabwe postbags strewn across the floor and a notice inviting folk to come and sing carols at St Michael's, but no sign of life. Solidly shut until two o'clock. A wise old man sitting by the roadside told me it was 'holidays' and it would not open.

I met a boy of fourteen with bites on his legs whose parents had died. Now he lived with his grandfather in the woods. He spoke ever so politely. 'Can you feed me, boss?'

I decided to wait for another fifteen minutes. Still the trucks roared by and the bus to Mutare full of people going home for Christmas. The hills were now rolling with thunder. The clouds, pregnant with rain, skirted the mountain tops, highlighted by the impending electric storm. I returned just in time to avoid the flash of lightning, which seared through the pine trees, still with my letter in hand. Troutbeck to Miami – forget it. But I had experienced a little bit of the nation's heartbeat and tonight when the silver moon shines down from a purple sky, mirrored on Dickson's Lake, I will turn in my bed and wonder where all those souls I met would be . . . Under the star-filled skies, ragged clouds and the jagged tree.

Hotel California

So I'm sitting here in 1999, in the bar of the Château Marmont, a funky Spanish colonial pile, looking down with smirking approval on Sunset Boulevard like an elder statesman of decadence, approvingly supervising the foibles of the inspirational. I'm thinking of California. I wish I could have been a guitarist in the Eagles, a bunch of musical artists who created a body of work that didn't fade away like so many boys of summer, but rather resonated year after year.

Some troubadours travel a road so well at precisely the right time that they become part of that road. They create a living record of their journey that continues to connect with people in a way that is deep and enduring. Ultimately these artists must be considered winners of a different sort of race. One measured in the long run.

I first met the Eagles back in 1974, whilst recording the Bee Gees album *Main Course* at the Criteria Studios in Miami. We had written 'Nights on Broadway' featuring Barry Gibb's falsetto throughout the song for the first time. In the next studio the Eagles were recording their album produced by Bill Szymczyk. Clearly musicians are influenced by each other's music. The Bee Gees vibe was heard by Don Henley and Glenn Frey, who went next door and wrote 'One of These Nights'.

The Eagles' body of work became the soundtrack for millions of lives. Fans all over the globe played Eagles music in their cars, their homes, at parties, during happy times and sad. They fell in love, broke up, got engaged, got married and started families with the band's music surrounding them. A lot of people did a lot of things to the Eagles. Some of these things were even legal. The boys in the band were drawn to leave their assorted home towns to chase the late twentieth-century American dream that drew countless hopefuls to the rocky gold country of California. 'Hotel California' explored the glamour of the dream and its more nightmarish side effects through the Eagles' vividly documented life in the fast lane. 'Life in the fast lane sure enough to lose your mind'. They also counted some of the casualties left on the side of that road. The best sort of travelling music for a generation of fans anxious to go along for the sweet, if sometimes dark ride. Checking into the Hotel California, you could lose your innocence and indulge in the sort of modern excess that brought on the Mercedes Bendz. When you are driving home from a new love, listen to the lyrics of 'Lyin' Eyes' or 'Tequila Sunrise'. They enunciate the foray into the night. The aching, yearning heart, all the passion and the newness in the beginning of a love affair. Stunning words that hit the mark not like a Britney or Aguilera, blank outlines distinguished by the draughtsmanship of those who colour them in. For me the Eagles captured the last picture show, tumbleweed towns, the desert and life in the fast lane. Since then only the speed limit has changed. I wish I'd been there for the ride.

From California I moved on to Austin, Texas where an army of musicians commandeered this affluent sprawling southern city armed with electric guitars and a sense of belief that verged on the delusional. I was there to sign bands to my RSO label. The city centre at night is something to behold, an almighty din of clashing riffs and unsynchronized drum patterns reverberating in the warm air. Hot-dog vendors and jewellery makers tout their merchandise as people stagger from bar to bar, out of the warm embrace of a semi-acoustic chanteuse and into the sucker punch of a hot-rod quartet. It is an urban Glastonbury.

Esther from Bordeaux

It had all started with a telephone call to a wrong number. I had asked for a Michelle but a voice, throaty and French replied.

'Non, I am sorry there eez no Michelle 'ere.'

Enchanted by the Gallic sounds at the end of the line I launched myself into my O-level French, once again attempting to deliver the little gems I'd learnt at the Whitefield Academy of Institutionalized Correction.

Her name was Esther. She was a model staying at a friend's house in London. She came from Bordeaux. We talked for two hours and then she had gone like a whisper in the wind.

It was not only the way she spoke that instantly captivated my heart, in the most beautiful of God's tongues, but what she actually said. Deep and soul-searching, kind and considerate, funny and sad . . . *Cette amour, si fragile, si tendre, comme une nage d'été.*

Two years later my phone rang. It was Esther. Once again, as she spoke I was thrown into a trance.

'Ello Davide, do you remember me? It is Esther from Bordeaux.'

My heartbeat raced, stirring a passion deep inside that had not been touched for years. My breath quickened and a flush crept across my face. We talked and talked. I was mesmerized by this stranger at the end of the line.

'Look, Esther, enough is enough; let's meet. I will come to Paris so we can sit across a table and I can see the face behind the voice.'

So starbursts and thunderbolts propelled me to the Eurostar at Waterloo Station. It was Friday 30 January 2004 and the ten thirty-nine to Paris stood on platform twenty-four. Already my soul felt connected to the lady from Bordeaux, but what would happen at the Gare du Nord? Who cared? My heart was bursting with curiosity and expectation.

Wearing my camel coat and old tweed cap, I sunk into my seat, coach twelve, seat forty-five. First class, had to be the best. Trevor Howard would have done so in *Brief Encounter* before meeting Celia Johnson. What is it with stations? The romance, people on the move. I felt like a peaceful *Day of the Jackal*, a predator of the heart.

Back on 14 February 1992, I had met this beautiful blonde girl on the escalator (Esther called it the electric stairs) at Baker Street Station at three forty-five p.m. Three weeks later I asked her to marry me. I was forty-six. Robyn was twenty-six, from Zimbabwe, quite beautiful. Together we lived on my farm. We had two children; Amy Rose, now aged eleven, and David English Junior, aged ten. They now live happily in Cape Town. I loved Robyn very deeply and still do, but five years ago we were divorced, not through lack of love but because she was homesick for Africa. Africa, where nothing is as bad as you feared and never as good as you hoped. Believe me, you can take the African out of the bush but you cannot take the bush out of the African. And here I am again, chasing another foreign dream along a railway line.

We're pulling out of Waterloo. I stare out of the window. There is a flurry of snowflakes and it is bitterly cold. Down in the street below, five men in hard hats are digging a hole. Well, one is digging and four are watching. We're building up speed. It feels strange to be going through Clapham Junction on the way to Gai Paris. Welcome to Brixton. Lowry figures, huddled and stooping, walk over a frozen Herne Hill. Penge East, where my pal Bill Wyman was born in 1935. Why am I here? Sometimes I feel that I'm clutching at straws. A watery sun filters through the trees. Branches, stiff as fingers, are poking towards the heavens. Whistling through suburbia, an old gothic church in the distance, stark against a mottled sky. The rolling countryside, woods bereft of leaves, naked trees. A running dog. Swanley and its pylons. Chocolate-brown fields dusted with snow. The steward minces down the aisle in a yellow jacket followed by the trolley dollies.

'Tu veut un Chardonnay ou un Bordeaux blanc, monsieur?'

'Better make it a Bordeaux, Mademoiselle . . . Si'l vous plait.'

Woods with deep, dark, frozen pools. 'Transports Henriques' lorries lumber by down the M2. All these bastards around me using mobile phones. 'Why can't they look out at the wonderful country-side?'

'Is Olivier there or is he going direct to St Moritz?'

What a load of bollocks. I don't seem to belong to anyone or anywhere, the insecurity of being the Hampstead Cavalier, liberty and freedom of spirit gone wild. The not knowing what lies ahead is very exciting. Although I think I belong in London, part of me knows that I don't really belong anywhere. Nobody is waiting for me in London, but a complete stranger is waiting for me in Paris. A girl across the aisle strikes up a conversation.

'Do you travel a lot?' she enquires.

'Yes,' I reply.

'Does it make you lonely?'

'I am a loner,' I say with a smile, 'but I'm not lonely.'

Outside the window, it is deserted. We enter the Channel Tunnel. On the other side, it noticeably feels warmer. The countryside looks smoother. Lost in France. The long tree-lined avenues. Memories of hitch-hiking to the south in 1963. We've just hit Lille. There is a lone golfer playing with an orange ball in the snow. France has more space. It's better laid out. The call of the wild. A solitary car silhouetted on a road to nowhere. Bleak, there is a building standing in the middle of a field for no apparent reason. Through Evreux and Dreux and finally arrive at Gare du Nord at two thirty-nine p.m.

There are some train spotters, not anoraks clutching the *Observer Book of Trains*, but Les Passionnes de Chemin de fer – elegant and civilized folk pursuing an interest regarded as perfectly reasonable.

Collar up, I clamber down from the train clutching my two

enormous bags and join the mêlée making their way to the barrier. Now . . . there are a thousand ways I could describe to you the next moment. Allow me to do my best.

I survey the sea of faces at the end of the platform, taking in the different features with a steady gaze and there in the middle of the throng is the face of an angel, ethereal and not meant for this world. She moves away from the madding crowd and runs towards me.

'You are Davide?'

'Yes, Esther. I have come for you.'

I drop my bags and open my coat. Her arms enter and take me to her. My heart leaps out of my chest and I instantly fall in love. I hold her tighter; she is slim but strong. I explore her gentle spirit and can feel her tenderness. She is beautiful on the outside. She is beautiful on the inside and when I look at her eyes, I feel like a little boy of six, totally out of control. We must be standing there entwined in the pale-green light of the station for a good ten minutes, totally oblivious to the outside world.

I have not stopped cuddling her since.

Love is a beautiful dream. I wanted to ask her how she knew it was me on the platform but I was scared it would disperse the magic.

She carried my bags and hailed a taxi. That afternoon she took me around Paris. In a blur of crazy traffic and leafy boulevards we walked through Les Jardins Tuileries, famously painted by Monet. Lovers strolled arm in arm. So did we. We fed the ducks and took in the beautiful buildings and exquisite sculptures etched in front of a January sky. We were two vivid colours on a pastel canvas, like the little girl in the red coat in *Schindler's List*. We drank hot chocolate by the lake. I couldn't stop kissing her. It really was like living in a film.

'Esther, you live in Bordeaux. Let's go there,' I said.

A taxi to Gare Montparnasse with its criss-crossing elevators, the greenish underwater light and the echoing throb of the expresses, impatient to speed to the Atlantic coast.

She held my bags and made me laugh. It was Friday night and

the train was very crowded, especially with soldiers eager to return home on weekend leave.

We staggered down the train to the bar, where we bought two bottles of red and a chocolate cake. On the way back I asked the soldiers if Esther could sit down. They immediately obliged with a big smile and a kind heart. We shared our wine and I made them laugh, doing my Elvis Presley impersonations. The train relentlessly rattled along the tracks. We returned to our places and she whispered in my ear about the past. The father of her child, Bob from Madagascar. How she had made love to him when she was very young. She was a mum at seventeen. Her little boy was called Eladji. Now she'd been seeing a Vietnamese DJ called Andy. We laughed kissed and cuddled non-stop. I didn't know to what degree she loved me, but if it was the same I felt for her it would have gone through the roof.

We were met at the station by her friend Katharine. She took me to the Hotel Burdigala. We drank wine and she was gone. Although our love affair was fraught with danger, we carried on blissfully living for the moment. I knew it would come to a terrible sad end, but at least we went for it. She had that stale French taste on her breath of cigarettes and wine. It would probably do my head in, but when she looked at me I melted. When we first met I sat in the back of the cab and stared at her, never felt so nervous. She called me an angel. 'You are the Lord of England. My heart and my head are open to you.' Blow me; I was fifty-seven years old. I was sitting in my hotel room in Bordeaux. Outside it was raining. A man walked his dog along a deserted street. Life was fantastic. I was waiting for the beautiful twenty-one-year-old French girl and I was the happiest man in the world. Some people fall in love with the picture. I got under the surface of the canvas and felt the heart. She took me around Bordeaux to see the magnificent eighteenth-century buildings. Down by the river. Les Meubles Maritimes. We danced through the night on a boat on the river Garonne. I met her friends: Cindy with a diamond in her chin and a ruby through her tongue. When she left me at the station she made the sign of the heart on the train window.

As I sped back to Paris I stared out at the countryside, but all I could see was the reflection of her face in the window. I met a deaf man on the train. He gave me a pen, which was also a cigarette lighter. I gave him five euros and I shook his hand, felt his strength and saw his smile. Bless him, take special care my friend. There was a fairytale chateau on the hill overlooking Two Rivers in the valley. We whizzed through Angoulême and Poitiers and on through Tours. I saw a tree on a pea-green hill. It stood stark against a blue sky. It was special. The French countryside had not changed since I walked through it in 1963. Green hills and gravy-brown fields. I saw a fire burning. The orange flames and the acrid smoke filtered away beyond the hills. Old buildings and rusty pipes. It's sad when they have had their day. The longevity of their life is over and they are abandoned. I love them and look to their history.

When I fall in love I am so crazy in the head and the heart, emotionally out of control. The last thing on my mind is sex. To tamper about in the physical department would break the magic spell. If sex comes, it must start in the eyes, then on to the heart and down to the todger. If it bypasses the heart, it is not love. The teapot is only the physical end to the feeling of love. If it is to pour the juices of love into the sacred cup, it has to brew naturally from the head to the heart, stirring all the emotions on the way.

I saw a psychedelic painted VW on a lonely road and thought of Donovan and Sunshine Superman. Everything I do or think of, you are there, Esther. If anything ever happened to me at least I could say that I had found love again.

It makes me sad; it makes me glad. I'm terrified of anything happening to the ones I love: Robyn, Amy Rose, Little Dave . . . Life is so fragile. You have to take care of the ones you love. The hopelessness of love. Give me time to miss you. Swept away on a flood of emotions across a fragile earth. Trying to clutch on to the sides, but being incapable of doing so and not caring anyway. Just give in and go with the flow. To champion the imagination. The French Connection, a decision, to settle down or chase wild horses.

The last time I held her in my arms I said, 'Esther stay with me for thirty years. Then I'll let you go.'

She replied, 'After thirty years, why would you let me go?'

So I went back to Bordeaux six months later to link hearts with the girl I truly loved. Very quickly there was a sense of tragedy to our fairytale. It was like living in a French film by Jean Luc Godard or François Truffaut. Esther was not at the airport when I arrived. Maybe I had fallen in love with an illusion, like a poster of Marilyn Monroe, never bothering to go deeper than the surface.

The airport was bland and clinically clean. I was happy to be anonymous, sitting on a bench watching the Frogs go to and fro like characters from a Jacques Tati film, long noses, black hair, stern features, players in this antiseptic building of marble and glass. But where was *mon amour*? My stomach turned and my heart ached.

Then the automatic doors opened and she was there, a vision on high heels, silhouetted in the afternoon light, radiant and beautiful. Once again I took her in my arms and felt complete.

'Sorry, Davide, the traffic was terrible.'

'I thought you had forgotten me,' I replied a little pathetically.

I felt like a kid.

'Are you crazy? Never.'

Again she insisted on carrying my bags. Boy, these French girls are strong willed.

'We must go and get my son. He is with my mother.' As Esther talked of her family, there was a sadness. Her dreamy disposition darkened.

'Tell me about your family, Esther.'

'It is not good,' she said.

The taxi took us to a slightly depressed area of Bordeaux. When we arrived at these flats painted in brown and cream her little sister was playing. I gave her a hug. When I met her mum she looked fine to me. I come from the school of positive thought, where optimism rules. Always look for the best in everybody and think they are great until proved otherwise.

As Esther went to get her son I drank coffee with her mum. There was tension in the air. Suddenly there was a terrible scream. Esther appeared holding her son.

'Look what she has done. She has cut his hair.'

The little lad stood there shorn of his locks. He smiled and didn't seem to care.

'This is my muzzer for you, Davide. She knew I loved his hair and now she has done this.'

'It's OK maman,' said Eladji. The little prince of three years old.

Her mother told me Esther was mad. She had returned from a modelling assignment in Morocco and gone crazy.

'Look Davide, she painted the walls.' I must say I liked the montage in the kitchen, an exhilarating exhibition of brush strokes, angry skies and orange flowers. Esther blazed into the kitchen.

'Come on Davide, we go.'

Her brother was in his bedroom up to no good and her little sister arrived. I found it terribly sad, having come from a broken home myself. I wanted to make things right between them. But it seemed hopeless. I had entered the troubled waters in the Basin of Aquitaine and now we would have to ride the storm together.

We returned to Esther's apartment where we sat on two plastic chairs and drank wine. Outside the shuttered windows high in the heavens the stars twinkled down on Bordeaux as my lovely girl unfurled her dark past.

Her father had tried to kill her when she was twelve. He had beaten, abused and stabbed her. He was sent to prison for five years. Her parents had separated. There was bitterness and sadness everywhere. She showed me her family photo albums. There seemed to be despair on every page. Esther had tried to take her own life on three occasions. The birth of her son had saved her. She lived for her little angel. She had met the father of her son when she was just fourteen. Later she discovered that Madagascar Bob had five children with five different mothers.

I listened, terribly sad, as the storm clouds rolled in, bringing more lurid details of her childhood days.

'Esther, c'est la vérité? You are telling me the truth?'

This really upset her.

'Of course, you think I make this up?'

It was so difficult to comprehend. Such a beautiful girl with such a sad past, and now she had met me. Poor girl, from bad to worse!

'But Esther, you have a wonderful boy and you are a great mum,' I reassured her. 'And now you have found pure love from the Lord of England. Just think, a lot of people go throughout life and never find pure love.'

Eladji appeared at the door, clutching a CD.

'You like Carole King?' he enquired.

I thought how amazing that a little boy of three should like the works of one of America's greatest singer songwriters.

'Fine, Eladji – put it on.'

Eladji's Carole King turned out to be karaoke, so instead of listening to 'Tapestry', we sang along to Tom Jones, The Rolling Stones and The Beatles. Just the three of us, the two plastic chairs, drinking wine, being tossed around in our own perfect storm.

I left Chez Esther at one o'clock and checked into the Hotel Trianon just down the road. It certainly was a room at the top, six flights of stairs and no Leslie Caron to greet me. The room was very French. A tall wardrobe in dark wood, a writing table with a reading lamp, shuttered windows and a large bed. I got into the bed and thought about Esther and her past. Emotionally drained from our deep conversations, I realized that we were two lost souls in the same boat. Every part of me loved her and Eladji and wanted to keep them, make them feel secure and warm, loved and wanted, because by doing so I would feel the same. To give and feel needed, what a wonderful feeling.

To say it was cold in my room at the top was an understatement. Put it this way: if there had been a fridge I would have happily jumped in to get warm. I got out of bed, put all my clothes back on, including my overcoat and cap, and lay there desperate for the morning to come.

At nine a.m. I went to her home and presented her with a silver elephant. It was Valentine's Day or as Esther called it, the Day of Love. She loved elephants and from time to time reminded me that her dream was to live in a castle in Sri Lanka with a white elephant in the garden. As I watched her open her present and the happiness it gave her, I cried my eyes out. An Edith Piaf song was playing on the radio as the sun filtered through the windows. I held her as tight as I could and for that moment felt the best I have ever felt in my life.

We spent the Day of Love on our two plastic chairs, talking and laughing. At midday we ventured outside to walk in the watery sun along streets and boulevards with wonderful-sounding names. Rue Montesquieu, Rue Voltaire, Avenue Jean Jacques Rousseau ... I pushed Eladji in the pram, blissfully happy. If the boys could see me now ... we went to a cinema to watch a French cartoon.

I wanted to spoil the little boy. There were no subtitles and I understood very little, but Eladji was in his element.

It was wonderful to see a child laugh. I thought of my children in Cape Town. How the sense of missing gripped me like a vice. My stomach tightened and my heart bled for my little girl and boy. How many sleeps before I see you, Daddy?

I had gone back to Cape Town to see my ex-missus Robyn and two children, Amy Rose and Little Dave. Robyn was pregnant but the father had sadly died from cancer. I sat outside in the sunshine and contemplated how fragile life was and how great it felt to be complete as a family.

And here I was cuddled up in a cinema with a mum and her little prince in a town in France.

Madagascar Bob should have been here and I should have been in Cape Town, but life isn't that simple. You can't analyse why marriages and love affairs don't always work. It just happens that way, as the momentum of life drives us down another road.

I left for England the next day, missing Esther terribly even before I had said goodbye.

So after six months I went on another daring raid to Bordeaux. It was the third mission in my French dream, not to break down the physical defences of the girl I loved – there had been no sex, although I'd have loved to do the business. It wasn't on the cards from Esther's perspective; she had been seriously damaged in that department.

'Davide, the men only want my arse or to marry me. They fall in love with my face. Well, fuck my face. I am not a box. I am not a machine. They fall in love with the illusion. For me our love is deeper. You respect me and I love you for it. Please take it time from time.'

Enough said, and anyway I was too crazy for her cerebrally. It's the same with all the birds you really fall for. Frightened to get their 'Bristols' out too soon in case you lose them and they run away.

I arrived at the airport. Once again she was not there. I felt totally lost and out on a limb. Some French boys were lolling about a bar showing off and looking at the girls' legs. I felt terrible. I had been up all of the previous night with shooting pains in my stomach. Maybe a combination of bad food and anxiety; I thought I was going to die. Just like Elvis Presley, dead on the toilet. I felt as though I was in an emotional wasteland. A combination of joy, tragedy and farce.

And there she was . . . walking towards me along the marbled foyer, her little prince Eladji clutching her hand. I took her in my arms, felt her heart beating and once again we were whole and back in our special world. We hired a Renault Clio and drove back to the Centre Ville past the beautiful eighteenth-century buildings. Once again she insisted on carrying my bags as we clambered the five flights of stairs to her apartment in Rue Franklin. 'Welcome home, my Lord,' she said, giving me another hug.

I emptied my case of presents. My gifts reflected her obsessions: two gold elephants, three Madonna CDs, some angels and stars, with a couple of England cricket tracksuits thrown in.

I played cricket with Eladji in the little apartment as Esther prepared dinner. She reminded me of my mother, a true Cancerian, wonderful homemaker, great mum, full of fun but also prone to waves of depression.

Eladji went to bed and Esther and I drank wine and had a heart to heart. Once again I absorbed her aura, so beautiful on the surface but a compendium of complexity on the inside. She told me again of her two attempts at suicide and how sadly they had failed. Her mother had sent her to a special hospital for two years where her mental state could be monitored. Though not properly delusional she had experienced a crack-up, what with her father's violence and mother's non-interest. A dejection that had turned into catastrophe, altering her moods, ability to sleep, appetite for food and any kind of pleasure. She had been sectioned because she had lost interest in her future and in living. I could imagine the Acute Mental Health building, small and brutish with steel-framed windows that could be opened only a fraction and walls painted in pasty pea-green.

'For my first night I was given my own room opposite the nurses' station, so they could make sure that I attempted neither to escape nor to harm myself. A nurse peered in the window every fifteen minutes.'

Esther unfurled her story with that wonderful animated French delivery, highlighting the mannerisms with hunched shoulders, cheeks puffing and blowing with that wounded hangdog look and outstretched hands. Just look at the Arsenal footballer Thierry Henry for these expressions. She smoked continuously, rolling her own cigarettes made of Old Holborn.

'During the first week I felt a sense of outrage, embarrassed at the sectioning. I had told hardly any of my friends. I received few phone calls or visitors.

'Then as the days dragged by I became more relaxed and more institutionalized. Along with a couple of other early risers I was the first up at seven a.m. I made tea, if there were any tea bags, cups and milk. I often had to ask a nurse to collect these from a locked cupboard. If left out, the cups disappeared and the sugar ended up strewn over the surfaces: the kettle kept getting stolen.'

I was captivated by her story. Our 'Franglais' was good and any time we got stuck for a word we resorted to the dictionary to capture the right meaning. Her hospital sounded remarkably like the setting of One Flew Over the Cuckoo's Nest.

After two years she was released, met Madagascar Bob, fell in love, and fell pregnant with Eladji, only for Bob to do a runner.

She insisted on looking after me and I felt exactly the same about her. It was very sweet: two loons who had each found their soulmate.

'You know, Esther, in a way I wish I was your dad and you were my mum.' How surreal was that?

She laughed. 'But tomorrow, Davide, it is your birthday and we will go to the sea.'

I returned to yet another hotel. The Hotel de la France. It was literally next door. I paid my euros up front to a bald concierge who looked thoroughly uninterested in any *entente cordiale* and checked into a room at the top, which would be next to Esther's room. Just a wall stood between us. We knocked on it, sending goodnight messages.

The next day we took off to the ocean. Just the four of us: the eternal optimist, the manic depressive, the little prince, and Clio driving along an arrow-straight road through the pines to the rolling sea. It rained. I held her hand all the way. The windscreen wipers metronomed to and fro. French songs crackled from the radio as we travelled through a bleached photograph of fading images.

Vincent Van Gogh, another tortured soul, should have been in the back seat. I would have loved to have met him. He would have been in his element. We would have stopped and he could have set up his easel in the forests and used the pastel colours to transform the blandness of the firs, no doubt, into a scene of mouth-watering beauty. He would have captured the intensity of a light piercing the grey skies.

'The skies are crying, look at the tears rolling down the streets.'

The lemon yellow façades of the farmhouses deep in the woods seemed detached from their own lime-green sides so that they appeared to float above the picture plane anchored to Van's canvas only by the deep greens of the front doors and shutters.

We finally swept into Le Cananou on a wave of nostalgia. I had hitch-hiked there back in 1963 with my pal Peter 'Bomber' Mellor. We had met some lovely French girls and danced barefoot in the woods to Françoise Hardy's 'Tous Les Garçons et Les Filles de Mon age'.

The place was deserted. The romance, sadness, fragility and tenderness of a French seaside town, out of season. Angry skies touched massive waves, which exploded onto flotsam and jetsam-strewn beaches.

'A perte de vue' – as far as the eye could see were mists dissolving far away into infinity.

We parked Clio and left Van in the back. Through the gloom we could just make out the neon sign of the Café Robespiere standing high on the cliffs. We staggered through the rain, Esther's *parapluie* being blown inside out. The Café Robespiere was right up Van's boulevard. 'I'm going back to get him. Tell him to call up his pal Paul Gauguin, they'd love it here.'

The proprietor of the All-Night Café Robespiere, Madame Delaspaul, was sat in front of a billiard table, a glass of absinthe on the table before her. A pall of blue Gauloises hung in the air, a huddle of soldiers, a few drunks and old lags from the town in the background. I'm sure Van would have painted this setting on the spot but Gauguin would have preferred to work from his imagination. They would have then had a violent quarrel as to its content and poor old crazed Van would have turned his rage upon himself.

As Esther fed Eladji, I watched her carefully. She was not like my pal Brigitte Bardot, with whom I had struck up a *liaison dangereuse* back in 1964. 'BB' had long, tousled hair, a 'come play with me' attitude and a quicksilver nature, a sex kitten who might either purr or scratch. She had a luscious pout with the sort of naturally bee-stung lips that women pay plastic surgeons hundreds of pounds to recreate. Brigitte only had to pucker up to the camera for it to fall madly in love with her. Then there was the baby face with huge eyes and round rosy cheeks, sexed up to the maximum with heavy make-up. Add to that a slim frame boasting a wonderful pair of curvy breasts, thick waves of blonde hair and a nicely rounded derrière.

Esther's looks were more fragile, more waif-like. She looked like a Gallic Kate Moss. But for both Brigitte and Esther, their magic transcended their looks. They both had attitude and a certain way of conducting themselves. Brigitte was wholesome and sexy; Esther's eyes were mesmeric, and she was slim and sensual with an amazing natural beauty. Being French certainly helped. Her slenderness meant that she could wear anything and encapsulate high-maintenance chic. A blouse costing one euro, a pair of jeans tucked into boots, a woolly scarf tied inside a fitted red jacket, all looked sensational. Nobody could look that great in a Bunbury sweater again. Her tastes were pure and simple. Beauty comes from within. Joy is not in things;

it is in us. Esther was neither a femme fatale nor a mythical nymphette, just a lovely person and a deeply caring mum.

But Brigitte's Riviera was in St Tropez with its cigarette-smoking cafe culture of sun, sex, sand and the inevitable sea. A world away from being banged up here in the Café Robespiere with my girl, Madame Delaspaul, the little prince, Van and Gauguin overlooking a troubled sea.

Refreshed and fed we made our way gingerly down to the beach. We were in the eye of a storm, but I was determined to leave our mark on my birthday. I found a stick and made the sign of a sacred heart – *le sacré coeur* – pledging my everlasting love, in the middle.

'We shall return here on 21 July for your birthday, Esther,' I promised.

'The sea will not have our heart. No waves are strong enough to wash away our love. Come here Davide.'

She led me to the rocks where we huddled under the nifty *parapluie* away from the driving rain. 'These are for you.'

She took two parcels from her bag and presented them to me, followed by a kiss and a cuddle. Inside was a teddy bear and a calendar depicting mums and their kids, tender and loving photos of sweet little faces, playing hide and seek, blowing bubbles or offering flowers to the less fortunate. It mirrored Esther's feelings perfectly. We drove back to Bordeaux after stopping to pick some mimosas. Very little was said; I knew our time together was running out. In my mind it was time to leave. I was emotionally drained and tired and the pains had returned to sear through my stomach. I cared deeply for Esther and Eladji and I wanted to do everything to keep them safe and secure. Her face and eyes still drove me wild and our hearts beat as one, but I could feel us spiralling to tragedy. We had been on the road to nowhere and shared true love, happiness and grief and now it was time to part – life moves too quickly for regrets and 'Je ne regrette rien'.

We returned to the flat and she baked me a chocolate cake in the shape of a heart. But she was unhappy.

'Davide, what is a cake without candles?'

'Don't worry, I love the cake,' I said, 'and remember, Esther, I will always be thirty-six more candles than you!' I took her in my arms and told her I was going back to England.

'But, Davide, you have only been here one day.'

It's true, I thought, at this rate I'd be home before my postcards arrived.

'Ah yes, but I have spent my birthday with the girl I love . . . *Quand le soleil se couche* – when the sun goes to sleep, I'll be gone!'

I returned to yet another hotel, the Hotel Clemenceau. When I left her building, sure enough she was there waving from the window just like my mother used to. I got up at four a.m. and drove through the deserted streets of Bordeaux. At the airport there were four Frogs wearing berets boisterously berating each other, still pissed from the night before. They were on their way to support France versus Wales at rugby.

'Let's see if they croak so loud on the other side of the pond.'

I climbed the stairs of Air France flight AF3413 and looked back one more time . . . and with a whiff of aftershave, Eau Sauvage, courtesy of Monsieur Christian Dior, I had gone. I felt like a damaged fighter pilot limping back to Blighty, emotionally shot to pieces.

> *A spitfire high in the mantle of the night above with just the*
> *moonlight on my wings.*
> *I dive into a dawning sky.*
> *Shattered, wounded*
> *Soon to die*
> *I follow the Garonne to the open sea*
> *And down below on a deserted beach*
> *I can see a heart*
> *Etched, out of reach.*
> *No golden strands of laughter now*
> *No flighty romance in the clouds*
> *Still dive and climb and weave and soar*
> *My Esther, to be remembered evermore.*

When I returned home, I turned on the TV. A film was about to start: *The Cockleshell Heroes* – a daring raid on Bordeaux. I thought, 'Surely not two in one day.'

So Esther, here I am still a sad old single dad of sixty on a farm in north west London and you a single mum of twenty-three in Bordeaux. Two people from different worlds who connected and found true love in isolation, lost to the world.

Before I had left the Hotel Clemenceau early that morning I'd left a note on my pillow. I knew she would come to find me.

'My darling, I leave you now with the same feeling of love from the first time I saw you. The little elephant will take care of you while I am away. Keep him with you always. He will keep you safe. Take care Esther, face and enjoy each day at a time. The winds from London will blow you kisses and cuddles for ever. When you sit in your chair and look at the stars outside your window high in the heavens, think of me, drink a glass of wine and smile. Feel secure in the knowledge that the Lord of England loves you and Eladji for ever.'

Le Fin

Lest We Forget

Just last year I stumbled across the Royal Air Force museum in Hendon. As a veteran from the film *A Bridge Too Far* I have always been fascinated by the daring deeds of the pilots and aircrew from World War II. I am in awe and have total respect for the young men who were shot down in flames beneath the bomber moon, young men who died too soon. How can we praise these brave young fellows who flexed their new and untried wings, like eaglets free and bold, a generation who gave up the flower of its youth, a sacrifice so quietly made that we might live in peace and truth? How can we tell of loyal men who worked long hours upon the ground in drizzling cold or tropical heat, to serve their crews in honour bound? All tears were shed long years ago but memories last for all our days and so with pride, I make my vow to keep my faith with them always.

Had I served in the war I would have taken to the sky, a battlefield of dazzling blue, as a Spitfire pilot, a man, no longer a boy whose youth passed in a day, locked into an airy silence shattered by the noise, exhausted, battle-spent, to fight your fear and keep courage still, to put from your mind the blood and death and flames and dreaming hope of life as young men will.

As I stand amongst the bombers and fighters in the museum, time has passed, and a full sixty years can melt in this day and we will not be able to repay the timeless debt we will for ever owe.

Sad September passes by and on this tranquil golden day my imagination glimpses the drifting haze of fading vapours across the sky.

The skies are empty now as darkness falls. The bare deserted runway scarred with weeds; across a lonely fen a night bird calls; the wind sighs softly in the whispering reeds. Where once the air vibrated to the mighty merlin engines' throbbing roar, disposal huts stand crumbling and forlorn, their broken windows open to the rain. The taxi track is fringed with waving corn, the echoing hangars used for storing grain; up on the crackling tarmac wander sheep; a derelict crew-room door creaks in the breeze. The silent world around is lost in sleep and stars are twinkling far above the trees. Those very stars which were a friendly aid to those who flew upon the wings at night, the crews who never begrudged the price they paid, to keep aglow the flame of freedom's light. There is no flare path now to show the way and guide the homing bombers to the ground. The old control tower stands in gaunt decay. In silence and in darkness wrapped around . . . A thousand bombers over the northern sea heading out for Germany.

Ginger Cox stands at the dart board, 'Steady' Eddy McGee writes to his wife, Nobby Clarke and Jumbo Johnson are playing cards and smoking pipes, and over the hangars rises a bomber's moon and the planes taxi out on runway five and sail off into the silvery night. Sandy Campbell checks his oil gauge, the Belgian coast is coming soon, Eddy McGee lifts his sextant, lined up on a bomber's moon and waves are shining far below as the Lancaster's flying high, come in along the Belgian coast, a thousand silver-shrouded ghosts. Flak flies up from Dresden and Cologne, Jumbo Johnson banks the plane, goes in low to drop his payload and turns to join the pack again and people are dying there beneath the bomber's moon. The city's a raging hell as the planes head out towards the northern sea, young men coming home from victory – over Belgium came the fighters flying high against the night; Eddy McGee saw them coming, closing in before he died and the young men shot them down, sending young men to their graves, shot them down into the North Sea waves.

Now it's '44 in bomber country. Mrs Cox dusts the picture and she cries: Ginger Cox in uniform, looking as he did the day he died.

'Hello chaps, this is the skipper. Belt up, ready for take off.' The plane zooms into the red dawn sky. Course navigator, 105 degrees magnetic. The Dutch coast ahead, then on to Germany, change course 095 degrees magnetic skipper. The silver snaking Rhine, loomed on the starboard, black puffs of flak greet the bomber boys into Germany. Into the valley of the Ruhr roar the chariots of death.

'Hello skipper, fighter, fighter, port quarter down, coming at three hundred feet. Prepare to turn port, go! Go! Go!'

The rattle of guns, the smell of cordite, sickening the nervous stomachs of the crews.

'Hello skipper, this is the rear gunner. Attack broken, attack broken fighter, veered to starboard, commence run in course. Navigator to skipper, four minutes to target.'

'Take run in bomb aimer, bomb door open, come in green marker, one degree error we can miss target by one mile.'

'Twenty-five seconds, twenty-four, steady, steady skipper, left, left, steady, bombs gone, bomb doors closed.'

'Hello gunners, keep eyes open for fighters.'

The Lancaster leaps forward. Relieved of its burden, diving, slithering, throttles slammed wide open. A volcano is raging below, with incendiaries and bombs creating a battered city; the flak is beginning to recede – the ground defence has been beaten. The rendezvous is reached. The surviving bombers turn course for home. That was how it was done. Young men with moral fibre helped by science and skill, and *esprit de corps* on a wing and a prayer.

The watchtower stands, although its windows are broken and bent; no more will young women climb those stairs or listen with headphones to the voice of a loved one returning from a raid and for those who did not return have a little cry. No more are summer breezes blowing. Will you smell the fragrance of their scent? The operation block is just a shell; the roof and doors are gone but on summer nights when all is still, men of the phantom fleet return, hoping to meet a friend for they have a story to tell . . .

A perfect touch-down on a deserted plain. Now a cornfield, a field with no name. They that have climbed the white mists of morning, they that have soared before the world's awake. Some that have left other mouths to tell the story, of high blue battle, quite young limbs that bled, how they thundered up the clouds of glory or fell to an English field stained red.

As I leave RAF Hendon I think about the Battle of Britain waged and won, valiant men and women their duty done. To eagles fallen, the glorious, the brave, in a tidy churchyard or some unknown grave, back then life was for the living as they diced with their fears and signed their honour in a clear blue sky, leaving a heritage of pride to fight or die. I think on how life was for the living.

So live for the day as though it was your last; don't wait for a false dawn or think of the past. But take every moment and remember the few who gave their lives so we can do the things that we do.

For Valour

Somewhere amongst the crumbling ruins of Wembley Stadium lies the memory of the only cricket team to have played beneath the Twin Towers – the Bunbury XI in 1980. We played a game to raise funds for Leonard Cheshire Homes. Ours was the curtain-raiser to a World XI v Rest of the World XI, but the rain swept in from the north to wash out the big event.

The eerie silence reverberating around the stadium where Matthews, Finney, Charlton and Beckham had once starred was shattered by the cries of Joel Garner leaping into action bowling to Rory Bremner, with Mark Nicholas standing at cover. Dennis Waterman patrolled the outfield as Roland Butcher, Chris Broad and Johnny Morris peppered the stands with towering sixes. Errol Brown and Joe 'The Hat' Cuby bowled with style as umpire Dickie Bird looked on incredulously and I, as the captain of this extraordinary outfit, watched in complete wonder.

Earlier I had sat down with group captain Leonard Cheshire VC, one of the greatest RAF heroes of the Second World War. He was sitting with another man, who was introduced to me as Norman Jackson. As with all war heroes they seldom talked about their adventures and group captain Cheshire, a paragon of modesty and understatement, was certainly no exception. Extremely reticent about the war, but very charming and enthusiastic about his charity, he thanked me passionately for putting on the cricket match.

After the game, as we were drying off, he sat down and joined me for a cup of tea. Speaking in hushed tones he said, 'Look, David, if you really want to know about heroics, let me tell you about my colleague Norman Jackson sitting over there. He was awarded the Victoria Cross for one of the most heroic acts of the Second World War. He crawled on to the wing of his blazing bomber at 22,000 feet to try to put out an engine fire.'

Even by the extraordinary standards of the men who have won Britain's highest award for valour, the astonishing bravery of Sergeant Norman Jackson during a bombing raid over Germany in 1944 is exceptional. Norman clung to the wing as the Lancaster tore through the night at 200 miles an hour under attack from a German fighter. He then plunged thousands of feet to earth with his parachute on fire but survived when his fall was broken by bushes. Norman did not have to be aboard Lancaster ME669 when it took off for a 1,000-mile round-trip to Germany on 26 April 1944. Aged just twenty-five, he had already completed his tour of thirty missions, but agreed to stay with the rest of his crew because they had done only twenty-nine.

After bombing the target near Nuremberg, ME669 turned for home but was attacked by a German fighter that set an engine ablaze with a burst of cannon fire. Norman realized that this could ignite an adjacent fuel tank and destroy the aircraft. He volunteered to climb out with a fire extinguisher despite the fact that the Lancaster was flying at 22,000 feet.

The plan was to release his parachute inside the aircraft and then crawl from the cockpit with two crew members paying out the cords. With the extinguisher stuffed inside his tunic, Norman emerged into the freezing, 200-mile-an-hour slipstream and lowered himself from the top of the fuselage onto the wing. He then threw himself forward and grabbed an air intake on the wing's leading edge.

Clinging on with one hand he subdued the flames with the extinguisher held in the other but, just as success seemed possible, the bomber banked sharply to the left and he heard the sound of cannon fire. The German fighter had returned and Norman was wounded in the legs and back. He lost his grip on the extinguisher, which was swept away, the engine burst into flames again and the slipstream lifted him off the wing and flung him backwards. Norman was now being dragged along on his parachute behind the twisting, falling bomber like a fish on a line.

His two comrades desperately paid out the cords to try to get him clear before they baled out of the doomed aircraft. Jackson suddenly broke free from the Lancaster but then realized that the fire had spread to the canopy of his parachute. The cords were also smouldering and he gripped the rigging lines with his bare hands to extinguish them. Because the canopy was torn and had holes burned in it, Norman was plunging to earth much too quickly, but he landed in some large bushes, which broke his fall. His ankles were broken, his hands and face were badly burned and he had shrapnel wounds in his back and legs, but he was alive.

Two fellow members of the crew of ME669 were killed when the aircraft crashed, but four others escaped by parachute and were subsequently taken prisoner. It was not long before Norman, who was in no fit state to escape, was also in captivity. He crawled to a cottage and knocked at the door but Allied bomber crews were hated in Germany. When the owner opened the door he spat at Norman and called him a 'Churchill gangster'. But the man's two daughters took care of him and bathed his wounds while their father fetched the police. 'I was lying there like a lord,' he later recalled. 'I began to think I was pretty lucky.'

After ten months in hospital Jackson made a good recovery, although his hands were permanently scarred. The full story of his incredible bravery did not emerge until the surviving crew members of ME669 were released at the end of the war. Norman, who had been promoted to warrant officer, went to Buckingham Palace to receive his VC with Leonard Cheshire. 'This man stuck his neck out more than I did; he should have the VC first,' Cheshire told George VI. But protocol did not allow it. After demobilization Norman worked as a salesman for a whisky company and he rarely talks about the war. 'If he goes to a reunion he never puts his medals on until he gets inside the building.' It's almost as if it's an embarrassment for him to wear them. He didn't think he had done anything out of the ordinary.

It is the most incredible Victoria Cross story that I have ever heard.

'The thing is, David, when he went out on that wing he did so knowing that he could never get back in the aircraft.' After listening to the group captain's story I had never felt so humble. We presented him with a signed bat. 'And this one is for you, Norman.' Unknowingly, Warrant Officer Norman Jackson VC walked forward to accept our signed Bunbury cricket bat. There was a semblance of shyness and a wry smile.

> Time after time, we saw the cost to all who fought so well,
>   yet lost
> For Norman a fiery plunge through space to some foreign
>   field or place
> We Bunburys doffed our caps
> To Leonard and Norman for valour
> But today, just two of the chaps.

The Little Window, Dave English and the Sundance Kid

It's the last Tube home to Mill Hill East. I'm surrounded by the debris of the day. Yesterday's *Evening Standard*, today's *Metro*. Some prick is barking down a mobile phone as though he is the only person in the carriage. As if we want to hear all his personal news and plans for the night. What a fucking intrusion on the privacy of a public place. Death to all mobile phones, emails, texting and websites. Please download all this shit into the North Sea.

A girl is slumped in the corner of the carriage. I ask her how she is. She looks up through eyes like rotating gobstoppers and mumbles that she has felt better.

I take a closer look at the newspaper. There is an interview with my hero Lord Attenborough. My hero? Well, it was Dickie who gave me a part in *A Bridge Too Far* on the strength of my two towering performances: a Head and Shoulders commercial and as a Dead Man in *Z Cars*. It was the start of my adventure from Cricklewood to Hollywood.

It's 17 April 1976, Deventer, Holland. I'm sitting in my trailer learning my lines. I've been up since five a.m. There is a lot of sitting around waiting for the little window in which I must try and capture my character Captain Andrews, First Airborne Parachute Regiment.

Us thespians are peddlers of dreams. In life you have to face terror and demons. As an actor, you go looking for these two things – to look for the danger, the chance to be spontaneous. You are nothing until someone is listening. So much of acting is vanity. I was always showing off at school, joking and mimicking. It builds your ego, which is crucial for an actor. You mirror who you are talking to. Then listen to the response. You shift your soul towards whomever you meet. You always connect initially from the inside out.

Then you take care of the outside, but always the inside first. You want the scripts to be like talking, not writing. Some of the most powerful things are not said.

When I write scripts, I first write from the heart. The second draft is from the head. As a playwright, first you play, then you write. Ideas go around your head like a kaleidoscope then they appear as one clear colour and you write it down. Let your mind be free. Free to go anywhere Then, as the ideas form and percolate, write them down. Keep faith in your talent. A writer writes when he wants to. A genius writes when he has to. Sometimes I find that the dreams of life are woken by the alarm clocks of reality. I paint pictures in my head. Pictures and paintings are like children. You learn to love them, then they leave you. The face of acting changes around the world. The British have Shakespeare, the French have Molière and the Americans have the Western. They are all national art forms.

Take Robert Duvall, Dustin Hoffman and Gene Hackman. They have all had long careers because they play characters, instead of just trying to be stars. It is clear that Robert Duvall likes the stage but prefers being in movies because he can get his character right, then move on. Why do the same part eight times a week when he can do it once on film and then try something else? As far as I'm concerned the only difference between the theatre and the cinema is that an actor has to speak up a little louder on stage.

In this country we are consumed by *I'm A Celebrity Get Me Out of Here*, get me into there . . . If you freely elect to make yourself available to the bright light on a dark stage, on the TV on a cold night, on the invitation of a great interviewer like Michael Parkinson, on behalf of your fans, then you must remember that if you do choose to enter the game, the very least you must do is to play it by the rules. There's no point in Meg Ryan getting a huge 'strop on' and refusing to answer Parky's questions. Celebrities must be prepared to share their lives with the fans who put them there.

The first thing I noticed about my pal Robert Redford was his arresting beauty. The focal point of his face is a perfect mouth and then his hair, the hair of a teenager, although on *A Bridge Too Far* he was forty years old. Then you notice he bites his nails, has a cluster of moles on his right cheek and has legs so thin that I wracked my memory to try to recall if they have ever been seen on film. He knows that his looks are his fortune: why else fly a make-up man 7,000 miles (taking him away from Richard Burton's *Exorcist II* in Hollywood) to look after your interests? Colonel Frank Gregg, the American military adviser on the film, was at pains to point out that nobody in World War II had his hair as long as Redford's. But despite his ministrations it didn't get any shorter.

It's a paradox that actors spend their lives struggling for fame and recognition, yet when they receive it, it can be nothing other than a continuing irritation. The bonuses of tables in restaurants and VIP treatment at airports are small crumbs compared with the deprivation of the basic human right of privacy.

When not working he sat in his room, read scripts and made phone calls to America. He hired a local tennis pro to play with him, jogged in the park at Arnhem and very probably counted the days until he could return to Sundance. We became firm friends. I taught him how to play cricket and he taught me how to be a movie star. He had an excellent eye for the ball and as a young man had excelled at baseball. He bowled left arm quick and as a batsman, smashed the ball to all parts in our impromptu cricket matches between takes. Robert Redford and James Caan opened the batting, Anthony Hopkins came in at three, Sean Connery at four, followed by Dirk Bogarde, Michael Caine, Elliott Gould, Ryan O'Neal, Gene Hackman, Edward Fox and the great Lord Olivier at eleven. Not a bad side and probably the greatest cricket team I've ever captained.

To play the part of Major Julian Cook, Redford was paid two million dollars for about twenty days' work. He is a rich man but not in the same category as Clint Eastwood, who by 1976 had made ten million dollars from the Dirty Harry pictures alone, nor Paul Newman, whose cheques by the same year from *Towering Inferno* were unlikely to be below the five million mark. The receipts from *All The President's Men*, a movie that Redford owned, probably helped him build a couple more ski lifts at his Sundance resort, but it was before that picture was released that Joe Levine issued the invitation to come to Holland.

Everybody on the set seemed to know that the invitation had a cheque for a million appended to it. I think it was Marlon Brando who once muttered something about 'making an offer you can't refuse'.

The fact is that Joe Levine needed Redford to ensure the film's success. He told me so. 'What the public want are stars, especially the public abroad. They want Steve McQueen, who's suddenly in a sort of semi-retirement. He doesn't see anybody. He doesn't see the public. He doesn't see his manager; he doesn't want to do anything because he's rich. He's too rich. He'd be better if he had some wrinkles on his belly. He'd be a better star. Redford now is number one because of *President's Men* and all the other pictures he's got. He deserves to be number one – he's sane, he's got both his feet on the ground and he's a hard worker.'

Without forcing him to name a sum, I enquired if Mr Levine didn't resent having to pay a man upward of one million dollars. He didn't. 'I do not resent paying him anything he can get from me. Good luck to him if he can get it. If I want him bad enough. Let's take Redford. The way I handle pictures is a little different from a major company. I have independent distributors all over the world for this particular picture and my distributor in Japan said, 'If you can get me Redford as part of your cast, instead of me giving x number of dollars, I will give you 2x number of dollars.'

By chance I had a drink with Jimmy Iwasaki, the Japanese man who bought the film, when he came over to Holland for a look at his investment. He was suffering badly from jetlag and after we'd polished off a couple of bottles of wine, he confessed that he'd never bought a major film before and he thought he'd probably paid too much. But he was a shrewd man and had calculated fairly exactly what any star was worth in Japanese box-office terms. Redford was in front, then came Charles Bronson, and then amazingly, Alain Delon. Later in the evening he ran out of cigarettes and offered a pal of mine an exorbitant sum of money for the 200 pack that he had

just bought from a duty-free shop in London and which was unob-
tainable in Holland. My pal accepted. Maybe Joe Levine didn't have
that difficult a job!

I asked Robert what was the highlight of his career. He told me
the scene that gave him most pleasure (and where he joined the ranks
of the cinema almighty) was with Paul Newman in *Butch Cassidy
and the Sundance Kid*. They are trapped. Behind them, their pursuers
are closing in. In front of them lies a hundred-foot drop into a fiery
river. They discuss the alternatives. Butch insists that they must make
the jump, but Sundance is adamantly opposed. When finally the
enemy is upon them and the alternatives no longer exist, he confesses,
'I can't swim.' He laughed his head off when he told me the story
and how much he'd enjoyed working with Paul Newman.

I was fascinated with the character Robert was playing in *A
Bridge Too Far*: one of the many unsung heroes of the Second World
War, Major Julian Cook. Cook it was who led his men – the third
battalion of the 82nd Army – in what a lot of people think was the
bravest single action of the war. One of the major objectives in
Operation Market Garden was the vast bridge across the River Waal
at Nijmegen. The American 82nd Army under General Gavin had
got as far as the south side of the river. The British XXX Tank Corps
had progressed by road almost to the southern tip of the bridge. But
the German strength on the northern bank was formidable; not only
that, they had almost certainly mined the bridge.

General Gavin summoned twenty-seven-year-old Julian Cook to
his headquarters and ordered him to get hold of some boats and
cross the river, under a smokescreen, but in daylight. It must have
seemed like a suicide mission. At 1515 hours on Wednesday 20
September 1944, Major Cook led his 260 men in twenty-eight small
boats – less than twenty feet long, with so few paddles that many
soldiers had to row with the butts of their rifles – into the teeth of
German fire. Cook, having previously informed his men that he
would stand at the prow of his vessel like George Washington, found
'those bullets started coming too fast and furious and I had to stay
out of their way. In fact, I had to row myself. As I rowed I prayed,

"Hail Mary, full of grace," over and over to myself.' Miraculously the mission succeeded – but at a terrible price.

At ten a.m. on Sunday 12 September 1976, Robert Redford plus a couple of hundred extras and as many cameras and cameramen as money could muster stopped the busy Rhine-bound traffic of the Waal for an hour to recreate the gallant action. Hundreds of locals and tourists gathered in the Sprokenberg Hotel by the side of the river to watch the scene. But one person who wasn't there was Major (now Colonel) Julian Cook.

It seemed odd as nearly all the other major characters portrayed in the movie had been invited to come onto the set and see themselves being acted out. General Frost had been to see Anthony Hopkins, General Gavin to see Ryan O'Neal, General Urquhart to see Sean Connery, Kate ter Horst to see Liv Ullman, Joe Vandaleur to see Michael Caine. General Mackay had come, so even had Taffy Brace and Andrew Milbourne – two regular troopers. But not Julian Cook.

Nobody had a very good reason why not. In fact Cook had written to Joe Levine offering any help he could give and you would have thought that there was no one in the world more fitted to advise on the events of that memorable day than the man who led the crossing. I think that someone, somewhere, had said that he was inclined to be a bit of a testy character and they thought it was problematic enough stopping the river traffic and sending the little boats out into the swirling current without any other worries.

So Cook spent that Sunday morning back home in South Carolina and it was there that he answered my telephone call a few weeks later. He wasn't difficult to find. I rang the 82nd Airborne press office at Fort Bragg but they hadn't heard of Colonel Cook. Their records didn't go back that far, but they advised me to call the adjutant general's office at the Pentagon, because if such a man existed, he was probably collecting an army pension. The Pentagon said they would see what they could do and when I returned home that night there was a message that Colonel Cook had called from South Carolina.

I rang him back, enquiring anxiously if he was the same Cook who led the Waal crossing. He was. He'd heard about the film, in fact he'd had a letter from the production company telling him about it. But then nothing more, until a neighbour who took the *New York Times* had shown him an article about the filming of the battle on the bridge at Deventer. He still didn't know if his participation in the operation was going to form part of it. By sheer chance another neighbour, Mr Hansen, who had lived in Holland and still got some Dutch newspapers, read about it one day and sent Cook a cutting. Undoubtedly pleased, Cook told his family. His children speculated on who would be playing their father; they suggested it must be Gabby Hayes or possibly Walter Brennan. 'No,' replied Cook. 'It's Robert Redford.' His children were amazed and very impressed, but Cook less so. 'I'd heard of him, but I've never seen him. I wouldn't recognize him. I'd have recognized Clark Gable.'

He had remained a full-time soldier until 1970, staying with the 82nd Airborne until 1947 and then serving in Alaska, Vietnam, Paris, Naples and finally Columbia State. Now he was a partner in a small business. He told me again of the reminiscences he had related to Cornelius Ryan. He had not been reluctant to undertake the river crossing: first intelligence reports had indicated they would have to scale down a cliff forty feet high to get into the boats and he was relieved when that proved not to be the case. He certainly didn't volunteer his troops to make the crossing. 'As a battalion commander I'd never volunteer my men nor ask a man to volunteer for anything.' And in the disputed area as to whether his men or the British got to the far end of Nijmegen Bridge first, he had no doubts. 'My men got there first – at seven fifteen that day.'

He didn't sound too testy on the phone. On the contrary, he was anxious not to say anything controversial, although clearly he was hurt not to be more closely involved in the film. But on one subject he was controversial. He retained no love for General Gavin. 'He didn't particularly care for me. He relieved me as liaison officer. He had no respect for me.' I asked him if Gavin thanked him for the deeds he did that day. 'No, he didn't. It isn't in the nature of the man to express thanks.' But his men did. They recommended Julian Cook

A kiss from my sister Annie in the back garden, Hendon, 1955.

Mum centre, Dad centre right, Grandpa top right, Grandma far left and me in my whites in front, summer, 1946.

A scene from
A Bridge Too Far,
with me as a hand-
grenade thrower,
leading the charge.
Robert Redford is
far left (away from
the danger!).

Off set with
Laurence Olivier.
'A word in your
shell like, m'lud.'

Silence of the Buns.
Me with Anthony
Hopkins.

Opposite.
Over the Top!
Me in action in
A Bridge Too Far,
Holland, 1976.

It's only rock 'n' roll.
Come and get me girls!
1976.

D.E. and B.G.
– face to face.

Left to right.
Barry Gibb, Linda
Gibb, Ian Botham,
Kathy Botham,
David English and
Eric Clapton at a
Cartier Polo Match,
1990.

Backstage on the
Bee Gees Spirits
Having Flown tour,
1979, with Robin
and Hugh Gibb.

Left to right.
Phil Collins, David English, Eric Clapton, Bill Wyman;
the first Bunbury game at Ripley, 1987.

Opposite.
Being presented with a Bunbury Bunny by Viv and Beefy,
Finchley CC, 1986.

E. C. (Eric Clapton) in the armchair, Castle Ashby, 1989.

for the Congressional Medal of Honour. It was turned down. He received a DSC and an award from the Dutch.

Redford, on the other hand, did volunteer to cross the Waal. It would have been possible to shoot with a stand-in and do his close-ups in the tank but he seemed happy enough as he came down from his dressing room in the hotel (followed closely by his make-up man and hairdresser, Gary, carrying two helmets) to join the extras for the master shot of the scene. No risk was involved, save that of a boat capsizing in the ever-increasing current, or of one of the special-effect explosions coming adrift and blowing up uncomfortably close.

The main camera operator, Peter MacDonald, had been assigned to travel with Redford in the boat, to get his close-ups and Cook's incantation. 'Hail Mary, full of grace.' MacDonald, like the rest of the cameramen and soundmen who made the crossing, was disguised as a member of the 82nd Airborne.

There was another camera present covering the scene, for the purposes of a documentary. Redford used his reflection in its lens to check his hair and make-up and then try on the helmets to see which was suitable. He asked the cameraman, Martin Bell, 'Are you running?' 'Yes,' replied Bell, and Redford turned away.

The director, Richard Attenborough, observed this with some fury. He strode up to the crew and asked what they thought they were doing. 'Can't you understand?' he remonstrated, 'Redford's meant to be a butch soldier in this scene and you show him checking his make-up. Now piss off.'

It was the first time the documentary director had been asked to piss off by a Knight Commander of the British Empire, but in fairness one could understand his nervousness. If I were shooting a twenty-five-million-dollar epic I wouldn't have another solitary soul on the set save the actors and technicians. Redford was the goose destined to lay the golden egg – at least the Japanese golden egg.

He had been treated with the awe normally reserved for visiting royalty from the moment he arrived on the location. As his Mercedes drew up and this pencil-slim young man with an arresting shock of flaxen hair and sunglasses that appeared to have been purchased at

Woolworths stepped out, Sir Richard abandoned directing for the time being and greeted him with a series of bear hugs, as one might embrace a parent after a decade's separation. It was the day of a parachute drop. A special hide had been constructed to keep those on the ground out of the view of the aerial cameras, but Redford was permitted to stand outside it – so if you see a blond, clad all in blue with reflecting sunglasses, amid the tangled parachutes, you'll know who it is.

It is Attenborough's nature to embrace his actors in the butchest (his word) of ways, and Redford grew noticeably less enchanted with these expressions of thanks as his stint in the movie continued.

His performance on the screen you can see. His performance on the set was one of reticence which even extended toward Ryan O'Neal, with whom he had many of his scenes, but who didn't prove to be his type.

Towards the end of his time in Holland he called round to the production office and invited the behind-the-scenes girls who bash away at typewriters and punch calculators out to dinner. None of the other stars did that.

In common with James Caan, Ryan O'Neal and Laurence Olivier he had the right to approve and disapprove publicity pictures taken on the set. I asked Robert if I could interview him for my local newspaper, the *Hendon Times*, back in England.

He smiled. 'No problem, Dave. Fire away.'

The Redford Transcript

DAVID ENGLISH: Watching you last Sunday, crossing the river at Nijmegen, I wondered if it actually helped you as an actor to almost live the part like that?

ROBERT REDFORD: Yes, it helps. There's not a lot of choice when you're going across a river with fifteen or sixteen boats and they are exploding detonators all around you and people are falling over the side and missiles are flying through the air – you don't have a lot of choice but to act like that. It's fairly tense, but I do believe it helps, yes.

DAVID ENGLISH: Is it the first time you've done this sort of picture?

ROBERT REDFORD: No.

DAVID ENGLISH: Information on Julian Cook, the soldier you're playing, is reasonably sparse. How did you go about sketching the character?

ROBERT REDFORD: Well, there was not a lot to sketch because he appears very briefly in the book. You just have to pretty much draw your own conclusions based on the facts that do appear in the book. There seems to be some difference of opinion: some people say he was a shit, some people say he was a good guy, full of courage. It is very hard to draw a fair determination from that, so you make your own choice.

DAVID ENGLISH: Does it intimidate you playing a man who's alive and well today?

ROBERT REDFORD: No.

DAVID ENGLISH: Have you had any experience of war yourself?

ROBERT REDFORD: No. Just day-to-day living.

DAVID ENGLISH: When playing a relatively small role like this with just a few pages of script in which to create a character, do you approach it differently from playing the lead in a picture?

ROBERT REDFORD: No.

DAVID ENGLISH: I asked the same question of Lord Olivier and he said he did find it more difficult to sketch a character from so few scenes. I wondered if you felt like that?

ROBERT REDFORD: No.

DAVID ENGLISH: When you are creating the character . . .

At this point a platoon of real-life British parachutists who had just landed on the heath where we were talking came by, and stopped to listen to the interview – or lack of interview as it had then become. One of them had a badly smashed-in face and Redford beckoned him to come over.

ROBERT REDFORD: Let's talk to somebody who's really doing it. What happened to your face? Did you land on it? That eye's a real beauty.

PARA: I got into a bit of an argument.

ROBERT REDFORD: Oh, it didn't happen in the drop?

PARA: Part of it happened in yesterday's drop and then afterwards I got hit in the bar.

ROBERT REDFORD: So really the most dangerous part of the war is in the bar?

PARA: Yes, afterwards.

And after his mate had taken the battered Para's photograph with Redford, who put his arm around him, joking, 'A couple of old friends,' he left, having the beneficial effect of making Redford forget that he was trying to give a monosyllabic interview.

DAVID ENGLISH: When you read the script, why did you decide to do the part?

ROBERT REDFORD: I can only tell you what connection I was finally able to make with the part. My uncle was killed in the war on a bridge outside of Luxembourg in a fairly heroic feat. And I think that since a large part of war is waste, waste of good manpower and a lot of courage. I was interested in the project from my standpoint and I think that is probably the best example of the blend of courage and waste, with games played by a few generals, than anything I can think of and it makes one wonder about all the other wars in our history or the world's history and how much of those wars were fought for the same feudal end or wars that we didn't even hear about, like this one. I never knew anything about this war; I don't think many people knew about this, but from that standpoint I found it a very interesting project. Beyond that, there wasn't much that attracted me to it, but that was enough.

DAVID ENGLISH: What is your attitude to films like this, great big multi-million-dollar, epic films, both as an actor and as a producer, as indeed you now are?

ROBERT REDFORD: Well, as a producer I wouldn't do it because I'm not interested in that kind of production as a producer. As an actor it depends on the part and project.

DAVID ENGLISH: Is it something that's good for the cinema? Is this sort of film good for the cinema?

ROBERT REDFORD: Absolutely, sure, because it's the truth, you see. I think it's being done authentically and I think like Westerns, like films about Indians, it's about time we started seeing a version of the truth. We were given a lot of propaganda during the war, which I suspect was good; it kept the morale up, but I don't know that it was always the truth.

DAVID ENGLISH: It is interesting that America has sheared off feature films about the Vietnam War.

ROBERT REDFORD: Guilt. Worried about their image.

DAVID ENGLISH: Could you see a time when America could approach the Vietnam War with a script like this approaching World War II?

ROBERT REDFORD: I think it's being done. There is a picture being made now called *Apocalypse Now*.

DAVID ENGLISH: Turning just finally to the script which you have read and which people will now see in the cinema – when you finished it, what was the overall feeling in your gut?

ROBERT REDFORD: With the script?

DAVID ENGLISH: When you finished reading their script.

ROBERT REDFORD: That it was a good example of this incredible waste and courage and that – well, I'm interested in people's behaviour under duress anyway and I think that a lot of . . . a lot of their courage was absolute panic and fear being manifested in some sort of action. They do say that when Indians used to attack the cavalry or covered wagons in a circle, when they would start to yell and chant on their attack, a lot of people for years felt that that was an attack cry; in truth it was expelling fear, their own nerves. It was a form of expelling; that interested me and I think that a lot of what happened in this crossing of the boats was just that – I mean, when you are being shot at and explosions all over the place and you know the odds are just incredible in terms of you making it and it has very little to do with your own skill, very little to do with your own abilities. It has more to do with your own luck that drives you in a way that you might be driven in which you wouldn't be driven in other circumstances – that interests me – I think this whole courageous feat of crossing the boats, they keep talking about it being the most courageous, heroic event of the war. I think there was no choice; whoever got across got across and if you call that heroic – fine – there is no choice, an order was given. 'Cross on the boats.' They were paratroopers and they were told to take boats. I don't imagine anyone was happy about it, but they had to do it, so they did. Some people made it, very few, and those people were called heroes – I don't know about all that; it's pretty grey stuff as far as I'm concerned.

DAVID ENGLISH: I suppose if one were in the war in that situation you would almost certainly have to be fatalistic.

ROBERT REDFORD: It's like gambling in Las Vegas. You have got to go preparing to lose and then you can have a good time.

Confessions of a Dedicated Englishman

I concluded the interview by asking his advice on screen acting.

ROBERT REDFORD: Well Dave, as you know, most directors give you an eye line to perform your dialogue. Watch Richard Attenborough – he'll put his hand up to the side of the camera as though that is the face of the other actor you're talking too. But I will always speak directly into the lens, using the little window as a mirror. To my knowledge it's unheard of amongst other screen actors. So remember, Dave, the secret is in the little window. Anyway, that's enough chat for one day. Let's go and play cricket; it's my turn to bat.

DAVID ENGLISH: Sure Sundance, anything you say!

The Little Window

On stage, an actor, after twenty years of apprenticeship, can learn to reach the depths of an audience at the moment he is employing the maximum of his technique. A film actor with equivalent technique will have developed superb skills for revealing his reaction to the little window, the circle of glass. He can fail every other way, disobey the director or appear incapable of reacting to his directions, leave the other actors isolated from him and with nothing to react to, he can even get his lines wrong, but if he has film technique he will look sensational in the rushes, he will bring life to the scene even if he was death on the set. It is not surprising there is something sinister about film. Film is a phenomenon whose resemblance to death has been ignored for too long. An emotion produced from the churn of the flesh is delivered to a machine, and that machine and its connections manage to produce a flow of images, which will arouse some related sentiment in those who watch.

Think of a favourite uncle who is gone. Does the apparatus of the mind which flashes his picture before us act in another fashion if we ask for a flash of Robert Redford next? Perhaps it does not. Film seems part of the mechanism of memory, or at least a most peculiar annex to memory. For in film we remember events as if they had taken place and we were there. But we were not. The psyche has taken into itself a whole country of fantasy and made it psychologically real, made it a part of memory. Movies are more mysterious than theatre. Even a clue to the indefinable attraction of the movie star is that he remains a point of light in the measureless dark of memory where other scenes have given up their light. He has obviously become a centre of meaning to millions, possessed of more meaning than the actor next to him who maybe is actually more attractive, more interesting – definition of the phenomenon frays as we try to touch it.

I deplore how self-critical actors are. We are this curious contradiction of low self-esteem and large ego. That's the common denominator – the chronic seam of insecurity that runs through us all.

The movie star may also suggest obsession, that negative condition of memory which we cannot resolve and so we lose confidence in our ability to estimate the present. Obsession is a wasteful fix. Memory when it can be free of obsession is a storehouse to offer up essences of the past capable of digesting most of the problems of the present; memory is even the energy behind the ego, sweetening harsh demands of the will when memory is good. But the movie star seems to serve some double function: the star needs memory and obsession – you only have to think back to Marilyn Monroe. The movie star is welcoming but mysterious, unavailable and yet intimate; the movie star is the embodiment of a love that could leave us miserable, yet we believe we are the only soul the movie star can love. Most essentially, the elusive nature of film makes the movie star a guide to bring us through the adventures of a half-conscious dream. It is even possible the movie star gives focus to themes of the imagination so large, so romantic and daring that they might never encounter reality: how can an adolescent have any real idea whether he will ever have sex with a beautiful woman or fight for his life? Of course we all fell in love with Marilyn Monroe, but it is possible that the dream life of the film exists not only to provide escape but to prepare the psyche for revelations that most likely will never come. For most of us Marilyn remains a fantasy through the looking glass of the little window.

I talked with Robert Redford at great length about the differences between stage and film acting. He told me that the need of a stage actor is to draw an audience together; his instinct is to simplify the play and concentrate it, give it a single crisp flavour. So theatre speaks powerfully or commonly, comically or at the height of hysteria; secretly it almost always speaks vulgarly, for almost always it says: 'We're here to tell you something about life. We've got a piece of the meat for you.'

Film, however, is shown to audiences who do not often react together. Some laugh, while others are silent, some are bored. We share the same time. They have come in on the movie at different places. For film always speaks of death. Theatre rouses desires between the living audience and the living actors: film stirs suicide pacts where each individual in the audience goes over the horizon alone with the star.

Movie stars are caught in the complexity of the plot, but they do not belong to it altogether, as stage actors do. It does not matter of whom we speak: whether it is Garbo or Hepburn or Marilyn Monroe, Julia Roberts or Meryl Streep or Robert Redford, the star is still one misty wink of the eye away from clear presentation. The charisma of the movie star speaks of associations with diverse thoughts with the dispersal of the story point into ripples that went out wider and wider, out to the shores of some fantasy land only the waves of the movies could wash.

David English

The Great Escapism

DAVID ENGLISH MBE

'We'll have Viv,' said Eric.

'We'll have Freddy,' said Alec.

'OK, we'll take Matt,' said Eric.

'And we'll have Bill,' said Alec.

'Jack, you keep wicket for me,' said Eric.

Fifty of the world's biggest stars stood in the yard. It could have been before the bell in a school playground. It was like a scene from the Great Escape, especially as my captain for the day was Alec 'Steve McQueen' Stewart. But instead of being incarcerated in Stalag Luft III, we stood in the playground of the Ripley Court School where the Eric Clapton XI/Bunburys had started in July 1986. Viv, Freddy, Matt, Bill, Eric, Alec and Jack were not Allied POWs but the icons of sport and showbiz. Viv Richards, Andrew Flintoff, Matt Dawson, Bill Wyman, Eric Clapton, Alec Stewart and Jack Russell. Instead of Goon Towers, Robin 'Badger' Ford and Bobby 'Boy' Baker marshalled their programme sellers and security men at each corner of the ground.

After a magnificent lunch in the school canteen served up by Ivor Powell, his lovely wife Lesley, headmaster Andrew and the dinner ladies – wonderful to see Mike Gatting, Adam Hollioake, Norman Cowans and co. sitting at the children's little table and chairs eating and drinking from Thomas the Tank Engine plates and Postman Pat cups – we got changed behind the gymnasium. Inside, instead of the running shorts and singlet of Master James Powell, aged seven, hanging on the hook, the blazer and flannels of the Master blaster Vivian Richards took pride of place.

As the boys got changed, to hear the banter and mickey-taking from the likes of Jack Russell and Dermot Reeve, Cubes, Andy Jacobs and Jon Batty reminded me of the conversations between the brothers in the hallowed secret circle at the Malcolm Marshall match. Sacred stuff for the ears of the assembled high and mighty only.

Outside in the compound the world's paparazzi were milling, ready to descend upon the superstars . . .

'Arfur, you've got to get us out of here.'

'Tell you what, El, there is a tunnel from this hut concealed under the stove. With a bit of luck we can burrow out beyond the wire and be in Switzerland by tea. It could be a journey fraught with danger; we'd better take some sandwiches. Jack kept a diary of one of our previous escapes. Jacko, show the lads.'

Squadron Leader Jack Russell took out a small notebook from his flannel's pocket showing an illustrated diary of an escape across war-ravaged Gloucestershire.

'Certainly, Skip,' said Jack. 'The prisoners' major preoccupation was lack of food. Ask Sgt Major Gatting. A man's eyes betray his hunger. Watch the eyes recede and narrow as they probe for the taste of remembered meals. Watch them again as rations are served, comparing size of portion, measuring width of bread slice. An empty belly is a very basic thing.'

'Thank you, Jacko,' I said.

'Gatt, you'd better take some pork pies and Branston pickle down the tunnel.'

By now, instead of the continental highways towards neutral Spain, Sweden and Switzerland being jammed with hundreds of fleeing cricketers successfully making their way to Blighty, the more sedate routes from nearby Guildford and Peaslake, Ewhurst and Shere were swollen with 4,000 punters bursting to get to Ripley's field to watch our titanic battle.

'Follow me, lads, I know a shortcut to the pavilion,' I lied.

So I led the breakout of the illustrious company through the woods, the sound of dead leaves crackling beneath our boots.

After twenty minutes I knew we were lost but I dared not let on.

'Arfur, are you sure you know where we . . .?' sighed E.C.

'Nearly there, El,' I reassured.

Then we were out of the woods and into a clearing, or should I say some bloke's back garden.

Inadvertently, we had stumbled on to the lawns of the Rev. John Phillips, rector of Ripley, who was enjoying a spot of cucumber sandwiches and lemonade with some local parishioners. It was a scene from a Noël Coward play. Disbelievingly, he looked up, openmouthed, with a hint of double-take, as fifty of the world's most famous faces trooped over his manicured lawn and disappeared through the hedgerow at the end.

'Nice day for it, vic,' piped up Bill, pulling on his twenty-seventh Benson and Hedges since lunchtime.

'Listen lads, we could lie low in the woods and wait until dark. Then we can walk along the railway line and hop on a train to Lubeck and on to a ship to Sweden.'

I surveyed the faces of the escapees and noticed a particularly pained expression on the 'Boat Races' of Bill, Eric and Viv. My time was running out. Then just as I thought I'd be sent to the cooler, we stumbled across the pavilion, which resembled the hut in *It Ain't Half Hot Mum*, standing on a parched brown field. The team photo taken, the captain tossed and the Eric Clapton XXV elected to bat.

It was 100 degrees Fahrenheit and the hottest day ever recorded in this country. Disaster had already struck. The ice-cream van blew up. The happy Mr Softies who had been waiting in a line for an hour turned into the nasty Mr Whippy as 1,000 flakes were scattered all over Surrey.

Aravinda da Silva scored seventy-two off thirty-five balls including eight sixes, one off Andy Jacobs' head. Eric at the other end laboured long and hard for his thirteen with the aid of two charitable dropped catches and despite being clean-bowled twice, only for umpire 'Hursty' (as befitting a former drinking companion of Oliver Reed and the Who's drummer Keith Moon), to call a no ball.

'I know what you're trying to do, Arfur,' muttered El darkly. 'Keep me out in 100 degrees for the entire innings you bas—'

Our surreal game blossomed in the heat and dust, watched by the mesmerized 4,000 crowd of mums, dads, grannies, kids and dogs. There were some memorable cameos. Eric Clapton, guitarist, played cricket whilst cricketer Mark Butcher played guitar. Freddy Flintoff, who had made the 800-mile round trip from Preston via Worcester

especially to make his Bunbury debut, scored forty-one in nine balls.
I had known Fred since he was fifteen, when he starred in my 1992
Bunbury English Schools Cricket Festival at Charterhouse School,
along with Liam Botham, Alex Tudor, David Sales, Ben Hollioake
and David Nash. What a year indeed!

'No problem, Dave, wouldn't have missed it for the world.'
Typical Fred, top man.

Aussie star Andrew Symonds was exactly the same. He had flown
in from Darwin earlier in the day. Symo didn't bat or bowl but was
happy to sign autographs and talk to everybody. Like the others, what
he did give was his time, a truly valuable commodity in a cricketer's
congested diary. Dermot Reeve and Rudolf Walker trudged back to
the pavilion, hastening the arrival of Sir Viv to the crease accompanied
by a reverential round of applause. 'C'mon soul brother,' he exhorted
E.C. who, suitably inspired, moved into double figures with a well-
run five before being given out when 'Hursty' finally ran out of excuses
on his behalf.

'I didn't get a wink of sleep last night,' El told my pal, Robert
Philip of the Daily Telegraph. 'One of my little ones is teething, so
I went out there and didn't know where I was. But I like putting
myself in situations where there is no safety net. It's great fun playing
with professionals because they look out for you: the only time
you're in trouble is playing against amateurs, because they're dangerous and they're out to win.'

Muralitharan bowled to Viv, who had been his hero since
childhood. 'This is the greatest moment of my life, enthused the Sri
Lankan master bowler. Murali's lethal spinners turned, stopped and
spat like a cobra. Viv took years off his life to combat the threat and
played masterfully, watching every tweak and deviation.

There was a hush around the ground as the two maestros
contested their skills in the searing heat. For them it could have been
a Test match on the St John's Ground, Antigua, with 60,000 baying
in the stands. Gravy on the disco and the Red Stripe girls cavorting
in the pool.

But no, it was just a small field in Surrey behind the Ripley Court
School. Mind you the bouncy castle had stopped bouncing and Peter

Baverstock's hot dogs and burger van had ceased to sizzle. All eyes were focused on this extraordinary encounter; you could feel the intensity of the battle of wits.

Anoushka, our opening bowler, sent down her bouncers to Kent's Robert Key and Mark Ealham. Dressed to thrill in minuscule bikini-top, micro-mini skirt and skyscraper heels, the Polish princess and her twin peaks had the boys in a trance.

'Blimey, you don't get bowlers like her down at Canterbury!' beamed Keysey.

Bill Wyman, bowling and fielding in a private cloud of cigarette smoke with a Benson and Hedges stuck defiantly between his lips, marked his run-up with a little pile of fag ash. But when he batted it was Bill who was on fire. Carrying his bat for an unbeaten forty-one in the service of the Alec Stewart Bunbury XXV, wily Will returned to the pavilion to bemoan in his best Michael Caine Penge accent, 'I'm the oldest f—g bloke out there and I've been fielding and batting all bleedin' day. Tell you what Dave, I'm sixty-seven and I don't need all this!' For the record, Billy batted from 5.35 p.m. to 7.09 p.m., which undoubtedly represents the longest he has ever gone without a filter tip in his entire life.

And so our Mad Dogs and Englishman continued to entertain the troops brilliantly in the midday sun. The auction at teatime raised a fortune for the two charities of the day, the NSPCC and Eric's Crossroads Drug Rehabilitation Clinic in Antigua.

Dermot Reeve, our auctioneer, was in his element. Standing on a rickety old table, he held a guitar above his head. 'And here we have it, ladies and gentlemen: Eric Clapton's guitar signed by the legend himself. Who will start me with £5,000? You sir, £6,000, £7,000, £10,000 I've got!'

Earlier El had delivered a quiet message in my 'shell like'.

'Look Arfur, I can't keep on signing these guitars. These punters buy up Fender lookalikes made in Taiwan from Ronnie's Music Shop in Tooting or somewhere. I sign them and then they flog them around the corner for £25,000. It's just not on and it's got to stop now. So read my lips, understand!'

'But El, this is a special day,' I pleaded, knowing full well that most of the boys had brought down guitars to be signed by the maestro. I knew for a fact that Dermot had a Ford Transit van parked at the back full of 'Fenders'. But E.C. was adamant. I saw his point.

For thirty years we had shared adventures and high jinks around the world. I had always badgered him into some exciting scenario or other ending up in E.C. sending me to my hamper. He knew I was watching him and at about 6.15 p.m. he weakened.

'OK Arf, this is the last time; line 'em up, but I'll only personalize the autographs, all right!' So the boys got their guitars signed. The Alec Stewart Bunbury XXV finally beat the Eric Clapton XXV by six wickets and a hefty sum was raised for two deserving causes.

For the second time in his cricketing career Eric announced his retirement. The first time was back in 1989. We were playing on this village green in Penn, Buckinghamshire. It was a week before he was setting off on a concert tour of Japan.

I put Eric in the gully. Gary Mason is bowling. First ball, whack, he breaks a finger. There are lawyers and underwriters leaping out of the bushes screaming 'Litigation!' As he walks off smoking a fag and clutching his damaged digit, a bumble bee stings him on the other hand. So we now have El with both hands in ice buckets. A twenty million to one chance, surely? Anyway, El goes off to hospital, meets a couple of very nice radiographers, signs a few autographs with his dodgy hand, has a glass of wine and comes back with both hands in bandages.

At the end of the match El announced, 'I've dreaded this day with every ounce of my being. But in years to come I'll probably look back on it with some kind of grim satisfaction, at least for having kept my word when I would much rather have been on a beach somewhere 3,000 miles away from David English. But underneath all his noise and chaos, there beats a heart of gold.'

Thank you, El. Believe me, in a couple of years we will be tunnelling *Back in* to Ripley's field for a rematch and another 'Great Escapism' from reality.

Cape Town Blues

I'm sitting in the Café de Cuba overlooking Fishoek Harbour just
outside Cape Town. To the left of me Ernest Hemingway pores over
his prose, chain smoking, deep in thought, eyes squinting beneath a
furrowed brow, searching for the next line. In the alcove, slouched
on a sofa of dazzling fabric, Che Guevara and Fidel Castro talk of
revolution in hushed tones, pulling on massive Havana cigars and
smiling behind their beards. Sexy young girls from Panama with
heads of tumbling curls wait the tables. Lips of scarlet, high heeled,
blouses bursting with ample bosoms and skirts so tight they fit like
a silken skin. Candlelight flickers to catch the gold in their earrings
and the ivory white of a flashing smile as they serve their masters'
every whim. Outside, beyond the harbour, lies the Indian Ocean
shimmering away to the Cape of Good Hope where it meets the
mighty Atlantic creating a diversification of currents, swells, flotsam
and jetsam. The air is filled with happy shrieking voices.

Not so in 1982 when I toured South Africa with the McAlpine's
Cricket Club. Back then apartheid split the beaches into white and
non-white, the same with trains, different carriages designated to
different denominations. On the face of it everything looked rosy.
There we were, a cricket team sweeping through Cape Town, Johannesburg and Durban. Tourists with eyes bulging in wonder at the
sights of Table Mountain, the wine fields of Stellenbosch and Con-
stantia, the massive beaches and drama of the high veldt.

But scratch the surface and you saw how the blacks and colou-
reds were bullied and looked down on by some elements of the
whites. I saw it with my own eyes: how the ethnics were treated like
second-class citizens. On one occasion our white hosts had invited us
to a barbecue. As per normal our McAlpine tourists (under the
inspired leadership of Johnny 'Dinger' Bell) mingled with everybody,
but during the evening the two faces of our hosts became evident.

One reasonably respectful, giving its black staff their orders, but later I heard the same woman berating a waiter and his wife.

How could anybody speak to a fellow human being like that, especially when they were called 'Welcome' and 'Beauty'? I was seething with anger and unusually for me consumed by a deep hatred for a fellow human being. I took Welcome and Beauty to one side and put my arms around them.

'Now listen, my friends, if anybody, and I mean anybody, ever speaks like that to you again just tell me and I'll really fuck them up.'

'No boss, I don't want no trouble,' said Welcome, cowering into the shadows.

I felt South Africa was a place where to be born black was to inherit a lifelong curse. A place where to be born white was to carry a permanent burden of fear and hidden rage. To me it was a place in which those who cried out for freedom were promised and rewarded with the gift of the cold and silent grave.

Fuck the white supremacy; to think that locking away Nelson Mandela on some island could shut them up. What a load of shit. Ask Ian Botham. The White Cricket Association asked him to bring his best pal Vivian Richards to play in South Africa on one condition, that they would make him an honorary white man! I'd have loved to have been in the same room when the Master Blaster received this request. Strangely enough, Viv declined.

When our touring party touched down at Cape Town on 11 February 1982 at the invitation of our marvellous benefactor A.J. 'Jimmie' McAlpine, I decided to go AWOL for a couple of days in the townships.

The shop window at the street corner was two-foot deep in eggs. Painted on that window in red: 'Mixed eggs: small, medium, large and extra large. Price 26c a dozen.' Out of the shop came a fearfully old, small, wizened woman, gaping at the world with opaque purple eyes. She could have been looking for some dark corner to lie down and die in. Her face had shrunk to a handful of wrinkles and her toothless mouth was open like an old thirsty tortoise. She gaped and felt her way out of the egg shop, carrying one egg in a black clawed hand. She walked slowly down the pavement, touching passers by to steady herself, then disappeared into a butcher's shop bursting with people and raw meat. Everyone in the shop gave way spontaneously to let the old woman reach the counter. There was always a deep respect for the very old in the township, even fear, for the old were so much wiser and nearer death. A black hand came through the thick curtain of sausages and five dirty fingers dug into a bowl of mince and pulled out a fistful of it, a well-judged pound for the old woman. She emerged from the shop with her eggs in one claw and her mince in the other. Now she was more uncertain. She had no free hand with which to steady herself: but a young Moslem in a red fez appeared, put his arm round her frail old back and helped her on her way.

It was Saturday morning in Hanover Street. A river of people, cars, barrows, buses, horse-drawn carts and small boys racing down slopes in soapbox carts; a bustling, laughing, hooting, whistling, shouting, chatting river of people; fat women with scarves around their heads laden with shopping bags. A turbaned sheik in long robes and a neat hairline moustache; pretty young coloured girls with large gaps in their teeth, men looking like King Farouk with smart suits and dark glasses, two little girls with coloured chalks, drawing pictures on the pavement. An old Moslem, blind in one eye, selling green ginger, garlic and chillies; young men with skinhead haircuts and brass studded belts ogling girls on street corners and girls swinging sexy backsides; men hurrying by with blocks of ice on their backs, or large bags of sweet potatoes or sacks with gallon jars of white wine; messengers, cripples, loafers, dope peddlers, men and women with haunting faces. People whose faces were the faces of Malaya, India, Sri Lanka, Mauritius, Mozambique, Africa, Western and Eastern European all blending with one another but each somehow retaining a shadow of its origins.

Children everywhere, shouting, laughing, whistling, teasing, darting between old men's legs, running between fast-moving buses and cars and missing them by inches with perfect judgement; children who all seemed too thin, too small, too old and wise for their ages, playing in dirty gutters, dark alleys and sitting in gloomy doorways with stairs leading straight up from the pavement to mysterious rooms. But children who were always laughing, playing with anything they could find and putting it to good use: discarded boxes, tins, old car tyres, pram wheels, hoops of iron, ball bearings, children playing hopscotch in the middle of busy streets, singing, skipping or kicking footballs made of rolled up newspapers. Poor underfed children, but cheeky, confident, happy and so emotionally secure in the bosom of their sordid surroundings. Everyone loved them. To them it seemed every adult in those busy streets was another mother, another father.

I played cricket with them up against dimly lit little shops that sold herbs and spices and aromatic joss sticks which Moslems burnt in their homes on certain nights to keep away evil spirits. I told them I came from England where we had won the World Cup at football. They had heard of Bobby Charlton and Georgie Best and sung out their names. We played soccer and held up all the traffic. Somebody had produced a ball and everyone started kicking it. There was uproar. Cars and buses hooted angrily, but it all ended in laughter when the ball bounced resoundingly onto a roof of a beautiful new midnight-blue Mercedes. A mentally retarded youth stood in the doorway of his home with an expression of anguished concentration, listening to a ping-pong ball, which he held between his thumb and forefinger close to his ear.

And then there was the ultimate case of the blind leading the blind: a drunken blind man being led through the crowds by a man who was blind drunk. People turned, gave way and roared with laughter at their disastrous progress. There was the general dealer who had so much in his shop and such a variety of goods that only one customer at a time could get into it. Banjos, guitars, Mandolins, prams and chairs hung from the ceiling. The shop window was price tagged as extra special bargains.

At a glance you saw glass vases, cups, kettles, lamps, razors, a scale, oil stoves, kitchen utensils, broom heads, fly sprays, chamber pots, mops, batteries, pots, pans, cheese graters, jars, torches, locks, clothes pegs, thermos flasks, rolling pins, egg beaters, knives, rope, porcelain ornaments of dogs, cats, birds, reindeer and squirrels, ash trays, rolls of linoleum in red floral patterns, belts, harps and mouth organs. I fully expected Ronnie Barker and David Jason to emerge from the set of *Open All Hours*. Instead, a little Jewish shopkeeper told me of his philosophy, his secret for success: 'If you've got it someone will buy it.'

Outside, it reminded me of Mardi Gras coming to Harlem, a touch of New Orleans, a little Louisiana and a lot of the back streets of Rio. A kaleidoscope of colour as folk in their silks of white, red, yellow, orange, green and blue danced and pranced with vivacity, unquenchable happiness and good humour. They were the spirit of the township come to vibrant, thrilling life. They turned the street into rivers of fire. They were madness gone sane, they were fantasy turned into reality, and they were a heartthrob that gave life to an otherwise dead city. They lived, they danced, they laughed, they drank, and they created happiness and infected everyone else.

It reminded me of my nights down at the Apollo Theatre in Harlem. As the only white man in the audience I marvelled at the sight of Marvin Gaye, Otis Redding, Smokey Robinson and the Miracles weaving their magic on stage whilst women knitted and chewed the fat and kids danced in the aisles to the 'Shooby Doo Wops' and tantalizing melodies. Back in the late seventies I went backstage and signed the Staples Singers to my RSO Record Label. Pop Staples could well have been a character from the township. He would have loved the vibe.

'Tell me, where do I find the music?' I asked the shopkeeper.

'You must go and meet the fiddler.'

I fully expected to meet a big Bill Broonzy, Memphis Slim, Lightning Hopkins, Muddy Waters kind of cat . . . Maybe a South African Robert Johnson. Instead, standing on the corner of Queen Victoria Street was a small, thin, emaciated man with large, moist eyes that looked like lights in his head. He had sunken cheeks and an Adam's apple made large by a thin stalk of a throat. His trousers ended above his bare ankles and his shoes were too big for his small naked feet. The sleeves of his jacket were too short, showing thin, brittle, transparent arms like those of an opium smoker. He must have had a beggar's licence because the police never picked him up and his way of begging was to place his oily rimmed hat on the ground to one side of him. When no one was approaching he would stand leaning against the fence as if fast asleep and his chest would rise and fall with an effort. But as soon as someone came along he would take up his violin with its one string, cup it under his chin with a dirty silk handkerchief, put his bow to the string and saw off a little tune.

Fascinated, I watched the fiddler. He didn't know a note of music and to be honest he couldn't even play the violin, but he went through the motions of playing and the little whine that came wavering towards you on the south-east breeze was tuneful enough to bring back a memory or touch your sympathy. I saw passers by remarking 'How pathetic!' 'The poor little devil, I must give him something.' His acting was spectacular. You could not walk past him and ignore him without it being on your conscience. If you didn't toss a coin into his hat you would walk off worrying about it, thinking that some terrible vengeance lay in store for you. I watched mothers giving their small children a cent to drop in his hat as a first lesson in human charity. Even tramps who were hard up themselves used to give him something. That was the little fiddler. Where he went after dark and where he came from early morning to start another day, no one ever knew. He was something of a mystery.

I went into the Cheltenham Hotel, run by a man called Charlie Terblanche. As soon as Charlie had taken over the Cheltenham, it had become the meeting place of all the characters, especially after five in the evening when they all pitched in for a drink, mostly for any number of drinks . . . and the strange thing about this situation was that Charlie Terblanche was an ex-detective and they all came to drink at Charlie's bar because many of them were ex-criminals who had had professional dealings with Charlie when he was on the beat. Yes, many of the men he had once arrested for murder, assault, robbery, housebreaking and theft were now his devoted customers; they respected him as they would someone very special and he loved them, too.

'What characters, man,' he told me in his rolling Afrikaans accent and he pointed to one and then the other. 'They're just Liquorice Allsorts.' By that he meant that in his Cheltenham bar you could meet up with hoodlums, drunks, dope dealers, pickpockets, beggars, queers, bores, chancers and no hopers. Some drank in confidential huddles, some drank alone, fixing their eyes on one spot, some were argumentative and some were happy and full of bawdy laughter, some drank with strange solemnity.

'Do you see that man there?' said Charlie Terblanche. 'I once arrested him for murder. He got ten years and now he's out again and on the straight and narrow.' Then he pointed to a tall man who drank his double brandies with a strange ritual. He was always alone and would never take a drink unless he could stand at his own special place in the bar, against the far wall. That was where he was now. He was a tall, sullen man who had a face of disturbed memories. He spoke to no one and looked fixedly before him. Each time before he raised his glass he first looked to the left and then to the right, then he would bring the glass slowly to his mouth, allow his eyes to roll around the rim and empty the contents with a single convulsive swallow.

'That man,' said Charlie, 'was one of the greatest safe-breakers in the business. The safe wasn't made that he couldn't open, except one. And that was a famous case, I can tell you. He and two others broke into a place in Long Street but the safe weighed 800 pounds and they couldn't get it open. They took it away with them, mind you! Just the three of them and you know how? They rolled it out of the shop on billiard balls! Now,' he said, 'I want to show you the greatest character of them all.'

It was the little fiddler, but now he looked a very sick man. His large eyes were brighter and wetter than ever, his neck and arms thinner, his breathing more laboured, with upward jerks of his chest. He sat at a table with his hat on, his violin on his left and in front of him a tumbler of Scotch whisky.

'He looks poor, but he makes more money in a day than the rest of them put together,' said Charlie. 'After every day begging he takes a taxi from the bottom of Queen Victoria Street to here, and he sits at the table till the bar closes and drinks nothing but the best Scotch.

Sometimes he buys drinks for everyone in the bar. Once he told me if I was short of cash he'd let me have some. But death is staring him in the face, I can tell you. He's riddled with TB. The doctor told him that if he didn't lay off the liquor he would die. But he told the doctor they knew nothing about life and that he would live it his own way. Now there's a character for you.'

Charlie Terblanche shouted to him across the noise of the bar. The fiddler took a deep, painful breath and looked up. It seemed that death really was staring him in the face and that he was staring back. But when he saw Charlie he raised his glass and smiled, a wonderful toothless smile that pinned back his ears with radiance.

It's almost closing time in the Café de Cuba. Outside the last caterpillar train to Muizenberg has just trundled by. Still the boys dive in the harbour, the moonlight picking out their glistening bodies. Twenty-two years later I had gone back to the township only to find it had been razed to the ground. Lost in the memory of the people who had been its lifeblood, I entered a bar next to a BP Station and a McDonald's where the Cheltenham Hotel and Hanover Street had once stood. Still in shock I challenged the barman to tell me the story. He told me the central government had made repeated requests to the city council and the landlords to upgrade the area. But to no avail. The government declared it a white area under the Group Areas Act and the wholesale relocation of the inhabitants had started, mainly to areas away from the city. The process had taken fifteen years and some 55,000 people had been removed. Towards the end the government felt the area had become so run down, it had turned into a slum on the doorstep of one of the most beautiful cities in the world. I felt devastated. Only people who never knew this township could have dismissed it as a slum. They would have never cared about the quality and vitality of the people who were its lifeblood. They would have reinforced their beliefs with snide remarks about dirty streets, peeling walls and drug trafficking. They would have seen the district only from the outside without ever caring about its soul. People like Welcome and Beauty. This approach had the seeds of inevitable tragedy because the spirit of the township was in the hearts and minds of its people. Not the houses they lived in.

While so many other South Africans I met on our cricket tour found pride and esteem in their cultural bonds with England, Europe and other parts of the world, my friends in the township were quite happy to be uniquely themselves and, in doing so, they fitted the definition of 'South Africans' more genuinely than anyone else. I'm sure there were many thousands of others just like them all over the country, but the people of the township were the ones who gave all of them definition and a unique character and approach to life. In the end, a happy, generous, wonderful community simply disappeared and the emptiness they left behind changed the whole life and character of Cape Town.

'Would you like another beer, sir?' enquired the barman.

'No thank you, I've had enough.' As I got up to leave, my eye caught the sight of an old violin in a case behind the bar.

'What is that?' I enquired.

'Oh, it was found in the rubble. Rumour has it it belonged to a bit of a character, who could play a bit. A mean fiddler by all accounts. The funny thing is that it's only got one string,' laughed the barman. 'Why, are you interested in music, sir?'

I couldn't imagine my life or anybody else's without music. It's like the light in the darkness that never goes out. The blues took me back to the old fiddler's side where it had all come to life. There's an old African saying that 'the roots of a tree cast no shadow'. That's how deep the blues goes. When you really listen to the music you understand. This was the one thing they could never take away from the black people.

'Yes, you could say that,' I said, turning for the door.

'Well, good night, sir.'

'Good night to you.'

And on a wave of nostalgia I had gone.

Robert Stigwood –
the Greatest Showman of Them All

'Ferry Across the Mersey' sang Gerry and The Pacemakers . . .

Well, it's 2 June 2004 and I'm sitting here with Bazzer Gibb on the Red Funnel ferry chugging across the Solent to see our old boss Robert Stigwood. An emotional voyage tinged with sadness for the man who was quite simply the most important pop impresario in the world. Now seventy, crippled with diabetes and a dodgy back, he is holed up as a recluse in Queen Victoria's old spread, Barton Manor, on the Isle of Wight.

'We must go and see him, Baz,' I had said. 'Give the old boy a hug and rekindle the memories.'

For it was Robert who took the Bee Gees, Eric Clapton and I on the worldwide adventure that was RSO. A magical mystery tour of shenanigans, hard work and laughter unrivalled in the history of popular music. We alight from the ferry and move through the harbour and up on to the main road out of East Cowes.

Although Robert has been one of the most important figures in international music, film and theatre since the early sixties, his enormous influence and his role in the careers of acts including Cream, Eric Clapton and the Bee Gees has never been examined in any depth; no one has ever written a biography of him. This is a great gap in the literature, because in terms of his significance on the music scene over the last forty years, Robert Stigwood is (after Rupert Murdoch) probably the single most successful and important Australian in the entertainment business.

We pull through the gates of Barton Manor, bought by Queen Victoria in 1845 as an extension to the Osborne House estate. There she accommodated equerries and other high officials including Empress Frederick of Germany, King Leopold of the Belgians and the Russian royal family. I could imagine Queen Vic canoodling with Prince Albert in the beautiful gardens, a walk through the rhododendrons past a thousand roses and into the woods dappled in sunlight to the secret bench for a stolen kiss.

Few people know of Robert's whereabouts on the island. Little is known of Robert's early life. Back in the early seventies he would recount his life to me over a bottle of J and B after 6 p.m. at our HQ high above Brook Street. It's important to me that I tell you his story.

He was born in Adelaide in 1934 and educated at Sacred Heart College. He began his career as a copywriter for a local advertising agency and then in 1955, aged twenty-one, he departed Australia for good. He hitched to England, one of the first Aussies to travel to Europe in this way, pre-empting the hippie trail by ten years.

He had an eventful trip and I know that there was an incident when he bravely climbed fifty feet down a rope ladder into the hold of a tanker to administer morphine to a seaman who had fallen through a hatch.

When he arrived in England he found a job in an institution for backward teenage boys, working primarily on nightshifts, overseeing the dormitories and preventing any flow of traffic after lights out.

Not long after that he met a man called Stephen Komlosy who went on to manage Lionel Bart (creator of the musical *Oliver*) and they decided to go into business together. They set up a small theatrical agency in Edgware Road and began building up a roster of actors. Among their clients was an aspiring young actor and singer called John Leyton (who went on to star in the *Great Escape* and *Von Ryan's Express*). It was Leyton's unexpected success as a recording artist that made Robert and his erstwhile associate Joe Meek into Britain's first independent record producers.

Robert realized there was a fortune to be made through record production. Up until then the pop music industry was highly stratified. Managers managed artists' careers and nothing else; agents only booked the artists; publishers only published music and recording companies recorded, manufactured, sold and promoted the product. It was rare for a manager to be involved in publishing or agency work and it was almost unheard of for managers, agents or publishers to be directly involved in record productions. Recording was still strictly the preserve of the major labels.

Robert decided to take on all aspects of the business. He would make records independently, and then get the record company to distribute them in return for a percentage of the selling price. It was the music business equivalent of the independent film production that had changed the face of Hollywood.

John Leyton, actor, became a pop star with the number one hit 'Johnny Remember Me', establishing Robert Stigwood, male model agent, as a record producer. Robert had made a distribution deal with Joseph Lockwood, managing director of EMI but soon realized there was a flaw in the deal – the minuscule percentage that EMI was paying meant that he was barely able to make a profit from his recordings.

Nevertheless the system he pioneered changed the style and direction of the UK pop charts for ever and his success with John Leyton was instrumental in expanding his business, becoming simultaneously agent, manager and producer, a role he evidently relished. Robert became fascinated by the business. He loved its trickery and tease and the apparent ease with which money could be made, and unlike his predecessors he expanded laterally. He didn't remain simply a manager or an agent. He moved into music publishing as well and into pop concert promotion. But his real contribution to the British music scene was independent record production.

He was in every way the first British music business tycoon, involved in every aspect of the music scene and setting a precedent that was to become a blueprint of success for all future pop entrepreneurs.

Robert's other big innovation was in the songs that he selected. British acts had conventionally covered US hits after they had become successful there, but Robert began making regular trips to America to find new releases he thought had potential and then rushing out UK covers by his acts before the originals hit the American charts.

For a few years Robert rode the crest of a wave of success. He lived extravagantly and spent lavishly. The small percentages he released from his production meant that he was largely dependent on agency and management commissions to maintain his cash flow and gradually his company funds dwindled. Robert also promoted concerts 'as a quick way to make a buck' and top up the books during slow periods. He specialized in summer seaside promotions, which were sometimes highly profitable, but were also notoriously risky since they often depended on the fickle English weather among the many other hazards of the business.

In 1965 Robert promoted a package tour headlined by notoriously difficult rock 'n' roll legend Chuck Berry (who famously always demanded payment in cash up front), supported by The Five Dimensions, the Graham Bond organization (with Jack Bruce and Ginger Baker), Long John Baldry and the Moody Blues. The tour was poorly attended and Robert lost heavily and copped a lot of flak from the industry when he over-hyped his latest new pop hopeful, an Anglo-Indian singer called Simon Scott. His heavy-handed promotion included sending out tacky plaster busts of Scott as a gimmick, but it backfired and made the hapless singer a laughing stock. The venture cost Robert a great deal and it was money that he could ill afford to lose.

His finances ran out halfway through the Chuck Berry tour and he called in the receivers owing some £40,000 to his creditors. EMI offered to bail him out but he refused because he was anxious to get out of the unfavourable deal he had with the company. He fought valiantly to maintain the illusion that he had kept his personal wealth intact, although in reality he was flat broke. Robert managed to fool enough people to keep his creditors at bay while he re-established himself. Within two years, be was back on top.

Robert's aggressive style and his drive to expand his management empire occasionally brought him into conflict with other entrepreneurs. He is the subject of one of the most famous stories in British showbiz, a fabled altercation between himself and one of the other big movers and shakers of the British pop scene, the infamous Don Arden.

Some time during 1966 one of Robert's staff made the mistake of discussing a possible change of management with one of Arden's top acts, The Small Faces. Not surprisingly Arden – a man you crossed at your peril – took exception to this, and in spite of the fact that Robert had never met the group personally, Arden decided to pay him a visit with some of his minders, to teach him a lesson.

Don Arden recalled: 'I had to stop these overtures – and quickly. I contacted two well-muscled friends and hired two more equally huge toughs. And we went along to nail this impresario to his chair with fright. There was a large ornate ashtray on his desk. I picked it up and smashed it down with such force that the desk cracked – giving a good impression of a man wild with rage. My friends and I had carefully rehearsed our next move. I pretended to go berserk, lifted the impresario bodily from his chair, dragged him on to the balcony and held him so he was looking down to the pavement four floors below. I asked my friends if I should drop him or forgive him. In unison they shouted; "Drop 'im". He went rigid with shock and I thought he might have a heart attack. Immediately I dragged him back into the room and warned him never to interfere with my groups again.'

Robert took on David Shaw, an ex-City banker, as his partner, giving him access to previously unavailable funds and expertise, and he gained some extra cash flow by subletting his offices to The Who's managers, Chris Stamp and Kit Lambert, although he had reason to regret that decision, becoming the butt of the pair's inveterate and often cruel practical joking.

He kept his Robert Stigwood Agency intact and began rebuilding his career as a manager and independent producer. In 1966 Robert made an important connection when he paid £500 to Stamp and Lambert for the right to become The Who's booking agent. This gave him the opportunity, soon after, to lure the band away from Decca and onto his own newly established Reaction label, for whom they recorded the famous single 'Substitute'. The recording was done on the sly, and was explicitly intended by the group as a means of breaking their five-year contract with producer Shel Talmy, with whom they had fallen out (the single's original B-side, 'Waltz For A Pig', was reputedly written about Talmy). Also in 1966 he became the manager of a new band comprising three of the best musicians from two groups that he had under contract – guitarist Eric Clapton from John Mayall's Blues Breakers, and bassist Jack Bruce and drummer Ginger Baker from The Graham Bond Organization.

His connection to The Who enabled him to get his new group, Cream, onto the bill for a major US tour supporting The Who in March 1967. Although the tour was not a great success it was an important showcase for Cream and enabled Robert to introduce the band to New York's music cognoscenti, helping to break them in the USA. (It was for this tour that Robert commissioned the Dutch art collective called The Fool to paint striking psychedelic designs on Eric Clapton's Gibson SG and Jack Bruce's Fender VI bass.)

Robert moved his recording activities to Polydor, where Roland Rennie, with whom he had dealt at EMI, had been appointed as the new managing director. Robert had apparently been forewarned that Rennie was moving to Polydor, and this was the major reason that Robert had been unwilling to accept EMI's rescue package. Rennie had been a key figure in breaking The Beatles in America; he had been sent to New York by George Martin and all EMI products were channelled through him for distribution by EMI's American partners. It was Rennie who struck the deal to license the first three Beatles records to the Swan and VeeJay labels, rather than to Capitol, who at first had no interest in the group.

Robert signed a much more advantageous deal with Polydor, with high percentages and substantial funding for his recording costs. This gave him the luxury of being able to take Cream to New York, where they cut their records with Atlantic Records' famed house producer-engineer Tom Dowd.

On 13 January 1967 Robert signed a career-making deal with his friend and colleague Brian Epstein to merge their two companies. The Beatles were by now off the road, and Epstein was tiring of the demands of his ever-expanding business. He was keen to reduce his involvement in the company he had founded in 1963, NEMS Enterprises, so he eventually struck a deal with Robert.

Why Epstein decided to merge with Robert is uncertain. There had been numerous other offers made for NEMS over the previous few years and Epstein was reported to have turned down more than one multi-million-dollar offer from American interests, so it is unlikely that he chose to become a partner with Robert simply for the money. They knew each other socially and through business, and Robert already had a reputation as a shrewd, tough operator.

Brian Epstein told The Beatles' publicist Alastair Taylor that Robert had originally offered to buy NEMS, but the deal eventually became a merger, in which Robert would have to put all his company assets into NEMS; in return he would receive a reciprocal shareholding, plus a salary, an executive position as co-managing director, and access to all of NEMS' now considerable financial and other resources.

It was a godsend for Robert, and it effectively placed him at the pinnacle of the British pop industry in one easy step, but Epstein seems to have been about the only person in NEMS who was keen on the idea. Alastair Taylor is reported to have exclaimed, 'You must be joking!' when Epstein told him of the merger. Epstein was also considering handing over his role as manager of The Beatles, but when the Fab Four learned of this they were outraged. They evidently disliked Robert intensely; interviewed in 2000 Paul McCartney recalled the group's angry reaction. 'We said, "In fact, if you do, if you somehow manage to pull this off, we can promise you one thing. We will record 'God Save the Queen' for every single record we make from now on and we'll sing it out of tune. That's a promise. So if this guy buys us, that's what he's buying." '

Consequently, Epstein stayed on as manager of The Beatles but he handed responsibility for most of his other acts to Robert.

NEMS had expanded rapidly, growing from fifteen staff in 1964 to eighty in 1966. Epstein had taken over the Vic Lewis agency in 1965 (bringing in Donovan, Petula Clark and Matt Monroe) and Lewis became a NEMS director, but many staff members found Lewis' abrasive manner difficult to handle. They could see the same problems arising, multiplied tenfold, when Robert moved in. His autocratic style would be a time bomb ticking beneath people who had stuck by Epstein through thick and thin.

Epstein told Derek Taylor that the merger with Stigwood would bring new talent into the fold and would strengthen the operation. Taylor remained unconvinced – Robert, he said, had 'a ruthless reputation, a cavalier style that upset more people than it pleased'. Epstein soon found himself at odds with his new partner – he was reportedly unhappy about Stigwood's spending, was upset by his renting a yacht for the Bee Gees, and was also angered by Robert's unilateral decision to send Alastair Taylor to America on a business trip, a plan Epstein overruled. It is claimed that Epstein subsequently decided that he didn't want Robert in the company.

Robert's next big break as a manager came only weeks after he started with NEMS. The Bee Gees had recently arrived from Australia with hopes of making it in the UK. Unknown to them, Ronald Rennie had already heard 'Spicks and Specks', thanks to the band's publisher, and Rennie had made arrangements with their Australian label, Festival, to release it in the UK. When, to his surprise, Barry Gibb appeared at Polydor's offices in London, Rennie immediately contacted Robert, who he thought would be ideal to sign the group to Polydor and manage them. Robert had just begun his eleven-month tenure with NEMS, to whom Hugh Gibb had sent an LP and acetates in an effort to sign the group. Robert signed the Bee Gees to a five-year deal in February.

Polydor released 'Spicks and Specks', but in spite of Robert paying for four weeks' exposure on pirate station Radio Caroline, the single flopped. Robert was undeterred, and with NEMS' resources behind him, he embarked on a concerted campaign (no doubt at NEMS' expense) to break the Bee Gees in the UK, assiduously wining and dining TV producers and DJs; according to the Music Web Encyclopaedia, he spent a whopping £50,000 promoting the group in 1967.

It paid off – within months their second single, 'New York Mining Disaster 1941', had become a major UK hit and the follow-up, 'Massachusetts', went top five in both England and the USA, the first of a string of Bee Gees hits through the late sixties.

Robert's future with NEMS may have been uncertain, but it was decided in dramatic fashion by Brian Epstein's untimely death in August 1967. Brian's brother Clive took over as managing director and Robert left NEMS to form his own company, the Robert Stigwood Organization, in December, taking the Bee Gees with him.

Robert's companies expanded into almost every field of entertainment. Over the years the Robert Stigwood Organization has promoted artists such as Mick Jagger, Rod Stewart, David Bowie and managed and forged the careers of acts including the Bee Gees, Cream, Blind Faith, Eric Clapton and Andy Gibb. Under the RSO Records label Robert recorded artists including Clapton, Yvonne Elliman, Paul Nicholas, Player and soundtrack albums for the motion pictures *The Empire Strikes Back* and *Fame* in addition to the films produced by his company RSO Films.

In 1973 Robert brought me in to start RSO Records. As president of the company I was responsible for the worldwide recordings of Eric Clapton and the Bee Gees. In the next ten years we made RSO into the world's number one independent record company achieving a still standing world record of five singles in the same week in the US top ten ('Night Fever', 'Stayin' Alive', 'How Deep is Your Love' and 'More Than a Woman' by the Bee Gees and 'Lay down Sally' recorded by Eric Clapton).

RSO's transition from rock management concern to multimedia entertainment empire began after Robert saw the Broadway production of the pioneering rock musical, *Hair*. He decided to stage it in London and it was a huge success, running for more than five years in the West End. He followed this with many highly successful productions; *Oh Calcutta!*, *The Dirtiest Show in Town*, *Jesus Christ Superstar*, *Pippin*, *Sweeney Todd*, *Sing a Rude Song*, *John, Paul, Ringo and Bert* (*Evening Standard* Drama Award best musical 1974) and the last of the Tim Rice/Andrew Lloyd Webber musicals, *Evita*. Both *Superstar* and *Evita* were successfully reproduced on Broadway, the latter picking up the Tony Award for best musical 1980. Later Robert produced stage versions of his two big film musicals, *Grease* and *Saturday Night Fever*.

Robert purchased a production company, Associated London Scripts – the company that subsequently developed the hit series *All in the Family* and *Sanford & Son* in the USA. In 1973 Robert moved into film and produced *Jesus Christ Superstar* as a motion picture in association with its director, Norman Jewison. He followed this with the acclaimed film version of The Who's *Tommy*. Robert chose

wisely, selecting iconoclastic auteur Ken Russell to direct. His out-
landish visual imagination provided a perfect filmic setting for the
improbable story. His casting raised eyebrows in some circles but also
proved to be ideal for the task. *Tommy* starred Ann-Margret, Roger
Daltrey in the title role, and featured Elton John, Robert Powell, Jack
Nicholson, Tina Turner, Oliver Reed, Paul Nicholas, Eric Clapton
and The Who. It became one of 1975's most popular films and
remains one of the most successful mergers of rock music and film.

RSO Films' next production became one of the biggest ever hits
in the business – the colossally successful *Saturday Night Fever*.
Written by and featuring the Bee Gees, the 2LP soundtrack album
made music history by becoming the largest-selling soundtrack album
and one of the biggest-selling records in history, making the Bee Gees
into international megastars. It was followed by another huge success, *Grease*, which launched TV actor John Travolta to super-
stardom. Incredibly, the songs were written 'to order' without the
group having seen the film, and according to Frank Rose's 1977
Rolling Stone article about The Bee Gees, at least four of the songs –
including 'Stayin' Alive' – were written in just one week.

Although he has enjoyed many great successes, Robert has also
had his fair share of flops as a producer. His two music blockbusters
were followed by a rare but infamous miscalculation. In fact, RSO's
next film turned out to be one of the biggest bombs ever made – the
execrable *Sgt Pepper's Lonely Hearts Club Band*. On paper, the
multi-million-dollar extravaganza looked like a sure-fire hit – it
featured the songs of The Beatles, and starred two of the biggest rock
acts of the day, Peter Frampton and the Bee Gees, backed by a
staggering list of rock and film greats in cameo parts. Unfortunately
for all concerned, the problems surfaced early and grew steadily
worse. Robert sacked original director Chris Bearde before shooting
began; the Bee Gees quickly realized that things did not augur well
and begged to be removed from the project, to no avail. Although
the new director, Michael Schulz (*Car Wash*) did a valiant job, the
film turned out to be a disastrous flop; lampooned by audiences and
critics alike, the unfortunate production is still cited as one of the
worst ever films. This was followed by the cult 'kiddie gangster'

musical *Bugsy Malone, The Fan, Times Square, Grease 2,* Peter Weir's *Gallipoli* (under the R&R Films banner) and the 1997 Golden Globe Awards best film winner, *Evita,* starring Madonna.

Not all these films were successful, however. *Moment by Moment,* which co-starred John Travolta and Lily Tomlin, came out only a year after *Saturday Night Fever,* but it was panned by critics, bombed at the box office and is generally credited with single-handedly turning one of the hottest stars in the world into 'box-office poison'. Five years later Travolta again displayed his now-legendary inability to pick roles when he agreed to appear in Robert's new film, an ill-advised *Saturday Night Fever* sequel, directed by Sylvester Stallone. Although perhaps not as bad as *Moment by Moment,* the movie was not a success and did nothing to restore Travolta's career, which languished until his 'comeback' in *Pulp Fiction* in 1994.

I hadn't seen Robert for twenty years and here we were going back to see the old master. When Bazzer and I arrived at the huge doors of Barton Manor we were shown into the massive lounge where Queen Victoria must have conducted affairs of the state and of the heart. There was a murmur at the door as Robert walked in, helped by two sticks and his French assistants. He looked terribly frail.

'So you've come to see me,' he laughed. 'Well, look at me, they said I'd never walk again.'

Robert sank into the armchair and lit up a cigarette. He chain-smoked all day as we reminisced. He spoke slowly and you could see the memories of the wild parties and mercurial business deals coming back.

We ate in the state dining room assisted by his staff of butlers, chefs and minders. He noticed my Bunbury tie.

'David, do you remember that night in New York?'

'Certainly do, Robert.'

We had gone to this swanky nightclub. Our party had consisted of Andy Warhol, Jimmy Page, John Lennon, the Bee Gees and Eric Clapton. On arrival at the door Robert was told he couldn't come in without a tie.

Quietly Robert went inside and a few minutes later we were

admitted. After a particularly boisterous night I asked him how he had got us in.

'I bought the club,' smiled Robert, 'on the one condition that nobody could enter with a tie on.'

My relationship with Robert had always been special, almost hauntingly so. To become the first president of RSO Records was a miracle, which shaped my life. I had been working as the press officer of Decca Records, responsible for the publicity and promotion world-wide of the Rolling Stones, Tom Jones, Engelbert Humperdink, Gilbert O'Sullivan, Dionne Warwick and The Moody Blues.

It was December 1972 when I arrived in my office; my secretary had a message for me. 'David, Gini Smythe, Robert Stigwood's secretary called you – she wants you to phone her back.'

'Hello, Gini. This is David English.'

'Hi, David, Robert would like to see you.'

'When?'

'As soon as possible.'

'How about lunchtime?'

'Fine.'

Sixty-seven Brook Street stood elegantly in a row of gleaming white Edwardian buildings. On the door was a shiny brass plate, 'The Robert Stigwood Organization'. I entered the portals of the man who was a legend in showbusiness. He was known to be a visionary with exceptional intuition for a hit. Above all he gave the young a chance to fulfil their talents in the business, riding a fine line between the controversial (*Jesus Christ Superstar, Oh! Calcutta, Hair, The Dirtiest Show in Town, Till Death Do Us Part* and *Up the Chastity Belt*) and the more conventional and brilliant household favourites of *Hancock's Half Hour* and *Steptoe and Son*.

He loved to surround himself with young, vibrant, radical and restless talent and would take enormous risks on their behalf to promote their energy and their hunger to succeed. If Robert Stigwood believed in you, you really were onto a winner – from the wilderness to a big star of stage and screen.

'Go straight up,' said the immaculately turned out commission-aire.

From the hall to the golden discs lining the stairway, the place was heavy with the trappings of success.

Gini Smythe, a lovely looker, met me with a warm smile. 'Go straight in, David. Robert is expecting you.'

From that moment my life was to take a massive step upwards.

The room was long, softly lit, heavily carpeted, tastefully decorated. Pride of place was given to a large oil painting of Ray Galton and Alan Simpson over the John Adam fireplace. Later I was to learn that while writing *Hancock* and *Steptoe and Son*, Ray and Alan would sit opposite each other from nine till five. At lunchtime they strolled around the streets chatting and observing. At 5.01 p.m. they left the office, never phoning each other in the evenings or at weekends with any ideas. Writing for the two giants of comedy was strictly nine to five.

And there, at the end of the room, sitting behind a huge glass table supported by four stone lions, was Robert Stigwood. Well dressed, a nice face, slightly florid with gold wavy hair. He beckoned me in a slow, soft Aussie drawl and shook my hand. Then, after a seemingly endless thirty seconds of silence from his end of the table, his face bathed in a pool of light, he looked across at me and announced, 'You're the one.'

I looked behind me thinking there must be someone else in the room. 'Me?' I asked.

'Yes, you're the one,' repeated Robert. 'I've decided to start my own record company, and you are going to make it the greatest in the world.'

Steady, Dave boy, I thought to myself. This bloke doesn't take no for an answer – keep your cool.

'Now, how much do you want?' continued Robert. 'What car? When can you start?'

My mind was racing. To Robert it was already a foregone conclusion that I'd join him. But what of Decca? What money could I ask for? Well, Johnny Hayes was the first £100 per week footballer so, '£100 per week and a BMW,' I said.

'A BMW? Isn't that a motorbike?'

'No, Robert, it's a car. £100 per week and I'll start on 1 January.'

'Fine,' came the reply, across the four stone lions. 'Now RSO Records – what logo would you suggest?' Talk about hitting the road running! My mind raced. I had read in Tony's *Evening Standard* that it was the year of the 'Red Cow' in Japan. 'Tell you what, Robert, The Beatles formed an apple. How about a red cow? It's lucky in Japan.'

'Fine,' came the reply. 'You can have whatever staff you require. You will build your own team, press officers, pluggers and secretaries . . . anything you wish. Thank you, David.' And with that Robert sat down to pore over some contract or other. I stood up and turned to leave the room. As I approached the door once again I heard that soft Aussie drawl. 'And, David, remember . . . You're the one.'

On 1 January 1973, high above Brook Street at number forty-six, and right opposite Claridges Hotel, I started RSO Records. Just me and the red cow. I was twenty-six years old. On my door it said:

D.S. ENGLISH
PRESIDENT

Eight years later the biggest-selling soundtrack album of all time was created. To date, 50 million albums have been sold. From the moment John Travolta was seen strutting down the street to the strains of 'Staying Alive', the phenomenon of *Saturday Night Fever* was born.

'Staying Alive' went to number one in the US charts and the film was a smash success worldwide. The combination of John Travolta's dancing and the Bee Gees' music created huge disco fever around the globe. To celebrate the success of *Saturday Night Fever*, Robert staged a massive garden party in the middle of New York. One thousand guests partied all night – all the beautiful people were there. I remember sitting at a table with Andy Warhol, Carly Simon, Paul Simon and James Taylor. Robert and the Bee Gees came over.

'Look, David,' said Robert, and there above Times Square was our red cow flashing in big red neon above the USA top ten.

CONGRATULATIONS TO THE BEE GEES, FIVE SONGS IN THE USA TOP TEN

To this day it still stands as a world record. RSO Records was now far and away the world's number one independent record label. Robert made a toast: 'To you, David, you made us smile, knocked down the doors and moved us on down the right road. I told you, you are the one!'

It was late when we left Barton Manor. Outside, the moon shone over the gardens and the dogs were barking. It was difficult to say goodbye. Barry and I gave our mentor a hug.

'Go on, Robert, throw away your sticks and walk.' I laughed. 'Tell you what, let's get the old red cow out and start again!'

'Now that would be fun,' laughed Robert. 'Thank you for coming to see me, lads. It was very special.'

We just managed to catch the last ferry. Bazzer and I sat on the top deck and looked back at the island. You could just make out the silhouette of Barton Manor under a starry sky. Stiggy the star-maker was probably sat in his favourite chair, his faithful labrador Marmaduke by his side.

'Did you see the twinkle in his eye when you said let's start again?' laughed Barry.

'You're right, I can see it now. Robert Stigwood presents . . .

'*Victoria and Albert* the musical, live at the Isle of Wight Festival. Music by the Bee Gees and Eric Clapton, one night only. Available on RSO Records!'

How Many Sleeps!

It's early evening as I stretch out in the old brown chair, high up in the hills above Harare. I am smothered by children. Two of my own, Amy Rose and little Dave, Chloe Avalon, the bundle of joy from heaven and Fari, Maidea the maid's little boy who resembles Viv

Richards and is convinced I'm his dad. I'm very happy to be so. My heart is like an African bus. There is always room for one more.

It is 2003 and I have been happily divorced from Robyn for five years. I am still crazy about her as a soulmate but we pulled in different directions. She had been homesick for her native Africa and after three years of being banged up in my cottage, a pretty prison on a track lost in endless green outside Mill Hill in North London, she had flown back to her roots along the dusty trails of Zimbabwe.

Ian Botham was my best man at our wedding. On the way to the church, Beefy, my confidante, had asked me: 'Loony, do you know what you are doing?'

'What do you mean?' I replied quizzically.

'Well, Loony, I don't think marriage is for you. David English loves everyone. He loves life. You can't be stuck with one person. It just won't work.'

'Charming,' I responded. 'Look, Beefy, you're married. And now it's my turn to walk up the aisle with my beautiful girl. Anyway it's too late now. The band are on their way and I've paid for the sandwiches!'

Three years later we had two lovely children: Amy Rose and David Harry, fruits from a true love affair.

There are people I know who have had a string of disastrous marriages and inappropriate obsessions with beautiful, unavailable women, but I met someone whom I genuinely loved and still do. She is my addiction and I can't stop cuddling her. I marvel at her powers of motherhood, her gentle spirit, iron resolve and endless patience bringing up three children. Yes, *three* nippers.

Young Chloe Avalon came as a surprise bundle of joy straight from heaven. It was mid June 2002 when I was awoken by a loud knocking at the front door. Still in semi slumber I ran down the stairs, tripped over the cat and opened the door. It was Robyn standing on the step, well and truly 'bunned up'.

'Inge, can I come in? I need your help.' Over a pot of PG Tips she unfurled her story. She had experienced a relationship with a fellow back home. Tragically he had died of cancer, leaving Robyn pregnant. She wanted to go ahead and have the child. Could she have it in England?

No problem. Up went the sign, 'The David English Maternity Home'. I called Edgware General Hospital and took my ex-missus down to meet the girls in the baby department. I booked Robyn in for a water birth.

The ante-natal classes were fun. I sat around in a circle with all the mums bulging at the seams with their Bunburys in the oven.

'Mr English, you've probably got a question you want to ask me,' piped up the super-enthusiastic midwife. 'Are you looking forward to being a dad?'

'Dad? Not me, love, we've already got twelve children. For this one I'm only the minicab driver!'

On 17 July 2002 Robyn gave birth to a beautiful bundle of joy that tumbled out weighing three kilograms. We went to the Births and Registration office.

'Are you the father?' asked the registrar.

'No love, I'm afraid he's deceased, but you can put my name on that certificate. I'd be proud to be her dad. Tell you what, we'll call her Chloe Avalon English!'

Robyn returned to her beautiful home in Glenlorne just outside Harare. It stood on a hill and had a bright yellow sun painted on its side. I found returning to England after visiting the gang particularly painful. It was the ache of leaving your loved ones. I never knew if it was best to say goodbye to the children or to leave in the heat of the night. On one occasion I was creeping out of my bedroom with my suitcases when I saw a little figure standing in the hallway. It was Amy. She had got dressed in her favourite red coat, put on her shoes and stood with a pink Barbie bag by her side.

'Daddy, I'm coming with you,' whispered my princess.

'Amy, you can't, sweetheart. I have to go back to England to work.'

'I'm coming, Daddy,' insisted Amy. 'I will tell the pilot I will sit with him.'

Every long journey starts with a small step. Amy Rose English was just three years old. It broke my heart. Saying goodbye to the children destroyed me; I had wandered into an emotional wasteland, not knowing where or to whom I belonged. I felt a failure that our marriage had not worked. The sense of remorse still tears through my belly. It was particularly confusing for the children as Robyn and I were always cuddling, laughing and getting on famously.

'Why is it, if you get on so well, you are not together?' they asked.

Amy used to call me to ask, 'How many sleeps before I see you, Daddy?' Instead of a calendar she thought in terms of sleeps before we were together.

Without your children, you have no foundation in life. You get through the day on a wing and a prayer. This insecurity drives you on to succeed, seized by sudden regrets for the road not taken.

Then you are out back on the street. Never lonely, just a loner. First you have to find love, a rare commodity. Fighting your way through the barren times in between. Many people are in love with the idea of being in love. The reality is often very different. You must find the words to express the feelings. Jesus Christ is the head of my house, the unseen guest at every meal, the silent listener to every conversation. I turn to him for advice and support and try to return his love and wisdom by helping others. Those less fortunate and disadvantaged. The biggest risk in life is not to take one. The people who make it are those that push that extra mile.

I once met Sean Penn. I could feel his confidence simmering inside. The same self-belief belongs to Ian Botham. He can get on a surfboard and stand on a wave and I think that is the parable for his whole life. He's always riding the crest.

Not all of us are as confident. I tell the young ones never to take a step backwards even to gain momentum. Always make that instant judgement, do what you think is right at the time. There is no point in looking back and saying, 'I should have done this, or that.' Too late for regrets, the moment has gone. Every ending is a new beginning.

The secret of survival at school with its playground culture is to get friendly with the dangerous ones. Always go to the core of the problem. Don't evade the inevitable. Hit the cancer on the head quickly. You are the only one inside your own mind. Only you know the pressures and what you must do for yourself and those closest to you.

Look after your friends. Link hands with them at the school sports day to make sure neither of you comes last in the running race and remember, fundamentals are the building blocks of fun!

The years have ticked by. Robyn, a wonderful mum, travelled with the children trying to find a home and peace of mind. I have rarely encountered such a dichotomy between a person's day to day restless spirit and the perplexed serenity of her mind as a mother, which has remained unimpaired. Zimbabwe, Cape Town, Johannesburg. This is Africa where nothing is as bad as you feared but never so good as you hoped. All that untapped potential and beautiful, gentle people, usually ruled by greedy, tyrannical megalomaniacs.

Often, I look out of my office window and a robin arrives and perches on my fence. Then I get the call. It always happens.

'Inge, it's getting dangerous here in Zimbabwe. I need your help. Amy is eleven, David is ten and Chloe just two. We've got to get out. Can you find them a good school?'

It's autumn as I drive past the chilling fields and scented meadows of Hertfordshire along the green and gold road to Edgegrove School. September and the rusty fingers of trees wave me on past the gypsy barrow laden with flowers and the old cricket pavilion out of season. An empty shell of a summer dream. In the back seat, resplendent in red and grey uniforms, are Amy and David. Chloe is in her car seat. Her turn will come soon.

After consulting many eminent educators as to the best school, I was universally advised to 'try the school between Radlett and Bushey in Aldenham Village'. So thoroughly recommended, all the roads seemed to lead to Edgegrove.

I made an appointment to meet the headmaster, Michael Wilson. At the end of a long gravel drive was this magnificent ivy-clad Georgian house. On entering the main portals I was met by an enchanting lady who gave me a tour. From that moment I was mesmerized by the 'home from home' warmth of Edgegrove. The atmosphere of inkwells and monitors, dormitories and names in gold leaf on the oak board of honour took me back to the gentle days of *Goodbye Mr Chips*.

At the end of my tour I asked my lovely guide if *I* could join the school. She laughed. 'Come this way. I will show you to the head-master's study. Oh! By the way I am Carolyn Wilson, the headmaster's wife.'

Before I met Michael Wilson I was already under his spell. I had flicked through his parents' guide where he had written 'perhaps one of the most important words in growing up is joy. Joy in learning, joy in discovering, joy in friendship, joy in activities, joy in helping one another. Also one of the most important words in teaching, joy is helping the young to achieve their potential joy in friendship of colleagues and pupils, joy in the partnership between home and school. In the middle of all the other things that have to occupy our minds – let us not lose track of joy.'

Michael Wilson was a tall, handsome fellow who had come from Kenya, so he understood my strong links with Africa. A first-class man who loved sport; you could tell he knew and cared for each one of his 270 pupils with a loving, father-like protective spirit.

Amy Rose and Dave English Junior were accepted into the wonderful warm bosom of Edgegrove School. Sometimes as I drive home from Edgegrove a fog hangs heavy over the ponds of Letch-more Heath. I'm moving slow motion through a black and white celluloid film of *Great Expectations*. I can see John Mills standing erect representing good values, decent and respectful. Bygone days of innocence and good manners when we sat around the table as a family and ate Sunday Roast with gravy and we doffed our caps and believed in Santa Claus.

Through the mist, names from the Edgegrove roll of honour appear, scholarships and exhibition places . . . Sinearavelou to Eton, James Daniel to Haileybury, David Mason Merchant Taylors, James Pears, Millfield, Edward Burrell, Harrow and Jonathan West Brook to Uppingham. What constitutes a school? Not ancient halls and ivy-mantled towers where dull traditions rule, not spacious pleasure courts and lofty temples of athletic fame where devotees of sport mistake a pastime for life's highest aim, not fashion or renown or wealthy patronage and rich estate.

Not one of these can crown a school with light and make it truly great. But teachers strong and wise who teach because they love the teacher's task and find their richest prize in eyes that open and minds that ask.

Michael Wilson's seat of learning embodies all these virtues. All those young hearts beating vibrantly eager to learn at the end of that lonely drive in that ivy-clad house. So now I live in number 1 Highwood Cottages and my ex-wife and children live next door but one. Tension Terrace? Crestfallen Heights? Not at all.

And 'How Many Sleeps?' All great songs start with the title. 'Yesterday', 'The Long and Winding Road', 'Night Fever', 'How Deep is Your Love?' 'Tears from Heaven', 'How Many Sleeps' – all heartfelt sentiments that we express every day.

I went to Miami and wrote the song with Barry Gibb. We invited Cliff Richard to record it and 'How Many Sleeps' became a big hit record.

'How Many Sleeps'

DAVID ENGLISH AND BARRY GIBB

Chorus 1

How many sleeps till I see you again
How many waves on the shore
How many wishes and how many prayers before
    you are with me once more

Bridge 1

I'll kiss you good night and I'll promise to write and
    I'll see you very soon
Are we looking at the same moon
Can I hear you when you call
I'll meet you in the same world
Oh Amy Rose I love you most of all

Chorus 2

Lions and tigers and crocodile tears
Things that go bump in the night
I'll be your hero, dry all your tears
Drove all your fears out of sight
And how do you find it so easy to leave me
Alone inside my room I will see you in the same stars
    and I will hold your face somehow
And the moment is for ever my Amy Rose
This is your daddy's vow

Chant

And I will meet you at the kissing gate
Remember the fish on the stone
I will meet you down at Amy's Barn
And you will never be alone
    How many sleeps till I see you again
How many rays in the sun
Daddy I love you as long as I live
Long as the rivers may run
And how many colours we see in a rainbow
And race that red balloon
We'll be looking at the same moon
We will never be apart
And the moment is for ever
My Amy Rose
You live inside my heart

Isn't Life Grand in Disneyland?

It is half term and time to take the nippers off to Fantasyland, courtesy of Uncle Walt's imagination. All is quiet on the Disney front. The Mickey Mouse Express tears across Northern France, where soldiers spilt their blood at Arras and the Somme in the First World War and twenty-three years later our boys battled their way to Dunkirk to be rescued by strangers in little boats.

In Main Street USA the Hotel Cheyenne stands lonely in the Frontier Ghost Town. High Noon beckons at LA Gare Du Marne La Vallée. The Disneyland railhead. In the Wyatt Earp Saloon, Doc Holliday is enjoying his first tot of whiskey as Miss Kitty adjusts her bloomers. So does Jules from Southgate, who has followed through in her Fruit and Looms after being scared shitless on the big Thunder Mountain accompanied by her six-year-old nephew, Ollie.

The Eurostar grinds to a halt on a lonely stretch outside Lille. Old French couples peer from behind net curtains to see the latest multitude of 'Looneys Anglais' who are preparing to wreak havoc in Fantasyland.

Little Lydia from Liphook dreams of pink and purple palaces and sleeping beauty princesses as Monsieur Lefevre (the local baker) takes another swig of red, shakes his head and stares at the crazed painted faces pressed against *les fenêtres du train*.

We are only people, after all. All the grans and grandpas from Rotherham and the Ribble Valley spoiling their grandchildren in dear old Walt's fantasyland. Just outside Paris and yet you could be a million miles away from the Eiffel Tower or Les Champs Elysées that no one will ever see. Too busy filling Mickey's pockets or goofin' about with Minnie.

The Mickey Mouse Express finally pulls into Toy Town and the throng surge from the train to check into the Hotel Cheyenne, to be billeted into rooms on streets called Cochise, Sitting Bull and Jesse James.

Then it's the long walk by the river and around the lake to Adventureland to fight with the thousands for a brief thrill on the Space Mountain or Star Wars. Kids play with instant new friends in Buffalo Bob's Saloon, crashing each other's heads with rifles and giant balloons. Uncle Reg from Basildon swigs his beer, a welcome anaesthetic to his weary limbs after queuing up for forty-five minutes a ride.

Old Alf from West Ham flirts with the idea of riding the Bucking Bronco.

'You must be eighteen years old to ride!' calls the Carnival Barker.

'Should be all right,' laughs Alf. 'Don't take the piss, I'm seventy-eight!'

I see an Albino and a crazy man in a tree. There is a boy in a tall velvet hat and everywhere, pretty girls with braids in their hair. I see a man with a ravaged face like Johnny Hallyday.

Isn't life grand in Disneyland?

Dad chases shadows of years gone by, the beautiful face has dissolved in the crowd before he can weave his magic web and make her laugh leading to a stolen weekend in Paris in a week's time.

It's evening and Walt smiles down beneath a Halloween moon on Kai aged five with his single mum from Camberwell Green, then exhausts himself on rides he's never seen. The student from Vietnam tosses pancakes to make an extra euro for Vicky and her kids over from Truro.

To be a parent you must have the patience of Job, but I wouldn't change it for the world. To snatch a cherished moment and sit down by the lake and catch the children's glee with candyfloss fingers and stars in their eyes.

A moment that lingers; Alf's been bucked off the Bronco and has lost his teeth. Time for tea in the Rainforest Cafe with Snow White and her seven friends.

All the single mums with firm bums and the married mums with big tums.

I'd love to meet Walt. I bet he adored children. He must have done. I'd like to take all these thousands of skipping, dancing, beaming, screaming 'Hairy Potters' on a spiral staircase to Neverland to meet him. We could ride Jumbo's Circus Train over the hills and bridges to Storybook land where Walt could meet us and lead us into his imagination.

Instead we'll stumble back, tired but happy through Tumbleweed Town to the Hotel Cheyenne, clutching ornaments and sweatshirts and fall into our beds and dream of sleeping dragons and flying elephants.

Isn't life grand in Disneyland?

Raid on the Wood

Where else can you bowl potatoes to Lawrence of Arabia, exchange banter with the England players whilst swigging Chardonnay from Ian Botham's box, debate the odds with two Pierses and make secret plans with Sir Vivian Richards for a night on the town? Answer? Lords Cricket Ground.

It's the Saturday of the Lords Test match in 2004. The secret is to hit St Johns Wood at the crack of dawn, park your car in the high street, no later than 6.30 a.m. for free all day parking and make your way swiftly to the simmering Gammon Rasher Cafe in Allitsen Road, for the mother of all fry-ups.

Lords Cricket Ground, the most precious piece of real estate in England, plonked in the middle of St Johns Wood, a Georgian Haven for diplomats and surgeons, theatrical agents, conmen, estate agents, the Sultan of Brunei, Russian hookers, Japanese au pairs, Chinese gamblers, rabbis, lotharios in chinos and loafers, Jewish princesses in Gucci and Prada, the American School, bistros, Elizabeth Arden, haute couture, diamonds, Ferraris, faded film stars walking fluffy white dogs with diamante collars, wheeler dealers spieling, perfumed pleasure sitting outside cafes, stilettos, ankle bracelets, thespians, lesbians, the Beatles Studio. How did Graveney, May, Cowdrey, Lindwall Bradman, Botham, Sobers and Flintoff from such diverse backgrounds come to contest their skills amongst this lot? And in the middle of the hoi polloi, the somewhat incongruous Gammon Rasher greasy spoon with its steamy windows, gingham table cloths and gurgling coffee pots.

'All right, Dave?' calls Joe from his sizzling kitchen.

'Nice day for it. Old Vaughany should score runs.'

A lovely lady, wide of girth wearing an apron and a huge smile, serves me with the world's greatest English breakfast, which I devour with relish, washed down by a large beaker of piping hot PG Tips. Then I'm on the move; you can get more done on foot between the hours of 7 a.m. and 10:30 a.m. at a Lords Test match than a thousand letters or phone calls throughout the season.

Out in the street you bump into Ace Snapper, Patrick Eager and a couple of lads from the Sky team. Into the ground at the North Gate by 7:30 a.m. where 'Barbados Pete' greets you, always with a story and a smile. Past the groundsman's hut. A quick gag with Mickey Hunt and his ground staff and straight into the Media Centre for a coffee with David Lloyd, Bob Willis and Paul Allott of Sky Sports. 'Morning Loon!' booms Beefy. 'I'll see you in my box later.'

'Morning Biffo,' laughs David Gower. He always calls me Biffo and I call him Chalkey. Names we picked up whilst flying in the same squadron.

I stagger round the journalists handing out my new Bunbury brochure, hot off the press. There's Peter 'Reggie' Hayter from the *Mail on Sunday*. John Woodcock from *The Times* and David Norrie from the *News of the World* – 'What's happening, Dave?' they ask. 'Any scoops?'

Then round to the pavilion, big handshake from the MCC doormen, up the stairs to the England and West Indies dressing rooms, where I leave a brochure on each of the player's places. Out of the pavilion. A quick chat with Big Dave in the Clerk of the Works Office, into the Lords shop to see my pal Alan Pryer to check up on how my books are selling, then on to Clive Radley MCC head coach for a swift cuppa and chinwag in the Young Pros' office.

'What's your latest gag, Anglesi?' asks the great 'Clifton' Radley.

By now the ground is swarming with spectators, some decked out in MCC regalia, others in shorts clutching eskies and blowing horns. There is a tidal wave of punters spilling out of St Johns Wood underground elated by the prospect of seeing Lara bat or Harmison bowl; they are marshalled by policemen on horseback and stewards in DayGlo jackets.

'Good morning, David.' It's Roger Knight, the genial and distinguished MCC chief executive. Time for another story and a prognostication on the day's play. Duck and dive into the ECB's main office to give my niece, England team liaison officer, Medha Laud a cuddle and to find my old mate assistant chief executive Hugh Morris and

Keith Tomlins, in charge of the UK's cricket academies, to talk about some up and coming young stars. There's David Graveney the super-amiable giant and chairman of the England Selectors who has picked the country's top teams for over 120 Tests.

'Tell me Grav, am I in?' I ask.

'Not this time, but it was close, Dave,' laughs D.G. 'But I'll be there to present the caps at your Bunbury Festival as usual; just send me the map.'

David Graveney has travelled thousands of miles to kick off my Bunbury Festivals over the years. A real star.

'Go and see Vaughany and the boys; they're in the nets,' said Grav.

The England lads are practising. I stroll across the Nursery End where I scored a hundred back in 1982, 17 September to be precise. I still look up at the roof of the then Groundsman Jim Fairbrother House to see the tiles I dislodged with six straight sixes. I remember Asif Din of Warwickshire batting at the other end trying to hit the aluminium chimney of the old Cricket School as a target. From seventy-five yards he remarkably hit the mark four times. The dents remained on the smokestack for years.

An official calls out, telling me to 'get off the grass'.

'Hey you. Leave him alone!' shouts Michael Vaughan. 'Dave's playing for England today. Didn't you know?'

I feel an enormous high at being able to contact the England lads at an immediate heartfelt level every time I see them. I have known them since they were fifteen and I feel a great surge of pride at their success. Vaughany, Freddy Flintoff, Marcus Trescothick, Steve Harmison, Matthew Hoggard and the entire England team all played in my Bunbury Festival and we have remained very close friends ever since.

When they see me they all stop practising and come over for a chat.

'Where are we going tonight, Dave?' ask the lads. 'We'll meet you after the game.'

The boys return to the nets and I actually have conversations with them whilst they're batting. It's quite surreal to see Freddy and

Tres driving, Vaughany cutting, keeping their eyes on the ball whilst still talking to me.

It's approaching 10.30 a.m. when I leave the nets and fight my way through the maddening crowd, acknowledging cricketing people I've known for the past forty years. Cricket is a small worldwide family and on doing a lap of Lords you can bump into Michael Holding, Dennis Lillee or even someone you played cricket with at school. I finally arrive at the Mound Stand; the wonderful Eric the Jamaican steward resplendent in his straw hat welcomes me.

'Good morning, David. Go straight up. Mr Botham is waiting for you in the box.' I'm greeted by Beefy and cricket's number one whiz-kid lawyer, Naynesh Desai. His brother Kamel, along with sports publisher Joe Cuby, does more for cricketers than anyone in this country.

'Morning Looney!' booms Beefy. 'Have a bacon butty and a cup of tea.'

One by one, Beefy's famous mates arrive. In 2004, three Pierses fell from grace. The West Pier in Brighton, Piers Morgan, the erudite and sharp-witted ex-editor of the *Daily Mirror* and Lord Jeffrey Archer, former chairman of the Conservative party and ex prisoner FF8282 from the North Sea Camp in Lincolnshire. Both Piers, Morgan and Archer are wonderful company and between them have raised vast sums for charity. Jeffrey is, quite simply, the best auctioneer in the business and a raconteur *par excellence*.

'Morning, Lord Archer.'

'Good morning, Bunbury. I trust all is well?'

'How did you escape from your prison, Jeffrey?' I ask. 'Rope ladder over the wall?'

'Certainly not, dear boy. I walked out the front door. Occasionally I'd take a stroll into Lincoln to enjoy a meal at Zuchinis. Especially after an inter-prison cricket match in which I umpired. I tell you what, Bunbury; we didn't play many away games. Sometimes the opposition, like the teams from Pentonville or Wormwood Scrubs, would get quite vociferous. On one occasion we were playing Parkhurst at home and their number three batsman, in for armed robbery, started to get a bit lippy. I had to step in and remind him that my opening fast bowler was a double murderer, which soon kept him quiet!'

The box is now filling up as the jugs of Pimms are downed with great gusto. Sir Viv and Allan Lamb arrive to be welcomed by much hooting and back slapping.

Out in the middle, England are fielding. Freddy Flintoff has spotted me and the word has gone round the field that the Loon is holding court in Beefy's box. Much waving and visible laughter ensues from the slip cordon – and this is in the middle of a Test match!

It was the same in 1976. I would turn up in my shorts when Middlesex were playing Essex and stand to attention in the grandstand. Keith Fletcher, Goochie, Kenny McEwan, Pont, Turner, Prichard, Hardie and the Essex lads would actually stop the game and return the salute.

At 1.30 with the sun fiercely beating down, a character approaches from the shimmering far horizon, a mysterious figure, not on a camel, but walking, elegantly dressed, immaculate in waistcoat and tweeds. It is Lawrence of Arabia, blond and piercingly blue-eyed. Gone are the narcissistic theatrically flowing white robes, enter stage right Peter O'Toole, cigarette holder clasped in right hand. 'David, my dear Lord Bunbury; how is Flintoff performing?'

Peter O'Toole loves Lords and the game of cricket with an actor's passion to entertain. I have often bowled to him in the nets at Finchley CC. He is an elegant batsman who drives with a theatrical flourish and a dazzling technique. The great hellraiser was a firm friend of ex MCC head coach Don Wilson. Don's favourite film was *Lawrence of Arabia*. On one occasion Peter asked Don to bowl to him in the nets. 'On one condition,' said Wils, 'that you tell me some behind-the-scenes stories from your historical epic.'

'Later, Donald,' laughed an impatient O'Toole. 'We can discuss Lawrence next week. Now bowl up!'

The following week, Don was sitting in his office feet up watching cricket on the TV, surrounded by bats, pads, clipboards and coaching paraphernalia. There was a knock at the door. It was Peter O'Toole.

'OK, Donald. I promised you that this week we'd talk about Lawrence. Please meet my co-star, Omar Sharif, and director David Lean. Now let us hear your questions.'

Wils nearly fell off his chair as the three legends sat in his tiny office talking about the film.

On another occasion Peter was feeling lonely at Christmas. He had just split up from his wife Sian Phillips and felt down in the dumps. He went to see his pal at Lords.

'You can stay with us,' said Wils. 'Can't be alone at Christmas, just won't do.' Months later, whilst Wils was coaching at Ampleforth College in Yorkshire, a smartly dressed pilot walked into his office.

'Mr Wilson, Mr O'Toole sends his best wishes. You are to come with me.' Wils was taken to a nearby airstrip where Peter O'Toole's private jet was parked on the tarmac. 'Mr O'Toole looks forward to having dinner with you in Nice where he is filming at the moment.' To repay the kindness of his Christmas party at Lords, Peter flew Don down to the South of France for a slap-up meal.

It's now four o'clock. The box is jumping, frantic banter, and nonsense rules as I take Peter O'Toole outside.

The ground is buzzing. The egg and bacon brigade resplendent in their red and yellow stripes sit upright in their MCC seats outside the pavilion. Opposite them in the Compton and Edrich stands the sunbathers sprawl, semi naked, soaking in the rays.

The grandstand is packed with celebrities. There are Elvis Presleys, a couple of Popes, the Pink Panther, forty-eight Nando's chickens and a row of bearded nuns well Brahms and Liszt, enjoying the action in the middle, which has now reached fever pitch.

Flintoff and Harmison are bouncing Lara and his boys into submission.

'Your turn to bat, O'Toole.' Momentarily play stops in the middle as the England lads and 25,000 spectators watch Lawrence take guard with a spoon. I bowl a potato, which he smashes to pieces with a single blow.

We are now live on Sky TV as a full-scale game takes place. Lamb and Viv are in the slips, Beefy at short leg, Tim Rice at mid-off and Archer and Morgan in the deep, standing on the seats in rows G and H. All we need is Quentin Tarantino there to film this surreal sequence – *Pulp Potato Fiction.*

I fizz another King Edward to O'Toole, who smashes it over the balcony out onto the field, narrowly missing Trescothick standing on the boundary. Vaughany valiantly marshals his troops distracted by the alternative test in the stands as 'Potato O'Toole' and our gang retire inside for our seventeenth bottle of Chardonnay and more hilarity.

It's nine o'clock when I finally stumble out of our box and wind my way through the debris of the day. Shuffling through scorecards, empty lunch boxes, spent bottles of Moët and a couple of Elvises worse for wear, I make my way out of the ground and along the Abbey Road. Past the Beatles Studios, where tourists still daub graffiti on the walls and walk barefoot across the zebra crossing.

But I remember in 1969 sitting in on the vibrant sessions produced by George Martin, clowning about with George and Ringo whilst John and Paul penned the lyrics of the *Abbey Road* album. The magical mystery of St John's Wood, a long and winding road from Penny Lane but a day in the life in the presence of the Lords.

I Believe in Miracles

I have a dear friend who lives in the West Indies . . .

'Sound of the sea came in at my window. Life heaved and breathed in me. Then with the strength of that turbulent soil . . .'

He is a genius. His name is Isaac Alexander Vivian Richards. Ultimately what makes sport such a compelling spectacle is the way it reveals character. It is a celebration of human spirit where the brave and the good, whatever their flaws, become heroes, and where the charlatans and faint hearts are exposed. The very same qualities of courage, ingenuity, daring and swift decision-making that made Viv the undisputed King of cricket were, I'm sure, also those that made him the proudest of West Indians.

Viv was not only the world's greatest batsman, he was the most entertaining player confidently wielding his bat in the middle. He was generous about his opponents, perceptive about his colleagues and self-effacing about his own ability and his magnificent star-studded record.

Yet the figures speak for themselves and not since Don Bradman or Garry Sobers has any single player had more influence on the game. Viv is the embodiment of the spirit and flair with which the West Indians and the Bunburys have always played cricket. He is a player of quite exceptional ability.

But on 11 July 2004 at Fenners CC in Cambridge, I bowled him out.

At 3.32 p.m. he swaggered to the wicket and took guard. 'Leg stump please, Hursty,' grinned Viv to our legendary umpire. He surveyed the field, chewing on his gum, then settled at the crease, smiling at me through the eyes of an assassin.

I knew that if I gave him any width, the ball would disappear over the spires of Jesus College. I ran in; the ball was on a length, ramrod straight. Respectfully, Viv played a forward defensive shot, bat and pads sealed together. The next delivery was fractionally down the leg side. That's all it took. With an act of wristy violence, he whipped the ball away to the mid wicket boundary, past a fielder who had hardly moved.

I ran in again, hardly athletic, more Telly Tubby top half, Douglas Bader bottom. The ball was slightly over-pitched. Viv went for an extravagant drive through the offside. But Jamie Theakston dived full length to stop it.

Cometh the hour cometh the man.

I turned and waddled in, giving my all.

I saw the big smile and the cobra quick eye shape up for the kill. Viv moved forward ready to hit the ball savagely across the line whatever the delivery, but I saw him coming and for a micro mini-second I held the ball back.

It was too late; the Master Blaster had committed to the stroke and I nipped it back in at the last moment, bowling him off his pads. I didn't know where to put my face. The ground went deathly quiet.

Three thousand people had come to see the legend bat, not some out-of-shape Bunbury curtail his innings for eleven.

As my players mobbed me, Viv walked proudly past. My mind flashed back to our friendship. This was the man I had shared the stage with, along with Ian Botham, for 189 nights during our world tour of the 'The King and I'. On the poster, Viv was the 'King' (cool on the stool), Beefy was 'I' (heat on the seat) and in the middle, in tiny letters, I was lucky to be 'and'.

There was the occasion of the Lords Test between England and the West Indies. The West Indies were batting.

'Brother D, where are you sitting?' enquired Viv.

'In Row G4 in the Mound Stand next to a lady in a pink hat,' I replied.

Sure enough, after batting for half an hour, Viv leant back and hooked the ball directly to us in the stands. After executing the shot, followed by the roar of the crowd, he visibly raised his bat to us with an enormous smile. What an incredible eye. To think he could see us clearly in a packed crowd from 100 yards. The same happened at Leamington Spa CC when we played together in a charity game. I arrived with four pretty girls. Viv was batting. He immediately spotted us sitting on the furthest boundary. The next six balls were deposited in our laps. Viv had the quickest hand/eye co-ordination in the history of the game.

'Sorry Vivi,' I said, trying to conceal my joy.

'Respect, brother; well bowled, brother D,' smiled my hero.

In the same week another miracle occurred. The Bunburys were playing against Lashings CC, raising funds for Alan Igglesden's UK Brain Tumour Trust. The remarkable David Folb, a modern-day Kerry Packer, had started his Lashings Club in 1979 from the Minstrels Wine Bar in Maidstone. Folby, a local entrepreneur, became actively involved in Lashings by signing South Africans Paul and Gary Kirsten.

Then, a master stroke, Folby invited the former West Indies captain Richie Richardson to join. Richie accepted. As well as raising the profile of the club himself, Richie introduced a collection of internationally renowned players to the local cricket scene, including

Desmond Haynes, Sherwin Campbell, Stuart Williams, Keith Arthurton and Junior Murray.

With Folby negotiating the kind of sponsorship deals that became the envy of world cricket, from its humble origins Lashings had, in a couple of seasons, moved from being a village side to one of immense strength. With David paying top wages, soon Brian Lara, Wasim Akram, Shane Warne and Herschelle Gibbs had joined Folby's fold, a collection of top professionals who, like the Harlem Globe Trotters, could entertain and still take on the best sides in the world. David Folb is a first-class man who supports me and the Bunburys 100 per cent. Our players mix and socialize and have become firm friends. We often combine forces to help each other raise vital funds for good causes.

Richie Richardson is the world's number one gentleman of cricket: proud, soulful and generous in spirit. Like all the West Indian greats he cannot be bought. If you are their friend it is for life. Respect for one's brother, one love. My love for the West Indians goes back some forty years. Viv Richards had introduced me to the brotherhood. I played and stayed in the islands for many years. I have spilt blood on the wicket in Barbados, felled by a bouncer, but later returning to drink Banks beer, tell gags, be rowdy and proud to be called the 'happy hooker'. 'De Englishman, he crazy man.'

I have helped the boys with their benefits and the West Indian lads in two Junior World Cups. On 27 July 2000 I staged the biggest charity cricket match ever for the late great Malcolm Marshall. Fifty Test cricketers played in memory of their lost brother and £50,000 was raised for Malcolm's young son Mali.

For me, the greatest honour was to sit in the tiny dressing room at the HAC in London next to Viv, Richie, Gordon Greenidge, Desmond Haynes, Michael Holding, Joel Garner, Brian Lara, Collis King, Alvin Kallicharran, Courtney Walsh, Curtly Ambrose and Clive Lloyd and be accepted as an honorary West Indian, but most importantly, their brother.

Back to Lashings and Iggy's day. As Richie and I strolled out to toss, he said, 'Thanks for coming, Dave. We'll always be there for you.'

On arrival at the ground, the Lashings lads were practising. Not a bad line-up. Allan Donald, Shoaib Akhtar, Wasim Akram, Waqar Younis, Henry Olonga, Franklin Rose, Vasbert Drakes, Jimmy Adams, Inzamam-ul-Haq, Curtly, Courtney and co.

'Morning, cousin,' called Courtney. 'You'd better have a good team!'

My Bunbury squad were not quite as strong. I had experienced a few cry offs. Over the years there have been some spectacular last-minute excuses for not playing. Here are some of my favourites.

'I'm filming in the Rembrandt Museum.' – Jamie Theakston.

'I'm just about to meet the Chancellor of West Germany.' – football agent Jerome Anderson.

Matt Dawson making love to Jo in Brisbane – not much conversation, plenty of grunting.

Ian Baraclough QPR FC sitting on the bog in Spain.

Peter Scudamore riding his horse on some field in Cheltenham.

'It's 5 a.m. and I'm in bed in New York.' – Sir Trevor MacDonald.

'Sorry, Dave, just about to go on stage in Buenos Aires.' – Barry Gibb.

'I'm filming a scene in EastEnders' – Leslie Grantham.

'I'm racing at Brands Hatch.' – David Smith.

'I'm just about to have open heart surgery.' – Ex FA chief executive Graham Kelly.

Lashings batted first and were giving us some fearful hammer. Big Sid Lawrence, my opening bowler, was getting smacked all round the park. Richie, Sherwin Campbell and Stuart Williams had put on 215 in 20 overs.

In walked New Zealand Test star Chris Harris, who continued the assault. I was running around like a blue-arse fly trying to curb the blitzkrieg when I realized I had lost a tooth.

'What's wrong?' enquired 'Harri' at the end of the over.

'I've lost my tooth,' I said, somewhat down in the mouth. I looked like an out-of-work pirate, which amused the players no end.

'No worries, Dave; my dad was a dentist!' laughed Chris Harris.

What possible relevance did that have? I thought.

Then the miracle. Like Moses parting the Red Sea, Harri marched through the players in a straight line and continued some sixty yards into the covers.

'Here it is!' he cried, picking up my denture with his batting glove. Spellbound, we watched the chirpy Kiwi return to his crease to resume his innings.

In over a square mile of turf, Chris Harris had walked straight to my tooth – off the peg – I'll never know how, a 10 million to one chance.

In the bar afterwards I gave Harri a big 'thank you'. 'What do you want to drink, champ?'

'Tell you what, I'd better try the dentist's favourite drink. Give me an aperitif!' (A pair of teeth.)

After the game we enjoyed the usual knees-up fuelled by a few Cockspurs and Mount Gays. Richie and Curtly supplied the music, playing brilliantly. Being in a band is being part of a team playing for each other with the sole purpose of making the best music – like playing in a cricket team, bonded by rhythm and harmony. Cricket and music go hand in hand. England batsman Mark Butcher is a fine guitar player; so is Aussie fast-bowler Brett Lee; England bowler Alan 'Spider' Mullally plays guitar and worships Bob Marley and U2 frontman Bono; Essex bowler Mark 'Ramble' Illott and ex England physio Wayne Morton are both competent guitarists. Graeme 'Foxy' Fowler is an excellent drummer, 'Tuffers' is a demon on the triangle, 'Freddy' Flintoff plays the cow-bell and Robin Smith is on tambourine.

Conversely, guitar legend Eric Clapton and ex-strangler Hugh Cornwell like to bat and ex-Rolling Stone Bill Wyman is an ace leg-break bowler. Phil Collins keeps wicket, Ringo Starr loves to field and David Essex is a gifted all-rounder. All these lads are Bunburys along with the late George Harrison, ex Spandau Ballet drummer John Keble – a superb wicket keeper, singers Donny Osmond and Paul Young and the incredible double Emmy award winner John Altman, the world's number one saxophone-playing off-break bowler.

What a night! At 2.15 a.m., after buying up most of the auction items, I managed to squeeze into my Saab and get on the road to Leeds wedged in between Tiger Woods framed prints, Sir Viv Richards' touring jacket and Curtly's signed guitar. I made my way to the M2, M25 and the M1, to the north. If I had been stopped I would have been wearing Pele's shirt, Lawrence Dallaglio's tracksuit and Geoff Boycott's signed panama hat.

The following morning was the finals of 'The David English Bunbury Cup', the foremost festival for U12/13 players in the United Kingdom. Over the years, as I've mentioned before, I have sponsored twenty Bunbury ESCA festivals and organized two Junior World Cups. Nothing has given me greater pleasure than to see the best U15 players in this country contest their skills, forge lifelong friendships and go on to win full England caps. Eight of the current England team were discovered at the Bunbury Festival. I remember them all vividly. John Crawley, Aftab Habib and Ronnie Irani, Middlesex 1987; Michael Vaughan, Oundle School 1990; Marcus Trescothick, Paul Collingwood, Vikram Solanki, Manchester United players Gary and Phil Neville, Bromsgrove 1991; Andrew Flintoff, Ben Hollioake, Liam Botham, Gareth Batty, Alex Tudor, David Sales, Steve Harmison, Charterhouse School 1992; the list goes on and on.

And now I've got the opportunity to see the even younger Bunbury players fulfil their dreams on the golden path to a full England cap. Over 100,000 boys from all schools, state and private, play their hearts out to be the best U12/13 cricketers in the country.

This is only made possible by my partnership with my second family, the English Schools Cricket Association. We are all Robin Hoods. To raise the money and expertise and give it to the children is the ethos of Ken Lake, general secretary of ESCA and his band of merry men, all unpaid volunteers, schoolmasters who give up their time to stir up the enthusiasm of the young, whom we seek to nurture. Nobody sees a young Botham or Flintoff quicker than a schoolmaster. Marcus Trescothick was spotted batting in the playground at the age of eleven. He went on to make six centuries that season before reaching twelve years old. Ask Michael Vaughan, Steve Harmison, Graham Thorpe, Ian Bell or any of the England players and they will tell you it was a schoolmaster who gave them their first chance. School is the best place for youngsters to be introduced to the magical joys of sport, and cricket especially. It is no easy task in an era when the dazzle of technology all too frequently takes precedence over the games field. These days time, space and inclinations are in short supply and the ESCA masters are the best unpaid talent scouts in the world.

Bunbury and ESCA have a huge responsibility to make sure that young men and women are given the opportunity to play and have fun and thrive. Independent schools, for so long the nursery of young cricketers, have now opened their doors more widely to share facilities and expertise with neighbouring state schools. I have had meetings with the heads of Eton, Wellington, Shrewsbury, Winchester, Millfield, Charterhouse and Ampleforth College and all have welcomed the state school children with open arms to use their resources and wonderful grounds whenever possible, an exercise that has been embraced wholeheartedly by ESCA and the excellent England and Wales Cricket Board.

The working partnership between Bunbury, ESCA and the ECB is a phenomenal success. Bunbury raises the sponsorship money; ESCA first spots the exceptional boy or girl player. Hugh Morris, the inspirational assistant chief executive at the ECB, is immediately informed and his coaches take over to fast-track that youngster, very often through their academy under the brilliant expert eye of director Rod Marsh and the U15 national coach David Parsons, to the professional game.

For me, cricket represents an opportunity for children to learn the importance of individual achievement within a team, leadership, respect for leadership and a healthy ambition to end up on the winning side. For the inner cities in particular it is a socially beneficial way of expending youthful energy during long summer days in an often dreary and overcrowded urban environment. It teaches you mental strength and attitude to combat the opposition's strength with teamwork. Dealing with and playing mind games.

I often have inspirational meetings with Richard Caborn, the minister for Sport, and his assistant private secretaries, Martin Niblett and the lovely Leonie Phillips. Richard's vision and enthusiasm is boundless. He recognizes that sport must be taken very seriously by politicians because it transcends so many aspects of government policy. Team games provide the basis for understanding how to win and how to handle losing, for building respect for players around you, for working together through days when winning is beyond you. Respect for each other, respect for authority, respect for the rules of the game, respect for the ethics of sport. I think that the world of sport can provide hope and in many cases careers for those who may not shine academically but have a God-given talent for sporting excellence, and a way out for some people who tragically find themselves on an escalator towards crime.

Look at the productivity improvements following national sporting success. The joyous reaction to national victories in the Rugby World Cup or Michael Vaughan's inspirational England cricket team against the world's best. It gives us a glimpse of how teamwork combined with individual virtuosity can produce courageous performances, however tough the opposition. I know that Richard, Martin and Leonie can think of no department of state that does not have to pay attention to sport and recreation, from health to education, from foreign policy to law and order, from providing opportunity for our disabled athletes to social inclusion. Government can be the enabler. It can help create the environment in which those committed to sport can flourish.

Do not let our young talents that spring up in the grey provincial corners of our nation be sludged down into the bog of daily life. Elitism in cricket went out of the window years ago. Our top players are split 50/50 from the state and public school sector. Botham, Gatting, Stewart, Ramprakash, Flintoff, Vaughan and Trescothick all attended state schools, many of which do not have the facilities of the independent schools.

Our Headingley final was a good example of 'the 'cricket for all' generation reaching the top. Millfield Preparatory School, Somerset, was to play Christ Church Middle School, Staffordshire. The pupils at Christ Church Middle School polished their cricketing skills by using a broken litter bin and two cones for wickets on the school's cement tennis court.

The boys at Millfield Prep batted and bowled all the year round on the school's indoor and outdoor cricket pitches. So it was not a great surprise that the private school team from Glastonbury beat the state school in the final. But not before Christ Church had trounced four other private schools, including Manchester Grammar, between May and July to break through to the final heat.

Playing in the final at Headingley, Yorkshire's home ground in Leeds, proved too much for Christ Church. They froze at the sight of the 'oppo's' tracksuits, overwhelmed by their reputation. The school where LEA per-pupil funding is £2,815 a year, lost by ten wickets to Millfield Prep, where annual fees are £15,180 for boarders and £10,245 for day pupils.

Chris Waghorn, the excellent headteacher of Christ Church told me, 'The team became overwhelmed when they found themselves standing on the wicket that they had been watching on television. They did not play anything like the way they are capable of. If Millfield invited us to play at their school we would go. We will take them on without the razzamatazz.'

Christ Church were the second state school to get through to the final in the cup's eight-year history. In 2003 John Taylor High School in Burton-on-Trent got through, but also lost. As well as practising on their concrete tennis courts twice a week, Christ Church used the grounds of the local cricket clubs Oulton Barlaston, Moddershall, Stone and Little Stoke. Although there were tears from some of the losing side – they are only twelve years old, for heaven's sake – both teams got on famously.

Finance was a problem. Christ Church had played three away matches costing £300 each time and two home games at Oulton Cricket Club, costing £100 each. New cricket whites for Headingley had cost £200. Being in the competition had obviously stretched Christ Church's finances. There was an inequity of funding and opportunities. I saw a couple of dads doing warm-up exercises with the boys, whereas Millfield had a cricket coach, a cricket manager and a head of cricket. After my ESCA pal Chris Twort, head of cricket at Millfield Prep, had congratulated Christ Church, I presented the trophy to the winners and pledged to buy Christ Church a £2,000 pair of nets.

'You should be very proud of yourselves. If you can get to Headingley by practising with a litter bin and two cones on a tennis court, just think how far you would go with nets and, more to the point, a proper school playing field. Anyway lads, the nets will prevent you from having to go and retrieve the ball from Stone High Street!' I laughed.

As I bade everyone farewell and drove through the gates of Headingley, I thought back to my week of miracles; bowling out Viv, losing and finding my tooth and watching twenty-two fine young men from different backgrounds do their best, playing the game they loved. Life is a pure flame and we live by an invisible sun within us.

If you can wake up in the morning and embrace the perpetual present and get paid for the work you enjoy, you have really cracked life.

Tommy, Where Art Thou!

It was late afternoon in 2003. Shafts of sunshine slanted across Central Park and a golden light fell on the Plaza hotel. Our cab pulled up outside the 57th Street entrance, its yellow paintwork shining in the autumn light. My friend Tommy and I had gone to New York to attend the Grammys. We were going to meet the Bee Gees, who were to be presented with the Lifetime Achievement award.

Barry Gibb was on the palatial steps to meet us. The cabby, all stubble and moulting hair, leaned out of the window. 'Hey mister, you and Tommy enjoy the show. Give Bazzer my love. Tell him I grew up with *Saturday Night Fever*.'

It was a chilly day. I was wearing my camel coat and Tommy his customary red velvet jacket and trousers.

I had known Tommy since 1961 when I appeared in the school play *The Dam Busters*. I played the part of Wing Commander Guy Gibson VC, DSO and Bar DFC, and Tommy was my faithful partner, always by my side. Tom and I had been inseparable ever since we filmed in the school gymnasium. Just me, my squadron and Tom.

It was great to see Bazzer. We embraced and went up to the Presidential Suite at the top of the Plaza. Just the three of us in this opulent suite in New York's finest hotel. The views were stunning. You could see across Central Park, all the way to Harlem. The vista took in 5th Avenue on the right and Central Park West on the left; it continued past the Wollman Memorial ice rink, the Metropolitan Museum of Art and Strawberry Fields, opposite the Dakota building where John Lennon lived. The Plaza was where the Beatles stayed on their first visit to the States in February 1964. I was there at the time. Press and public alike besieged the hotel for five days. I remember two teenage girls managed to smuggle themselves up to the fifth floor inside a gift box before being thrown out. John Lennon retained his affection for the Plaza to the end of his life; Tommy and I used to join him and Yoko at the hotel's famous Oyster Bar.

After a short rest Tommy, Barry and I went down to the Palm Court restaurant to meet Robin and the Bee Gees' entourage. A harpist performed as we enjoyed afternoon tea.

It was the night of the Grammys. A wonderful, joyful occasion tinged with sadness. We had lost Maurice in life's great adventure and Barry and Robin would accept his award posthumously.

7.30 p.m. Showtime. We arrived by limo at Madison Square Garden. All the razzamatazz was there to greet us; the aroma of Chanel No. 5 hung in the air, red carpets, sparkly shoes, paparazzi with a million cameras flashing, TV crews – the glitz that welcomed the world's greatest recording artists.

There was Alicia Keys and Sheryl Crow, Beyoncé and U2. Backstage we met Bruce Springsteen, who epitomized rock 'n' roll and all its glorious rebellious and rollicking spirit. A true reflection of everyday American life – the wild, the innocent seen through the eyes of the common man. Barry, Robin, Tommy and I sat down and laughed with the 'Boss', whose songs had captured the technicolour images of suntanned summers at the New Jersey shore, painting for us Fender-driven *West Side Story* on rain-slicked streets under the bright moonlight and humbled us with stark narratives of the harsh realities and entrapment of living on the fringes of society. There was also Simon and Garfunkel with their brilliant lyrics, angelic vocals and stunning harmonies.

We met Christina Aguilera, Britney Spears and Eminem, rapping about White America. To me, he seemed to be torn between the roles of victor and victim, a schizophrenia that reaches its peak in a tribute to his mother that's simultaneously apologetic and full of suffering. Eminem met Tommy. So did Norah Jones.

Norah is the daughter of a dear friend of mine, the world-renowned sitar player, Ravi Shankar. Tommy had been with me when I wrote and recorded a song called 'Ride Raj Bun' with George Harrison and Ravi Shankar. And now there was young Norah, whose mixture of sounds harked back to when Patsy Cline and Billie Holiday reigned, when Laura Nyro was in her prime and when Carole was King. We caught up with James Taylor and my great friend Carlos Santana, whose guitar playing soared like an eagle and whose fondness for collaboration with the young players showed us that the blues was more than some old man with a guitar talking about his troubles. Outside in the arena the euphoria had reached fever pitch. It was time to go.

'And now to receive a Lifetime Achievement award, please let me hear it for the Bee Gees, who during their lifetime have made enormous contributions of artistic significance to the field of recording. Ladies and gentlemen, Barry and Robin Gibb, and to collect the award on behalf of their late great father Maurice, Adam and Sammy Gibb.'

We were standing backstage ready to go on. What a line-up! Bob Dylan, Simon and Garfunkel, Maria Carey, Bruce Springsteen, U2, Avril Lavigne, Puff Daddy, Destiny's Child, Christina, Britney . . . The world's greatest artists on parade.

'Oh! My God!' I froze.

'What's wrong?' said Barry.

'I've lost Tommy!'

'Tommy who?' asked Bruce Springsteen.

'You know, Boss: Tommy . . .' I blurted.

The line-up became flustered but hadn't a clue who or where Tommy was.

'Tom Hanks, Tom Dowd, Tommy Motolla, Tom Cruise, where's Tommy?'

'What does he look like?' asked Bob Dylan.

'You tell them, Bazzer,' I pleaded.

'Well, he's wearing a red velvet jacket and trousers. He's got a brown face and he's two inches tall.'

Yes, my little pal Tommy had been my mascot since the sixties. For forty-three years we had been inseparable. He had spent most of that time thrust deep into my pocket nestling in my groin. He had stood over me at night on my bedside table and shared all my love affairs and adventures.

I was devastated. To see all these superstars searching for Tommy on their hands and knees was quite surreal.

Paul Simon was moved by my despair and sense of loss. On stage he announced 'And this song is for an old friend, Tommy . . .'

'Old Friends' started so softly, two quiet chords taking turns and then Paul alone singing 'Old friends sat on their park bench like bookends' before being joined in harmony by his oldest of friends, Art Garfunkel. The memory of Tommy reverberated long after the song was over, like an echo without end, the sound of voices singing from a shared soul. Not a day goes by without my missing Tom and thinking about our times together.

Tommy, where art thou?

My Friend in the Forest

It is October, the month we see our breath reflected in the air as we labour to build bonfires in the garden. As night falls you see that particular shade of blue in the sky unique to this time of year, that touch of melancholy, which brings a pang to the heart and a tear to the eye. It is autumn, quite the most beautiful and saddest of seasons.

Beauty and melancholy seem to arrive at the same time. The colours on the trees are glorious: rusts, reds and yellows, far more picturesque than when they are merely green. And yet that is because the leaves are dying, their life cycle complete. Not that it doesn't renew itself – those leaves will be made into compost, which itself will be used to tempt forth new life and so each generation passes itself onto the next. Then there's the whiff of woodsmoke in the air and the slight chill reminding us that harsher times lie ahead. Autumn is a memory of the lost warmth of summer and a warning to prepare for winter.

Not far from where I live, somewhere off the beaten track, there is a wood. I must have driven past it a thousand times. Sometimes a pall of smoke rises from the trees. I feel drawn to this wood high on the hill. One day, I climbed it. A wind whispered through the trees, bringing a feeling of calm and love on the breeze.

I heard a voice drawing me to the trees and when I entered its enchanted clearing I discovered Jesus hanging from the cross. I stared at him and felt his pain. I desperately wanted to lift him off his cross and comfort him. I sat amongst the leaves and focused my gaze on his tortured features. Once again the voice came to me ever so clearly: 'And when they came to the place called the skull, they crucified me in between two criminals, one to the right and one to the left and I said, "Father, forgive them for they know not what they do . . ."

'And the people stood by watching, but the rulers scoffed at me, saying, "He saved others, let him save himself, if he is the Christ of God, his chosen one!"

'One of the criminals who were hanged railed at me, saying, "Are you not the Christ? Save yourself and us!" But the other rebuked him, saying, "Do you not fear God, since you are under the same sentence of condemnation? And we indeed are suffering justly, for we are receiving the due reward of our deeds, but this man has done nothing wrong." And he said, "Jesus, remember me when you come into your kingdom." And I said to him, "Truly I say to you, today you will be back with me in paradise." '

I listened as the voice continued. 'It was now about the sixth hour and there was darkness over the whole land until the ninth hour; and the curtain in the temple of Nazareth was torn into two.

'I cried with a loud voice, "Father, into your hands I commit my spirit," and having said this I breathed my last breath.

'The Roman soldiers mocked me and gave me vinegar to drink. "If you are the King of the Jews, save yourself!" '

I sat there transfixed. After his final breath I could feel the heavens on earth, floods and fire and columns of smoke. The sun turned to darkness and the moon to blood.

The terrible day of the Lord had come. His last words of prayer shouted into a dark heaven. 'Father, into thy hands I commit my spirit.'

I knelt in the dampening leaves and bowed my head in prayer.

'In thee Lord do I seek refuge: let me never be put to shame; in thy righteousness deliver me! I incline thy ear to me, rescue me speedily. Be thou a rock of refuge to me, a strong fortress to save me! Yes, thou art my rock and my fortress: for thy name's sake lead me and guide me, take me out of the net which is hidden to me, for thou art my refuge.'

I looked up and told Jesus of my deep distress and sorrow at seeing thousands killed by the elements of nature. The tsunamis and earthquakes, especially the little children who suffered and died and never stood a chance. It couldn't be right; what justice was there in this world?

Then his voice.

'I will take them to paradise, the young and the maimed, the blind and the lame.'

To me paradise evoked an image of exotic bliss, of unending joy and celebration.

'These people will head the guest list in the Kingdom of God.'

I asked Jesus to give me more power to help the sick and the needy. And he said, 'David, go to the window that shines.' I walked to the edge of the wood and in the distance I saw a window glistening on the side of an old building. I walked across the fields, drawn by the radiant light.

When I arrived at the building I discovered it was a monastery. The place was deserted, the front door swinging in the breeze. I climbed the stairs and walked along the corridor, trying to estimate the whereabouts of the room with the shining light. My heart was beating fast, my palms were sticky and the back of my throat was dry. I found the room and walked in. I went to the window and looked back towards the Hill of Hope where I had shared those moments with Jesus. Just then a brilliant light pierced the room. On the wall was an inscription.

'David, may you always have an angel by your side, watching out for you in all the things you do. Reminding you to keep believing in brighter days, finding ways for your wishes and dreams to take you to beautiful places. Giving you hope that is as certain as the sun, giving you the strength of serenity as your guide. May you always have love and comfort and courage and the ability to help others. Have the courage to change the things you can change, the serenity to accept those you cannot change and the wisdom to know the difference.'

When You Wish Upon A Star
in the Land of the Midnight Fun

'Some day whenever the spring breaks through you'll come to me out of long ago warm as the wind, soft as the kiss of snow.'

Through the swirling snow, just north of the Arctic Circle came a red glow piercing the gloom.

'Hey Rudolf, with your nose so bright, what's so special about tonight?'

'Listen you elves,' panted Rudolf, 'now the midnight sun has lost its strength, we must generate our own Northern Lights. Get the candles so we can prepare the landing strip.'

Santa Claus was busy in his workshop making toys. He would deliver his special parcels down chimneys throughout the world.

'That's right, Rudolf, we have some very important visitors arriving from England.'

Santa, Rudolf and the elves lit the runway and stared towards the heavens. There, for a tantalizing moment, was a twinkle coming towards them.

This celestial light was in fact the magical Monarch Airlines flight 932 from Nottingham, carrying 100 little brave hearts, mums and dads, ten doctors, six paramedics, England cricketer Phil deFreitas and his lovely missis, Katie. Alice in Wonderland, Andy Pandy, the world's number one sports writer Robert Philip and his curly companion, award-winning Aussie photographer Phil Brown, a couple of clowns and yours truly, dressed as an oversized elf.

Our plane was full of laughter and nonsense. The stewardesses were dressed as Christmas fairies and even the pilot joined in the fun: resplendent in red velvet Santa hat, he opened the flight deck door to announce, 'Good morning ladies and gentlemen, boys and girls, I am Captain Dancer, and this is First Officer Prancer. 'We've been flying at 35,000 feet over the land of the lakes. Now children, if you look down below it seems that Santa is preparing a very special welcome for you.'

All over the UK children are bravely suffering from life-threatening illnesses and many of them have just one wish. These wishes are varied, often expensive and many families are not able to afford to make these wishes come true. However, thanks to the charity, *When You Wish Upon A Star*, over 10,000 wishes have already been granted to children who are poorly.

I am proud to work very closely with the charity. Last year my Bunbury cricket team staged two games raising vital funds. *When You Wish Upon A Star* is not government-funded and every penny that we raise comes from voluntary contributions. The more money we receive, the more wishes can be granted. The most popular wish worldwide is to visit Father Christmas. So we chartered an aeroplane to take our little heroes to have 'a banter with Santa'.

When we landed, Lapp Guides welcomed us in their traditional costumes. There are in fact more reindeer than the 200,000 people sprinkled across the Arctic wilderness which is Lapland. The temperature was minus six as the sun began to rise. We would get only two hours of light. It was breathtakingly beautiful. The snow was deep and crisp and even. It was like entering a Christmas card.

We boarded the sleighs and were soon being pulled by teams of reindeers with red ribbons tied to their antlers, streaming in the wind. There were plenty of 'Oooh!'s and 'Aaagh!'s as we whizzed through the enchanted forest lit by flickering candles and bonfires.

I cuddled a little girl who lay there motionless, tucked up in her blankets. Little Sophie, aged three, had had half her brain removed to combat the epileptic seizures that threatened her life daily. The last operation – her seventh – performed at Great Ormond Street Hospital – was a big risk but she came through, though she will have to go back after Christmas for yet another operation.

She would never get better. She lay there as if in a manger, with the face of an angel. Her eyelids were heavy and maroon, her skin as pale as porcelain. I told her she was going to meet Santa. There was a flicker of a smile.

'We'll enjoy Sophie as long as we can have her,' said her mum and dad, Julie and Matt Byrne.

We also introduced the locals to cricket. 'How long did you say a match lasted?' asked Santa's helper and wicket keeper Airo Lukkiven. On being told 'five days' by Phil deFreitas, Lukkiven said, 'That's a pity; we get exactly two hours of daylight in Lapland at this time of the year.' Only the presence of a team of doctors, nurses and paramedics plus the row of wheelchairs parked alongside our buses provided the cruel reminder that some of the youngsters would never know another Christmas. Little George on the sleigh in front was having the time of his life: terribly disabled, he kept giving us the thumbs-up sign followed by a broken smile and an extra loud 'Whoopee!'

Soon we arrived in a clearing where we sat on reindeer skins and logs around a roaring fire. Our friends introduced us to the Lapp Initiation ceremony. We were flicked around the face with a reindeer tail and black charcoal was rubbed into our noses like red Indians. We were told we would become kinder people and in our next life would return as reindeer. For many of these children, the next life was just around the corner.

It was so invigorating, we all went potty. Children were flying all over the place on small sleighs and kick sledges. It was a winter wonderland of snowmobiles, husky rides, snowball fights, skidoo rides and quad bikes. Children suffering from leukaemia and tumours, cerebral palsy and epilepsy, forgot their pain for a day as they tumbled down a slide sending them hurtling through the snow and landing in a huge drift.

Now thirteen and a daredevil on skis, Larvell Gisby had beaten non-Hodgkin's Lymphoma. After Phil the photographer had broken the world record for consuming seven reindeer sausages, he pulled Larvell's sister Yasmin around on a sledge. Mum Julia recalled the heartbreak of the past three years. 'For the first twelve months we lived almost entirely in hospital because although Larvell knew he was ill, he didn't let on until he had difficulty breathing, so the first course of chemo was very, very heavy. He's missed two years of education and equally importantly, of his childhood, but he's been so brave about it all. He's never cried, moaned or groaned during any of the treatments, even though he's had injections in every vein in his body. Now we've been told he'll grow into a strong man and that he'll even be able to have children of his own one day. It's a true Christmas miracle.'

We huddled together for warmth, sitting around the fire eating sausages, drinking hot chocolate, singing carols and watching our two hours of day turn into night. It was so beautiful with twinkling lights and fires and the sound of children's laughter and screams as they chased each other in the snow. We had wheelchair races, fixing skis to the bottom of the chairs. I talked to a little lad who kept taking photos of me and laughing.

'I bet you're looking forward to meeting Santa,' I asked. 'And what's so funny?'

'Yes David, I am looking forward to meeting Santa, but my name is Kimberley,' said the little girl without hair.

'Now children,' cried Jeremy and Pogo the clowns. 'Who wants to meet Santa?'

The children went mad. 'We do!' they roared in unison.

'Well, he'll only come if you sing "Jingle Bells" very loudly,' ordered the clowns.

By now Santa was well on his way. He had left his village on the slopes of Mount Korvatunturi, which he had built with his elves, to make gifts for the children.

No one can remember how Santa came to Lapland. It's no good asking the old man himself. He just smiles and is silent. Perhaps he himself no longer remembers. He just lives in his village with his elderly wife surrounded by hundreds of elves and reindeer. It is said that the other elves are former guardian spirits of households and forests who, over the years, fled from the modern cities and industry of the south to the peace and quiet of the village. Santa and his elves work diligently all year long from January to December making presents for children around the world.

'Jingle Bells' was now being sung at fever pitch as the excitement was mounting to a crescendo.

Suddenly there was a flurry in the clearing as Santa appeared on his sleigh, being pulled by Rudolf.

The children screamed and yelled as he climbed out of his sleigh and sat in the middle of them.

It was very emotional and humbling to see all the children go up to meet this special man they had travelled all this way to see.

All these little brave hearts with life-threatening illnesses who throughout the year had suffered extremely painful treatments, long stays in hospital and lots of difficult medical procedures, behaved just like any well child would. Oh! To be four years old, normal and healthy again! To watch the kind old man with a white beard listen intently to the hopes and dreams of children who were mesmerized by this giant who secretly visits them every year eating their mince pies before quickly disappearing back up the chimney. You could see he was visibly moved as he gave them each a present and listened to their stories. With a tear in his eye the miracle worker told the children how he and his elves have vacations in the summer.

'There is more spare time then anyway, because the sun does not set at all. Letters arrive in huge numbers at my village. There are no roads so an aeroplane from the General Post Office brings the mail by special delivery. I read all the letters and each of your wishes is recorded in a huge book. I receive letters from all over the world. Sometimes the little writers make spelling mistakes but my elf scribes manage to put them right. Only now and then do they have to ask the professors at the University of Helsinki about a word or two.'

By now the children were getting tired and cold. It had been a long day filled with great fun and emotion. They kissed Santa good-bye. He was the best medicine they could ever have received.

'Listen, my friends. I won't be seeing you for a while,' smiled Santa. 'You will all be tucked up asleep in your beds when I come down your chimneys with your presents. But take special care and remember I love you all.'

Twenty hours later we had returned to Nottingham aboard our

good aeroplane Monarch, with 100 sleepy heads, their hearts glowing beneath the layers of vests and jerseys.

'When you wish upon a star, thank you for taking us to Santa in Lapland afar.'

My special thanks go to Barbara White, the founder of When You Wish Upon A Star and her special events manager Margaret Rowarth, who also made this adventure very beneficial to the mums and dads who came to Lapland to get away from all the hospital trips, the treatments, the drugs. Barbara gives them the chance to forget, but, and this is the best part, a day to remember.

And if I could be granted one wish . . .

It would be to build a magical hospital in Lapland courtesy of the National Elf Service where I could take all the little brave hearts to be cured from their pains by Santa's magic touch – I would call it 'Heals', a sanctuary where we could find a small measure of peace, that we all seek but few of us ever find.

'When I was small and Christmas trees were tall . . .'

Three Days in Budapest

God bless Hungary with prosperity and good fortune; extend your protective arm when it faces the enemy, torn by fate since ancient times; bring to it glad years to come. Its people have suffered enough for the past and the future. 24–26 February 2005 – Freddy Flintoff's stag weekend, sixty-two marauders holed up in a castle overlooking the Danube. Would Budapest and its glorious baroque past ever be the same again?

I first met Andrew 'Freddy' Flintoff at the 1992 Bunbury ESCA Festival played amongst the leafy cloisters of Charterhouse School. The tall, thin lad from Preston was in terrific company. In 1992 the U15 Bunburys produced some real stars. Freddy was joined by Liam Botham, Ben Hollioake, Alex Tudor, David Sales, Owais Shah, David Nash and Gareth Batty.

The boundary was ringed by cars owned by the proud parents, who sat on blankets, ate picnics and shared every nerve and emotion paraded by their young pretenders.

Colin and Susan Flintoff were a joy. Down from Preston, they were passionate about their boy, modest about his tremendous potential and 100 per cent supportive of his ambition to play for England. Over the years it has been my privilege to meet the parents of all the young Bunburys. They deserve enormous admiration and recognition for transporting their offspring thousands of miles up and down the country, washing flannels, lifting spirits and being present on far-flung grounds to give the unique rock-solid parental support required at this fragile age of fifteen.

The tall, slender lad bowls with an unbridled enthusiasm, rapping Sales on the pads. The slips go up; there is a massive appeal. The umpire says 'not out' and the bowler without a flicker of petulance returns to his mark ready to tear in for the next ball. This is the spirit of Bunbury cricket. Fred hasn't changed since then. He is a gentle giant who cares more about his fellow players and the team ethic than the fulfilment of personal glory.

Not yet exposed to the hurricane of first fame, at thirteen he scored 213 for the Harris Park Cricket Club in Preston before moving on to St Anne's in Blackpool, where he terrorized the bowling attacks, once scoring 222 out of 319 for no wicket declared. Blackpool, noted for 'fresh air and fun' received some serious damage as windows in local homes were smashed by a rampaging Flintoff pulling and driving with murderous power.

Thirteen years later, nothing has changed. He is Little John to Vaughany's Robin Hood, the England captain always turning to him to break a partnership or to dislodge an Aussie or two, exactly as Brearley had turned to Botham.

Fred and I have been close friends ever since. I love every bone in his body, not just for his talent to devastate any opposition but his caring for his teammates, determination to win and ability to turn a game by a moment of brilliance. He is massively generous on and off the field and a captain's dream. Ask Nasser Hussain and Michael Vaughan.

He still drives 300 miles to play for the Bunburys.

'You've never let me down, Fred.'

'Wouldn't miss it for the world, Dave.'

Our last game of 2005, Freddy drove the length of the country with Rachael and Holly to bring his magic and help raise funds for Great Ormond Street Hospital.

As his Harley-Davidson Land Cruiser entered the car park of North Middlesex CC, 1,000 children besieged Fred. He duly signed their bats, shirts, shoes, arms and heads, taking three hours to move from the car park to the pavilion, where he presented the trophies and shook the hands of another 1,000 adults, dignitaries and the mayor of Haringey.

Last year Margaret Rowarth from When You Wish Upon A Star called to tell me of Aidan Duffy, a little lad of ten with a brain tumour. Aidan's special wish was to meet Freddy and the England team. I immediately called Fred, the man with a heart the size of Old Trafford, to tell him of Aidan's wish.

'No problem, Dave. Bring him to Trent Bridge and I'll take care of him.'

That day Freddy took Aidan to the nets, where he watched the England lads practising their skills, then on to the dressing room where all his teammates signed Aidan's bat and had photographs taken with him.

Freddy made Aidan feel special, like a king for a day. After the terrible, gruelling treatment for his tumour, he and the England lads had given the youngster the best medicine. A month later Aidan Duffy was given the all clear; the tumour had been vanquished.

To think that twelve years after the Bunbury festival, I'd be sitting next to Fred, crutches by his side (one week after an ankle operation) surrounded by sixty-two mates drinking beer out of brown bottles, overlooking Budapest, just seven days before his wedding, is the stuff of dreams.

It's five a.m. 24 February 2005 when I arise. Britain is gripped by the icy fingers of winter. Inside my body is boiling. Two days earlier I opened my window and 'in flew enza'.

Drove through the deserted streets to Heathrow. Just the early-morning brigade of sand gritters, newspaper deliveries, neon lights and traffic cones. Combination of pain and tiredness. Lost my way. Drove past the Bombay Dreams, Pinner High Street three times. Arrived at airport at six-thirty a.m. Saab into short-stay car park. Found a lonely trolley, pushed bags into terminal. Straight into disabled toilet (more room) to sort out tickets, passport and to see a couple of friends off to the coast.

Met Rob Key and pal Nev, Dave Norrie of the *News of the World*, checked in; pretty BA girl Bonnie wanted to join us on our adventure. Two hours on tarmac. Ice on wings. Lots of laughs with lads. Took off, had a few beers, landed in Hungary two hours later. Christian, our taxi driver, took the scenic route from airport past the famous Ferencváros football stadium where Puskas once paraded his skills, and into the city of two million inhabitants, situated in the middle of Europe roughly halfway between the Atlantic Ocean and the Ural mountains.

We entered the breathtakingly beautiful city, its fascination invit-ing us with an irresistible urban energy derived from centuries of rich history. There was a sharp contrast between the twin cities of Buda and Pest, divided by the powerful flow of the Danube. As Chris-tian steered his yellow Mercedes along the cobbled streets of Pest, I could imagine the Soviet tanks rumbling along the same avenues in the Revolution of 1956. Revolution . . . Communist symbols are destroyed, new parties formed, political prisoners released. The Rus-sians invade to suppress the revolution, killing 3,000 people. 200,000 Hungarians flee the country. I could see. But the Red Star was taken down in 1990, marking the revival of democracy. We leave the Art Nouveau world of Pest and drive across the Chain Bridge, the first permanent link between Buda and Pest. Excitement reigns inside the cab. 'Can't wait to see Freddy and the boys.' We whiz past baroque buildings, then the Royal Palace and up to the castle on the very top of the hill, the Hilton Hotel. We pile out of the car and send Christian away with a firm handshake and a pocketful of florins. And there stands our Colditz, a masterpiece of conservation; not for its bland 1970s Hilton facade but for the way it encompasses the

Gothic remains of an old Dominican monastery. King Matyas and his Jesuit priests would turn in their grave at the sight of Freddy's sixty-two stags running riot through the vestry.

And there on the top step is our leader, King Freddy I of Preston. Crutches thrown into the air, devil may care, massive hugs, into the bar to meet the other fifty-eight. Presented with a tour shirt. We left the same bar three days later. What a team! There was Vaughany and Jimmy Anderson, and Dave 'Rooster' Roberts, Lancashire's physio, to keep an eye on the Man From Ankle. It was Rooster who nursed Beefy Botham along all those 5,000 miles walking and making fortunes for Leukaemia Research. Gus 'Little John' Fraser, Mal Loye, Glenn Chapple, Warren Hegg, Neil 'Harvey' Fairbrother and all the Lancashire CCC lads. The legendary Farouk Engineer, Fred's dad Colin, plus all his pals from the north west, supported by the charismatic and extremely convivial top sponsor Paul Beck – a wonderful blend of mad, free spirited, cavalier, generous souls banged up in Budapest!

1,000 beers quenched. On to the coach. Drive from Buda to Pest for our medieval banquet at the Sir Lancelot Tavern. Served by beautiful wenches with ample bosoms and endless jugs of beer and wine. Very tasty fare, some eaten, some flung. I'm sitting opposite Gussie Fraser talking about the amazing rise in excellence of Andrew Strauss's batting when he is hit on the side of the head by half a pig. So pigs do fly when you are Hungary? This is followed by a volley of potatoes and a large beetroot. The mother of all food fights ensues. Serviettes are donned as makeshift helmets. Poor Gussie and Rob Key are in the firing line as Jimmy Anderson's out-swingers cannon off the wall. The restaurant is split into two. We are definitely the Pests. Across the Danube corridor are the Budas, families enjoying a quiet night out. Directly behind me are a besotted couple deep in conversation, making plans for the future. As the man gets down on bended knee to propose, I watch him take out the ring. Sadly the most important moment in his life is shattered as a wayward off-break lump of mash from the England captain passes between the pursed lips of the lovers. A barrage of carrots and leeks are followed by Freddy's in-swinging handfuls of Goulash, which strike a replica suit of armour sweetly on the helmet. I swear I see two eyes rotate beneath the visor.

Eva Bartok, a serving wench, ducks and weaves with platters of reinforcements remarking that 'most of her customers tend to eat the food, not throw it'. The stags retire from the battleground to the bar to be serenaded by the minstrel Mal Loye, with a rousing version of 'I Am the Wild Rover'. Further refreshments, back on the battle bus, covered in mixed vegetables to the Irish pub in Vaci Utca, the inner town. It is crammed to the gills as Hungary's number one band are about to take the stage. The singer resembles Joe Cocker's dad, a man mountain whose head touches the ceiling. It is a blues-driven set led by some extremely nifty guitar playing by a Jimmy Page look-alike. Gussie is in his element bopping to the music that drives the Magyars crazy. Fred, semi-comatosed, is talking to the cigarette machine, which surprisingly talks back to him.

The stags, refreshed and fed, decide it's time for some artistic stimulation. A difficult choice – a foray into the night to savour the culture of the Ferenc Liszt Museum and the Budapest Fine Arts Gallery or the sultry delights of the Hallo Bar or Marilyn's. Hot girls, cold drinks, topless and titillating. Surprisingly a visit to see the work of the well-known Hungarian artists Lesbi and Sado Mazo just nicked the majority vote.

Decadence in the confines of small rooms, breathy promises of undying love, table dancing, girls up poles, poles up girls, girls with candles, high-heeled sandals, bare botties, erotica, champagne and lots of laughs.

The next few days were a blur, a concoction of celebration to King Fred soon to be wed, great moments of singing and hilarity, team bonding. A kaleidoscope of camaraderie, all the stags away from their old deers. What a strange ritual! Go away with your mates, get plastered, paint the town red, the final few days of your liberty as a single man, the end of an era and the start of a new dawn, but in Fred's case, a new Rachael and their lovely little Flintstone, young Holly.

A Touch of Frost

In my life, I have had the great pleasure of knowing two Frosts.

One, Sir David Paradine Frost OBE, author, producer, columnist, star of *The Frost Report*. In the late sixties David was probably the most famous man in England, more so than the prime minister. I worked closely with him in the seventies producing TV specials on the Bee Gees. I also played cricket against him. He was a determined wicket keeper for the Lords Taverners, talented and typically very competitive.

I went to war with the other Frost. Major General John Dutton Frost CB 1964, DSO 1943 and Bar 1945, MC 1931, was one of the greatest British heroes of World War II. When military men gather in clubs and reminisce, the name Frost is spoken in terms of awe.

As an actor in Sir Richard Attenborough's film *A Bridge Too Far*, I played different parts as a member of the famous APA (Attenborough's Private Army). I met and became firm friends with General Frost, who gave us great technical advice and an insight into the horrors of Operation Market Garden. I kept an account of the making of the film entitled, 'The Boys from the Bridge'. General Frost gave me vivid details of the battle but never discussed his own heroics.

After making the film I met Frost's batman Dennis Wicks, who had actually saved his life at Arnhem and whom Frost hadn't seen since the day after that, thirty-three years ago. They had been living a few miles away from each other for the past ten years. Because Frost was wounded and Wicks wasn't, when the Germans captured them they had been sent to separate prisons. Wicks managed to escape but in doing so was wounded and eventually had to have a leg amputated. He remained in a British army hospital until 1947.

'Why didn't Frost get in touch?' I asked him. He didn't seem to mind. 'You must remember things were different then. No matter how close you were to somebody, if you went into action together and he got killed your first thought was, 'I'm glad he got it and not me.' Besides, I've been out of circulation since then. Some people keep reliving those days. It was just a phase in my life. I wanted to get on with other things.'

To Frost, the memories were less painful. He was standing on the balcony of the house he and his men had held for four sleepless days and nights (armed only with sub-machine guns and the portable anti-tank PIAT guns against the fleet of Panzer Tiger tanks that were slicing their stronghold into pieces), watching the film-makers recreate the ordeal. I suggested to him it must be somewhat upsetting.

'Surprisingly, not really. I've always found in life that you forget the bad things and always remember the good things. And there was a wonderful sense of glory, if you like, here. Surprisingly enough we didn't have a great number of people killed. I think it was sixty out of a battalion, but about 250 were wounded. One of the reasons for that was that we ran out of ammunition towards the end of the battle and had nothing left to fight with.'

It wasn't really the original house that we were in – that had been razed to the ground by the Germans. Nor was it really the bridge that had been destroyed as well. We were standing on a house built for the film near Deventer Bridge, which was playing Arnhem Bridge. But the action around us that boiling May morning was so vivid that it could have passed for a genuine battle, were it not for the presence of a film crew of 300 men busying themselves about the location. Even General Frost forgot that the location was make-believe. 'This very house,' he said, indicating the one we were in, 'was the last one that was unburnt and still standing.'

Richard Attenborough had gone to great pains to make it seem authentic. His sketch artist, Michael White, had combed photographs and paintings of the original battle and, in conjunction with the director, had made a cartoon strip of the action, as seen from various angles. They knew that the Germans had used twenty-four vehicles in the first assault on Frost – which he had repelled – but they decided to cut it down to sixteen for the film. 'We had to bring it down to a reasonable length,' Attenborough explained, 'and we had to contain the action, which might in fact have taken three-quarters of an hour, within about four minutes. In a subject as complex as this you can't afford more time, and anyway dramatically it wouldn't work.'

Before they even thought about camera angles, they made models of all the different vehicles and worked out logically how it would happen. Then they measured the bridge and, using all the vehicles that were needed for the charge and the drivers that would be operating them in the film, they rehearsed on a disused airport for eight days. In the light of that actual experience, they redid the storyboard, gradually fitting in the cameras. 'We wanted the action to be the dictating factor, rather than the cameras.'

One of the problems of being an actor in a scene like this is that the action can be more important than your performance. In the cutting room it can be more tempting for the director to use the take that has the best times and most spectacular background, rather than the best delivery of the lines. Anthony Hopkins, a man usually associated with more verbal and deep-thinking roles, like Pierre in *War and Peace*, was playing Frost. He didn't seem too troubled by the possibility that he was subordinate to the explosions.

'I've never really worked on anything quite like this. You get on, speak your lines, and get off as fast as you can. You simply have to do as you're told. Dickie Attenborough seems to have worked it all out beautifully. If he directs me and says, "Do this or do that," I say, "Okay, fine." Because when you have the tank charge and the army on the move, there's not much you can do. I don't think it matters a damn about the lines because it's all going to be post-synched anyway.'

Attenborough was more concerned. 'Without question I think you must go for the performance. No matter how exciting or powerful the action is, if the credibility of the performance lapses, then the whole thing goes out of the window. The audience is no longer subjective; they are able to disinvolve themselves, and so the whole scene doesn't work.'

Frost was watching Hopkins play his thirty-one-year-old self, watching a man who was making a permanent record for all the world to see of the four days that turned him into a hero. In years to come, long after he has died, people who have never read the book or even heard of Arnhem will flick the late-night movie on their televisions and see this performance. As with seemingly all things, he was nonplussed about it.

'I think he seems to be growing a little bit more like me every day. I hope he doesn't mind me saying that. He's like all the soldiers, I mean, actors. I look at them now and completely forget that they're actors. They seem to me to behave and look very much as our own soldiers did. And I think it's the same with their commanding officer. He seems to be biting out his orders and that sort of thing better all the time. We have a word or two after every scene. But it's hardly my place to give him instructions. That's for the director.'

Frost did, however, give Hopkins one piece of advice. 'I had to do a scene where I was running across the street under gunfire. I was running fairly fast as I thought he would to get under cover. General Frost said to me, "You know, you're running too fast." I said, "I'm running too fast?" "Yes," he said. "You wouldn't run that fast. You'd have to show the Germans and your men contempt for danger!" That's the kind of courage that's beyond my comprehension. I don't understand that kind of courage.'

Without doubt, Hopkins' meeting with Frost was of great value to him. For in his acting I noticed he introduced just a suspicion of parody – not enough to be disrespectful, but sufficient to remind us that thirty-one-year-olds aren't like that today. And I am sure he must have got his inspiration from the general himself, who was considered, even then, a little bit of an eccentric.

Frost's batman, Dennis Wicks, recalls that 'When the order to go to Arnhem was given, he breezed in one day and said, "It looks as if we're going to another party. Can you get my dinner jacket cleaned and brush up my golf clubs? They can follow us in the staff car." In other operations he used his hunting horn – he was the master of some hunt – as a rallying call for his men when we landed. We always jumped side-by-side."'

Even today, Frost rejected the free accommodation that was offered him by the film company, preferring instead to live in a Dormobile, which he parked by the banks of the river at night. 'It's got a little kitchen thing in it, and I can brew up in the morning.' If not quite the party he expected, he did look back at the battle as one might remember a cricket match.

'During this particular battle we found that the Germans fought with great chivalry and I hope that's depicted in the film. They were extremely meticulous about not shooting at our wounded. Our stretcher-bearers were always given a clear run, whether they had wounded with them or not. And when the doctors arranged a truce with the Germans – once the flames got a real hold of the building and we had run out of water, it looked as if our 200 wounded would be burnt alive – the Germans came in themselves and took a lot of risks to get us out. In fact the building collapsed as the last chap was brought out.'

Wicks remembered the moment. 'The last chap they brought out was an injured German prisoner we had taken earlier in the battle. The roof began to cave in, so they dropped the poor bugger and ran. I could see there was a minute left and I didn't want him to be roasted alive so I went back in and got him. A German officer saw me do this and gave me a packet of fags.'

Frost's bravery and stubbornness in the face of overwhelming odds was extraordinary – Wicks told me about the moment when the German commander approached Frost to discuss surrender after five days of shelling his depleted troops with an entire panzer division at the other end of the bridge waiting to advance. The commander walked towards Frost clutching a white handkerchief.

German: There is no point in continuing this fight. We are willing to discuss surrender.

Frost: Sorry, we haven't the proper facilities to take you all prisoner. We'd like to but we can't accept your surrender. Was there anything else?

An amazed German, knowing Frost only had a handful of men left, returned to his panzer division, which continued to bombard Frost's house.

But on the other side of the road from Frost in a schoolhouse, helping him to hold the north end of the bridge, was Captain Eric Mackay and fifty Royal Engineers. And at one stage in the battle when they were exchanging fire with some Germans who had taken refuge in a nearby house, the Germans asked for a truce by coming out with a handkerchief tied to a stick. To this day Mackay thinks they were genuinely trying to surrender to him.

Today he is Major-General Eric MacLachlan Mackay CBE, chief engineer, British Army of the Rhine. He isn't portrayed directly in the film: again, an amalgam character performs some of his deeds. And just as there is a degree of competitiveness among film stars, so is there among generals. It was my impression that Frost was none too keen for Mackay to be featured in the film.

The two men are very different. Frost is very Wellington and Sandhurst, patrician, a little vague, a little deaf and gracefully plays down his role in the battle – in all our conversations he never once mentioned that he was severely wounded and near to death himself. Mackay on the other hand is ten years younger – a twenty-two-year-old captain at the time, an alert, precise scientist, reeling off his memories with the speed of a sub-machine gun. He knew just what he was in for, from the moment the airborne armada left England.

'When I went on this operation I knew it was doomed to failure as any experienced paratrooper would have. We knew that we would either be killed or captured: it would have been a miracle if it had been a success.'

When I asked General Mackay about the tank charge that Panzer Captain Grabner made on his and Frost's positions at the beginning of the siege, he asked, 'Captain who?'

'Grabner,' I replied, and explained whom I meant.

'Oh, him,' said Mackay. 'I never really had the opportunity to ask him his name.'

(Approaching war from history books, one never realizes that the participants were rarely aware of the names of the people they were fighting against, or even dealing with, save the superstars like Rommel and Patton.)

General Mackay could remember the details of that tank charge, however, as if it had happened ten minutes earlier.

'One of my lookouts said, "There's a couple of armoured cars gone past the window." I rushed over there and sure enough they had gone past. There was nothing we could do about them – we had no anti-tank weapons. The next things that came along were half-tracks. These are open at the top and you can look down at the drivers. Well, all my men were marksmen so I said, "What you've got to do is shoot the drivers and then we'll shoot the rest of them as they get out." Obviously the same thought had occurred to Colonel Frost on the other side. So as these Henchel half-tracks arrived, we shot the leading people and they stopped. Nothing happened for a moment. Then another one came along and we shot those drivers and they stopped. Then the third one ran into those two and then people started to come out and we killed them as they came out. One went on fire and went into reverse and more people crashed into this lot and so it went on.

'We were fighting from the first-floor window. I looked down and one of these half-tracks had come up to us and was looking face-to-face, about six feet, into the commander's face when he took out his Luger and shot at me. The first bullet went through my helmet, the second hit my binoculars and the third missed. He was killed and all the crew underneath were killed. The driver was wounded, went on and hit the school on its north wing. The same thing happened later on. We killed them before they got to us.'

Listening to General Mackay, I was almost convinced that the British had won at Arnhem. They certainly had in terms of spirit, but only in those terms. Just five men escaped from that schoolhouse. But before they left, they gave the Germans plenty to remember them by.

'It was on the Monday night (the second night of the siege). The enemy set fire to two half-tracks against the wall of the schoolhouse. We thought we would get burnt out, but eventually we put the fires out. Suddenly there was a tremendous explosion in the southern wing: an anti-tank grenade had attacked us. I was in the wing at the time. It was blown away and everybody was killed except me. I was brought round some time later. It was all quiet around the house. One of my soldiers came up to me and said, "We're entirely surrounded by Germans." I said, "You're imagining it." But I went round to look, and, on the grass outside the school, were a lot of Germans, sixty or seventy of them. They were casually setting up mortars and machine guns and chatting among themselves, obviously thinking we'd all been knocked out by the explosion. So I gave orders that everybody should man the windows. We had fourteen sten guns, six bren guns and a lot of grenades and when I shouted our war cry, "Woa Mohammed", we dropped the grenades, and as soon as they exploded, which was four seconds later, we opened up with the sten guns and bren guns. This killed them all. You couldn't see the grass for dead Germans. The effect of this was that as their infantry started to attack us, they had to wade through the bodies, and of course they were so slow getting through the bodies that they themselves got wounded and killed and this made more bodies, one on top of the other, until eventually there was such a mass of bodies between the school building and the end of the garden (which was guarded by wrought-iron fence) that no infantry attack could reach us, because they couldn't wade through the bodies outside.'

One German had managed to get through earlier in the attack. He stuck his sub-machine gun through the schoolhouse window and started spraying Mackay's men with bullets. Mackay edged along the wall towards him, hoping he wouldn't be noticed. 'I got to the window, stuck my revolver in his mouth and pulled the trigger. The top of his head would have been blown off if he hadn't been wearing a helmet. He didn't cause us any more trouble.'

But even when they were no longer assailable by the direct approach, they were under almost constant fire.

'We didn't have time to be afraid. It was going on the whole time. One used to get hit two or three times a day. A favourite thing the Germans used to do was to fire rifle grenades through the windows. They'd go behind you and explode on the ceiling. The result was that the whole of your back was full of shrapnel. You had these bits of metal sticking out of your vest and the blood congealed on that. It was very unpleasant.'

Mackay and five of his men got out. He removed his badges of rank and when he saw the Germans coming, having no ammunition left in his revolver, he lay down and pretended to be dead. A sharp dig in the ribs with a German bayonet brought him rapidly to life again. He was taken prisoner, but shortly afterwards escaped and managed to reach the safety of Allied lines by paddling downstream in a small boat.

He wasn't decorated for his gallantry at Arnhem. There were no survivors of sufficient rank to recommend him for a medal. But he came away with the greatest prize of all – his life. There were innumerable acts of exceptional courage by all those men at the bridge. Lieutenant J. H. Grayburn stood in full view of all enemy tanks to personally direct the withdrawal of his men from an untenable position to the safety of the main defensive perimeter. He was posthumously awarded the Victoria Cross.

As the strains of the Pete Murray show rang out from the trucks and vans that had brought the equipment to the bridge at Deventer that cloudless May day, there was an air of levity about the proceedings. People knew the sad story they were about to tell: but film-making is a cheerful business. Coincidentally Mackay and his men had been listening to the BBC when they were holding the bridge thirty-two years previously. 'We heard the six o'clock news and the BBC said everything was going according to plan. There were a lot of ribald remarks like, "What plan?" Then the following night, Tuesday, we turned on the news again and they said that we'd been relieved. We were amazed, because at the time we were being attacked by Tiger tanks.'

Richard Attenborough was instructing Anthony Hopkins (Frost) in the less-than-method task of shouting 'Hold your fire!' at his men. Attenborough can, on occasion, be very theatrical-camp – I hasten to point out that he's a happily married knight with a loving wife and three bonnie children – but today was a camp day. 'Tony, dear, I don't think you should move quite like that . . . what's that Peter, darling? Robin, my love, can you pan just a little to the left . . . Whenever you are ready, sweetie.' These epithets are more profuse when he's in a good mood, and today, ahead of schedule and with weeks of good weather predicted, he was exceptionally buoyant. The insurance on a picture of this size was costing Levine more than $500,000, but with so many expensive stars participating in exterior action, any sustained period of rain would cost them a king's ransom (not that there are many kings around these days as rich as Joe

Levine). The payments to stars for doing extra days' work are known in the industry as 'overage'. On this picture it was known as 'over-rich'.

Despite the cohort of assistant directors, attendant upon Sir Richard and anxious to fulfil his every command, he preferred to orchestrate the tank action and even instruct the drivers himself. He approached the stolid German Fred Williams, who was playing the tank commander Captain Grabner.

Sir Richard: Fred, I've changed my mind. I think in this scene you should give the command to move off, go forward. What would that be in German?

Fred: Weiter.

Sir Richard: What does weiter mean?

Fred: Go forward.

Sir Richard: Would you be content using that word?

Fred: Bitte?

Sir Richard: I said, would you be content using that word?

Fred: Weiter, Weiter, Weiter.

Sir Richard: (holding up three fingers) Fine. Just say it twice.

John Richardson and his special-effects team threaded unseen wires across the bridge and in and out of the tanks which, hopefully, would cause fires and explosions, controlled by a box of tricks behind the camera.

The real General Frost watched the whole process with fascinated interest, chatting happily with the crew and learning as much as he could about the art of making epics. The unreal General Frost, Anthony Hopkins, sunbathed on the roof with us actors from Attenborough's Private Army, swapping theatrical reminiscences and doing hilarious Olivier imitations. (I've never met a former National Theatre player yet who doesn't have at least a passable Olivier imitation in his repertoire.) Hopkins was on the verge of becoming a big international film star and the not-much-younger members of Equity that sat with him were eager to pick up a few tips. He had no regrets about leaving Britain to live in California. He was clearly fed up with the English stage. 'Once it was an actor's theatre: now it's just a director's theatre. Intellectuals come down from Cambridge and foist their theories on the audiences. That's not what drama's about.'

A solitary, middle-aged American woman was walking among the smouldering tanks. It was Cornelius Ryan's widow, Kathryn. She had helped him to research *A Bridge Too Far*. She had watched him die as he wrote it. He lived for only two months after it was published.

'He wrote the book with the knowledge that he might not live to finish it. But with that dogmatic "I will do it" attitude that so characterized him. He refused at the end of his illness to take any kind of medication that might cloud his mind. It was his total ambition to finish this book.

'What we're doing today would have excited him so much. I keep seeing him in my mind's eye as he was before he became ill with cancer. I can see him bounding around the place, going up and down, looking in the lenses, thoroughly enjoying every moment of it.'

Ryan had also written *The Longest Day* and *The Last Battle*.

'He used to say, "Anyone who reads my books and thinks that they're about war has not read my books." He's talking about men and women and nations caught up in a disease. Just as he had a disease called cancer, people were caught up in diseases called wars. His books are always anti-war. They show the futility of war. At the same time they show the dignity of the human being and the courage of the human being. I understood his intense preoccupation with people. It was people that he cared about, because he had grown up and become a reporter in wartime. He was always fascinated with the fact that the academic historian would say, "The general ordered the attack at nine o'clock and by noon the hill was taken." He wanted to know how many babies were born during those three hours, what the weather was like, how frightened were the people, how many young men died unnecessarily, was the attack even necessary?'

A few minutes later the tank we had been leaning on to talk was ablaze with fire. Grabner's charge was under way. A fleet of German Tiger tanks, 88s (or 'sobbing sisters' as they were known to the British troops) half-tracks, kubelwagens and other assorted hardware rose up over the shimmering brow of the curved bridge. They began blasting away at Anthony Hopkins and his men. Hopkins warned his troops to hold their fire, not to waste their precious ammunition. As the leading tanks came within range his voice rang out, 'Fire!' and all hell broke loose. Actors I hadn't even noticed until then appeared at various windows, on rooftops and from balconies, and a storm of bren guns and PIATs and grenades, sten guns and machine guns and ordinary 303s let fly at the approaching Nazis. Now every man with a weapon was firing it full blast, and the tanks thunderously blasted back at the British paras. Two kubelwagens crashed into each other and burst into flames. Duggie Robinson, the chief stuntman, fell from one of them and bounced along the road. Actors dressed as Germans were falling dead and wounded out of their vehicles. Others began to retreat and crashed into each other, just as General Mackay had described. Eventually Fred, alias Captain Grabner, whose cries of, 'weiter' couldn't have been heard two inches away, such was the din, caught a bullet in his chest and slumped across the turret of his tank. The British had held on.

Attenborough yelled, 'Cut', and then anxiously cupped his hands and called down to the bridge, 'Is anybody hurt? Take up the ambulance.' But the message came back that nobody was hurt. Not this time.

When my war ended in 1976 I kept in touch with General Frost right up until he passed away.

Now, when they show A Bridge Too Far on the TV each Christmas, I think back to that sweltering summer when we marched down the long dyke roads behind Anthony Hopkins. The grinding of the tanks, the camaraderie, the banter. And our very special friendship with an extraordinary man.

Frost, Maj-Gen. John Dutton, CB 1964; DSO 1943 and Bar, 1945; MC 1942; DL; farmer; b 31 Dec. 1912; s of late Brig.-Gen. F.D. Frost, CBE. MC and Elsie Dora Bright; m 1947, Jean MacGregor Lyle; one s one d. Educ. Wellington Coll.; RMC Sandhurst. Commissioned The Cameronians. Sevt. 1932; Capt., Iraq Levies, 1938–41; Major and Lt-Col, Parachute Regt, 1941–45 (Bruneval

raid, 1942; Oudna, 1942; Tunisian campaign, 1942–43; Primosole
Bridge, 1943; Italian campaign, 1943; Arnhem Bridge, 1944); Staff
Coll., Camberley, 1946; GSO2, HQ Lowland Dist, 1948–49;
GSO2, Senior Officers' Sch., 1949–52; AA&QMG, 17 Ghurkha
Div., 1952–53; GSO1, 17 Ghurkha Div., 1953–55; Comd, Neth-
eravon, 1955–57; Comd, 44 Parachute Bde, 1958–61; Comdr
52nd Lowland Div./District, 1961–64; GOC Troops in Malta
and Libya, 1964–66; Comdr Malta Land Force, 1965; retired,
1967. DL West Sussex, 1982, Cross of Grand Officer, SMO,
Malta, 1966. Publications: *A Drop Too Many*, 1980; *Two Para-
Falklands*, 1983; *Nearly There*, 1992. Recreations: field sports,
polo, golf. Address: Northend Farm, Milland, Liphook, Hants
GU30 7LT. Club: Army and Navy.

Died 21 May 1993.

The Silver Screen, Steve McQueen and the Boulevard of Vivid Dreams

Films, like music, have always played an important part in my life.
Movies or scenes from a movie have had an influence on my
behaviour and my point of view.

It all began at the age of seven when I stormed the Gaumont
Hendon to absorb the cinematic wonders of the Saturday Morning
Pictures. The sheer joy of sinking deep into the plush velvet seats
dressed as Batman flanked by my gang of Roy Rogers, Superman
and King Kong and firing aniseed balls from my Mark One catapult
at the bald pate of Reginald Dixon, the resident organist, was only
eclipsed by the prospect of 'walking the dog', in the yoyo competition
before the feast of film took us to wonderland.

We would fidget through Woody Woodpecker, Zorro and the

Lone Ranger before marvelling at the double feature of *Sink The Bismark* and *The Adventures of Flash Gordon*.

It wasn't easy to leave the cinema. The forty-by-forty-foot images that appeared on the screen became the other people in my life. The giant faces of the film actors would become the new members of my family. Sometimes the movies would reflect the beautiful side, sometimes the frightening elements and most enjoyable of all, the humorous character of my celluloid extended family. For example, Gary Cooper, Humphrey Bogart and Clark Gable were the pals I wanted to have on my side when I grew up. As for the beautiful Marilyn Monroe, Jane Russell, Ava Gardner and Audrey Hepburn, they gave me my first taste of glamour, almost too good to be true.

Fred Astaire and Ginger Rogers provided the best in black and white screen entertainment in those wonderful RKO musicals. Great tunes sung in black, white and silver setting, very Art Deco. Through the eyes of a seven-year-old those sets were the ultimate nightclub, with silver and white palm trees, big winding staircases and penthouses overlooking the skyscrapers, Gunga Din, the G-men, gangsters and car chases offered my kind of excitement. I marvelled at the images of lonely trains in the wilderness such as in the beautiful opening sequence in *Bad Day At Black Rock* in 1955 when the Southern Pacific Streamliner thunders across a dusty plain. And the big cowboy films. John Ford's unerring eye for the spacious beauty of the American West or the melancholic loneliness of small towns. *High Noon*, *Shane* and *Stagecoach*.

Then suddenly there was a close-up of an unusual face. This cowboy was totally different. In just one close-up this man could express six or seven different and sometimes contradictory emotions and seemingly insightful thoughts. In a split second I knew that we were dealing with a strong and different kind of cowboy hero. He was interesting, unusual, appealing and sensitive all at the same time. He was rugged, decidedly different and unconventionally handsome.

He sat on a hearse riding shotgun next to Yul Brynner. Vin the hired gunman would make sure the coffin reached Boot Hill. The film was *The Magnificent Seven*, the actor, Steve McQueen.

It was 1960. Three years later, POW Captain Virgil Hilts had attempted to enter Switzerland astride a motorbike jumping over a barbwire fence. Then there was the poker-playing Cincinnati Kid and in 1968 Detective Lieutenant Frank Bullitt driving through the streets of San Francisco as cool as an iceman. Steve McQueen was street-wise, animal-like, non-intellectual and hip. In fact he brought a new meaning to the word hip. He was super hip.

I finally met him in 1971 at the Record Plant in Los Angeles. We were producing a Bee Gees album when he walked into the studio. I shook his hand and he just stared at me with his intense steel-blue eyes. He was seductive and threatening. I was mesmerized. His look was chilling. I felt he knew everything about me in a split second.

'Blimey, Stevie Boy,' I blurted. 'I'd love to see you ride that bike in London. I bet you could jump over my house.' There was a pause. Then still holding my hand, the greatest movie star in the world suddenly cracked up. He immediately mimicked my accent, put his arms on my shoulders and called me 'Limey Dave'. Steve came to our sessions for the next few days. We became good pals. He took the piss out of me and I told him jokes. He claimed he was tone deaf but when I gave him a guitar he had a very good sense of rhythm and was a brilliant mime. In return he took me for a drive in his Shelby Cobra, an experience I'll never forget for the rest of my days. Put it this way: I was glad I was wearing brown trousers!

One day he brought his great pal Bud Ekins to the studio. Bud was the stuntman who performed all of Steve's dangerous riding scenes including *The Great Escape*. I took Bud aside to ask him about his pal's passion for cars, bikes and high speed. Bud laughed. 'Tell you what, Limey Dave, nobody knows how he treats some vehicles.' Apparently in the film game it was the custom while on location for a local automobile agency to let the production company borrow several of their new cars to be used by the movie executives and of course the stars. When Steve wasn't needed on the set, he'd round up his pals and go for a drink. He would often go off the main road with the new car at top speed and beat the hell out of it until it could hardly make it back to the set.

Bud continued, 'One time when I was with him, he drove a brand-new Ford convertible, with only thirty miles on the speedometer, at top speed for such a long stretch of the Texas highway that the engine began to smoke and eventually caught on fire. He slowed down and shouted to me, "Bud, when I tell you to jump, jump!" We did jump out of the car just as it burst into flames. Steve sat on the side of the country road at a safe distance from the burning vehicle and laughed his head off. The car burnt to the ground before the local fire truck arrived. The next day the local newspaper headlines read, "Movie star Steve McQueen narrowly escapes death in burning car." '

Many years later I became great friends with the Surrey and England cricketer Alec Stewart. He reminded me of Steve; a certain facial resemblance and the same steely resolve to succeed and 'push it as far as it would go'.

I would have loved Steve to have met Alec. Maybe to play together in a Bunbury game.

4 a.m. pitch black on a Sunday morning. The phone rings. I reach across the bed over my Brazilian girl and pick up the phone on the second or third ring.

'Hello.' It is Steve McQueen.

'Hey Limey Dave,' says a hushed but urgent voice. 'It's Steve. Hey, what's happenin', you wanna go with us? I'm meeting Bud and Don and some of the other cats up in Palmdale at Du-par's. We're headin' out to Mojave Cross-country Bike Race. We'll have breakfast there.' His voice gets seductive. 'Eggs over easy, bacon, hash browns, hot coffee, it'll be a blast. Watch the sun come up over the desert. Get next to nature. Can you dig it?'

'Yeah OK Steve, but let me wake up a little, okay?'

Steve continues non-stop. 'We'll chase some Jack rabbits across the desert. Do some wheelies in the sand, hot, sweaty. We'll have a ball.' Pause. 'Yeah, I know your ol' lady's gonna be pissed, so's mine. Hey, we gotta make it. 'Bout noon, when it's too hot, we'll take off and head to a funky little Mexican place I know near Pear Blossom. Guacamole, refried beans and some brews. Okay? See ya in about thirty minutes, my place.'

'Yeah, okay Stevie, but give me a little longer.'

Steve interrupts, 'Dave, bring that cricketer dude, Alec Stewart. Perhaps we can play a little.'

I hang up the phone. The Brazilian rolls over. 'Let me guess. It must be Steve McQueen. He wants you and Alec to go out with the guys, right? Well . . . okay. See you about dinner time, if I'm lucky.'

I kissed her goodbye.

When the first frost descends on summer's roses, I drift off to Paris along the Boulevard of Vivid Dreams to my apartment on the left bank of the Seine overlooking Notre Dame.

I invite Françoise Hardy around for an aperitif. I knew her in the sixties when she was the embodiment of the French pop creation. I found her lyrics to be whimsical. She was a creature of moons and tides. Her song 'Tous les garçons Et Les Filles de mon age' – having boyfriends and girlfriends while she had no one – touched me. I wrote to her:

Françoise, here is the deepest secret no one knows.
Here is the root of the root
And the bud of the bud
And the sky of the sky of a tree called Life
Which grows higher than a soul can hope
Or mine can hide.
It's the wonder that's keeping the stars apart
I carry your heart
I carry it in my heart.

I told her that many people will walk in and out of her life, but only true friends would leave footprints in her heart. 'Come to me, Françoise, for tomorrow night could be your last first kiss.'

I always pull her leg. She was always far too gorgeous a creature to be sounding so sad and self-pitying in the first place.

I wish Joni Mitchell were here. I'd love to produce an album of them together in this very room. My apartment is at the top of the building, a studio, very light and airy with wonderful views over

Paris. I can see the sunlight slanting through the rose window of Notre Dame, leaving a kaleidoscope of colourful ripples on the Seine, which flows past Argenteuil to Le Havre and on to the open sea.

Argenteuil, where Claude Monet bought a house from his pal Edouard Manet so he could dedicate himself to his twin passions of painting and gardening. During the summer of 1872 Claude invited his friend Pierre-Auguste Renoir to come and paint. Cézanne, Degas, Pissarro and Bazille soon followed. Imagine all those impressionists together, 'The Wild Brushes'. A house full of romantics and visionaries. Their love of nature would have opened their hearts – the sight of the river and the beautiful countryside. They would have set up their easels on the banks of the Seine and would have painted spontaneously with importance given not to the details but to the whole, to the overall impression that reality awakens in the mind, free of reflections or second thoughts. Monet and Renoir were fascinated by water and strove to make their palette express the special effects of light on the surface of the Seine.

I'd have invited the impressionists to get a boat to sail up the Seine to my apartment where they could have painted pictures to Françoise and Joni's words.

Joni plugs into their paintings. Most of her best work comes out of depression. 'All romantics meet the same fate some day – cynical and drunk and boring someone in some dark cafe'. My impressionist lads would have livened up the ladies. They loved to visit cafes and dance halls to exuberantly paint the thrills of the city. They flourished on the long tree-lined boulevards and the wide sidewalks lined with restaurants, crowded at every hour of the day by pedestrians and carriages.

So the melody comes first and perhaps the most beautiful tunes are sad and the lyrics follow the mood. But, 'Do not get too melancholic, girls,' declares Eduard Manet. 'Just look at my picture, Bar at the Folies Bergère; it is full of life, full of fun.'

Just then there was the sound of a commotion down in the street. The noise of a high-speed machine screeching to a halt on the cobbles.

Cézanne went to the window. 'There is a man on a motorcycle waving his arms. I think he wants to come up.'

Seconds later there was a knock on the door. It was Steve McQueen.

'Hey, Limey Dave, I'm on my way to shoot a movie. I'm playing some cat called Papillon. Thought I'd call in to say hi!'

Steve was embraced by Joni, Françoise and the Wild Brushes. I gave him a massive hug.

'Steve McQueen, you son of a gun!'

'This calls for a toast!' roared Pissarro above the hubbub.

'Let's open a bottle. It's time to celebrate our collaboration.'

'We will call our album, "The Boulevard of Vivid Dreams!"'

Hit the Road Jack

My allegiance to the Gaumont Hendon Central ended many years ago, not because of disloyalty (one can never be fickle with film), but because our cinema was pulled down to accommodate a brand new, state-of-the-art health and fitness club. To think, our palace of panavision pictures and technicolour dreams was replaced by a sweatshop for the Mercedes Benz and BMW brigade.

Our escape, where, for just three pence, we could run amok chasing each other around the auditorium with our Robert Hirst macs buttoned at the collar dressed as Batman, was now full of vacuous bodies pumping iron, wearing skintight lycra, watching MTV and worrying about emails, broken nails and bleached hairdos – and that was just the men!

In 1992 I switched to a new pleasure dome, the name of which I cannot divulge for risk of jeopardizing my ongoing scam. It was a windswept Wednesday in Whetstone as I moved gingerly through the rain to the box office. Staring through the window, I jokingly asked for 'one OAP ticket for Clint Eastwood'. To my amazement the assistant, totally uninterested, complied with my demand. From that day on I have had to assume the character of a man twenty years my senior.

My golden days of cinematic indulgence start at the Turkish Cafe with a very tasty haddock, chips and mushy peas washed down by an ice-cold Dr Pepper. Then straight over the road into the foyer of the cinema where I hobble and limp clutching popcorn like a sixty-five-year-old.

I nearly came a cropper on one occasion when I tripped over the light fantastic, performing an Olympic-style header into the 'pick and mix' display after sprinting to see the start of *The Matrix Revolution* in multiplex theatre six. The usherettes looked on incredulously as my guise was blown. Momentarily, I had changed from Old Father Time into Linford Christie.

'Are you all right, Mr English?' they enquired, genuinely concerned, lifting me out of the sweet shrimps and Liquorice Allsorts.

'Yes, yes,' I mumbled through a sweet tooth. 'I really must stop taking those steroids.'

Every week I sit with the oldies, as happy as Larry, discussing current affairs. I feel very much at home with the elderly. I listen and learn, marvelling at their wisdom, experience and stories. Before each performance, we are given a cup of tea and a biscuit. Very often I am the only person in the theatre.

'Ready when you are, Mr English?' enquires the projectionist.

'Roll 'em,' I growl, à la Cecil B. DeMille.

My OAP impersonation has lasted for twelve happy years. All was well until *Ray*, the fantastic biopic of Ray Charles, came to our screens. The film was progressing perfectly. Ray Charles Robinson was a sightless man with more vision than anyone could imagine. He could hear like we could see. He could be blind and still afraid of the dark.

I was sitting next to Mildred, a deaf lady from Friern Barnet and Harry, her toy boy, aged eighty-four, from Potters Bar. Ray Charles had Georgia On His Mind when suddenly, the film ground to a halt, plunging us all into darkness. A voice crackled through the tannoy, asking us to evacuate the building as quickly as possible. It had to be a bomb scare. All hell broke loose. Wheelchairs and zimmers were making for the exit quicker than mercury rising on a summer's day.

I went into my SAS mode. 'Don't panic ladies and gentlemen. We now know what it must have been like to be Ray Charles,' I joked through the darkness. 'Don't worry I'll help you all to "Hit The Road Jack"!'

Once again, the usherettes looked on aghast at the sight of me lifting and carrying my old friends out of the theatre and into the road. It was a false alarm but my ruse was finally rumbled. As we returned to the theatre, the manager announced, 'Well done, Mr English. For this we really will make you an honorary OAP!'

My Boots Are Full of Blood

On Tuesday 21 September 1976 I was about to work with the world's greatest actor. Six-thirty a.m on location. Make-up, maximum wound and blood-up, at seven. On the set at seven-thirty. Camera running by eight a.m. David English to act in some powerful scenes with Lord Olivier, climaxing in the line, 'My boots are full of blood.' Heady stuff, cricketer meets screen legend, Oscar material.

My time on *A Bridge Too Far* was coming to an end. I was spent physically, mentally and emotionally after careering around in those heavy para uniforms in 100-degree heat. Trying to remember my lines, keeping in character and running the cricket team between takes, and now sitting on the top step in Kate Ter Horst's house surrounded by dying soldiers, stretchers, oil lamps, field dressings, medics and bloodshed. My legs shot to pieces, 'my boots are full of blood'. I had to deliver the line to Lord Olivier, who played Dr Spaander, an elderly Dutch doctor who intercedes with the Germans on behalf of the British.

I had become close friends with Laurence during the film. I listened to his stories and marvelled at his wisdom. He batted at seven in my cricket team (between Dirk Bogarde and Robert Redford) and was a canny off-break bowler, landing the ball on an immaculate length, between the rubble and the dying.

In the film, crammed to the last reel with stars, it was improbable that any one of them should actually stand out, be more revered than the rest, and create a greater magic on the set. But one did – Laurence Olivier. It wasn't his doing. He behaved in a manner that would attract a minimum of attention. In fact, if he hadn't been who he was, I doubt if he would have attracted any attention at all.

An indication of the popularity of any given actor in Holland was the amount of attention they attracted when waiting for their bags at Amsterdam's Schiphol Airport. They knew Redford all right and Ryan O'Neal was undoubtedly the best known of the Americans – Holland had been duly saturated with *Peyton Place* over the years. And, of the rest, Sean Connery will remain until his dying day as 007 and be persecuted no longer by Dr No, but by an over-affectionate public. Nobody noticed Olivier. The man who by almost unanimous acclaim was considered the greatest living English-speaking actor in the world, and nobody noticed him. Perhaps it was something to do with the plasticity of his face and his rimless specs, but I doubt it. He's just not the sort of person you recognize. He arrived at the airport wearing the suit that he had been given for the part. He was to perform one of the most dramatic and poignant scenes in the film with me, formerly a star of the Head and Shoulders commercials, a sheep in *Joseph and the Amazing Technicolour Dreamcoat* and a dead man in *Z Cars*. Mind you, in the last six months in Holland I had become an expert in dead acting.

He had been wearing the suit for the past week – both socially and at work (he'd been in Manchester rehearsing *Cat On A Hot Tin Roof* with Natalie Wood and Robert Wagner). He explained to me why.

'David, if it's meant to look well worn, it's better to wear it: there's no other real way. You can always press a suit but you can't do what's happened to this one.'

And indeed it did look baggy, well-worn and very much part of him.

The other thing Lord Olivier did in preparation for his part was to acquire a Dutch accent. Olivier is a master mimic. Even if he couldn't understand what he was saying, with his ear for a foreign tongue and his trained capacity to remember lines, he used to give curtain speeches in the language of the land in which he was playing, when he went abroad on tours with the Old Vic. To play Doctor Spaander in *A Bridge Too Far* he brought with him a cassette recording of some spoken Dutch, which he played in his hotel room in the evening. 'You just have a shot and guess what you think will be right . . . and you get a friend of a friend to do a bit of Dutch gentleman talking English on a tape . . . spouting a few of the lines you've got, so that you will have some sort of comparison. Just very simple ways like that.'

One morning when he was rehearsing a scene with Liv Ullman (Kate Ter Horst) and she was surrounded by some little children to whom he was meant to be the family doctor, it occurred to him that after bidding her farewell, he should gently pat the head of one of them and bid the little girl a child-like 'bye-bye'. He found a Dutch woman on the set and was at pains to find out the right word for such a gesture – 'glenchie'. And it was duly incorporated in the script. Small touches, like the wearing-in of the costume, but nevertheless he was the only actor whom I observed approach his part with such care, and his part was almost the smallest.

He may have escaped at Schiphol without notice but when he arrived on the set there was a buzz that ran through the crew, Attenborough's Private Army and the other leading actors that was so evident you might have thought you were in the presence of royalty. It was a buzz that even extended to the director. 'When he comes on, everybody in the unit is open-mouthed. His fascination as far as the watcher is concerned is sheer magic.'

When Attenborough went to visit him on his first night in the hotel, Olivier proudly showed him the worn-in suit. 'It works well, doesn't it? One believes I fit into it.' And then Lord Olivier showed Sir Richard his shoes. 'I wore those in the garden. It's English mud but I don't suppose it will matter, will it?'

Olivier, incidentally, refused the luxury of a suite in Amsterdam or even a comfortable set of rooms in Arnhem that many of the actors had been eager to insist on, and settled instead for the spare corner-bedroom of the old Keizerskroon Hotel at Apeldoorn, with no armchair in the room, nor any radio or television, and a bed that took up most of the space.

Attenborough had reason to feel indebted to him. He was one of the first people who agreed to play in the film and undoubtedly the allure of his name made it safe (to use his own phrase) for other stars. Not only that, it was his name that had enabled Sir Richard to get his first venture into directing, *Oh! What a Lovely War*, off the ground. 'I owe him an enormous debt. I needed superstars to raise the money for it and he not only agreed before seeing the script to play in it but also set a reasonable fee for his services which I was able to quote.'

In the current film, one gathered, Olivier was doing rather better. He was a man who had several times made a fortune and then lost it – often by sinking it into ventures of his own like the ill-fated *Romeo and Juliet* with Vivien Leigh. Not only that, if he had stuck rigidly to films in the fifties and sixties, he would be a great deal richer than he was in 1976. But instead he forsook Hollywood for the classical pastures of the English stage, eventually steering the new National Theatre to its launching pad, and for this his remuneration was paltry. He took time off occasionally to play cameo roles in films, but both his time and his health acted against many of these. Recently he had been seen in a scene-stealing and perceptive role as Professor Moriarty in *The Seven Per Cent Solution*. He only took a couple of days. 'I don't know if it worked or not. I told them, "If it's no good get someone else".' His health at times had been so bad that it was questionable if a film company would get medical insurance to cover him. On *A Bridge Too Far* he eagerly sought a chair to rest his bad leg between takes. Joe Levine worried lest his health should let him down before he came back to complete his part in the picture some three months later. But, as it turned out, it was Levine who had to go into hospital, and Olivier managed to cram the production, direction and starring roles of a succession of Granada television plays into the intervening period.

But, in his seventieth year, he was worried about money and as he chattered amiably to visitors and crew on the set, he ruminated about how he was going to pay the school fees of his youngest child who was about to join the other two at Bedales and joked that he even had to send his wife (Joan Plowright) out to work in the West End. He may have got the rumoured quarter of a million dollars for his Polaroid commercial in the States but he had never sought a tax exile and the English exchequer is not kind to its own.

His first scene was opposite Hardy Kruger, who was playing a Nazi general (what else). Olivier had come to ask for a ceasefire so that the Germans could take prisoner the British wounded and, hopefully, tend them in their hospitals. Kruger pointed out that the Germans were at war and, indeed, winning. Olivier replied that he wasn't concerned with winning and losing, just living and dying. He pleaded for an hour's ceasefire, adding, 'And then you can kill us all if you want to.' On the first rehearsal he produced a magical half-smile on this phrase, part cynical, part fawning. I wished the cameras had been turning; it added so much to the line and the character. I needn't have worried. On the succeeding eight takes he repeated the exact mannerism at the exact moment, as if it had been written into the script. Kruger was equally impressed. 'I've always been a fan. Unfortunately, it's the first time in my life I've worked with him, but it's been a fantastic experience all morning.'

If you have the opportunity to observe a dozen of the world's most popular film actors at work, it does make you pause and wonder what their gift is. In most cases it appeared basically that they were attractive – not always pretty – primarily people who could signal emotion to the audience with a degree of fluency. But in the case of Olivier you were dealing with something else. James Agate once wrote that he was 'a comedian by instinct and a tragedian by art'. I suspect, however, that his art was his instinct. And in film acting, he was perceptively aware that the camera could convey the slightest detail of the human face, details that are lost on the stage. As a young man he would always seize the opportunity to don a false nose, most famously in the film of *Richard III*. He did so again as Moriarty in *The Seven Per Cent Solution* and also, by a mere dropping of the mouth, indicated immediately the lowliness and humility of Moriarty's character. In *Oh! What a Lovely War* his puffed-out cheeks communicated the bluff buffoonery of Sir John French. It was funny and it was intended to be. Kenneth Tynan once wrote, 'He cannot play old men without letting his jaw sag and his eye wander archly in magpie fashion – in short, without becoming funny.' But there is nothing funny in the plight of Dr Spaander in this film and in Olivier's portrayal you can almost sense the weariness of a man who has been under Nazi domination for the past four years.

Attenborough was aware that Olivier's techniques, such as false noses or certain props, had not been substitutes for characterization. 'It is perfectly true that he likes to use these things as a base, but they are only a base. It does not in any sense whatsoever indicate a superficial characterization.'

Bizarrely, Attenborough felt freer to give him closer direction than almost any of the other actors. Perhaps because he knew him better: possibly because he relished the sheer joy of working closely with the great man. In an early scene where Olivier asked a local Dutch woman, Kate Ter Horst, if the British wounded may be accommodated in her house, he enquired, 'Is your husband not yet returned?' He knew her husband was in the Resistance and would not return. Attenborough reminded him that the question is thus pointed.

'I know. Didn't I make that clear?' worried Olivier.

'Oh, sir,' responded an abject director.

It is a far cry from the days when David O. Selznick would send anxious memoranda to Alfred Hitchcock, the director of *Rebecca*. On 13 October 1939 he wrote, 'Dear Hitch, today's rushes were, I thought, all right, but frightened me from the standpoint of tempo more than any we have had so far. Larry's silent actions and reactions become slower as his dialogue becomes faster each day. His pauses and spacing on the scene with the girl in which she tells him about the ball are the most ungodly slow and deliberate reactions I have ever seen. It is played as though he were deciding whether or not to run for president instead of whether or not to give a ball.' It got worse: 'For God's sake speed up Larry . . . While you are at it, you will have to keep your ears open to make sure that we know what the hell he's talking about.'

He wasn't writing about some ingénue from the English stage. Olivier had become an international star of some stature with the release of William Wyler's *Wuthering Heights*. But as a result of Selznick's memos or, more likely, Hitchcock's direction, or, even more likely, Olivier's talent, *Rebecca* got Olivier an Oscar nomination as best actor and the film won the Best Picture Oscar in 1940. But it, and the war, spelt the end of Olivier's honeymoon with Hollywood. And in 1976, thirty-seven years later, here he was once more a major box-office star – in addition to being the biggest serious theatre draw in England and, most recently, one of the most successful actors and producers on British television.

People have often said that Olivier really wanted to continue as a major film star after the war and was disappointed that this was not so. I asked him if it was true.

'No, I don't think career-wise I could have been more lucky. I don't regret anything from my career. I've made mistakes but in a long life you learn not to regret them so much.'

At the time we spoke, *Marathon Man* had not yet been released, but the 'word' on it was good. Olivier gave no indication of the joys and terrors that were in store for an unsuspecting public. However, in his usual deprecating manner, he did warn me that, 'It will lose me what remains of my public (a) the Germans and (b) the Dustin Hoffman fans, when they see me sticking needles into his teeth.'

I wondered if many of the technicians working on the film – measuring Olivier's focal length from the camera, keying his lighting, getting him to alter position for framing – remembered they were dealing with a considerable director. When Orson Welles did a cameo in a movie he was at pains to let the crew and the director know that he had forgotten more about the art of movie-making than they were ever likely to learn. Or rather, he hadn't forgotten. Other people have forgotten. Olivier's lack of interest in all things technical might have led one to believe that he had no knowledge of anything but acting. In fact, his trio of Shakespeare films, *Hamlet*, *Henry V* and *Richard III* have never been surpassed in the screen versions of that great writer. It took some courage to restage the Battle of Agincourt in your first film as director and more courage if you chose to demonstrate most of the stunts yourself, as he did. He appeared variously on the set with a crutch and later with his right arm and then his left arm in a sling – a legacy of showing Irish extras how to jump out of trees on to their victims. But on *A Bridge Too Far* he was happy to leave all that to Richard Attenborough, especially since his character only appeared in a few scenes, rather than throughout the picture.

'When a character runs all the way through, you've got an intimate knowledge of a great many things that happen to him. In this instance you just have an intimate knowledge, we hope, of a very few things that happen to that person. One only needs to know the things that have a bearing on the story. You don't have to know where he went to school or the colour of his father's beard. In this case you're particularly in the hands of your director and in this particular case it's a very nice and good thing to be, because he carries the whole story in his mind and knows exactly what's required of your piece of it, and he's able to advise you pretty well exactly how to do it. Anyhow, the medium belongs to the director. In this medium, I think the actor serves the director rather than in the theatre medium where, possibly, the director serves the actor.'

Despite the vast sums of money that tumbled into the pockets of those lucky enough to be cast in *A Bridge Too Far*, most actors hinted at the insecurity they had had when they were poor – an insecurity that goes with the job – but none more than Olivier. Never at any time did he suggest that he had done enough to reach the pinnacle of his profession and sit back and relax. I was reminded of his contemporary, Sir John Gielgud, who even at the end of his life, so it is said, when he was out of work, would write to theatre managements saying that he was John Gielgud, an actor, and was there any work going? Olivier always left himself vulnerable to the stings of his profession. In the third year of his vastly successful Othello, he lost his nerve. 'I had this irrational fear of forgetting my lines, making a fool of myself in public. So I went to my surrogate parents, Sybil Thorndike and Lewis Casson, and told them of it. "What should I do?" I asked them and Sybil replied, "Take drugs, dear boy, we always do." '

The day of my scene was another scorcher, this one seemingly hotter than any that preceded it. I followed the route map that the assistant director had given me the night before, to a new location. The road became narrower and more winding until it eventually dissolved into a mud track, brittle from the unceasing sun. I drove through a small village, then a copse and there before me was an old Dutch church and, beside it, an elegant new vicarage.

I walked through the churchyard and discovered all the gravestones were made of papier-mâché and held up with wooden sticks at the back. The church was just a shell with nothing but scaffolding inside. But the house was very nearly real, with several fully furnished rooms. Only its rear wall was a slab of wood.

Laurence Olivier was dozing under a tree. 'David, I can't understand why they didn't build a real house and donate it to the village.'

Beside him, working on a tapestry, sat Liv Ullman. She had flown in from New York the previous day and was still feeling jet-lagged. 'In Hollywood they're calling this a "Hi there!" picture,' she told us. 'There are so many stars in it that they think we only have time to flit across the screen and say "Hi there!" ' She looked at the assembling crew. 'I've never worked on anything like this before. There must be about three hundred men here. On Bergman films we usually have a crew of fifteen in all.'

Miss Ullman, soft and friendly with penetratingly beautiful eyes, was playing Kate Ter Horst – a Dutch woman who turned her home into a sanctuary for the wounded and dying British. The whole neighbourhood around her house in Oosterbeek, a suburb of Arnhem, had been turned into a raging battlefield as the might of Harzer's weaponry decimated Urquhart's paratroopers. To give refuge to the British was to face certain exile and possible death from the occupying German forces. She had five small children to care for, and her husband was away with the Resistance, yet she opened her doors and shared her food and her blankets and everything she had with the men of the First Airborne Division.

Richard Attenborough perched on a camera-crane high over the scene. On a cue from him hundreds of extras dressed as paratroopers filed past the gates of Kate's house while she and her children waved and blew kisses and the local villagers clapped, held orange scarves high and showered fruit and presents on the troops.

Opposite the gates of the artificial house, out of range of the cameras, a crowd had gathered to watch the scene. To the forefront of it a trim Dutch lady in her sixties, her silver hair clasped back in a bun, sat beside her husband. Both of them were on the edge of their chairs, eagerly taking everything in. As Liv ran down the garden path to greet the troops, the lady wiped a tear from her left eye. Even in 1976 Kate Ter Horst found the memories of these nine days in September 1944 too painful to watch.

'Was it just like this?' I asked her.

'I think the house is too big and too glamorous,' she replied. 'But the soldiers look so real. I can remember our excitement at these unknown British liberators like a long green serpent coming towards us. Maybe they are marching too quickly. When we first saw them, they were moving slowly, almost like ghosts.'

Mrs Ter Horst and her husband, Jan, briefly greeted Miss Ullman and then left. She hadn't really wanted to come. She knew it would upset her. I went to visit her at her real home. Indeed the film-makers had made it too large and they'd put the church on the other side – for technical reasons – but that apart, it was a very fair recreation. We sat in the back garden and talked. Not so much of a garden, more a shrine. Thirty-two years before, the bodies of sixty-four British soldiers had been buried there.

On Sunday 17 September 1944, Mrs Ter Horst had been to the 900-year-old church next door to worship and then taken her children for a swim in the Rhine, just at the bottom of the hill. They returned to the garden but quickly made for shelter in the cellar as British fighters attacked the ack-ack position behind her home. When the noise died down, they came out to see the sky filled with gliders going overhead. She thought then that the four years of Nazi occupation were at an end.

'Suddenly a jeep raced in front of the house. We hadn't seen a car racing for all those years, and this was a jeep, a new thing to us. An English doctor in his battledress got out and he said, "I'm probably going to have some injured. Would it be possible to leave them here?" We were glad to have them in.'

The house became an island in the sea of battle that raged for the next nine days. Every inch of the floor was covered with wounded men and when they were able to walk, they had to go and lie in the garden to make way for more wounded. When they died, they were buried in the garden.

The food ran out and the surgical supplies were low. 'After a few days it was not even possible to go out and pump the water, there were so many snipers around. The chalk kept coming down from the ceiling and they had no water to clean the instruments. The doctors even managed to amputate a man's leg without the proper instruments. They had to read from a book how to do it, not being proper surgeons.

'One man had been shot through the chest and was lying on a stretcher at the top of the house. He gave me a piece of Dutch money for my children. It was printed in orange and in the middle was a portrait of our queen, Wilhelmina. That meant a lot in those days, although it wasn't even worth two shillings. I took it down to the children in the cellar and I said, 'You have to pay for that.' So they did little drawings. The next day I went upstairs with them but the man was no longer there. Where he lay was a huge hole in the double brick wall. You can imagine what I thought. I never saw him again.

'Three years later I heard from him. I asked him how it was possible that he wasn't killed that day. He told me that in the morning the doctor had ordered all those who were able to walk to leave the house to make room for the wounded waiting outside. He said he saw the look on their faces and he thought, 'Well, I've had my share of morphine.' So he left. He was taken prisoner by the Germans and six months after the war was over he turned up on the doorstep of his parents' house in England. They didn't recognize him, he was so thin and white. They thought he was dead.'

Bereft of material help for the wounded, Mrs Ter Horst did the only thing she could. She gave them peace. 'The wounded soul can be as dangerous as the wounded body. You have to get a kind of rhythm of breath going again.' So she went round the various rooms at night and read from the Bible, 'a psalm written for fighters', psalm 91. 'Thou shalt not be afraid for the terror by night; nor for the arrow that flieth by day.' Afterwards she wrote, 'The words of King David spoke straight to our hearts and we understood what at any other time would have remained concealed from us.'

Andrew Milbourne was one of the wounded lying in her house. A direct shell hit on his Vickers machine gun had shattered his arms and hands.

'I seem to remember this lady, blonde, fair, and to me in my stupor at that time from loss of blood, sometimes as being an angel. And something I'll never forget, never ever forget. The reading of that psalm. When I hear it to this day, it's very hard to keep the tears back and I think of the lads and the courage of those Dutch people. God, what they went through to try and save us.'

In 1976 Mr Milbourne was an area manager in the Ministry of Pensions in Newcastle. He had two artificial hooks instead of hands. The Germans tried to kill him, and then they saved his life. Dr Warrack hadn't sufficient equipment to operate, so he handed Andrew over to the Germans.

'I was put in this room where they were making coffins. I can remember shouting, "I'm not dead, I'm not dead." It was like a slaughterhouse. I was put into a long queue that kept moving up the corridor. They were like ghouls, those German doctors, covered in blood. They put my arms into something. My father had taught me to count in German when I was a little boy – he finished up his time on the Rhine after the first gaffe. The doctor said to me, "Number," and I started to go, "Ein, zwei, drei, vier . . ." He was dropping ether meth on to a gauze over my face. And then I had guillotine amputations. You know the brain is a marvellous thing. It will not let you remember all the vivid things you went through at that time, because if you did you'd go stark raving mad.'

Milbourne had been taken to the refuge of Mrs Ter Horst's house by his friend, Corporal Terry Brace, who was a stretcher-bearer. In 1976 he worked for Reed International in Maidstone and the two men still saw each other as often as they could. Brace worked very closely with Kate.

'We would discuss what sort of attention different kinds of wounds needed, but she had a quality over and above her attentiveness. Something you just can't explain. You know that Bible quotation, "Cometh the hour, cometh the man." With Kate Ter Horst it was "Cometh the hour, cometh the woman." Everywhere you looked it seemed as if every building was having a direct hit except Kate Ter Horst's house – apart from some blast damage. It seemed as if there was a divine wish that this house should be spared.'

After those nine days of waking nightmare the British retreated, surrendering their wounded. The Germans drove Mrs Ter Horst, like her neighbours, out of her house. She took her five children and a few possessions in a hand-drawn cart and spent the winter in exile. But after the war she returned to her battle-scarred home and since then it became a place of pilgrimage for the men who were there and survived. She erected a memorial in the garden to the sixty-four who were buried there. After the war, their bodies were taken to the British Cemetery at Oosterbeek, not far away.

I went there on several occasions and nearly always met veterans of Arnhem who had come back to show their wives and children the graves of their dead comrades. They all knew of Kate, even if they had never been to her house. She was as much a part of the First Airborne as General Urquhart. And they all had stories to tell of British and Dutch courage.

They proudly pointed out the graves of Captain Ernest Queripel and Lieutenant John Grayburn, both of the Parachute Regiment, both of whom were awarded the VC for the manner in which they lost their lives at Arnhem. One veteran suggested to me that the graves were primarily those of the older soldiers. 'Those of us who were a bit younger were agile enough to duck and avoid some of the bullets.' But that wasn't so in the case of two paras: 55115323 T. Gronert and 55115324 C. Gronert. They were twins. They joined up on the same day. And, at the age of twenty-one, they both died on the same day – Sunday 17 September 1944.

Every year since the war, the men of the former First Airborne

Division, together with the local Dutch, have held a reunion in Arnhem. It is on the Sunday nearest to that fateful Sunday – 17 September. There is a service in the Oosterbeek graveyard. In 1976, Dr Graeme Warrack, the man who asked for a truce for the wounded, read the lesson and laid a wreath. More than 3,000 people attended, about 200 British and the rest Dutch. Afterwards there is a traditional dinner. Although regimental reunions abound, very few battles are commemorated in this way with the local inhabitants.

After the twenty-fifth anniversary, the senior officers of the paras decided that the war was now far away and the time had come to abandon this formal ceremony. They had a meeting with the Dutch people who were responsible for organizing that end of the reunion and informed them of their decision. When they heard this, the Dutch vehemently disagreed and some of them broke down and cried.

'It must go on,' they insisted. 'You must come back every year. Nobody must ever forget Arnhem.'

It was nine-thirty a.m. on Tuesday 21 September 1976 when I delivered my immortal line to the great lord. The interior of Kate's house was littered with bodies. The dead and the dying. I sat at the top of the stairs and on Sir Richard's 'Action', I looked down at my shattered legs and declared, 'My boots are full of blood.' Although Laurence was sympathetic to the line, I could see in his eyes that my delivery had not rung true. I was not helped by the fact that the entire crew were trying to distract me. Assembled behind Dickie they offered obscene gestures and stifled laughter. By take three, four and five, the nerves had set in. It is not easy to deliver an isolated line, far better to get 'a run at it', with some lengthy dialogue.

'My boots are full of blood', was now sounding like Tommy Cooper. 'Boots, blood, full of, just like that!' Lord Olivier's expression tightened, biting his lip. Under his breath, he reminded me he had to be back in Manchester to rehearse Cat On a Hot Tin Roof.

Outside the war was raging. The incessant gunfire and shelling was deafening. I could hear ambulances and jeeps. Stretcher after stretcher, carrying the wounded, appeared through the acrid smoke.

How surreal was this? Just our film crew stuck on a staircase in a house in Holland made of plastic and plywood, in the presence of a lord directed by a knight.

It was take fifty-two when Laurence finally blew a gasket. 'For fuck's sake, David, get the fucking line out!'

But I had gone. A gibbering wreck. I felt as though I was in *Apocalypse Now*, all those mad leering faces laughing at me, tripping on LSD.

I had drifted off to the stirring, swirling strains of Wagner's 'Ride of the Valkyrie'; a swarm of US Army choppers clattered out of the rising sun and over the sparkling South China Sea to strafe a ramshackle fishing village known to be harbouring Viet Cong guer-rillas, wide-eyed dope heads, wild sprawling madness of the first rock 'n' roll war. I could hear voices coming out of the mist. I was in the middle of the battle, the bravura and foolhardiness of combat fighter jets screeching overhead, explosions scorching swathes of jungle, but it wasn't Marlon Brando's crazed Colonel Kurtz bawling at me, it was Lord Olivier . . . It was not Director Francis Ford Coppola inducing a sort of madness, it was Sir Richard Attenborough. I was awoken from my reverie.

My voice had now reached an insane high pitch, prompting Dickie to cut, walk towards me and declare, 'Look David, if I'd wanted Norman Wisdom for this part, I'd have asked him!'

No Man's Land

Beneath the silent stars a breath of ice washes moon-pale grass. To harbour peace while waiting life is held in winter's sleep. To awake to that wonderful muffled hush that descends in the night, casting an unearthly super real glow from behind your curtains. The sheer unadulterated joy it would bring to my children who have never seen snow. Ask any child at Christmas for their wish and they will offer the heartbreaking and soulful felt response, 'Let it snow,' and 'Can we meet Santa Claus?' which is certainly one in the eye for every toy manufacturer who brainwashes them with super cyborg dollies, laptops, play stations and Harry Potters.

But my kids are in Durban, sweating in the humidity with their mum probably flat out on surfboards fighting off the sharks.

When I was a child we used to spend Christmas with my Uncle Bill on the moors of Yorkshire. He lived in a big mossy house on a frozen lake surrounded by snow-covered woods. We would give all our old toys to charity shops and then travel up the A1 from London in our yellow Ford Consul. We usually arrived in the company of a very friendly AA man who would be invited in for mince pies by Auntie Rita, who looked after us all. These mince pies were bought from the Hovis travelling van because the house was in the middle of nowhere and there were no shops and even though it had its own railway station, the trains no longer stopped there.

And in the morning we would sledge down the hill on to the frozen lake; when the ice cracked, it made a sound like a gunshot. There would be footprints of deer and foxes on the ice and sometimes marks that looked like the prints of the abominable snowman.

On Christmas Eve, people would arrive with snowflakes in their hair, bearing cake and carol books and fiddles. Late into the night, we would sing songs by candlelight and dance Yorkshire reels and tell stories of bygone Christmases when Uncle Bill's kilt caught fire and grandma Waffy got pissed on mulled wine.

And then it was time to go to midnight mass in the little church, where everyone had been christened, married and most of us would end up when . . . Anyway, my mum would always attempt the high notes in 'Hark The Herald', and get a bit giggly and a bit tearful and as we left, she would empty her purse into a box for starving children in Africa. We would end up pushing the Ford Consul up the last steep hill, while the stars above us had never seemed starrier. And life would suddenly all seem so clear and still and wonderful, as though the universe was holding its breath.

We would lie in our camp beds trying to stay awake to see Father Christmas, which was as likely as lassoing the moon. We would wake up to feel the weight of our pillowcases and open them to find tangerines and walnuts and a few precious things wrapped up in Christmas paper like a Hornby Dublo train set or a cricket bat.

In the morning we would open our presents by the tree decorated with candles and cotton wool. We only had one main present each and then a few little things and we'd all share the pleasure of each other's presents being opened. We would unwrap our presents quivering with anticipation and making a note for thank you letters.

Fifty-three years later times have changed. I'm banged up in the soup kitchens of the Seaman's Rest, fighting off the *Big Issue* sellers for a bowl of broth and a crust of bread. Then the shared joy of wearing an ill-fitting hat, pulling a cracker with a blind Spaniard with no teeth and watching Morecambe and Wise's Christmas Spectacular on TV. From my Tony Hancock mindset, I escape from railway cuttings, East Cheam to revisit memory lane. For the two weeks at Christmas, the whole country comes to a standstill. Companies are shut down. There's nobody to telephone. For me, it is like entering no man's land.

I return down the long and winding lane to West Hampstead with its higgledy-piggledy world of bedsits, dashed hopes and broken egos. It is the bewitching hour when I pull up outside my old house at number twenty-six Kingdon Road. I am drawn to it like an old friend. It is the house that Dave built and as I look up, filled with love, at its slightly faded superstructure, the memories come flooding back.

In 1971, as a record mogul of twenty-five, I was earning the princely sum of £100 per week. I was still living with my mum and sister in Golders Green. We existed happily in an airy top-floor flat above Rabbi Horowitz and his family. It was time to move out and make a killing in the property market. I refused to pay rent – rather invest in my own bricks and mortar, but where?

West End Lane was the yellow brick road, which swept me and my pals to the lofty fleshpots of Kensington and Knightsbridge. From the top of Finchley Road, through to St John's Wood and on to the West End. West Hampstead was the soft artistic underbelly nestled between haughty Hampstead and the vastly impersonal ambassadorial shrines of St John's Wood. It was a hotbed where students and actors, musicians and poets could afford to flourish. Everyone of consequence had started there at one time or other: actors Tom Conti and Emma Thompson, England cricketer Norman Cowans and old Luigi, the property magnate who ran the Charlotte Patisserie, which doubled as a hostel for nurses and au pairs.

One Sunday morning I drove down the lane exploring the side roads. There was an old 'For Sale' board outside number twenty-six Kingdon Road. I knocked on the door and was met by an Indian gentleman, who took me up to his flat. On one side of the room, a lady was breastfeeding her baby in the corner. On the other side were live chickens in a run made of wire. I couldn't pull up a chair to negotiate terms because there was no chair in the room.

'How much do you want?' I enquired.

'£5,000,' replied Mr Alan Rais, the owner.

'I'll give you £4,250.'

Mr Rais nodded, his wife beamed and the chickens crowed. The deal was done.

Three weeks later I moved in and set up my palace with utmost speed. Big leather chair where the chickens had roosted, another in the breastfeeding corner and my drum kit in the alcove. The bed was an all-purpose adventure playground, strong and springy. Now I needed some horizontal joggers to try out my furniture and fittings. West Hampstead, you couldn't go wrong. Between 'Kevin Costcutter's' open range and 'Shamrock' the dry cleaner's was the golden half mile. Swedish, French, West Indians, Japanese, birds of every denomination would pound the pavements on the way to the Tube station. Clutching A to Zs and looking lost, they were ripe for the pull.

Kazumi Yamashita (sounded like a motorbike) sashayed towards me in ridiculously teetering high heels. She wore a leather miniskirt under a tightly fitting coat. She had beautiful black hair, beautiful red lips, beautiful teeth, perfect pale complexion and a beauty that would last her into old age. The only trouble was, being Japanese, her command of English was somewhat limited.

'Where are you going?' I asked.

'Half past ten,' came the reply.

'What is your name?' I continued.

'Yes it looks like rain,' she agreed.

I tapped her on the bottom. She smiled and we were on our way to twenty-six Kingdon Road.

Kazumi had many Thai friends. She brought them around to my Temple of the West Hampstead Buddha, caught in the rays of the Siamese sun. I was fascinated by their passion for cleanliness, fastidiously soaping themselves from head to foot while all the time wrapped cocoon-like in their sarongs. A ritual not made easier by the confines of my tiny bathroom. Then to see them sit cross-legged on my Axminster, freshly showered, appreciating their golden skin far exceeding their country's finest silk. I discovered their unity between nudity and love. The Thai girl believes that the beauty of the body can only be seen within the context of romantic love. So consistent is she in that belief that the act of offering herself unclothed is to make love.

I was under the spell of a girl called Tui, but already I felt that the ecstasy had two notes of sadness in it: the knowledge that it could not last and that this particular rapture would never be repeated.

Tui stood before me stark naked. She tossed her hair and flexed her body, a lovely contained form, shapely and tanned amongst the greys and greens of my flat. She had the face of a full moon, her hair as crimson dark as a raincloud. Her complexion would have poured scorn on a jasmine. Her lips were like the flower of a pomegranate. Her neck was like that of a dove and her feet were as pretty as a lotus. She had magnificent eyes, large and black and glowing. Her lips glistened, glorious, bright and beautiful. Her cheeks were like dazzling jewels. Her waist was like that of a heavenly bird. There was no one in the world whose beauty could compare. Boy, if this was to be the life of a bachelor, I had struck gold in the Orient.

My Eastern experience with Kazumi continued for a year. Each Wednesday she'd come and stay with me wearing the most exotic outfits imaginable. She had an affection for rubber and leather, a penchant I told her was probably best to pursue within the confines of my knocking shop, not on the Jubilee Line with the rush-hour bowler hat brigade. She never divulged her profession or where she lived.

'Where do you live, Kazumi?' I enquired.

'Woodge,' she replied.

'What, St Johns Wood?'

'No! No!' She giggled like a geisha. 'I live near lots of men who shout something called, "Come on sweetheart, give us a flash," and "Get 'em off!"'

I discovered that my Japanese flower in fact lived in Woolwich next to the Arsenal. Each Wednesday the soldiers used to hang out of the windows to admire her outfits. Believe me, the one-piece all rubber with high-heel flippers caused quite a sensation in the barracks.

My flat was number three. The rest of the residents in Tension Terrace consisted of Sandy O'Rourke, a poofter accountant on top at number four, Mrs Noble, an elegant octogenarian, all regency chintz and Dresden china at number two, and the occasionally desirable Eva Jacobson, a Swedish nymphomaniac, alcoholic, in the basement. I can assure you, after a bottle of Portuguese Chianti from the Bohemian shop on the corner anybody looked like Marilyn Monroe.

Whenever my squad was depleted I used to venture to the Vikingman's Club in the basement for a bit of action amongst the candles and incense. A fatal mistake, as Eva would return the compliment by ripping her clothes off and lurching up my stairs to claw on my door when her third bottle of vodka had kicked in.

Directly across the street stood a German who wore a vest and shouted at me like a captain from his panzer, his feet seemingly being nailed to the floor in a twenty-four-hour vigil, the perfect Neighbour-hood Watch. Actor Bert Kwouk, who played Cato in Peter Sellers' Pink Panther films, lived at number thirty-two. Elizabeth, Dire Straits' shapely publicist, sunbathed naked on her roof garden next door. Herschel and Lloyd, the brass section from the wonderful band FBI, hung out in the corner house. Georgina, a star musician with the Royal Philharmonic Orchestra, operated from number nineteen, playing her cello with a wonderful touch, long into the afternoon.

And then there was the retired brigadier who was billeted at number eighteen amongst his medals and memories of fighting the Japanese in the Burma jungle. His strong dislike of Kazumi and my Eastern cousins was highlighted by the occasional military rant of 'Will the man spanking the Oriental please keep the noise down!'

Over the next twenty years, as the other flats in my house became available, I bought them up with great relish. To become a landlord was an edifying experience. I advertised for punters for free in the magnificent *Loot* Newspaper. Over the years I have signed up some memorable tenants. However, not all of them were suitable.

There was the lady who suffered from narcolepsy. In the middle of a sentence she would nod off. The twenty-five-year-old bachelor, sports jacket with leather patches and grey flannel trousers seemed perfect, until he asked me, 'When can I install my drums?'

The percussionist for the BBC Light Orchestra would certainly not have impressed my neighbours.

A couple of high-class hookers enquired about the basement flat.

'Dearie, do you mind if we install a red light over the front door?' enquired the ladies from Mayfair.

But my favourite tenants had to be Mike and Siobhan. By now I had moved up to the penthouse flat of number four. There, I could sit on my roof and survey the shenanigans of NW6. Mike Pretious worked for Burton's the tailors. He was a buyer and a first-class bloke who always paid his rent on time. Tall and angular, he possessed a slightly stooped posture with an engaging smile and a Piscean's sharp sense for observation humour. He was also a true Sporting Sam who fanatically studied the form and knew everything there was to know about horseracing.

Mike lived in my old flat, number three, with its large double lounge, double bedroom, bathroom and split-level kitchen. One day he asked me if he could sublet his flat, letting out the large lounge. No problem. We both advertised for the ideal tenant. Siobhan sold Creda cookers. She was half Irish, voluptuous with a robust sense of fun, great heart and overall sexy demeanour. Cohabiting meant that Mike would have to share the bathroom and squat on the khazi surrounded by knickers and tights drying on a line over the sink.

Although they lived in their respective kennels they met in the kitchen to share meals and chew the fat. After three months of living in the same flat, Mike, the eternal bachelor, asked Siobhan to marry him. So the tipster and his lady from Tipperary left to set up their own life.

Love continued to spring eternal in Kingdon Towers. There was the beautiful Austrian countess whom I had encountered when her leather coat had got stuck in the lavatory door at a party in Maida Vale. Our sometimes torrid love affair lasted for three years. She gave me a solid gold shamrock embedded with a diamond. She also presented me with a golden horse, which she smartly reclaimed when our love dwindled.

I met Celia whilst walking down Sumatra Road. We sat on a wall, drank champagne and lived life as one for eighteen months.

Eric Clapton was a regular visitor. He always sat in his favourite armchair. To this day 'the E.C. sofa' still sits proudly in flat number four. Barry and Linda Gibb called in from time to time and his brother Robin visited with the milkman, bringing me two pints from the Kilburn dairy. It amused him no end that my fridge was bare save for a piece of cheese, a year past its sell-by date. The mice used to march out in protest and much to the consternation of my female friends my football boots remained safely in the oven. The entire Aussie cricket team used to troop up to my room at the top to drink my beer and leave a signed shirt.

But now it's Christmas 2005 . . . People don't hang out any more. They're buried in their streamlined world of IKEA and laptops. I look up at my old friend, twenty-six Kingdon Road, and want to embrace all the memories of those I loved and lost between its walls before returning to my pals at the soup kitchen in no man's land, somewhere between nowhere and goodbye.

Back to the Bridge – in Search of Dickie

It's early Sunday morning. Richmond Green looks resplendent ringed by Victoriana and fifteen varieties of trees, which sway gently in the breeze. All week the whisper of anticipation has held the town in rapture. The Bunburys are coming to do battle with the mayor of Richmond's Invitation XI, raising funds for the Shooting Star Hospice. Who would be playing? Bremner, Theakston, Frank Skinner, Mark Ramprakash, 'J.B.' and 'Benno', the Lions from Surrey CCC, Michael Brown and Jimmy Bruce the Hampshire Quickie.

Rumours of Billy Connolly gracing the crease are rife. The organ grinds out some Beatles tunes and the monkey in an embroidered waistcoat dances in a frenetic style. Elderly ladies with arthritic hands and cornflower-blue eyes erect stalls, going about their business with passion and a beating heart, as the solitary man leans on his bicycle, surveying the scene, absorbing the grandeur and the prospect of the Battle Royal, two o'clock start.

As the publican of the Cricketers opens his doors, sunshine glinting off the brass taps, fit men emerge through the trees, pulling along kit bags covered in sponsors' logos. They are the professionals who once again will be giving up one of their free days to play for the Bunburys. They live in the washing machine of the game, spinning non-stop, one day, four day, twenty–twenty, C and G, one-day internationals, Test matches, free day, Bunburys, the constant cycle of cricket, and yet five of them will squeeze into a motor and drive 250 miles each way to bring their magic to our Bunbury games, stamping their class as professionals on the day, entertaining the crowds with dazzling dexterity and high-powered performance, doing the job and leaving with a 'No problem, Loon, give us a call any time'.

I park my Saab, bursting with kit, behind the beer tent and go in search of Lord Attenborough. He lives just off the green on the corner of the square. I had to go and find him. I was drawn to Beaver

Lodge, which stood dark and ivy-clad. I rang the front doorbell. There was no reply. I thought about Dickie. He wanted to act and, if you want to act, the best thing you can do is win a scholarship to RADA. Of course he did precisely that.

His mother took him down to London, which in 1941 was a less than pleasant place to be, being visited nightly by the Luftwaffe but, undaunted, her seventeen-year-old son auditioned successfully and was awarded the Leverhulme scholarship at £2.50 a week. His luck continued. When he was nineteen he got the part as the frightened stoker in David Lean's film *In Which We Serve* and when he arrived on the set, a familiar face greeted him with the words, 'You won't know me; I'm Noël Coward. You, of course, are Richard Attenborough.'

In 1968 he directed *Oh! What a Lovely War* at the end of Brighton Pier. Paradoxically, it was where he made his name as the treacherous Pinkie in *Brighton Rock*. He made a dramatic exit from the film, over the railings and into the sea. He was desperate to get the role even though he knew he didn't look right. He had a round, cherubic face and the character had to look pinched. He achieved the look by dieting and exercise, evidence of the tenacity and ambition of a man who gets what he wants. In a surprisingly short time, Dickie had become a film star. 1,500 people belonged to his fan club, which he felt obliged to close down as it was occupying too much of his time. He posed among starlets and was feted at fetes.

After a two-year stint in the *Mousetrap* he partnered Bryan Forbes in producing films of better intent than those that were generally made at the British studios. Films like *The Angry Silence* and *The L-Shaped Room*. He expanded his horizons in America and played opposite Steve McQueen in *The Sand Pebbles* and *The Great Escape*.

After snaffling up the Oscars for his direction of *Gandhi*, in 1976, as I have described, he reached the pinnacle of his career by directing Dave 'the Loon' English in *A Bridge Too Far*, who was by now creeping through the hedgerows to the tradesman's entrance of Beaver Lodge.

I peered inside. The kitchen was still. I rang the bell once, twice.

Inside a silhouette stirred, skirting the scullery. A pyjamaed figure was staring at me from the shadows, somewhat bemused. It was Dickie. The good lord came to the window of the door, rubbing his eyes and peering at me. 'Good God, it's David English.'

'That's right, sir.' I smiled, standing to attention and saluting. 'David English reporting for duty.' We stood in the kitchen and in the half-light embraced the moment like two reuniting old soldiers. 'We're playing cricket on the green.' I said.

'I know you are,' smiled Dickie. 'I'll be over this afternoon.'

Sure enough at 4 p.m. when the game was at fever pitch he appeared, small and dapper, wearing a blazer, cravat, grey flannels and a pair of loafers. He walked towards me parting the crowd rather like Gandhi in his film. For three hours he talked to everyone, still anxious to please, signing autographs, sitting toddlers on his knee, chatting to the mayor and enriching the whole occasion with his very special charm.

I asked him if he had any acting jobs for an old out-of-work cricketer. 'Dickie, how about a sequel, *A Bridge A Bit Further?*'

He roared with laughter in that true Attenborough way.

'Dickie, do you remember you gave me compassionate leave from the Bridge?'

1976 and Holland sweltered in the hottest summer in one hundred years. Running around in those heavy-duty paratrooper uniforms killing Germans every day certainly took its toll. I had done two months on the film, taking part in most of the action sequences, particularly leading the charges down those lonely Dyke roads. As 'the cricketer' on the film, I was given the job of hurling the hand grenades whenever necessary, in any of the hairy battle scenes.

I went to see my director. He was in his production office planning the next day's set-ups.

'Sir Richard, is there any chance of returning to Blighty for a spot of leave?'

Dickie looked up from his map. 'Don't tell me, David; England are playing the West Indies at Lords?'

'Blimey,' I thought, 'am I that transparent?'

'I will arrange for a car to take you to Schiphol Airport tomorrow morning. Go and enjoy your cricket and when you return I have a very special part awaiting you.'

What a great man. I flew home to England to watch David Steele take on Clive Lloyd and his mighty West Indians. Ten days later when I returned to the Bridge, Dickie gave me my wonderful part acting opposite Sir Laurence Olivier.

Back on Richmond Green I sat with Dickie, brothers in arms, watching the game.

'Are you happy, David?' he enquired. I told him how working on *A Bridge Too Far* had changed my life. How the film had acknowledged all the gallantry, all the selflessness, the comradeship and the instantaneous bravery that was involved in the Battle of Arnhem. It showed the stupidities, the misjudgements, the egotisms, the jealousies, the pressures and the powers that are brought to bear, which don't really relate to that battle, let alone the war, but are of a political nature. I hoped that when people left the cinema there was no question whatsoever that anybody could believe there was anything glamorous in war.

That's why I started the Bunburys, to give the kids something as beautiful as cricket – the greatest of all sports, the one in which the values and ideals of sportsmanship achieve their highest expression. Nothing in my own schooldays gave me half the pleasure of playing cricket. The game offered an escape from the servitude of the classroom into a whole of light and colour and adventure. How enthusiastically I rubbed my cricket bat with linseed oil at the start of spring. How proudly I pulled on my white flannels. How anxiously I scanned the horizon for the rainclouds that would wash out the big match.

In the simple game of bat and ball, which I learnt in the street, the playground and on the school playing field, I found an enduring metaphor for life itself. Just as in acting Dickie had learned the virtue of teamwork, of courtesy towards opponents, of being stoical in defeat and gracious in victory most of all, in cricket you learn respect.

At seven-thirty p.m. the shadows had lengthened, the game was won and the day was done. One final embrace of my pal Sir Richard. 'David, thank you for coming to get me,' he smiled. 'See you soon.' And with that, he turned and disappeared through the trees, back to the sanctuary of that Queen Anne house on the corner of the green.

PART TWO

Bring on the Bunburys

Welcome to the World-Famous Bunburys

One year a funny thing happened on the way to a charity match for Warwickshire's Trevor Penney.

We were playing at Blossomfield CC and I had got well and truly lost in the maze of roads surrounding Birmingham.

When you're lost the best person to ask is a taxi driver.

'Blossomfield CC?' I asked the West Indian cab driver.

'No mate, you're miles away,' replied the cabby, 'follow me and I'll put you right.'

We must have gone everywhere. Sutton Coldfield, Solihull, West Brom, through Balsall Heath and Dudley.

I then spotted a police car parked by the side of a bombsite. 'Perfect,' I thought, 'ask the Old Bill.'

I got out of my vehicle and climbed over some rubble, but was stopped instantly in my tracks by a scene from a Hollywood film. A squad of armed police officers had four rough-looking geezers up against a wall. It could have been a moment from *Get Carter*. Machine guns stuck in their backs, the men were being searched, arms and legs splayed against the wall.

The middle of a drugs bust was probably not the best time to ask for directions but I picked my moment anyway.

'Excuse me lads, do you know the way to Blossomfield CC?'

'F—k off mate,' snarled the sergeant, 'can't you see we're busy, these boys are going down for ten.'

'But it's an important cricket game,' I continued undeterred.

'Who's it for?' bawled the copper without relaxing his full NYPD SWAT arrest mode.

'Trevor Penney.'

'Old Trev,' said the sergeant, pulling away from the villains with a huge smile on his face, 'one of Warwickshire's finest, why didn't you say so. Here Len, you take over while I take Mr Bunbury to Blossomfield.'

Leaving the 'Usual Suspects' pinned up against the wall the policeman led me to Blossomfield CC in his car, blue light flashing and siren wailing.

Beefy Botham Takes the Trunk Road to the Bunbury Festival

IAN BOTHAM

When Dave published his highly successful *Bunbury Tales* I was proud to be included in them as one of the main characters – Ian Buntham. Unfortunately though, one of his other major successes, the Bunbury Cricket Festival, hadn't been initiated when I was young and therefore I wasn't privileged to take part in that event. I did have a trial for an England Schoolboys X_1 but didn't make the squad as I was evidently judged not good enough. I was, I confess, a bit put out by this lack of faith in me by the selectors but it did have the effect of making me all the more determined to succeed.

David English and I go back a long time together. I met him when I was a raw recruit on the Lord's ground staff. We have shared many an adventure, one or two of which *can* be recounted. David would be the first to agree that where there's a camera he longs to be. On one of my walks to raise money for Leukaemia Research he accompanied me across the Alps – I wish I could say step-for-step!

At the beginning of each day there would be D. English esq. among the starting line-up, which also included Eric Clapton, smiling at the cameras. And at the end of a gruelling 25 miles or so there he would be again swinging jauntily towards the finishing line as I hobbled wearily onwards. It took me a few days to suss out the fact that after a mile or so he would drop back and hitch a lift, for a while appearing by my side occasionally to crack a joke or two, then drop out of sight again to await a further lift to the finishing area where he would lurk in the crowds and join the weary walkers just in time for the TV cameras at the end of the day. I judged this to be 'not quite cricket' and bided my time.

On the last day we entered Turin preceded by two magnificent elephants. I suggested it would look great if Dave rode on one of these. It was quite a long way through the streets of Turin to the great square. Dave, mounted high on the front elephant, enthusiastically waved to the crowd but the waving soon faltered and a rather strained expression appeared on his face. Not being used to riding elephants he hadn't chosen the best place to sit and was astride the rock-like ridge of the elephant's backbone, bouncing up and down at each ponderous step. Need I say more?

On a more serious note, Dave has supported me on most of my fundraising events for Leukaemia Research and has kept up our spirits by his cheerfulness and unfailing source of jokes and anecdotes. I wish him well; and success to all the aspiring young cricketers in this year's Bunbury Festival.

For Brother 'D'

SIR VIV RICHARDS

I constantly enjoy the camaraderie of meeting up, on the special fundraising Bunbury match days, with David, many notable players, celebrities, and all the willing supporters. It is very reassuring to know that, apart from raising much needed charity monies, so many young and aspiring players benefit from our aching limbs, 'enjoyment and anticipation' on such match days!

As you may be aware I am a man of few words and during my playing career, fortunately, my bat did most of the talking. I was never able to 'get a word in edgeways' when in the company of David English, but there again, he did say it all for us!

Well done to David and the Bunburys for all their many worthy fundraising successes and it has been a pleasure to be invited all these years – my support is always there for you.

The Bunbury Spirit of Cricket

P.C.J. SHELDON
(Chief Executive, Surrey County Cricket Club)

We read a lot these days about the 'Spirit of Cricket'. And rightly so. There can surely be no cricketing institution that embodies this spirit more than the Bunburys. On and off the field, the Bunburys represent all the good things about this wonderful game of ours. They make the game inclusive, not elitist; they make the game competitive but lots of fun; they bring broad grins to those who watch and the very biggest of smiles to those who benefit from all the money raised through their exploits. A great formula that works.

But, however good the formula, it could not work or continue to thrive without dynamic leadership. I first met David English in 1994, when he approached me to run a game at the Oval to recognise the fiftieth anniversary of the D-Day Landings. Although I often rued my decision to agree to stage the game, it gave me a real insight into the unique qualities of this extraordinary individual, who is larger than life; who passionately believes anything is achievable; who never takes no for an answer; and whose energy and belief in what he does is indefatigable. He is everyone's (or almost everyone's!) friend. I am pleased to count myself as one of them.

As we move in to the celebrations for the twentieth anniversary of the Bunburys, it gives us a marvellous opportunity to double our efforts to support this great cause. And I suspect the now venerable doctor is already planning the next twenty years! Let's hope all of us privileged to be part of the Bunbury family can emulate some of the 'English' enthusiasm.

Camaraderie and Humiliation

FRANK SKINNER

It was a poor delivery. It pitched halfway down the strip and bounced twice before it reached me. I had danced down the wicket to meet it, like a younger man at a railway station, bounding towards his returning lover. But she daintily evaded my welcome and skipped past me. I froze, deciding not to turn; feeling there was no need to trouble my eyes when my ears would tell me all I needed to know. I just looked at the bowler and waited. I could hear the distant hum of traffic, a clink of glasses in the pavilion. My eye caught that of an opposing fielder in a sequinned beret. He had entertained the crowds, the players and, indeed, himself all afternoon with his Frank Spencer impression. And I mean *all* afternoon. Don't get me wrong, it was good, uncannily accurate, funny even, but most of all it was long. I never thought I'd say this of a Frank Spencer impression, but it was positively Wagnerian. Anyway, I caught his eye (the only thing I caught all season) and he looked at me with a sense of profound pity, as if my mistimed sweep encapsulated all mankind's thwarted dreams, all our shortfalls and should-have-beens. It was almost as if he was, for that moment, truly Frank Spencer, a man who, having spent his life hanging from a double-decker bus on roller-skates and crashing through Mothercare in a supermarket trolley, now stood by, deeply moved, as another simple man crashed to humiliating failure.

Then I heard it – the sound of leather against wood; a sound I had hoped to create with ball against bat was now being created, a few yards behind me, with ball against stumps. A great cry went up. I counted ten 'Owzat's and one 'Ooo! Betty'. I was out. Oh, yes, one other thing. The bowler was eighty-six years old. Did I mention that? As I marched, bat under arm, back towards the utterly insincere 'Hard Luck's of my fellow Bunburys, an opposition player said, 'What a bowler! He'll be in the Ashes next year.'

'Ugh!' I replied. 'He'll probably be in the urn.' It was unsporting and unkind but, hey, I was in shock.

Two hours later, in the bar listening to Mark Butcher's rock band, I was already claiming to be the victim of exaggeration and that the bowler was, in fact, only eighty-five.

Thus ended my first season with Team Bunbury, where camaraderie and humiliation walk hand in hand.

The Bunbury Cricket Club

JEFFREY ARCHER

Bunbury was of course a figment of Oscar Wilde's imagination. The Bunbury Cricket Club, on the other hand, is a reality, but only because of one man, David English.

Over the past twenty years David has shown all the qualities needed to fund, organise and run such an outrageous club. He's mad. But it takes a particular brand of madness that turns into an obsession, and then ends up benefiting so many other people's lives.

David has every right to be immensely proud of raising over nine million pounds for different charities during the past twenty years, while at the same time skippering an XI that continues to search desperately for teams they can beat.

But it is not his team or his fundraising ability that he can be most proud of, but his service to the game of cricket, for which he was awarded an MBE. If you look at the great players in the past and present English squad, so many of them were nurtured, developed and came to fruition thanks to Bunbury's endeavours. Names such as Vaughan, Flintoff and Trescothick spring to mind, and heaven knows how many more youngsters are waiting impatiently in the wings.

Let us therefore raise a glass, or a tankard, to the Bunbury Cricket Club and to its founder, Dr David English MBE.

The Incredible Bunburys

JOHN INVERDALE

There are some rock stars you can't really see playing cricket. The guys from ZZ Top for example, unless it was in an attempt to re-create the era of W. G. Grace. Then there's Meatloaf. Have they invented a pair of whites that would fit him? And what about Eminem? You'd probably pay good money to hear him appeal for an lbw decision . . . 'How was that you mother— son of a— umpire.' I mention this because even though all of the above, and many more, have to the best of my knowledge never adjusted their boxes and walked out to bat on a crisp English June morn, if there's anyone around who could persuade them to do so, it would be David English. Since that famous day 20 years ago at Ripley in Surrey, when the first Bunbury match took place, David has managed to cajole at various times the likes of the Bee Gees, Eric Clapton, Phil Collins, Bill Wyman, David Essex, Ringo, George Harrison and Elton John to take the field alongside people who really can play the game, from Richards, Botham, Warne, to Vaughan, Lara, Flintoff and dozens of others. And I confess that while the real cricketing aficionado would crave a scorebook entry that read 'c Botham b

Warne' as the ultimate accolade, as a huge Bee Gees fan, I dream of hearing Richie Benaud summarising an innings at close of play, and including the following: 'Inverdale st Gibb R bowled Gibb B 127.'

The Bunburys are now a cricketing institution, and an institution that most of us would be happy to live in. But never mind the fact that almost every England cricketer for the past two decades has played in a Bunbury Festival; and never mind that as a way of encouraging the playing of the sport and the raising of standards, it's done the sport an almost unparalleled service. Just consider the fact that in those two decades, more than £9,000.000 (it always looks better with the noughts) has been raised for children's charities and for cricket through a whole array of Bunbury matches and functions, and you realise that this is a very special organisation. We all have ideas but very few of them ever progress much beyond that. David English had a dream 20 years ago, which he has made into the most marvellous reality. All you need to say to people who don't know much about the Bunburys is that Bill Wyman took the only ever-televised hat trick at the Oval while playing for them. 'I see,' they will say, in a Winnie the Pooh kind of a way, not seeing at all. In that curious world where showbiz meets sport and sport meets showbiz, the Bunburys occupy a unique position – a place where hip-hop meets long-hop over a cucumber sandwich. But there is still so much more to achieve – so many more young cricketers to develop into England players. And there is still that dream xi that English has so far patently failed to get on to the field of play: Timberlake, Greenidge, McCartney, Lara, Bono, Flintoff, Hucknall (wkt), Warne, Williams R, McGrath, Stewart R. He's clearly not trying hard enough. Maybe sometime in the next 20 years . . .

Bunbury Debut at Last

DARREN MADDY
(Leicestershire CCC)

I always heard that David English was a bit mad but didn't quite realise to what extent until I got the chance to meet this legendary man.

It was during the tour to South Africa in 1999/2000 that I finally met him at the Wanderers Stadium during a practice session. He was keeping an eye on all his boys when I was finally introduced and he told me that he remembered me playing at an ESCA (Bunbury) Festival when I was 15. I tried to explain that I hadn't played in that tournament and instead tried to impress him with my musical knowledge (which was non-existent at that stage) hoping that would be enough to finally secure me an invite to play a Bunbury game.

Five years later and at the tender age of 31, I got that invite and made my debut in his team. Having missed out at playing in that festival all those years ago I relished the chance to play and become a Bunbury. Still 'the Loon' insisted that he could remember me playing when I was a young lad.

Well I'm sorry to say that it wasn't me, and having missed out at representing the Midlands and England Schools when I was a kid, it was probably the incentive I needed to knuckle down and work harder. I'm sure that looking back now it was a good thing and without that knock-back I wouldn't be writing this article for you today.

My experience in your team is a memorable and a very enjoyable one. The day was exactly what I was hoping for and I was extremely proud to wear the Bunbury cap. More importantly, you helped put the fun back into the game, which I believe is a vital ingredient to the success of a county cricketer.

I'm looking forward to playing in many more games in the future and I just hope that I won't have to wait another five years for my next invite!

You are 'the original Loon' and I'm glad that our paths finally crossed.

Tony Blair

10 Downing Street
London SW1A 2AA

Once again, I'm delighted to be able to lend my support to the Bunbury English Schools Cricket Festival. This year, the festival has reached a milestone, as it is the 20th festival to have been staged. Everyone involved with the event can be rightly proud of this achievement.

I would like to pay tribute to the excellent work the festival continues to do in raising funds for the English Schools Cricket Association and other very important national and international charities. Cricket is a great uniting force and I hope England's historic Ashes series victory this summer will encourage many more young people to participate in the sport.

The festival also continues to provide a golden opportunity for young cricketers to show their talents. I was very interested to learn that many of the England's victorious Ashes squad have participated in the Bunbury Festival. I hope this will inspire all of the youngsters involved this year to believe that they can take their first step towards representing England in the future.

I wish everyone involved with the festival an enjoyable and successful few days.

My Bunbury Debut

GRAHAM GOOCH
(Essex CCC and England)

Playing cricket with ten others is sometimes quite nerve-racking, but turning out with 24 on your side is particularly frightening.

This is how I made my Bunbury XI debut at the Metropolitan Police ground, Imber Court, 31 August 2003, under the watchful eye of the skipper and top Bunbury David English, and his multitude of celebs.

He commanded me to bat at four, a tall order considering I hadn't picked up the willow for a few years. As I strode to the wicket I crossed Robin Smith, the out-going batsman, an ex-England team-mate and ferocious hitter of a cricket ball. I thought to myself, would I be able to hit the ball hard enough to call 'Wait!'?

I arrived at the crease, asked for my guard, was it one or two, it had been such a long time. I settled on one, and looked up to face the bowler. He was a giant Metropolitan Policeman, all of 6'5", looking mean and nasty and obviously scenting the scalp of another old has-been! After playing and missing at my first ball, he stood in the middle of the pitch and gestured the ball towards me, saying, 'Here it is, it's red and it's round'. I thought 'OK'. Anyway, next ball he pitched it up and I launched the kitchen sink at it. Fortunately it cleared mid-off and found safe ground in the tennis courts 100 yards away. As he followed through, I felt quite proud of myself, he stopped right next to me and I couldn't resist the taunt, 'You know what it looks like, why don't you go and fetch it?'

I enjoyed my brief spell back in the middle courtesy of the Bunburys; it was an honour to be out there with all of David's other celebrities and supporters. Fielding with 24 players is somewhat easier than I remember with 11 and it was a thoroughly enjoyable experience.

David and his Bunbury XI raise millions of pounds for good causes and this day was no different. A substantial sum was given to the Milly Dowler Memorial Fund, a very worthy cause.

Thanks Dave for the opportunity, put me down for the number four slot again!

English Puts Alec in a Stew

ALEC STEWART
Surrey CCC and England

Having had a long tour of Zimbabwe and New Zealand, the last thing you want welcoming you home is contact from a certain David English! The fact that he is asking for an article for his book quickly softens the blow, especially as it's for such a good cause. The only problem that then arises is the choice I am given for the subject to write on – England's winter tour or David English claiming the wicket of Alec Stewart in a benefit game in 2001! I mean what a choice! A few words on the tour: there is still room for improvement, which I can assure you all the players are working on.

As the above couple of lines do not really make a great article, the 'David English school of bowling' had better get a mention!

So that everyone is aware of the importance of this unforgettable piece of bowling, it took place at the famous Test ground known as the Fosters Oval. With a ground capacity of 16,000 I would estimate that there were nearly 15,983 empty seats to witness the occasion. For those of you who can remember the ball that Shane Warne bowled out Mike Gatting with at Old Trafford, which is often referred to as 'the ball of the century', this delivery from D. K. (after Lillee) English was just as good – or so he'll tell you! I've played a few games at the Fosters Oval in my career to date, and have faced some truly great bowlers, including Richard Hadlee, Malcolm Marshall, Curtly Ambrose and Waqar Younis to name a few, but having

True love with my missus Robyn, 2000.

Amy Rose English, aged 11,
Edgegrove School.

David English Junior, aged 10,
Edgegrove School.

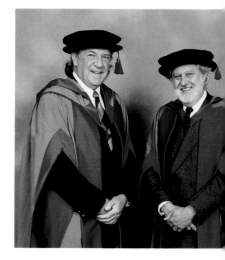

Our MBE day at the Palace, 2003.

With Lord Putnam receiving an honourary doctorate from Middlesex University, 2003.

The Loon meets her Majesty, 2003.

Father and daughter, Amy Rose.

Chloe Avalon – a little angel
from heaven.

Esther from Bordeaux.

In the office at work and play, 2005.

Opposite top.
Lamb and Beef in search of the pink trombone, 1999.

Opposite bottom.
With Frankie and Viv at the Oval 2003.

Bremner and the Bunburys at Blenheim, 2005 – he kills me every time!

Opposite.
E.C. and 'Arf' at Ripley, 2003.

On top of the world
the England Bunbury l
after winning the Ash
Trafalgar Square, 200
the Loon is top right

Staggering, with Fred
Flintoff, in Budapest, 2

to face David English on a 'flat Oval wicket' in a Benefit Game is something I hadn't encountered before, especially as he was off his long run bowling at 'genuine medium very slow'! Having survived an over and a half from the demon bowler I was beginning to feel a little confident until I had to cope with this 'brute of a ball'. It pitched five inches outside leg stump, hit the seam and then went straight past my immaculate forward defensive shot and knocked out my off-stump – the most unplayable ball I have ever faced.

As I slowly marched back to the pavilion in a state of shock, one memory, which will stay with me for a long time, was the look of total ecstasy on the face of the bowler!

David, I hope this article is what you wanted – you're a great bloke, a great entertainer and most definitely a great bowler!

Please support the Bunburys who do so much for cricket and worthwhile causes.

A Heart of Solid Gold

ERIC CLAPTON

I had such a great time at David English's birthday party last year (2003), seeing old friends and cricketing cronies, that I decided I would like to revisit that part of my past. I was also touched by how much love was expressed towards him by his friends and colleagues. We all know (those of us who have had reason to find out) what a royal pain in the arse he can be, but underneath all that noise and chaos, I know there beats a heart of solid gold. So it was that, having observed how dejected and morose he looked at the end of that particular evening, I decided to take action, and proposed we play one more game together, for old times' sake (what have I done?).

The game would be played in Ripley, where the first ECXI game was played in 1987, between David and his Bunbury Team and me and some sort of reconstituted ECXI. God knows who will show up and how it will turn out, and to be honest, I'm dreading it with every ounce of my being. But I think when it's all over, in years to come, I'll be able to look back at it all with some sort of satisfaction, at least for having kept my word, when actually I would much rather be hiding in the pavilion, or on a beach somewhere 3,000 miles away.

Whatever happens, I know we'll have fun and a lot of laughs, and he'll be in his element, I just hope and pray I don't break any fingers.

I would like to thank all those who have given their time, support and energy to this event, especially Ivor Powell and Guy Pullen, and most of all David English, for making me wish I could actually play this game of cricket . . .

A Personal Commentary

RORY BREMNER

It's not every day you get to see top-class cricket entertaining the crowd in a relaxed style full of fun and incident.

But you may be fairly certain that during any Bunbury's fixture at least two or more of the following will happen.

1. David English will mistime a drive and shout 'bollocks', loudly.
2. Someone will ask where Eric Clapton is.
3. Someone will ask who Joe Cuby is.
4. Bill Wyman will bowl with a ball in one hand, a fag in the other.
5. Someone will say 'I didn't know Bill Wyman could bowl.'
6. Someone else will answer, 'He can't.'
7. David English will tell a joke. If you laugh, he will carry on for forty minutes.

8. If you don't, he will carry on for an hour and a half.
9. Rory will mistake Gary Mason for Syd Lawrence.
10. Joe Cuby will come on to bowl. He will combine the style of Paul Adams with the bowling skills of Thora Hird. At least two batsmen will get out needlessly through a combination of complacency, poor shot selection or helpless laughter.
11. Someone will try to impersonate the Test match special team. This may feature Tony Blair, Nelson Mandela, Victor Meldrew and Ian McGaskill.
12. A television celebrity will be clean-bowled. After a brief discussion lasting three minutes, no ball will be called, the batsman will be reinstated and the bowler taken off for trying too hard, the celebrity will then either be out next ball or scratch around for seven hours scoring 2.
13. A Test player will be bowled by
    • David English
    • Joe Cuby
    • One of the teletubbies.

One thing is sure, the players will have turned out for no other reason than to have a fun game of cricket and raise some money for charity. The fact that David English has not been off their phone all week and has kidnapped their children is neither here nor there.

Enjoy the day!

Is He W.G. in Disguise!!!

GERAINT JONES
(Kent CCC and England)

The first encounter I had with Mr English will be an everlasting memory of mine. This meeting happened during my first season of first-class cricket in 2003, which also coincided with Mark Ealham's benefit year, and it was at one of Ealy's functions that Dave's and my paths crossed.

Ealy had organised a cricket match at the school where his dad Allan teaches and as we had some time off a few of the boys offered (were told) to play in the game against a Bunbury eleven. I knew of the Bunbury organisation but up until then had not participated in any of their events. I had heard Rob Key and the lads in the Kent dressing room talking about this madman named English who was in charge of the Bunbury brigade. With the start of the day being fairly hectic and my timekeeping not helping things, I walked up to the pavilion, spotted Ealy and was promptly told the toss was taking place, with the girl in the bunny suit in charge, but not to worry as we were fielding first! A quick change, a glance at our furry-eared friend striding off the pitch and the game was under way. Being a gentle affair, I had been told previously by Ealy that my keeping was not required, and he had lined someone else up so I was left prowling at cover point. The game was progressing well with my side taking a few wickets and the oppo scoring their share of runs. It was after one of these wickets that in our customary huddle someone muttered in a hushed voice, 'It's English, lads look after him!' Look after him? What are they on about? Keysie was on my side and fielding near by so I quickly sided up to him to enquire exactly what 'go easy on him' actually meant. With his cheeky grin all I managed to get was 'just watch'. After the third time the stumps were demolished only to be quickly followed by the umpire's shout of 'no ball' I started to get the message, and that famous line 'they have come to watch me bat son, not you bowl' sounded in my head! Unfortunately Dave was yet to get off the mark so my guess was that it may continue until at least a single was snatched somewhere. That single very nearly happened the following ball when he got everything together and squirted one my way in the cover direction. With some quick thinking required to somehow get Dave up the other end I made my way towards the ball. Any further thought was taken away when out the corner of my eye I noticed Keysie hurtling in my direction. The next thing I knew Rob had performed one of the best sliding tackles I have ever witnessed and playing the ball and not the man luckily he had booted the cricket ball 60 yards towards the boundary thus English was off the mark. It had worked. Dave was scampering up the wicket, but that then left Keysie on the ground grinning away at me! It then clicked that I now had to go and fetch the ball! Who was this man I had yet to meet?

Since that day I have had the chance to meet David again and get to understand the huge amount of effort he has put into Bunbury cricket and the positive influence it has had on English cricket. You only have to look at the current Test and one-day team, then go through the record books, to realise that nearly everyone was first noticed performing great deeds at the Bunbury under-15 carnival. Had I not been on the other side of the world in my youth I too would have hoped to have been influenced by the Bunbury spirit from an early age.

So thanks Dave for all you have done for cricket in this country, it has made a huge difference. Keep up the great work.

Dagnall's Diaries ... Aged 28½

CHARLES DAGNALL
Warwickshire CCC

'Dave this is Charlie Dagnall. He plays for Warwickshire.'

'Charlie boy!!! Great to see you, brilliant, this is Brian Close, Lloyd Honeyghan, Dave Smith, Frazer Hines, Jimmy Adams and you'll meet the rest later, anyway do you bat, course you do, you can open with Shaky, they've got a West Indian opening bowler, that shouldn't worry you, by the way did you hear the one about Prince Charles going to open a factory in Newcastle????'

This was the first sentence ever spoken to me by David English. It was like being hit in the face by 15 stones of long-haired blancmange.

Of course this was all very new to me in 1999 at Dunnington

CC in Yorkshire. Dunnington had eleven players. The Bunburys had 23. When it was our turn to bowl, none of the fielders moved . . . not even when the bowling changed ends. Five slips turned into five mid-ons (why stop good conversation?).

Throughout the day I witnessed a plethora of mini events . . . the lunch which never ends ('come on Fraser finish your quiche would you?'), Lloyd Honeyghan the former world boxing champ getting bowled three times in one over yet all the deliveries just happened to be no-balls (for Lloyd came and went when he wanted to), John Hurst lighting the biggest, fattest cigar whilst I was appealing for an lbw (I've still never had a decision from him yet) etc., etc. This, I found, was all routine in any Bunbury day.

The one thing that struck me most, however, was that the moment I walked into the dressing room as an unknown quantity, I was treated like family by cricketing peers and celebrities alike. Since that day, and many Bunbury games later, I have met rock stars, prime ministers, page-3 girls (bonus) and great sportsmen and crick-eters, many of whom I would never have dreamed taking the field with, and have made many friends along the way. And most impor-tantly, millions of pounds have been raised for worthwhile causes along the way.

All this is because of one man.

'Charlie boy, did you hear the one about the American ship that docked in Liverpool . . .!'

From Hollywood to Hollywood

JOHNNY ALTMAN
(Emmy Award-Winning Musician)

This is the story of a typical Bunbury season – the sort of thing you come to expect as standard fare as a regular team member of ten years' standing.

Our little tale opens in the movie capital of the world in March 1999. I had just returned from the last two Ashes Tests in Australia and was about to witness the rebirth of my illustrious victim B.C. Lara in the exciting Caribbean dash between West Indies and Australia. But first I had some work to do, which is why I sat in the bar at the Sunset Marquis Hotel, West Hollywood, awaiting the arrival of our esteemed skipper D. English (after a tip-off from another Bunbury, John Cousins). What followed was six months of surreal mayhem – from which a few highlights in chronological order – with no comments!!!!!

David English (travelling with the Bee Gees): 'So Mickey [addressing reformed hellraiser Mickey Rourke] did you ever know Barry Gibb when you lived in Miami?'

Mickey Rourke: 'No, but I think I burgled his house a couple of times!'

David English (on microphone left on unwittingly in the Polo Lounge of the famous Beverly Hills Hotel): 'Good morning everyone – have you heard the one about . . .'

John Altman (to Viv Richards at Antigua airport): 'I hear you might be playing for the Bunburys this year.'

Viv Richards (to John Altman preparing to bowl in the Winston Davis Testimonial Game): 'How do you want your field maestro?' (Still can't believe that one).

Receiving a telephone call at 2 a.m. on the morning of the World Cup final from my sons, 'Dad we told the gateman at Lord's that we've been left two tickets by the Australian team, and all he said was "Nice try son – on your bike".'

D. English to J. Altman: 'Let's try and put together a Bunbury band with Mark Butcher and some great musicians to round off this year's PCA dinner at the Albert Hall.'

The Mark Butcher England band, with a host of cricket and

music superstars, brings the house down at the Albert Hall on 29 September 2000.

J. Altman hits the winning run against Essex and John Major's xi!!!

J. Altman dismisses Nasser Hussain and Alec Stewart in the same week to give him three England captains in four days.

And adds three more Test players and three county caps to give him nine first-class scalps in two weeks!

What is going on!!!!! And the final twist – back to LA in time for five one-day internationals between Australia A and India A (total coincidence) during which I get the chance to show some of the Aussies Shaq O'Neill and the other sights of Hollywood. If you can imagine a field in the middle of the San Fernando Valley where you can find Barry Richards, Michael Holding, Allan Border, Ian Chappell, Ravi Shastri, Paul Hogan and twelve other spectators watching a game being beamed to fifty million viewers in India, you'll understand why it's so bizarre being a Bunbury – it's never just a simple game of cricket. (And was that really a percussion section of Foxy Fowler, Phil Tufnell, Robin Smith, Ben Hollioake and Andrew Flintoff on stage at the Albert Hall? Next you'll be telling me that Mark Illott, Wayne Morton, Bill Wyman and Paul Carrack were there as well. I must have dreamt the whole thing, unless . . .?

And so it came to pass that on Christmas night 1996 I was regaling a group of partygoers high in the Hollywood Hills with stories of how I would best like to spend my summer.

Not for me the villa in the South of France, no jetting off to exotic climes. No thank you very much. I want to drive for three hours to a field in the middle of who-knows-where and proceed to humiliate myself for several hours in the company of athletes far greater than I could have ever aspired to be. Having achieved this first objective, I then love to retrace my steps home swelling on each blunder and occasionally savouring any small success that may have come my way. For I am hopelessly addicted to playing cricket.

Let me qualify that last statement. In my younger days I really could play cricket. An infrequent flashback to the Bunbury field of play – driving Lillee and Edmonds for four, getting the wicket of

Brian Lara, taking four wickets in two overs – reminds me that 'Once upon a Time . . .'

However, one thing I shall have to realise and finally accept is that I will never again take a catch. For a while I sincerely believed that the reflexes that made my school's first slip, way back in the days of W. G. Grace, would magically return, and as I watched total novices to the game turn up without any kit and proceed to make like Mark Waugh, I hungered for the ball to come flying towards me. I knew I would hurl myself sideways and grasp the ball in mid-air to the amazement of Joel Garner or Brian Lara or even Bill Wyman, whom I've seen take some spectacular catches, some off my bowling! Unfortunately the only diving I seemed to be doing was out of the way of some ferocious shots from the likes of Nasser Hussain and Mike Gatting. Even worse, the simple dollies don't ever stick. I can say with all modesty that my last successful catch in a cricket match occurred when Harold Wilson was prime minister and when Pakistani Test newcomer Hasan Raza was minus fifteen (or minus fourteen depending on whose birth certificate you believe).

At least I am now comfortable with this fact, unlike the time skipper David English had to restrain me physically from walking off the Oval in disgrace after missing every ball that came anywhere near me.

So pick me this year, Captain, and I promise I won't let you down in the field.

Important Stepping Stone

ANDY FLINTOFF
(Lancashire CCC and England)

Playing in the Bunbury Festival is a great opportunity for any young cricketer and also an important stepping stone to going on to greater things. It enables talented young men to test and express their ability against the best players in their age group. I have fond memories of the two festivals I played in and still remember receiving my first North of England cap from Wayne Noon and David English at Charterhouse.

A lot of guys I played with and against have gone on to successful county and international careers and that bears testament to David's and their hard work that goes into such an event.

The chance of representing your region at a young age is a great thrill. During the festival some players will shine and make names for themselves and be selected for the England team at the end of the week. To the others I want to say, don't be discontented, never stop trying and believing. Your day will come, not all pros are childhood stars.

David, the work you do for young cricketers and various charities is magic. I thank you for giving me the chance to play in the festival and for your many phone calls, not to mention your friendship.

PS: We're still going to Brazil!

David English – Minister for Cricket

MICHAEL PARKINSON, CBE

Writing about your festival I am afflicted by nostalgia, and not a little jealousy. What wouldn't we give – we elderly gentlemen who are now asked not to play cricket but to write about it – to be in your shoes? It is the loveliest and most complex of games and the only conclusion I arrived at after playing it for most of my life, was that I gave it up too soon.

So if I can offer any advice to you young men who are just embarking on your careers, it would be to play cricket as long as you can and don't let anyone dissuade you whether they be wives, babies, girlfriends, bosses or those sad souls who just don't understand the game. You will never be happier than when the sun is shining, there is the smell of cut grass in the air and the game's afoot.

David English, whose brainchild this festival is, epitomises what it is to be cricket-mad. He can be loud but he is not boastful, so I would like to write a line or two about him. His enthusiasm for the game is exemplary, his love for it inordinate.

We are all fond of spouting the cliché about putting something back into the game we love and, in the main, do nothing practical about it. David English did and still does. It is because of his abiding passion and his desire to make sure cricket has a healthy future that the festival exists.

Sadly, cricket like most sports in Britain is generally neglected by politicians and the education system. David tries to do his bit to change the present situation where people succeed in spite of the system and not because of it.

Would that more politicians shared his concern and energy; would that he was Minister for Cricket. Now that would be something. In the meantime my admiration for him is unbounded, my best wishes for you and the festival unstinted.

Make the most of every golden moment.

Father and Son Reunion

PHIL DEFREITAS
(Leicestershire CCC and England)

After seventeen years I have reunited with my adopted father, David English, on the cricket field. I finally made my debut for the Bunbury Cricket Club in July 2003, a match with twenty-five players a side which ended up being a fantastic game of cricket with David bowling the final over. The opposition needed four runs off the final over to win the game. Once again, my adopted father bowled a magnificent over, which tied the game, and then he whispered in my ear, 'That's how it's done son.'

Looking back over the years, I was one of the first to be labelled as the next Ian Botham and, unsurprisingly, I found this to be a heavy tag. I became a high-profile player at an early age. Playing for England I felt the pressure and needed support, which wasn't always available. I wish I had been backed more but I was left on my own to deal with the ups and downs of the game.

Looking at the present England set-up, the support network is much improved. I had to teach myself and made mistakes but never gave up. I have lost track of the number of times I was dropped and came back. My determination to succeed was largely down to the guidance and influence I received from Ken Higgs. He was a tough man who told it to me straight. He would always give me advice when I asked for it. He saw that I desperately wanted to make it and told me to believe in myself, make sacrifices and go for it. This advice and encouragement have left their mark. So, when approached by younger players telling me how hungry they are to succeed, I always try and back them in the same way that Ken backed me.

I have never been shy of voicing my opinion and have occasionally fallen foul of cricketing authorities. My bluntness and straight talking may have cost me a few more International appearances, but my cricket is honest and I have worked hard. When I see people cutting corners and making excuses, they fool no one but themselves. And, after so many years of playing professional cricket, I have finally been granted my first-ever benefit for the year of 2004.

Finally, I would like to congratulate David English (my dad) for receiving his MBE, which he thoroughly deserves.

Your son

Daffy

(1 September 2003)

Better Late Than Never

CHRIS SILVERWOOD
(Yorkshire CC and England)

'Better late than never' is a term that springs to mind for more than one reason whilst writing this. Firstly, why am I still waiting to get my first Bunbury cap? Secondly, the amount of time it has taken me to put pen to paper. And, last but by no means least, a recent car journey I shared with the Loon in London.

As most of you know, David is never short of a word or two but you could have heard a pin drop the moment Brands Hatch came to London. After overtaking the seventh car on the bounce passing numerous bollards on the wrong side of the road and almost visiting some old lady for a quick cup of tea and a bun, we arrived safely but somewhat shaken at the Hilton. The only word muttered went something like, 'F—k me, I didn't realise Nigel Mansell was driving us.'

The look of horror on the Loon's face was priceless and the silence in the car was golden and, believe me, after an hour of him whittering in my ear in the hotel, I was praying for the car back!

David, as always, it is a pleasure to see you. And though things usually get daft when we meet I'm glad this trip was no different. Keep up all the good work pal.

Best wishes

'Spoons'

Long On to Long On ... Waterloo 1815, Wembley 1966, Chesham 1999

WILL MACDONALD

Such is the dream world of Bunbury's cricket, a wonderful happy world I was lucky enough to chance upon when I met the overwhelmingly gorgeous but slight and retiring David English who greeted me with the words, 'Fantastic. Innit marvellous. Well done Willy – now next Sunday, Southgate, you're opening the bowling. See you there. Well done. Bye.'

Ever since then my Sundays have been filled with the joy of playing alongside international cricketing heroes, meeting some of the nicest people in this big old bad world and, occasionally, getting a wicket. Here, for what it's worth, are some of my 1999 Bunbury memories awards:

The Oliver Reed best match preparation award: Keen as mustard for my Bunbury's debut in May I turned up extra extra early. I had held off the wicked sauce the night before and polished each and every shirt button for the huge match that was Phil Tufnell's testimonial. Unfortunately I turned up so early there was only one person at the ground when I got there.

As the lank-haired, shabbily dressed, arse-scratching groundsman came over to greet me, the awful realisation dawned on me. It was Phil Tufnell. By then it was too late. 'Hello mate, fanksfrcoming. Lesgofrafewliveners,' said the Cat as he dragged me to the bar and oblivion.

Two hours and 13 bottles of wine later I took to the field surrounded by internationals. I returned legless and wicketless and scored a solitary boundary – cut off the one man more half-cut than me – Tuffers.

The Salvador Dali award for most surreal cricketing moment ever: Playing in sub-zero temperatures at Gloucester in Mark Alleyne's benefit, whilst we were being painted for Channel 4's *Watercolour Challenge*, as I batted with floppy-hatted tea-obsessive Jack Russell who was at the time being interviewed by 1970s' actress Hannah Gordon.

The Justin Langer and Peter Bowler annoyingly-nice-Australian-who-also-played-the-innings-of-the-season-and-caught-the-catch-of-the-season award: Michael Lynagh.

The England–San Marino great start award goes to Nasser Hussain, who three balls into his tenure as England captain is dismissed as useless while medium-pacer buffet-bowler Will Macdonald, it being his testimonial, reserved the right to sulk and stay in.

The Toto Scillachi flash in the pan award: In dismissing England cricketers Mark Butcher, Alan Butcher and Chris Cowdrey I sparked the back page headline still resonating today, 'New Botham is 33-year-old posh boy'.

The Frank Bruno best laugh in the world ever award: Lloyd Honeyghan.

The I'd rather be stuck in a lift with Bernard Manning and a box of snakes than hear the joke about the wire-brush and the Dettol again award: Dave English for 'Helmet Gleaming'.

The Rourke's Drift glorious failure award and David and Goliath small-time hero award go to me for failing to hit a last-ball; Peter Such full toss for the winning run at Chelmsford, but hitting a last-ball; Ashley Giles Yorker, Chinese-style through my legs, for the winning run at Ripley.

The 'Why have you turned up at a cricket match in a purple velour hand-stitched suit and matching cravat?' 'Because I'm an actor' award: to Stephen Tompkinson.

The Bunbury player with the worst highlights to represent England award: Ronnie Irani.

The Chris Lewis late arrival award goes to me for turning up at Robin Smith's testimonial so late that as I walked onto the pitch the last over was about to be bowled. In true Bunbury style David English brought me on to bowl it, and without breaking stride from the M3 I handed my car keys to the umpire who passed me the ball. Six balls and 26 runs later it was tea.

The John Altman worst excuse for not attempting a catch award: John Altman for 'But they're the fingers I play the saxophone with.'

The annual Leonardo DiCaprio best-looking Bunbury award: 3rd, Ian Baraclough; 2nd, Robert Duncan; 1st, Joe Cuby.

The Green and Gold Sweater

WAYNE 'NED' LARKINS
(Northants CCC and England)

Having known David English for more than 20 years, I had never played for the Bunburys, but the scene was set one Sunday afternoon in May 2000 at Finedon Dolben CC. I had been asked along with fellow Northants cricketers to play for my old teammate Winnie Davis, who tragically had fallen while playing with his children and was now paralysed. The day was a great success, making thousands of pounds for Winnie, and everybody thoroughly enjoyed themselves.

While I was enjoying my Evian water and cucumber sandwiches during the tea interval, the Bunbury skipper came over to me and said, 'Come on Ned, you're a natural Bunbury, you like a drink and to socialise [I don't know where he got that from] how about playing for the Bunburys at Chesham CC against David Thomas XI, another fine man cut down in his prime?' I did so, the die was cast, and I have not looked back since. Now, the next story may make you giggle . . .

As you can imagine, there is a lot of rivalry and good spirit in the dressing room (great crack) and this particular Sunday at Radcliffe CC was a prime example. Steve (Thomo) Thompson, footballer extraordinaire, had scored 18 n/o the week before batting middle order and very pleased he was too, but it all changed when the captain, David English, walked in and said '15 Thomo please'.

Batting 15 out of 17 was not what Thomo was expecting after his gallant knock the week before. Having fielded in the pouring rain and wind for 35 overs he was now on the look-out for someone to take it out on. It happened to be Frazer Hines and the vicar from *Emmerdale*, who put on a very good partnership but not very quickly though, and as the overs were running out and we were getting behind the clock, Thomo was getting more and more frustrated.

This was his chance. 'You can see why they bloody kidded him off in *Emmerdale*, can't you? And as for that bloody vicar, he's well cast, isn't he?' Thomo paced up and down, growling, but we tied the game, thanks to a career-best from Frazer (using my bat). The captain trying to be diplomatic said, 'Thomo you can open next week'. Thomo retorted, 'You can piss off, I'm not bloody playing.' We were all creased up in the dressing room. But after a shandy or two he turned to David English and said, 'I'll be there skip.'

One week later we were at Goodwood House, Neil Lenhams XI. Thomo was first there working on the theory, first to arrive, first to bat, the theory worked, we fielded first and we were set 210 to get in 35 overs. Thomo was opening with Paul Taylor. He seemed quite concerned, not his normal jovial self during tea, very quiet. Slipping off quietly to get his pads on I could see it was getting to him but I kept quiet.

The score after 6 overs was 35 without loss, Phil Tufnell 35, Thomo 0. I mentioned this to the captain and he said, 'Come on Ned, we had better tell him to play a few shots.' We watched 2 more overs go by; the score was moving on to 45 without loss. Phil Tufnell 45, 10 overs now gone. Thomo still had not troubled the scorers.

'What's this, a five-day Test Thomo?' shouted the captain. Next over, Thomo edged two down to third man then holed out at mid-off. 'Couldn't get the strike! Skip, couldn't get the strike.'

On taking his pads off, with sweat dripping from his face, he said, 'Look at this Ned,' and protruding from his ankle was a swelling the size of a cricket ball. I looked at him, and we both burst out laughing. He then proceeded to shout from the dressing room to the wives, 'Come and look at this swelling girls!' 'Obviously self-inflicted,' one of them shouted back.

I put my arm around his shoulder and said, 'Well, let's go and have a drink and you can talk me through that 2 you got.' Thomo looked at me and said, 'It's all about bonding Ned.'

And that word 'bonding' for me sums up the Bunbury spirit. That day at Chesham CC, when I put on the green and gold sweater for the first time, was a very proud moment for me.

I never thought Sundays could be so enjoyable, meeting and playing with and against big-hearted people from all walks of life. What a wonderful way to make money for charity.

Thanks David (Skip).

The Crazy Gang

ANDY SINTON
(Spurs, Wolves and England)

With it being two years since my last appearance for the Bunburys, I eagerly awaited my return to action on 20 September 1998, when cricket's version of the Crazy Gang travelled to play at Puttenham in Surrey.

Having spent two hours travelling in the car, thinking about all the good times I'd enjoyed with the Bunbury's and hoping I would mark my return with a few runs and a wicket or two, I arrived at the ground to find half the square under water and the rain getting heavier by the minute. Oh well, I haven't played for two years so one more game wouldn't matter, I was thinking to myself.

But meeting a few old faces and friends over a glass of wine, it started to become apparent that we *were* going to play. They are joking, I thought to myself as I took a quick look outside. Then it came back to me – this is the Bunbury's, I should have known better. Next skipper English came in and said, 'We are fielding,' with a huge smile on his face. 'Come on boys let's get a win' were his last words to us as he led us out – as if the league championship was at stake. As the rain kept coming down and the puddles on the square got bigger, I was back in action for the Bunbury XI.

I was given a few overs bowling by captain English in which I bowled quite steadily and took one wicket. Thankfully, I managed to escape the ritual given to every bowler when he took a wicket for the side. The successful bowler would be carried by his teammates and dropped into the largest puddle on the square leaving him drenched from head to toe. Only myself and big Gary Mason escaped. I can understand why Gary was left alone but I'm not sure how I got away with it as well. We then went in to bat. I was due in at the fall of the first wicket. I stood outside the pavilion to get used to the light, which was pretty poor to say the least. It wasn't long before my services were required. This is what I'd waited two years for, although I'd have preferred a better wicket to bat on. You know no matter how many times you've played cricket for whatever team, at whatever standard, facing your first ball is always a bit nerve-racking. I was delighted to steer mine away for a single. I was away.

I managed 16 before being bowled playing an awful shot trying to push the score along. David (Captain) English was whacking the ball to all parts as usual and he took us through to the end, where the scores were tied.

I must say that despite the weather I really enjoyed myself, and I look forward to getting my whites on a few more times this summer – hopefully not on waterlogged pitches.

The Bunburys are a great bunch of guys brought together from all walks of life by their love of cricket. I'm sure cricket's 'Crazy Gang' will entertain lots of people again this summer come rain or shine and hopefully because of this many less fortunate people than ourselves will benefit from it.

My First Bunbury Festival

ROD MARSH
(Director of the ECB National Academy)

I had heard so much about the Bunbury Festival from different sources I thought it too good to be true. How could one man manage to organise an event for Under-15 (or should I say 15 and under) cricketers that has the blessing of every county, every region, every coach, every school and it seems every cricketer in England?

I really didn't know what to expect when I arrived at Billericay in Essex in July 2002. There was never any doubt of my attending the Bunbury Festival. David and I have been mates for almost 30 years and for those of you who know the man, when he asks, you always seem to say yes.

It was particularly easy for me to say yes on this occasion as being at the festival was a very important part of my job as Director of the ECB National Academy. From the 2002 festival we can almost be assured will come several players who will find their way through the system to the Academy. From the Academy we would expect these players to challenge strongly for an England position.

Perhaps the greatest surprise I received from this, my very first, Bunbury Festival was the fact that each of the 4 regions seemed to have 2 spinners. People keep on telling me England needs some spinners. Since the festival I am able to say that England has some very good spinners. At the moment they are a little young to represent their country at the highest level, but time will heal this. Young spinners are being encouraged and this can only be good.

To see so much talent at the festival should have come as no surprise as one of my old mates, leg spin coach Terry Jenner, has been working with the young wrist spinners for a few years now and of course he was on hand to see his charges conjuring up all of their tricks in order to impress the 'spin doctor'. TJ has a very good programme in place and nothing would give him more pleasure than to see a leggie bowling out Australia.

I don't recall who won the festival and, to be honest, it doesn't matter. What is important is that young people are given the opportunity to come together and compete and learn in a very special environment. The eyes of England are on these youngsters and if they want to play for England badly enough they will do the necessary work and will make it through.

Mind you, they will have to be good as there are a whole new group of boys in 2003 who will be doing their utmost to play for England. Don't you just love a bit of decent competition?

Bunburys in Bombay?

MOHAMMAD AZHARUDDIN
(Ex Captain India)

There are precious few opportunities for Test cricketers to relax these days, except when they play for the Bunburys.

I have appeared only once for the side but it ranks among the highlights of my career. I scored 91 in no time and spent the rest of the time laughing and joking with rock stars.

That beats batting with Sachin Tendulkar et al, I can tell you. Not that there is anything wrong with my Indian teammates, you understand; it's just that they are not as good company as the likes of Bill Wyman and Eric Clapton.

I've also been trying to get Sachin involved. It might not improve his batting but it would sure improve his singing.

It has been some time since my debut, but I would love to be involved again soon. Perhaps David English can arrange a game in Bombay or Calcutta. The Bunburys in Eden Gardens . . . Now there's a thought.

The Bunburys, Manchester United and England

PHIL NEVILLE
(Manchester United FC and ESCA)

Hi Dave. This is Phil Neville wishing you and all the lads competing in this year's Bunbury Festival all the very best of luck. I have great memories of the festival. I represented Lancashire and the North and enjoyed making new friends from different parts of England and pitting my skills against lads of similar ability at the very highest level of the game. I particularly enjoyed the social side of the festival.

Sadly, I haven't played cricket for a long time, because of my football commitments with Manchester United and England. I only get 4–5 weeks off in a season and normally head straight for the beach!

It's very disappointing, but when I've finished playing football I'll start cricket again. I think English cricket has improved immensely and we have now got a team to be proud of. Central contracts have helped to keep the best players fresh and hungry for a challenge. I'm sure England will play well this summer and beat the Indians! The preparation for football and cricket is similar in a way because both sets of players have to prepare for massive games. It's probably a bit more intense for a footballer, because you have to learn set pieces, corners and free kicks, and plan how you will mark certain opposition players. With cricket it's different preparation, but in terms of fitness I think it's more or less the same. Footballers are slightly fitter but a fast bowler who has to bowl thirty overs in a day might disagree with me. A cricketer's power of concentration is greater as he may have to bat or field for eight hours in a day, whereas a footballer only plays ninety minutes.

When I left school I played for my club side, Greenmount, along with my dad, brother and cousin. I played every Monday, Wednesday, Thursday, Saturday and Sunday. I hadn't played very much for my school team and went from Lancashire Schools to Greenmount, where a few of the United lads enjoy playing cricket. Dwight Yorke, Brian Lara's pal from Trinidad, fancies himself at the game. Ryan Giggs, Paul Scholes and of course Gary, all played at a good level. Mark Bosnich, ex-United and an Aussie is also a keen player.

Sometimes when it's snowing outside we go in the gym and play. It's a good laugh! I think it would be a great idea to play the Bunburys in a charity game.

When you're playing at U-15 level just go out and enjoy playing! I certainly did. I had no pressure from my parents or coaches and I ended up playing at a good level. If I had not played football I'm confident I could have played cricket professionally. My best advice to you is, 'As long as you enjoy whatever you're doing in life, you will end up doing it well.'

Bunbury Achievement

GARY NEVILLE
(Manchester United FC and ESCA)

Hi, this is Gary Neville. I have great memories of playing in the 1999 Bunbury Festival. I batted quite well in the first game, scoring 40 odd. But when I was fielding at second slip I dived for a catch and dislocated my finger. This ruled me out of the festival and put me out of the England team's selection process. Although it was an achievement getting to Bunbury, it was very disappointing to get injured.

I don't play cricket any more. I did until I was 18 or 19 whilst playing for United, but when I joined the first-team squad the club would not allow me to play, particularly as we only get four weeks off between seasons.

English cricket is good today and it's healthy for the country when the England team are strong.

I play football for England and I know how difficult it is to represent your country and have the respect of the nation because there is a lot of cynicism surrounding sport at the England level.

The English cricket team has a lot to be proud of. Their results in 2004 and the up-and-coming series against Australia will be fantastic. It is great that England can now compete with the best in the world.

Training with Manchester United is totally different from training with the England team. Having spoken to a lot of cricketers recently I have realised how well educated they are in fitness and nutrition. Also, the England cricketers have actually trained with United.

Football is physically more exerting, with high pressure over 90 minutes. Cricket is more energy-sapping, particularly when played over a whole day in a hot climate. I fielded in a 50 overs game in 30°C and, believe me, it is hard work.

When I left school I wanted to play cricket as much as football. I absolutely loved cricket and played six days a week at Greenmount CC, where I made some great friends.

Hopes were dashed when I had to stop playing at eighteen. To be honest I was gutted. I'd love to play a charity game against the Bunburys, but because we now play football 11 out of 12 months a year that would prove difficult.

Quite a few of the United lads play cricket. Dwight Yorke is always going on about the West Indies and Mark Bosnich used to rib us 'big time' about the Aussies. I hope that England can put one over him this summer.

My advice to you lads is to practise and never let anybody discourage you from your ambition.

To get to where you want to be you are going to experience a lot of heartaches, joy, trouble, nervousness, tension and anxiety. Probably there will be times when you get depressed, you will suffer upsets and knock-backs during that period of getting there, but the main thing is that you have the desire and the will to carry on practising and carry on playing. Don't let anybody stop you. At the end of the day being a professional sportsman is the greatest job in the world. It means getting paid for something you love doing, and for that it's worth sacrificing the things that 15-year-olds usually do. You can't do those things that your mates are doing because you will need all your energy for the mental and physical training required of a professional sportsman.

To be honest, going down the pub, wine bars and nightclubs is a 'no no'. At the age of 15–18 you have to dedicate your life to your profession. Then, if you don't make it at the end of the day, at least you can say you gave it your best shot.

To David English, keep up the good work; and to you lads, do your very best you can, *now*.

(September 2004)

Keeble Runs a Wright Marathon

IAN WRIGHT
(Arsenal and England)

Yes, you heard it here first. John Keeble ran a million miles for me.

In 1996, whilst unable to make runs for myself due to injury, he stepped in with the Wrighty pace. I was then out after 89 – a personal best for me – and he was run out first ball. As a result of his reaction we may need armour-plated dressing rooms next year.

Being with the Bunbury bunch was a personal break for me. What a great set of lads. However, there are drawbacks in everything, and standing next to Gary Mason in the slips, resulting in buckets of his sweat falling all over me, is one of them. So next season I'll remind myself to bring a shower cap and an umbrella.

On a high – and dry – note I would personally like to thank Mr Bunbury himself, David English, a great friend and special guy to know, who has worked tirelessly for the Bunbury causes; and also all those who have supported the Bunburys. Special thanks too from my wife Deborah and son Stacy.

See you next season . . .

(September 1996)

First Ball Blues

JOHN KEEBLE
(Spandau Ballet)

Here we come, walking down your street,
We get the funniest looks from everyone we meet.

Hey, hey we're the Bunburys,
The coolest cricket team in the land,
And we're too busy laughing
To run anybody out . . .

We've got so many players,
The stars from stage and screen,
Askin' how much we want it,
We'll take in any team . . .

But enough of lyrical songs of battle, and on to cricket . . .

As ever in the depths of winter, I have been spending time

watching our national side travel to warmer parts of the globe – i.e. anywhere – in order to further reduce their batting averages (to somewhere far below average . . .) and enjoy locally prepared pitches with the consistency of a good custard, whilst facing the sort of dobby bowling that is almost impossible to hit anywhere – especially when the ball is covered in bird's finest and the outfield is more akin to 'deep impenetrable tropical jungle' than the pen spaces beyond cover point.

It appeared at times that the only way we were going to hit a four in Zimbabwe was to arm our batsman with a suitable blade . . . No, not a Fearnley or a Surridge, I was thinking more along the lines of a machete or scythe in order to cut a swathe to the boundary rope.

That is of course, pre-supposing that the delivery had passed within an inch or two of the stumps . . .

I am sorry, but as I write we are days into a fledgling 1997 and England have just completed their tour of the former Rhodesia (nuff said). I trust that the boys will turn it all around in New Zealand . . .

The Bunburys, on the other hand, are going into another season a team very much at their peak.

Competition for the seven places at cover point is as fierce as ever and most of us have spent the winter rubbing in the linseed oil with impassioned hands – a few may even have attended to their cricket equipment . . .

Last year, as ever, provided many memories and fabulous days. My own personal favourite moment was, without doubt, the catch I took from the bowling of our skipper to dismiss the redoubtable Ken Barlow at Worcester.

The perfect leg cutter, a big nick and the ball safe and sound, nestling in the very end of my black Kookaburra gloves, as I sprawled in front of Tom Moody at second slip (or maybe it was third slip).

Other high points were: the two catches I took at Blenheim Palace, racing in from the deep backward square leg in pads and gloves to complete two more dismissals for the 'Cuby Leg Trap'; connecting sweetly to lift Shaun Udal over long on for six runs (sorry

Shaggy!); and the simply marvellous time I had keeping wicket to Sam Fox. There are few greater sights in all of world cricket.

The lowest point was without doubt the game at . . . er . . . now, where exactly was that place? It matters not, but at this particular game, I had volunteered to run for Ian Wright, who had a slight calf strain. Being a lifelong Gooner and all-round team man, this was of course no problem and I ran as Wrighty accrued fifty-odd. Finally, he skied one to cover and we crossed. Thus I began my innings proper at the non-strikers' end.

I was run out first ball, without facing, having run for Wrighty for an hour . . . the culpable batsman at the other end shall of course remain nameless – Jerome Anderson – and I commenced the long walk to the pavilion with a face full of thunder and entered a dressing room reminiscent of the *Marie Celeste* . . .

Unfortunately, this is where details get a bit sketchy, but what I do know is that I took some considerable time to calm down and, how shall we say . . . get it out of my system! Still, enough of the past and on to the next innings.

It just remains for me to thank you for supporting the Bunburys. For without you our efforts would be meaningless.

And finally thanks to the skipper and the lads and lasses of the Bunbury clan who make it all such a gas!

PS: I still can't quite remember which game it was, but I think I must have dropped my bat at some stage. There seem to be a few dents in it . . .

PPS: The only thing I do remember is that they had a very nice dressing room . . . Keep on keepin'.

(September 1997)

We Will Not Be Beaten

LEE DIXON
(Arsenal FC and England)

Camaraderie, team spirit, togetherness. These are all words used when describing the qualities a set of players have when taking part in team sports. However, it is true that other factors – including skill, fitness etc. – perhaps play a bigger part in the success of any team.

In July 1997, I was persuaded (press-ganged) into playing cricket for the Bunbury X1 (Bunbury 17 in some cases) by Mr David English. I had spoken to David on numerous occasions about playing, and immediately knew that this man's enthusiasm would be infectious on a bunch of would-be cricket super-stars. I was not mistaken. David epitomises the camaraderie and enthusiasm needed to play as a team. Playing for 'his' team with these ingredients is a pleasure. I speak for all my celebrity team mates, I'm sure, when I say that taking a relaxed break from our high-pressure occupations by playing for the Bunburys, comes as a welcome change.

But make no mistake, we take our cricket seriously and we will not be beaten (even if it does mean bending the rules a little by fielding 19 players)!

The main object of all this of course is to raise money. Doing it in this light-hearted sporting way is fun for all, and in the Bunburys, David has produced a money-making machine, having already raised over £9m for charities. But we want more!

Thank you for your support.

David English

To Cap It Off

JACK RUSSELL
(Gloucestershire CC and England

At the beginning of the 1998 season I was delighted to receive a call from the Chairman of Selectors, David. No, not Graveney, English. Having been involved with Bunbury cricket for a number of years (always for the opposition), and the fact that I announced my retirement from international cricket only a few months before, must have been key reasons in his considering me for selection. Sources tell me that it was a 'touch and go' decision. What I think swayed the issue was my personal intervention (from mid-off) with his batting during a match at Stowell Park (Lord Vestey's XI) the previous season. After all, us left-handers must stick together. He was playing the captain's innings, in a torrential downpour, but was still very receptive to a word of advice. It's always tricky attempting to 'time' the ball when it's skidding off mud!

I think David knew in his heart that my selection would not be a straightforward affair. For openers, the match was at Archdeacon Meadow against a Mark Alleyne Benefit XI, containing a high percentage of Gloucestershire players. Now, just give that some thought for a minute. Remembering that part of my job was playing for my country is to give my teammates grief by bawling and shouting at them and generally badgering them to achieve a high standard of performance, especially when we are in the field. So there were bound to be one or two of them out to get me. Especially the bowlers!

And to add some spice to the occasion, I had agreed to judge the paintings for Channel 4's programme *Watercolour Challenge* – at the same time!! I thought it would be a case of just popping over the boundary boards a couple of times during play to pass an opinion; then five minutes at the end of play to present the prizes. Oh no, no, no. I was to discover nearer the time that the filming schedule was a long one. The first ball was due to go down at 2 p.m., but filming started at 11 a.m.!! . . . and was scheduled to continue until after the close of play. In for a penny . . . as they say.

The Bunbury xi fielded first. Amazingly I wasn't required by Channel 4 for the whole session of 40 overs. David was so delighted he gave me a bowl!! (David Capel kept wicket – immaculately, I might add.) I was privileged to field in the covers with Michael Lynagh (now he is quick!); in addition to swapping duties with Leslie Grantham between square leg and deep square leg (so that he could keep an eye on his children). This meant that I had to make up filming time during our innings. By the time I had studied three paintings in depth, passed opinions and completed the necessary interviews with the delightful Hannah Gordon, our innings was coming to a close. I had to bat at No. 11. Serves me right!

But this was just the start of a fabulously enjoyable season. My Bunbury debut was followed by several visits to Lord's that season. Firstly, to the World Cup Final to paint the 'Winning Moment' for NatWest, followed by a Benson & Hedges Super Cup with Gloucestershire, to collect my first-ever winner's medal with my County.

Then, to cap it all, another visit later in the same month to pick up the NatWest Trophy. Wow! What a year! I'll argue to the end of time (and beyond) that this is the greatest game on earth!

PS: Just imagine how far you could hit the ball if we played on the moon?

PPS: This was drafted following the immediate after-effects of anaesthetic for a knee operation. Skipper, don't worry; I'll be fit enough to bowl during the next Bunbury season – if selected!

David English

The Bunbury Spirit

PETER HAYTER
(*Mail on Sunday*)

Strange things happen after an invitation to play for David English's Bunburys. They happened to me.

There I was, for instance, having just reached an extraordinarily impressive eleven on my way to what I felt sure would be an outstanding debut century and feeling rather pleased with myself at that, when a message came over the public address system that cut me to the quick.

'Would Peter Hayter please now get himself out,' said Chris Cowdrey, more by way of an order than a request. 'Roger Daltrey has just arrived.' The words were polite enough. But the message they contained was chillingly clear: 'No one has come here to watch you bat, you boring four-eyed git. Now kindly piss off so we can watch someone interesting.'

I shuffled off to be replaced by the lead singer of The Who . . . and wondered where my life had gone so terribly right.

The next thing that happened was just too strange, even to me, to take in. Stephen Tompkinson, a fellow debutant that day, still cites it as the reason he knew the Bunburys were for him. (Or at least he did as we drained our seventh bottle of Petaluma Riesling on the morning of New Year's Day 1999 en route to the England's final Ashes Test at the SCG, having stopped off to have one for the road at what turned out to be Sydney's only gay breakfast bar.)

The innings of our opponents had just started when their opening batsman pushed the ball well to the left of me at mid-wicket. Setting off for an obvious signal, he even suggested nonchalantly to his partner: 'Looking for two, here' . . . not loud but loud enough to hurt.

Then suddenly and quite without warning, a surge of power

seemed to course through my veins. It was as though I was taken over by the spirits of Jonty Rhodes, Derek Randall, Colin Bland and Clive Lloyd all in one. I swooped, collected the ball in one hand and threw down the stump visible to me from side-on at a distance of twenty-five yards, all in one timeless movement. What is more, and this I really cannot explain, just prior to releasing the ball I called across to the batsman, 'You're out, matey . . .'

Those who have seen me fielding in most forms of cricket know that whatever was in possession of my body then, it certainly could not have been me.

And only later, after opening the bowling for the first and only time with nine slips, three gulleys and four short legs and using an orange with which to do so, did I realise what that thing was.

The spirit of the Bunburys is hard to define and impossible to describe. But it is a phenomenon understood and appreciated alike by fellow players and the countless thousands who have contributed to Bunbury cricket merely by their presence.

And it stems from one man, David English.

If anyone else asked you to play cricket for him, then informed you that you would probably be going in at number 18 out of a probable 32 starters, you would almost certainly tell him where to place his bat handle.

But English is a man who is very hard to say no to. And this ability to get things done spreads through Bunbury cricket to his involvement in the ESCA Under-15 school cricket programme behind which he has been such a driving force for so long.

You will all have read about and heard of the great cricketers produced by the system and helped by this tournament. They all owe David a debt of gratitude; so do the Bunburys.

Good luck to the cricketers here. Work hard but always enjoy what you do. Without the fun, cricket is just another sport.

All the best, Dave.

And can I have my cheque now, please?

Eventful Days Out for the Bunburys

LLOYD HONEYGHAN
(Former Undefeated Welterweight Boxing Champion of the World)

Well, I got a call you know! Audley Harrison called me and I went to visit, David English and I went to Ripley. Got my cousin Tony, son Junior, Lloyd Junior, Monique, Bianca, we all got in the 'Honey Bunny' car. Went all the way down to Ripley. It was a lovely day, met some lovely people down there, Hollioake, some lovely English chaps, Dirty Den, it was a lovely day, what a fantastic bunch of people, and this bowler had the cheek to try and bowl me out. He bowled me and what he didn't know, he overstepped his mark, obviously it took the umpire about five goes before he got me out, but all I can say, 'Brave Man'. Then, we went to Exeter, fantastic day, down there playing. Bowled a terrific ball, Sky TV down there, captured, terrific day! Spent the weekend down there, the night down there with the kids, we had a great time.

The next day we travelled all over the country. David got me, me and the bear. Then we went to York, now York is fantastic; we had a great terrific time up there. I fixed the 'Honey Bunny' car before we went. I put in petrol, put in oil, took it to my mechanic for a service. Up there after the match everybody in the Caribbean Tent had a wonderful time. I went outside to check the car, the tyres were 'Blinking Punctured', and so I stayed outside before the sun went down. Outside fixing it, a bloody photographer came outside and took my picture, so what happened, I fixed the puncture, changed the tyre back in the boot, went back inside filthy as muck, went back to the hotel. We all went outside and climbed a hill and started rolling down the hill, fantastic in the restaurant after. Up 'til all hours in the night talking, David English and I.

Now . . . coming back to London the next day, I got up, mind you, my tyres punctured, I put air in the bloody tyre. I don't know why I put air in the tyre that's punctured, but I blew up a punctured tyre and put it in the boot. On the way back to London, I had a 'Blow-out'; luckily I put air in the punctured tyre. Took the tyre off in the middle of the motorway coming back on the A1, in the middle of Sherwood Forest, put on the punctured tyre that I had put air in, there was a little bit of air left in it, it managed to take me to a petrol station, I was bloody happy, had the kids with me. Then I bought one of those quick patch things that you keep the air in the tyre with and then foam comes out and seals the hole that got me home. 'Bloody Hell' . . . It's hard work working for the Bunburys, but also enjoyable.

David English called me again on another mission. Down to Cambridge, John Major bowling the first ball, 'Bloody Hell', that was fantastic! Mind you I didn't see Emma Noble, mind you she's spoken for, so better behave myself or I'll get myself into trouble! Good day down there, made the last runs, won the match, running so fast . . . it was the last bowl, last run to win, crossed the line, I fell over and nutted the floor, I almost knocked my bloody self out, mind you I was a bit concussed, but we managed to win the match by the last runs, the last ball. Terrific day. Came back to London, happy as anything, our last game, we made it to Goodwood, lovely day out, the sun managed to shine out, just about won the match, but I got the shock of my life, I got three trophies, couldn't believe it. The Royal Mail gave me a trophy, Umpires and Best Player, 'must be having a laugh' . . . I got 'The Funniest Joke' trophy, that's a joke! I got 'The Bunbury Trophy', I got 'Players Trophy', I got three blinking trophies, I couldn't believe it, and I was speechless. First time I've been speechless in my life, I was gobsmacked, but anyway, I had a fantastic summer playing for the Bunburys, what a fantastic guy Dave English is, what a fantastic man, the Bunburys, all the people that come in, you know, all the players, all these famous people, actors, actresses, coming to play for the Bunburys. You know, you feel like you know them, they're so friendly, everybody's so friendly, it comes in like you know them, there's no animosity or anything between anybody, everybody just leaves the 'Celebrity Thing' at home and everybody comes out and has a great time, Hmmmmm!

By the way, before we go, I got to tell you a story, I got to tell you a joke, as I got the trophy for 'The Best Joke of the Year', here we go . . .

Lloyd's Joke

There was this man walking down in Wales, and he sees a farmer, the man says, 'That's a nice cat you got there' to the farmer, so the farmer says 'Eye,' he goes 'You know I can read animals' minds.' The farmer goes, 'Can Ya, all right tell me what the cat is saying.' 'Well . . . the cat's saying that you gave him some milk this morning in a lovely bowl and he went out and caught a rat and brought it in the house, and you was upset,' he goes.

'Bloody Hell! That's true, how did you know that?' 'I told you that I can read animals' minds,' he goes. 'Well what about the dog's then,' he goes. 'Well the dog went out and crapped in your garden, you were very angry because he peed and crapped in the garden and you were really upset about it.' 'Bloody hell, you're fantastic, how did you know that?' 'I told you, I can read animals' minds.' 'Well let me tell you something,' said the farmer . . .

'Don't listen to the sheep, they're bloody liars, the sheep are bloody liars, don't listen to the sheep, they're bloody liars. Don't listen to what the bloody sheep tell ya, they're flippin' liars.'

Lloyd and the Honeyghans, King of Rap Reports

For Whom the Phone Rings

LESLIE GRANTHAM

All actors, whether successful or not, live for the day that the call will come from Hollywood. All actors live for the day that the phone will ring . . . All actors live for the day that anyone will ring them.

And when the phone does ring, your stomach tightens in expectancy, your throat goes numb and your brain ends up on the floor. So, if the call from Spielberg eventually did come you probably wouldn't get the job, because he'd think you were a raving lunatic, and he's got plenty of those already in LA.

I've put those opening paragraphs in just as scene-setters really, so you can picture my kitchen one morning as I start the daily routine of finding work that will keep me in close proximity to the phone. This morning, like all other mornings, I'm having breakfast, reading the papers, when out of the blue the phone rings, and sure as eggs are eggs, the throat, stomach and brain do the predictable. Sweat bursting on the upper lip and hand trembling, I reach for the shrill-sounding piece of equipment and thrust it to mouth and ear. It's not Spielberg, it's some bloke muttering, 'David English speaking.' Sounds as if he knows me, mentions some woman, 'Will you do it? What's your address? I'll send the stuff,' and the phone goes dead. As soon as the phone leaves your hand you become normal again. Trouble is, I didn't have a clue who he was, what he was on about or who the woman was. What had I gotten myself into? Was it a film? Was it the Foreign Legion? Or was it double-glazing?

Three days later I knew, it was none of the above; it was a cricket match, against Surrey. That's right, Surrey. I'm an actor; I'm not a cricketer, yet here I am playing against SURREY ... Alec Stewart and the rest. Now I knew how Daniel felt when he entered the Lion's Den.

How do I go about getting out of this? Out of all the reasons I could think of to get off the hook, the only one that looked like working was *suicide*. Trouble was the chemist was fresh out of arsenic. So the fateful day arrived, and I duly made my way to Esher, where I was to meet these other cricketers who 'David English speaking' had rounded up to play against Surrey.

And what a bunch: Sid Lawrence, Gary Mason, Dave Beasant, Robert Duncan, Johnny Keeble, Tony Meo, Neal Foulds, Steve Smith-Eccles, John Altman, Joe Curly Cuby, 'David English speaking' and me. If I've forgotten anyone I apologise, but that day was a traumatic one for me. I can't tell you much about the game, although I must have done okay, as I was asked to play again . . . this time against a Norma Major X1. Again the roll call was long and worthy, yet when I arrived at the cricket ground two men, obviously body-guards to Mrs Major's husband, approached me, reaching into their inside pockets. I anticipated their next move and raised my hands into the air . . . but it was my autograph they wanted. Probably for John . . .

Then, after the match, I was invited to the next one at Blenheim Palace. Again, the roll call was magnificent: Allan Lamb, Bill Wyman, Clive Mantle, Rory Bremner – I wish he would get a proper job, you can't make a living being someone else all the time – Ian Wright and Lee Dixon. Mind, that is one of the downsides to the cricket; you have to rub shoulders with Arsenal footballers.

Whether it is my sense of humour or lack of it that gets me picked, I feel at last that I am no longer intimidated when I walk into the Bunburys' dressing room and meet Richard Illingworth, Allan Lamb and all those other cricket legends. Although I am still over-awed when Devon Malcolm or the like is chucking one down at me – but at least I'm having a bloody good time.

That one phone call from 'David English speaking' has not opened my doors to Hollywood, but it has certainly opened up a whole new world where I meet the loveliest people – both cricket-wise and of course the public who come through rain, wind and weather (sounds like something from *Rawhide*).

To David and Janis, who travel thousands of miles trying to take a decent photo of me, and great photos of all the others, I would like to say thanks.

And finally, to 'David English speaking', who is without doubt one of the nicest guys you could wish to meet: your phone call is the one I wait for now . . . sod Hollywood.

A Message by the Rt Hon Richard Caborn MP

(Minister for Sport)

I am delighted to provide my wholehearted support for the Bunbury Cricket Festival.

Going for dinner with David English is always a pleasure – but invariably ends with him having extracted another promise or another favour. And it is his ability to do that which has propelled Bunbury to being one of the biggest and most enjoyable charity sports tournaments around.

Many top-class players have played in the festival over the years and I'm sure this year's teams will be hoping to emulate their achievements.

Here's to another great tournament – and another dinner with the famous 'Loon'.

Enjoy the cricket.

Best Wishes for More Success

SHAUN UDAL
(Hampshire CCC and England)

It is always a great pleasure to be in 'the Loon's' company. Whether you have had a bad day, feel down in the dumps or are simply cheesed off, he has that rare special way of making you feel good again, as if you are the most important person in the world.

It is that enthusiasm he has taken into the Bunbury Cricket Festival and that's the reason it has been as successful as it has.

So many good cricketers have come through the festival to be county players and, indeed, Test cricketers. Endless amounts of work go into making the Bunbury Festival the success that it is, and without the effort of a certain David English none of it would be possible. Belatedly he received the MBE in 2003 and there has never been a more deserving person.

To 'the Loon', many thanks for being a friend and I look forward to more Bunbury games; and to the festival of cricket and indeed the youngsters who play in it, enjoy the game and play with a smile, it's the best game in the world! With best wishes for more success,

Shaun Udal

And I Thought Wicket Keepers Were Supposed to Be Mad!

JONATHAN BATTY
(Captain of Surrey CCC)

My first memory of 'skip' is when I was an impressionable teenager at a Bunbury dinner in Oxford. Up on stage bounced the maddest, craziest, most nutty person I'd ever seen. Within seconds everyone in the place was in stitches. But we were also left with the important message of what the Bunburys are all about.

Fast forward ten years or so and I find myself batting with 'skip', feeling a little nervous about facing the Barmy Army's finest, and looking like I'm swatting flies as opposed to batting. I was being completely outshone by the elegant 'Goweresque' left-hander at the other end!

Moving on again to 2003, playing in a Bunbury game in the beautiful village of Ripley in Surrey, I'm sitting on a bench by the pavilion, minding my own business, and there are suddenly hundreds of cameras pointing in my direction. Not quite able to work out why, I try to look cool (very unsuccessfully). Suddenly, Mark Butcher comes bundling towards me with a pen and some records, he goes straight past me to the chap sitting on my left . . . Suddenly it all makes sense. It's the great Eric Clapton sitting next to me and I'm too scared to speak!!!!!! What a huge honour and privilege for me to be involved with the Bunburys, champion people working for a champion cause! I always look forward to getting called up.

Good luck 'skip', I know where to come for some advice when I win the toss!!!!!

Knighty, You Bat 5, 7, 9 . . .!

NICK KNIGHT
(Warwickshire CCC and England)

One of the most common questions I get asked these days is, do I regret retiring from one-day International Cricket. Of course the answer is 'no', but ask me that very same question at 2.00 a.m. whilst I'm settling into the Sky Studios with my old mate Charlie Colvile and you may get a different answer. It is at this very early part of the day that I'm writing this article for my great mate David English (Skippy) and his beloved Bunburys.

Well, talking of regrets and cricket . . . I cannot get a run for the Bunburys and doesn't Skippy let me know about it. During our innings, wherever I go, I keep hearing him, 'Knighty, you bat five, Knighty, you bat seven, Knighty, you bat nine' . . . as wickets tumble – of course, I'm already out.

Playing for the Bunburys is just great. I love it because you meet so many different people, all with the desire to enjoy themselves; and if there is one word that best describes David English, it is 'fun'. My Warwickshire team mate Neil Carter and I played in 2003, and after the game we decided that if you were ever feeling low about your cricket, pick up the phone for five minutes to Skippy and it will all be sorted. My wife is always getting on to me about reading more. Well, I bought Skippy's book, first book I've read for years. Having said that, I've now had it for six months, and I'm only just through the introduction; it's a start though.

Dr David English MBE – what a tribute and, of course, fully deserved . . . a ceremony to remember. As in fact is the ceremony to receive your Bunbury cap and shirt . . . the greatest moment in my Bunbury career? My 'ceremony' was in a car park in Shropshire. Okay – setting not ideal but full of emotion and meaning!!

Skippy you're a great mate. You played a big part in my benefit year in 2004, for which I'm so grateful. Can't wait for the next match against the Bunburys. I know you won't be worried about it. Certainly, when I come into bat, you know exactly what to bowl and where to put the field. Thanks for giving me the opportunity to be part of the Bunburys.

Cheers mate.

This Is Bunbury Cricket

ANDY JACOBS
(Talk Sport Radio)

When David first asked me to play for the Bunburys last year, I was apprehensive. I hadn't played cricket for a long time and I wasn't ever that good but I can honestly say that playing for the Bunburys has been one of the highlights and great pleasures of my life. It starts with the 'skip' and continues with the wonderful camaraderie shown by all. I've made some good friends, had a great time and have got hours of material for my radio show out of it. We even got to do a live broadcast from Alconbury for the Lashings game. Of course, the highlight for all concerned was the Eric Clapton game at Ripley. I still get goosebumps when I think of changing next to Sir Viv and walking out to field with Alec Stewart and Murali etc.

When the season ended at Hove I was genuinely sad and I just can't wait for next May to come around (if selected). On the match pages you'll find a selection of my notes and observations on each game I'd played in, which formed the basis of my Monday Bunbury report on Talk Sport. Of course, we are also grateful to David for being one of our favourite studio guests. He's Mike Dickin's favourite, which, if you know how grumpy he is, is quite an honour. My favourite English radio moment this year came when we mentioned we'd had Barry Johnston (son of Brian) on the show and he told us that Brian was buried in his Bunbury sweater. Very touching and we expected David to be quite emotional but, quick as a flash, he said, 'That's nice but where's he buried as we're a bit short of sweaters.' Jonners would have loved it and Paul Hawksbee and I cracked up on air in the BJ manner.

(September 2004)

Zimbabwe Memories

DAVE HOUGHTON
(Derbyshire CC Coach)

It's always a pleasure to run into old friends. Having just made the 'big move' from Zim to Derbyshire, it was a pleasant surprise to bump into David English in my first week. To catch him in after-dinner speaking mode was an extra bonus!

There are some really great stories to listen to, of a life really lived, of personalities met and friends made. But most important to me is the work done for charities. The creation of the Bunbury Cricket Club, hosting hundreds of famous names from all walks of life, and the raising of over £8 million for charities, singles David out as a very special man.

Our association goes back a few years, to his organisation of the 'Save the Rhino' matches out in Zimbabwe. He brought out some 'great' names – Lillee, Thompson, Gower to name a few. Cricket was played, beer was drunk and money was raised – another enjoyable and successful exercise.

Dave's association with Zimbabwe continued with his marriage to Robyn, and his involvement with junior Zimbabwe teams – notably the U-15's, whom he sponsored to the 1996 Junior World Cup.

Dave, keep up the good work! Fundraising is never easy, but most rewarding. I wish you and the Bunburys a very successful year and look forward to catching up during the course of it. I'll make sure I'm not driving this time, so we can drink the fixture back properly!

Best Wishes,

Dave Houghton

Steve Waugh, The Iceman Poeth

When people talk about Steve Waugh, they highlight his extraordinary commitment and sheer bloody-mindedness in the heat of a battle – 'If you want someone to go and bat for your life, you'd send out the iceman,' said Beefy Botham. Eighteen years, 168 Tests, 10,927 Test runs at an average of 51.06 – a marvellous Ambassador for the proudest form of Test match cricket, the traditions of which he holds most dear. All fantastic accolades for Australia's finest.

But for me, being 'the Loon', I've always enjoyed his humour and sense of the abstract.

I've known 'Tugga' since 1986 when we first toured England. That year, I took the Eric Clapton XI to play Allan Lamb's XI for his Benefit. When our tour bus swung into the gates of Northamptonshire CCC, Australia had just beaten the county side after a hard three days.

'Whatto, AB,' I called, as the Aussie charabanc was leaving.

'Blimey, it's English,' shouted Allan Border. All the Aussies, Merv Hughes, Dean Jones, Steve Waugh, the whole side, piled out to meet Eric, David Essex and the boys.

'Fancy staying to watch AB and have a few beers?' I enquired.

'Tell you what, better than that, we'll join in!' roared the Aussie Captain.

The entire Australian side alighted from their coach and got changed back into their whites.

'I'll play for you Dave,' laughed Steve Waugh, 'I fancy giving Denno a bit of tap!'

So Steve Waugh made his Bunbury debut, opening the batting with me. It was hilarious to watch him whacking Dennis Lillee and his teammates around the county ground. After the game Eric played his guitar as both teams enjoyed a thousand beers and a singsong way into the early hours.

Since then, every time I meet Steve, he reminds me of this game and wants to know how the Bunburys have developed. I'm sure now he's retired, he'll come back and play for us along with fellow Aussie Bunbury players Matt Hayden, Shane Warne and Justin Langer.

David English

From the PCA

RICHARD BEVAN
(Group Chief Executive, Professional Cricketers Association)

David,
Your recognition is thoroughly deserved – many congratulations. On behalf of the PCA's members, I would like to thank you for your unstinting support of our organisation and our members. Your contribution to the PCA has significantly furthered our aims of protecting the interests of professional cricketers in England and Wales.

Keep Those Strides Up

MIN PATEL
(Kent CCC and England)

What more can there be left to say about a man who has just had his life put into print in the shape of an autobiography – not a run-of-the-mill type book either, but with contributions from the good and the great of the world of acting, music and sport. Let's be honest though, we are not talking about a run-of-the-mill kind of guy. It's an extraordinary talent to reduce people to tears of laughter while they hand over lots of cash, and this is precisely what you have done over the years, to the huge benefit of countless charities and cricket beneficiaries.

In what is a fairly gruelling summer on the County cricket circuit, I know the Kent boys (Walks, Keysey, Symmo and I) enjoy participating in the Bunbury games and will long continue to do so. In return Davey, all I ask of you is that you actually stay the distance when we're on a night out. Our last social evening finished for you about thirty seconds after we'd entered the 10 Rooms Nightclub. I don't know if you'd forgotten your belt, or your braces had become detached, but somehow your strides had gathered down by your socks. I think the bouncers probably felt that, for your own safety, it may have been time to head back to English Towers. To be fair, I don't think forty to fifty P. Diddy wannabes were too enamoured at the sight of a half-naked fifty-something lunatic starting an audition for the Full Monty!

Long may you bring laughter to all who are lucky enough to meet you; and money to those who most need it. Lastly, I must congratulate you on receiving your MBE – nothing short of what you deserve. Well done mate!

PS: I'm still waiting for the Bunburys' tour to South America. C'mon Dave, you know it makes sense!

Meeting of the Loons

PAUL PRICHARD
(Essex CCC and England 'A')

It's funny how life sometimes turns full circle without you really noticing. It's 1986 . . . the old but far roomier visitors' dressing room at the Oval . . . another rainy day, which means another madcap day in the Essex room of that decade. Ray East constantly taking the 'Michael' out of the 'roomy' (room attendant), David Acfield so incredibly happy he will not have to face Sylvester Clarke today. Keith Pont constantly telling silly jokes and doing impersonations (mainly of Allan Border), Derek Pringle and Neil Foster having an argument over the speed of paint drying. Norbert Phillip still not arrived as he has got lost in London, JK Lever asleep, David 'Ether' East just generally keeping constant flak from anyone about anything. Keith Fletcher reading the paper, Goochie answering his pile of mail and Alan Lilley whilst trying to have a serious conversation (normally with Goochie) muttering sentences such as 'it's gonna be dark tonight' and 'ninety-nine times out of ten I would have caught it'. Meanwhile, a young Paul Prichard sits quietly in the corner, normally with Brian Hardie, trying to agree on the best pub to spend that night's meal allowance in.

So, on a rainy day, in a dressing room full of loonies, all you need to happen is the biggest one of all walking in. Enter one David English. 'Hello boys, did you hear the one about the Japanese submarine and the geezer with the cufflinks?' Forty-five minutes later the dressing room is still in hysterics – Ackers still looking out of the window at the rain and enjoying it even more. After the stand-up routine came a serious question. 'Boys, I'm writing a book and need some ideas for cricketers' names. I've got Viv Radish and Ian Buntham, any more ideas?' Allan Border took the brunt of the stick, names such as 'Boring Border', 'Badger Border', 'Herbaceous Border' were being put forward until the umpires called it a day and we all retired to the Tavern for a couple of lagers and some more jokes, hence the reason not one Essex player can claim the right to having helped David in the starting of the Bunbury's, but all can claim the right to have supported him in one way or another since.

How have I gone full circle since that day at the Oval? Well, after being lucky enough to be part of eighteen years of successful first-class cricket with Essex and having the honour to captain the Club for a while, it was time to retire and look for a second career.

Fortunately for me, the position of Cricket Manager at Gray Nicolls became available shortly after my retirement and after a couple of interviews I was lucky enough to be appointed. I soon learned that Gray Nicolls and ESCA Bunbury's had had a very good relationship for many years,

with Gray Nicolls supplying the regional clothing and caps
for both the U-14 and U-15 Festivals.

Having played in the ESCA Festivals in 1978 and '79
and a few Bunbury games over the years, it was now a must
to travel to Shrewsbury in 2003 for the annual ESCA-v-
Bunbury match on the Sunday, but I was not sure which
side to play for. After a few slogs, a few lousy off breaks and
a couple in the bat it was back to Shrewsbury School and
out to dinner with the man himself. A couple of bottles of
wine, numerous beers and a dance and a chance meeting
with a couple of Russian wrestlers later, we had not only
bridged the gap of nineteen years' cricket but kept the
British booze market afloat and also done our bit for world
peace.

From a personal point of view, a great tribute must go to
both David himself and the ESCA staff as a whole, for the
massive amount of hard work put in to give so many young
cricketers such great opportunities. To me, it is not only
about those of us lucky enough to have played for ESCA
and gone on to higher things, but also about the guys who
do not expect to play in such competitions, yet do and
whilst doing so enjoy every minute and every success, no
matter how big or small.

From a Gray Nicolls point of view, it is a great pleasure for
us to see the best young players in the country at this vital age
group wearing Gray Nicolls clothing along with the Crown
and Three Lions. Being a proud and traditional English
company we value our association with ESCA and Bunbury
greatly and hope it will continue for many years to come.

Good luck to all those taking part in future Bunbury
Festivals; and David, I look forward to a quiet Sunday night
in Nottingham and numerous more fun days in the famous
Bunbury colours.

Best wishes,

Paul

Bunbury Festival To Full England Cap to Play for England

MICHAEL VAUGHAN
(Yorkshire CCC and England)

It's a long way from Oundle in Northamptonshire to the BNS Stadium in Dhaka, which is where I am writing this article on England's tour of Bangladesh.

When I made my Bunbury's debut fourteen years ago back at Oundle, I was probably unaware that I was taking the first steps on the mad road to life as an international cricketer. Of course, not everyone who takes part in the Bunburys goes on to pursue a career in professional cricket, but the festival has a fantastic track record in producing high-class players, and the likes of Messrs Trescothick, Flintoff, Thorpe and Read are all Bunbury Old Boys.

I'd like to think that a handful of the players involved in this year's festival will go on to greater things, as we have. And I am sure that many of you will be asking yourself the question, what does it really take to succeed at the highest level? You need to be able to bat or bowl – that goes without saying – and it's essential these days to be a good fielder if you want to cut it in the professional game. If you can do all three, like Andrew Flintoff, then you'll be an even more attractive proposition to the talent scouts. But, there are three other priceless qualities that all young cricketers need if they want to turn a pastime into a profession: talent, determination and a good attitude.

What sort of talent are we looking for in the England team? Well, it's no secret that English cricket is crying out

for more spin bowlers – particularly wrist spinners – who
are far more prominent overseas. So my message to all of the
'leggies' at this year's Bunbury Festival is: stick with it and
don't lose heart if you can't always pitch six balls on a
length or find a flipper to go with your googly.

We need express pace too. Quick bowlers are always a
handy weapon for a captain to have in his armoury when
the ball is old, the pitch is flat and the opposition are 250–2.
That's not to say that the next generation of England
cricketers all have to try and bowl like Shane Warne or Brett
Lee. We need inventive, adaptable batters with sound
techniques who are as fluent in the reverse sweep as the
forward defensive, and also know how to play on different
types of wickets – seamer-friendly 'green-uns' or turning
tracks.

And let's not forget the 'keepers' either. Wanted: more
young stumpers with fast hands and nimble feet, and if they
can bat too, all the better.

Talent, however, will only take you so far. These days
all the best cricket teams put in the hard yards in the gym
and the swimming pool to ensure that their fitness levels are
on par with other international athletes. Whatever you may
hear from pundits on the radio and TV that it wasn't like
this 'in my day', believe you me, the pace of the game has
increased in both Test and One-Day cricket and you need to
be super fit to win.

So, we want young players with an appetite for hard
work and the desire to improve their fitness levels as well as
their cricketing skills. But there is a third quality, which is
an absolute prerequisite for success in international cricket:
mental toughness. This is a word you often hear bandied
about in commentary boxes and it is best defined as an
ability to withstand intense pressure. Where does that
pressure come from? It can come from within – knowing
that you have to make a half-century or a hundred to get
your team out of a hole. It can also come from without. Just

try being a Pommie cricketer standing on the boundary in front of a noisy Australian crowd when a high one goes up off the bat – and you'll know exactly what I mean. Or pressure can come from the media – as often happens when a player is going through a bad run of form and there's a cry for change in the selection policy.

And the opposition won't be short of a word either. There are plenty of teams who like to dish out the verbals. And as long as it is kept within the limits set by the umpires, it's all good fun and part of the package that goes with professional cricket.

So, that's my vision of England's cricketing future: a group of highly talented, hard-working, mentally disciplined individuals all vying for places in the international team. I like to think we've got good players with those qualities representing England right now but the next England Captain will need them too – and the more he has to pick from, the better our chances of taking the English game to a higher level.

Good luck with this year's festival and a big pat on the back from me to ESCA and, of course, my great pal David English and his team of organisers. It's a fantastic event and I'm sure that in the future you'll all treasure the memories of taking part – whether your cricketing future lies on the village green or in the Test arena.

All the best,

Michael Vaughan

(September 2004)

Bunburys for England

LORD MACLAURIN OF KNEBWORTH, DL

I am delighted to be able to pen a few words for David's book.

I write these words as the retiring Chairman of the England and Wales Cricket Board. I have been Chairman for the past six years and we have concentrated our efforts in that time on the development of cricket at all levels. Our grassroots programme has never been stronger and our International Team has been performing better and better.

I write this note just before our team leaves for the Ashes tour of Australia – let's hope that the team acquits itself well.

Over the years, I have been fortunate enough to follow the progress of the Bunbury Schools Festival. It offers marvellous opportunities for younger players to get noticed for the first time and one hopes that they will progress from the festival into county cricket and then the very best on to the England Team.

It gratifies me to see players who have taken part in the festivals over the years progress to the England side.

On a personal note I would like to thank David English for all that he has done for cricket in this country. I have thoroughly enjoyed working with him over the past six years and hope that this exceptional festival flourishes for many years to come.

(December 2004)

The Bunburys

THE RT HON JOHN MAJOR, KG, CH

The Bunburys are unique.

In their teams will be found some of the greatest players in world cricket, icons from earlier decades and celebrities of every kind with variable cricketing skills – all joined together by a love of the game.

But it's not always cricket as one *expects* it to be. The Bunburys play firstly for fun – and nothing is quite what it seems.

Are there eleven players in the team? Not necessarily. Can a batsman be given 'not out' if caught bang in front first ball on his birthday? Of course he can. Are there really sixteen fielders on the pitch? Very likely. Such eccentricities may infringe the strict Laws of Cricket but never the Laws of Entertainment.

In a world that often takes itself too seriously, the Bunburys are the supreme antidote: only rain or fog – or anything else – that *stops* play is taken seriously and then only for a brief moment. It's why they draw such crowds and carry cricket to those who otherwise might never watch it.

These days all too many schools – alas – play no cricket. This makes the Bunbury English Schools Cricket Festival even more important and David English's role in it has been pivotal for two decades. This year is its twentieth anniversary and, with luck, it will be a vintage season.

Who know how many future Ashes winners may play? Who will the stars be? These are games to enjoy for their own sake and also to glimpse some cricketing future.

Have fun – for that's the Bunbury creed.

(January 2006)

The Bunburys – A Force for Good and a Force for Fun

DAME NORMA MAJOR

Since 1989, David English has been bringing his Bunbury team to Alconbury in support of Huntingdon Mencap. The funds raised have contributed hugely to several local projects that help people with learning disabilities. All those involved with Huntingdon Mencap are immensely grateful to David and his players for their generosity and commitment. The Bunburys fixture is a hugely popular event and has become part of the annual landscape in Huntingdon. Generally, the weather has been kind to us, but even when it has not everyone has remained good humoured and a lot of fun has still been had.

But David's interest stretches beyond charity matches and I congratulate the Bunburys on the twentieth anniversary of their involvement in the English Schools Cricket Festival. Many fine players – adults and school players who later became household names – have participated in these games and everyone has enjoyed them and benefited from them.

I am a huge admirer of the Bunburys as a force for good and a source of fun. May the sun shine on the anniversary.

(January 2006)

A Damn Good Year... 2001

CHRIS ADAMS
(Sussex CCC and England)

The MCC is widely regarded as the premier of cricket clubs and it was a lifetime ambition fulfilled when I finally joined the elite. However, equal in honour and perhaps greater in pleasure was my long-awaited introduction to the world-famous Bunbury Cricket Club.

Abinger Hammer was the venue, myself and Richard Montgomerie had received the call-up by the legend himself, Dave English. A cracking ground, fabulous weather and, if my memory serves me well, I managed to get a few runs on the day. But what most people don't know is that I nicked the very first ball of the game to the keeper, only a faint one I might add but none the less a nick. Horrified at the embarrassment of it all I soon realised that nobody had appealed, in fact the bowler was already turning to deliver the next ball. I duly dispatched it to the boundary, one bounce four. Thank you very much I thought, Mr Boycott would have been proud of me.

Although I only recently became a Bunbury I have had the pleasure of appearing against them on several occasions. One game that springs to mind was an Allan Warner benefit match against the Bunburys. 'Jack' Warner was a teammate of mine at the time and an old colleague of us both had agreed to represent the Bunburys – the great Michael Holding. So picture the scene when at number 4 for the Warner XI out walks a cocky, impetuous youngster by the name of C. J. Adams. On to bowl came the legendary Michael Holding. What followed may have been a coincidence but looking back I'm not so sure. Michael

marked out his usual run-up and then pushed off the
sightscreen to deliver the first ball. He absolutely tore in at
a great speed and then proceeded to deliver the slowest,
gentlest pie of all time, which I launched over cover for four.
Chest out I wandered down the wicket and prodded the
wicket, pleased with my superiority over this once great
bowler. Michael then marked out a much smaller run-up,
about 15 paces. Got him I thought, his great pace is no
match for my skill so he is just going to bowl tight to stop
me scoring. The next delivery speared in at such pace I had
barely begun to bring my bat down when two of my
precious stumps were uprooted and sent hurtling somewhere
in the direction of Spondon, about three miles away.
Valuable lesson learned: respect your opposition, especially
if they happen to be a legend of the game.

Great memories, great times; let's hope this year will
bring many more great days. Good luck to all you
Bunburys, let's make this year one to remember.

All the best,

Grizzly

The Great Man

ROBERT KEY

(Kent CCC and England)

'Bobbie Boy, how are you? You're playing for the Bunburys at Windsor Castle in a few weeks, wear something smart as the Queen may be there, I'll send the details over the next few days. See you then.'

This was the phone call I got in 2001 from the great David English.

Since then I have played for the Bunburys a couple of times, meeting the likes of Rory Bremner, John (Grammy) Altman, Jamie

David English

Theakston and Anoushka, a Polish super model. The latter certainly had the best shape with or without the ball.

I have only played two games but for the past God knows how many years Dave has organised hundreds of these games, bringing some of showbiz and cricket's greatest together on the cricket field and all for charity.

Enjoy the festival on and off the field as it gives you the opportunity to represent your country but also, and more importantly, you meet friends you will probably have for life. I roomed with Owais Shah amongst others at the festival and I still see him as a good friend today. Neither of us got in the England side that year so if you don't, remember it is not the end of your career; it's probably a good omen, if the selectors are still the same. Good luck to those who get in. Play well.

Life as We Know It in the Twilight Zone

JOHN RICE
(Hampshire CCC)

It's strange how, when you start from a false premise, the very best of travel instructions are no longer viable and become rather tenuous . . . and as a consequence logical thinking goes straight out the window.

Turn right at the T-junction the directions definitely stated – then take the 2nd right and follow the lane to Halcot CC. From that moment it all got a little bizarre!

Every right turn became a possibility, as everything on the supplied photocopied map started to make little sense. Whether it be a small track, a very minor side road, someone's driveway or a footpath over a stile – they all became distinct possibilities as the time wore on – even left turns were looking promising.

Did I have the rogue map once again, or was it just bad luck, or had I suddenly become inept at map reading. All the possible turnings to the cricket club, so I thought, were viewed from both directions – was it once or twice or three times, who knows? Back and forwards, back and forwards!

The first Bunbury match of the season against the Northants Sporting All Stars X1 supporting Tony Penberthy's benefit, and I'm lost in the middle of Northampton – missing valuable drinking time. I'm in Halcot but where is the— ground?

Hang on – is that the Leader? It looks as if he too is looking for what appears to be a non-existent turning!!

Then in conjunction with a hand signal strongly resembling the 'Fugitive' attempting to master the butterfly stroke, he slowed down and was about to begin his manoeuvre left. (Such a hand signal has not been seen in Northampton since the indicators on cars stopped flicking out of the bodywork!)

Whilst the Captain it seemed was contemplating pulling in, to take another look at his map, I arrived at his side. Vigorous hand signals continued in an agitated manner as he realised another car was too close for comfort and proceeded to quickly wind up his window! A tad anti-social I thought!

The season had not officially started, but 'lofe as we know it' as a Bunbury was already beginning to enter the 'Twilight Zone' – in the nicest possible way of course. (What I really mean to say is that life tends to surge with a great deal of extra energy when you are lucky enough to be in the presence of the ever-ebullient David English!)

'Ricey . . . it's you! Thought I was gonna be mugged . . . pull in . . . come 'er . . . brilliant . . . marvellous.' Opening the rear door of his car I was aware of blazers, blazers and more blazers! And then the process of being presented with the very first Bunbury blazer began . . . the Bunbury motto rang out, 'A Bunbury stands for freedom . . . and a Bunbury does his best.' Magic! What an honour and a privilege!!

So here we are, in the middle of Northampton, the time
12.11 p.m., in a gravel lay-by next to an electricity sub-
station and pylon, with what is now a fair amount of
interest being shown by the locals, slowing and passing in
their cars, intrigued, squinting and wondering, and
seemingly becoming a little distressed as to why they had not
been informed about, what appeared to be, an upmarket car
boot sale!

Issie arrives, appearing out of nowhere, also lost, only to
hear the Skip stating that 'it suits you sir' and suggesting
'you ought to be a model Ricey . . . Armani and all that . . .
yeah . . . superb . . . What size did you want? 46 long . . .
Try this, 44 long . . . how about a 46 reg . . . brilliant Ricey,
marvellous . . . Fantastic Johnny Boy.'

And so the season was about to begin! (And what's the
moral? Never forget the Englishman's Philosophy: 'From
every potential tragedy a window of opportunity opens.')

And by the way . . . It was left at the T-junction.

Best wishes,

John Rice

Sir Loon

ROBIN SMITH
('The Judge' – Hampshire CCC and England)

It always gives me great pleasure to do anything for David English
(the Loon) and when he asked me to contribute a few words towards
his book, it gave me great pride to be able to do so.

I can't help feeling that at times all the wonderful work that
Dave continues to do goes unnoticed. He not only raises large
amounts of money for various charities, but has also spent years

developing the well-organised and respected English Schools U-15 Bunbury Festivals.

I would like to take this opportunity to wish all those playing in the festival lots of luck, and like so many others who have also taken part, I hope to see a few of you coming through to play for England.

One of the most enjoyable Bunbury fixtures was the day organised to raise money for the great Malcolm Marshall's son Mali. I was fortunate to captain Malcolm's side against a powerful Bunbury team, which boasted many International captains, and was captained by Sir Viv Richards. Had it not been for Dave, many of us would not have enjoyed that wonderful experience and I know the money raised has helped to ensure that Mali is being raised and educated in the way Malcolm would have wished.

David's work is endless. I don't know where he gets his energy and never-ending enthusiasm from. If he could bottle and market it, he would make a million – but knowing him as I do, it would all be donated to charity.

I have shared so many enjoyable times with Dave and have just recently purchased his autobiography, which is also giving me great entertainment.

I wish everyone involved in the Bunbury's great fun ahead and look forward to calling my mate Dave 'Sir Loon'!

Beep for Beefy

DAVE ROBERTS
(Lancs CCC and England Physio)

Going mental on one of Beefy's marathon walks around the UK, me as 'Physio' and Dave English as 'entertainer'. Yes, that's what I remember about the great Botham walks raising millions for Leukaemia Research and latterly the Noah's Ark Appeal. I'm sure we did some good along the way but we also had a great laugh.

The 'Loon' was trying to sell his house in London to Joe Cuby on the Aberdeen–Ipswich 'East coast walk' – and doing so in the break of the Radio One show (broadcasting the whole walk from a van), when in-between, English was on the microphone (where else) telling jokes, making wisecracks and giving out his hotel and room number to any female aged between 16 and 60!

The microphone was still *on* when Joe Cuby offered *less* than Dave was happy with and it was a source of great amusement to Beefy, the support crew and walkers listening in on the unfolding conversation – where, to be honest, Joe held all the aces!

Every night Dave would entertain the crews at the team dinner and dear old 'Crash' Lander (sadly now departed) would hold count at the 'fines' meetings. Hard work to keep everyone going for 35 days on the trot, but we managed it and now all we remember is the 'banter' and the humour.

English 'can get to where water can't', and one place he has got to and will remain is in the history and tradition of the Bunburys.

David Had Us in Stitches for the Whole Week

MAL LOYE
(Lancashire CCC)

I first met David English when I was 15 years old. I was invited to spend a week playing at the Bunburys Schools Cricket Festival, under David's supervision!! David had myself and every other boy in stitches for the whole week with his sense of humour.

I thought he was great . . . until . . . last year at the 'PCA Award Ceremony', when I was approached by David, who looked me straight in the eyes and said, 'Has anyone seen Mal Loye?'

I've Had more than a Few Laughs

DARREN GOUGH
(Yorks, Essex CCC and England)

*Everyone who has seen me play will know that I always enjoy
myself on the field and try to play the game with a smile on
my face. And I can safely say that I've had more than a few
laughs when I've been given the opportunity to turn out for
the Bunburys in a charity game. I've made plenty of friends
playing for the Bunburys and I'm sure that all the young lads
taking part in this summer's festival will do too.*

Best wishes,

Darren Gough

Great Chance to Establish New Friendships

ANTHONY MCGRATH
(Yorkshire CCC and England)

The Bunbury Festival is a fantastic event; I have many happy
memories of my week there. It was my first chance to see and play
against the best players in the country. There is strong competition,
but also an opportunity to establish new friendships, some of which
will be lifelong.

In my particular year Marcus Trescothick, Vic Solanki, Paul

Collingwood and Phil Neville (Man. Utd) were all starting their careers with style.

So I am sure you will have a great week. Keep working hard but most importantly enjoy your cricket.

Good luck lads, and well done David English!
Anthony McGrath

Memories of My Bunbury Debut

RICHARD DAWSON
(Yorkshire CCC and England)

The Bunbury Festival is a highlight in any young cricketer's career and I've got good memories of my Bunbury debut. Michael Gough, now at Durham, and Richard Logan, currently at Northants, were among my contemporaries then. Both have gone on to make professional careers.

Best wishes to everyone taking part this year.

What Some People Do in the Course of Duty

MARK EALHAM
(Kent, Notts CCC and England)

Picture this . . . David English, sitting on a rock in the middle of Africa writing a benefit article, and who for? Me! Couldn't quite believe it, a cell phone call to my little village of Elham explaining that at any moment, while writing his

masterpiece, one of a selection of local wildlife could pop up
and make a feast of Mr English.

Of course, this wouldn't be the first time that Mr
English's life has been in danger. I'm sure he has feared for
his next breath on many occasions standing 22 yards away
from some of the fastest bowlers in the world, although
unfortunately I cannot include myself in this category. I'm
just a friendly 'pasty-faced pie thrower', to quote some of
our more knowledgeable international journalists.

What some people do in the course of duty. And what a
duty! I take my hat off to you David; for all that you do for
your causes. Thanks to you, the Bunburys have brought a
little bit of that African sunshine to many lives. I must also
mention the help and support the Bunburys give to cricketers,
young and old(er), to aid their development at an early age
and to enable 'crusty old pros' to go on a little bit longer.

David, you know that at any time you can call upon my help
as a man of Kent, not a Kentish man. It is an absolute pleasure
to be associated with the Bunburys, I await your call . . .

In any case, Mr English survived and the masterpiece
arrived, with a photo of the man himself still in one piece,
to the great relief of all those he has helped over many years.

All the best,

Mark Ealham

Kippered by the Skipper

ALAN BUTCHER
(Surrey CCC and England)

After a successful Bunbury debut at Billericay the Skip dangled the
irresistible carrot of Bunbury sweater and cap. A good lunch, fun on

the field, ladies sharing the dressing rooms, it was impossible not to want more. The Skip being a shrewd man knew I was hooked.

'Can you play at Shenley Butch? It's for Weeksey, need a good side, be fantastic to have you. Champers, smoked salmon the whole works you'll love it.'

Unfortunately the match coincided with Surrey's NUI fixture with Essex.

'Sorry, Skip,' I tried to explain. 'I've got to work. I've got to do a presentation at Guildford. I'm not going to be able to make it.'

'Don't worry Butch, come along after. We always field first, get your presentation done, come and have lunch and a bat.'

I wavered, the lure of cap and sweater too much for me.

'Well maybe I could if—'

'Great stuff Butch see you Sunday.'

And so it was that a 160-mile round trip, from Coggeshall Essex via Guildford and on to Shenley, saw me enter the car park on the hottest day of the summer in time to watch the profusely perspiring figure of the Skipper walk off at the end of the Bunbury innings.

Champers, smoked salmon ... all gone and the prospect of fielding in the stifling heat; this wasn't how it was supposed to be. I'd been done like a kipper.

The Skipper being a perceptive man noticed my disappointment. 'Take the new – ball Butch.'

This brought about the most fearsome opening pair on show for the Bunbury's all season. Or at the very least the shortest, roundest pair of left arm trundlers in Butcher and Robinson, supported by the hungriest most predatory fielding side I've seen in a long time. Well, certainly the hungriest anyway.

Needless to say, we lost – to cap a terrific day's travelling. Still I earned my sweater and I'm looking forward to next year.

David English, The People's Champion

RONNIE IRANI
(Essex CCC and England)

I would like to take this opportunity to thank David English for all he has done, not just for the youngsters involved with the Bunbury Festival but also for the people throughout the cricketing universe!

He always manages to put a wonderful smile on the top international players' faces and give a laugh to the genuine cricket supporter.

As many people reading this article will know, David English has got a huge heart. He's not just a roaring fast bowler and left-handed batsman, but also a people's person. He is a man who will do anything for anyone, a 'people's champion', with total belief not only in himself as an individual but also in others.

My international career has had its ups and downs ever since I made my debut in 1996, but the likes of the David Englishes of this world have always rubbed off on me that I have to reach for the moon and if I fall short I will get the stars!

Just lately I have been given the opportunity of representing England again, and even though the highest level is very testing in all departments, mentally as well as physically, the rewards are of mighty proportions! If at first you fail, you must try again and that's what it's been like for me in my international career. Hopefully I will be able to continue in this vein.

A couple of years ago I was asked if I would ever play for England again, and as a pro you give a standard answer, 'of course I would like to if things go well and I can get some runs on the board and take a few wickets, and it starts to happen for you and all of a sudden you get a lucky break.'

You think it is an uphill battle and you're not going anywhere. It is strange how things work out sometimes. Reflecting on my

2002 season with Essex and England, it was one of my best seasons ever.

One old boy told me once, 'Mr Irani, it is like rubbing away at a stone, just keep rubbing and eventually it will become smooth.'

Mr English has done a lot of rubbing over the years and, let me tell you, he is one of the smoothest people in the game of cricket!!

Good luck pal and don't forget about my benefit year 2003. Looking forward to your company again and again many times over.

(September 2002)

A Fantastic and Relaxed Way of Raising Vital Funds for Charity

ADAM 'THE TYLOON' HOLLIOAKE
(Surrey CCC and England)

There are two things that spring to mind when I think of the Bunbury Cricket Club. The first is the fantastic and relaxed way of raising vital funds for charity; the second is, it is run by an absolute raving loony!!!!

Every time you pull on a Bunbury shirt you are guaranteed a fun day out and of course endless hours of banter with the other Bunburys.

David just recently approached me about organising a charity/memorial game for my beloved brother Ben, and as we spoke for hours on the phone about how we would go about it and who we would get along, I told David he was a tycoon. He was probably not used to me calling him that, as I usually call him 'the Loon'. Quick as a flash he replied, 'OK, from now on you and me will be known as "the Tyloons".'

So, from one tyloon to another, may I wish you another successful season and thank you for all the kind dedications in your book/brochure and the setting-up of the Ben Hollioake Scholarship.

My Pal, The Loon

DAVID LEATHERDALE
(Worcestershire CCC)

Some 27 years ago when I played my first game of cricket for Pudsey St Lawrence CC at the ripe old age of eight, it was difficult to imagine I would be writing this résumé now.

Having watched, in the crowd as a 13-year-old boy, a certain I.T. Botham score a now famous hundred at Headingley; having played in the same side as the very same seven years later, where I had the fortune, or is that misfortune, to meet 'Mr English'; and now having Beefy as patron of my benefit year – these are the sort of things a young aspiring cricketer dreams about.

The first time I met 'the Loon' was as a raw 20-year-old in my second year as a professional at Worcestershire CCC. The occasion was Phil Neales' 6-a-side benefit day, where cricket was secondary and fun was the order of the day, an event that still continues today. One thing I have learned about 'the Loon' is: always expect the unexpected. But it still came as a huge surprise to see Dave opening the batting with Bill Wyman, and Eric Clapton sitting with his pads on batting at three.

Names like these are more associated with a wooden stage than a grass one, but they are what has made the Bunbury dynasty what it is today.

As a 35-year-old with greying hair and 17 years' professional cricketing under my belt, and still a couple more to come, I hope, the friendships built up and enjoyment received will live long after my legs have died.

With the help of people like the Loon and the Bunburys, many more young committed cricketers will get the chance to experience the world of professional cricket, as I have.

Congratulations to the Bunbury's on your Silver Anniversary, 25 for those not old enough to know, and long may it continue.

(October 2003)

From the Front Line

MARK AUSTIN
(Presenter ITV Evening News)

Stories from the war zones . . .

'Tell us some stories from the war zones and throw in some sporting tales,' said David English when ordering me to bash out an article for his book.

Well, the truth is, I can never really understand why I swapped the life of a sports correspondent for the world of war reporting. It was such a great life covering England's Test tours in the eighties as well as all the Olympics and World Cups and other great sporting occasions. But for some reason I decided to opt for a more dangerous life in the world's hotspots.

Sure enough, there've been some hairy moments . . . Coming under rocket attack in Afghanistan (I hit the deck as my fearless cameraman carried on as if nothing was happening. What is it about cameramen?) . . . Being marched into a field at gunpoint by rebels in Africa . . . And ending up in a minefield in Bosnia. But happily we extricated ourselves from those tricky situations and life went on.

And anyway, I much prefer focusing on the great moments I've witnessed first hand over the years.

Single best sporting moment . . . The 100 metres Olympic final in Seoul, 'won' by Ben Johnson in the fastest time ever recorded in the world. Then finding out three days later that Johnson had cheated – cheated his opponents, cheated the sporting world and cheated everybody watching. It was a huge story but one I'd rather not have covered.

Best cricketing moments . . . Botham '81 of course, but also Botham's hundred in Brisbane in 1986/7 and, dare I say it, Viv's 56-ball century in Antigua.

Which brings me to the Bunbury CC . . . and charity cricket matches. And I'll never forget being asked by D.I. Gower to play in one of his testimonial games when I ended up batting with Eric Clapton! After he ducked and weaved his way through a particularly lively over from Imran Khan he walked up to the wicket and said, 'Bloody hell! I'd rather come with you to a sodding war zone!'

It's fun being a Bunbury!

I Could Have Been a Contender

CLIVE MANTLE

What a depressing thought – six months without cricket – six months without the banter and the badinage – six months without the Bunbury's. One consolation – six months for my fractured rib to heal!! I can then continue to throw my sad, unfit, 40-year-old frame around far-flung pitches and try to convince Test players, past and present, that I could have been a contender, whilst they applaud sympathetically, calling 'Great by Clifton' and 'Unlucky big man' but laughing quietly to themselves that the poor deluded giant at deep mid-wicket can't even act, let alone catch a ball.

But I had my moment in 1997. Sadly only able to play four matches because of filming, my greatest as a Bunbury came at Hampstead during our final game of the season. I had resisted the allure of the Ryder Cup in the Pavilion and was eagerly fielding hoping to catch Skip's eye for a bowl. (McCague and Mantle opening sounded good to me – but Skip went with Malcolm and Giddins. What was so special about them?)

Late on in the innings I made a desperate, badly timed and ill-advised dive at a lofted pull to deep mid-wicket, and as I landed I knew instantly I had done something horrible in my rib area. My only worries at the time were that I had dropped the catch and, even worse, that my wife and my agent would not let me play cricket again because of the danger to my physical well-being. Amidst the pain of the ignominy of the split catch and the pain of the fractured rib I stood my ground, mercifully not having to field for some ten minutes whilst I tried to gather my composure. By now the opposition were cruising to victory, although with only one wicket left, two excellent batsmen were punishing our brave bowlers mercilessly. Just as I was wondering what excuse Skip would make if he did offer me a bowl now, their Captain, thinking obviously he was perfectly safe hitting to me, lofted a mighty, high, spirally, spinning pull. I thought, 'Oh no – not me please,' but yes, the sky visibly darkened a notch or two as the ball ascended. It stopped in the air at the top of the arc, decided who it should fall towards, and chose me. 'Oh no – not Clive please,' the team muttered under their breath – but down it came. The rest of the world had ceased to exist for me, all I could imagine was the reaction if I dropped it – I still shudder to contemplate. The ball was fizzing in the air, spinning cruelly, that sound the only palpable noise other than the doom-laden thundering of my heart calling for pity.

And then I caught it – I caught it – I actually held on to the ball, and the game was won. The game was won, the season was over and I held the ball. All I then remember was 26 fully grown men running towards me, disbelief written large on their faces.

Amidst the congratulations and plaudits, each player managed to crush my ribs even more, but the pain was only evident later, for in that moment – for once, and once only – I had been a contender.

Fun-Filled Bunbury Days

GRAEME HICK
(Worcs CCC and England)

What do we do when we finally say, 'That's enough, and I'm hanging the boots up'? Are we happy ('at last it's over') or are we sad ('I wish I could carry on, I enjoy it so much but the body can't take it'); or do we sit there totally lost pondering over our next step.

We sit there no doubt and reflect upon what has gone, the highs and lows and the fun that we had along the way. I feel the most important things we take into retirement are the friendships that we have forged over the years.

Through David English, the Bunburys and the game of cricket we have had the opportunity of expanding those friendships into other walks of life. Where else would you be entertained by Ian Botham, Leslie Grantham, Sam Fox, Ian Wright, Michael Lynagh, Gary Mason, to mention a few. I have always found it enjoyable and interesting meeting people from the other fields. A magnificent effort by David English has turned the Bunburys into the success it is, which means great fun days (even in the rain?) and many generous people out there making great contributions towards the various charities that the Bunburys support.

I look forward to my next appearance for the Bunburys and hopefully help raise more money for the worthy charities.

Wonderful Day at Worcester

JOHN ELLIOTT
(Chairman of Worcs CCC)

I first met David on a beautiful summer's day in 1979 in a benefit match for Vanburn Holder versus Vic Lewis's XI on the County Ground at Worcester. I was behind the stumps and David scored 50 plus for Lewis's. Soon I realised this was a man of character as the jokes and banter flowed between us during his innings, something I have always remembered. During the evening David got up to his usual cabaret stint. He made the day most successful.

From then on David became very good friends with the players and committee at Worcester and entertained at many functions for the beneficiaries.

In 1983 I asked David to open a fete on behalf of the Club's fundraising and again we had a wonderful day.

The real highlight of our great times together was when Worcester signed Ian Botham and Graham Dilley in 1987, and from then on David and his celebrity friends enjoyed some exciting times. In 1988 I organised a pro-am 6-a-side cricket match on the County Ground for Phil Neale's benefit and David entered a team, including Eric Clapton, Ian Botham, Bill Wyman and Jeff Lynne. They enjoyed their cricket and the entertainment we had in the evening was unforgettable.

Another wonderful Saturday was Worcestershire versus Leicestershire at New Road. Graeme Hick and David Gower were playing. Our guests for the day included Elton John, George Harrison, Eric Clapton and David English. The members were amazed when they saw the police protecting three red Ferraris in the car park. Pink champagne flowed all afternoon.

Amongst some of the most enjoyable times was when David

brought the Bunbury Cricket Club to play against the beneficiaries to raise money and entertain the public with some famous stars, including Rory Bremner, who was tremendous on the loudspeaker system.

I would like to congratulate David on the tremendous job he has done for the England junior sides in arranging the many festivals. He has proved to us all at Worcester his great love of the game and the effort he has put in to make the Bunbury's so successful.

We have all come a long way since those days in 1979. I am now Chairman of the Club and David and his friends will always be welcome to enjoy our hospitality at Worcestershire for all the good he has done for English cricket.

Well done David. Hope to see you during our centenary year.

Following in the Footsteps – Maybe!

MATTHEW P. MAYNARD
(Glamorgan CCC and England)

Once again it gives me great pleasure to contribute to Dave's diary. I was fortunate to play my first game for the Bunbury's last season in aid of Courtney Walsh's benefit. It turned out to be a tremendous day although the weather was not what you would call ideal for cricket – that horrible thin rain that absolutely drenches you!! Most sides would probably have just cancelled the game but it is testament to David English, the Bunbury's and Courtney that the game went ahead.

It was great to see 'Syd' Lawrence playing and bowling spin in tandem to Phil 'the Cat' Tufnell. These two, apart from David 'the Hit man' English, were our best bowlers on the day (unfortunately our strike bowler Joe Cuby was a little under the weather after a night on the ink!!) and after Syd had taken 3 for 10 off four beautifully directed and flighted off-spin, I questioned why he hadn't taken up spin some 15 years earlier?!! The most enjoyable aspect of the day for me though was batting with David Ward – formerly of Surrey CCC. He's one of the nicest blokes I've had the pleasure of meeting through my career and also one of the sweetest hitters of a cricket ball. We just stood and delivered for about 10 overs in which time David played some of the most scintillating shots you could wish to see. I was very tempted to offer him a chance of playing First Class cricket again there and then!

At the end of a deserving victory for the Bunbury's everyone went their separate ways, looking forward to their next game for this great team . . . I certainly was.

My first taste of the Bunbury Festival came last year when my son Tom represented the West.

I couldn't quite comprehend how big the festival was and also how much effort David and his team of organisers put into it. Shrewsbury School was an excellent setting for the tournament and I thoroughly enjoyed watching the games.

There are certainly a good number of players who have 'what it takes' to become professional cricketers. The telling point, of course, is how these youngsters fare when they are seventeen, eighteen or nineteen years of age. If they still have the desire, bottle, commitment and, no doubt, luck, then I'm sure a number of them will be able to emulate the likes of Flintoff, Crawley, Vaughan, Hussain et al. and not only go on to play first class cricket but go on to gain full International caps.

The Bunbury Festival gives the players a great opportunity to test their skills against the best players of their own age. And, although scoring hundreds and taking five fours at fifteen is no guarantee of future success, it does give the players an enormous amount of confidence in their ability. I will be watching this year's festival with added interest to see if my lad can score a few. As this Maynard is getting on a bit it would be nice to see another Maynard play for Glamorgan at some future date.

Good luck to all the players, enjoy the festival, enjoy your cricket and have fun.

To Dave, 'the Loon', and his crew, keep up the wonderful work that you do to give the youngsters the best possible chance of making it.

(September 2004)

My Bunbury Debut

MICHAEL LYNAGH
(Aussie Rugby Legend)

I was thrilled to be invited by David English to participate this year in a number of Bunbury games and managed to play in the final game of the season.

David at the time seemed quite desperate to get me to come down to West Hampstead Cricket Club to play and I was very surprised to see 28 players ready to take on Allcorners in the cause of furthering the Bunbury name and also of course great charity.

It took me back to the heydays of Lillie and Thomson in 1974, when the opening bowler had a 6 or 7 slips in place and nobody in front of the bat. But we had actually 26 slips and we still managed to drop a catch.

I thoroughly enjoyed playing for the Bunbury Cricket Club, humbly titled the World's No. 1 Celebrity Cricket Team, and after spending a day with David English and his cohorts, I have no doubt that this is a very apt title.

I even managed to have a 50-odd run partnership with the man himself, which basically meant me standing at one end and David hitting the ball and running without even calling or looking in my direction. It took all of my powers of mind reading and reacting to David actually appearing at the same end as myself, to ensure that I was not run out on numerous occasions.

If I am invited to play for the Bunbury's next year, which I sincerely hope I am, I will insist that I am placed in the batting order, so as not to coincide with David's very haphazard running technique.

I do indeed look forward to next season's festivities and playing a role in the Bunbury drive to raise money for various charities throughout the year.

See you all next year.

(September 2000)

Biffo

DAVID 'CHALKIE' GOWER

David English, or 'Biffo', is a friend and a colleague who does tireless work for charity. So, it was only fitting he received a special award at last year's PCA event to mark his services to the game.

The Bunburys enjoy themselves, wherever they are, at any time. Most parties slow down at some stage but not, it seems, this one! The fact that they are still going strong is down to everyone involved, buoyed, as they all are by the camaraderie that is a major feature of Bunbury cricket.

However, I don't suppose anyone would mind me singling out David English as the most important factor in all this. He has been 'Biffo' to my 'Chalkie' ever since he made his name as a dead German in *A Bridge too Far*, i.e. years before we even met. Everywhere we meet around the world we are straight into the routine of retired Wing Commanders, with no disrespect, I promise you, to the genuine articles.

Yet behind the fun façade is a man of real substance. The Bunburys raise millions through their efforts and David has also been the driving force behind the inception of the Under-15 World Challenge, due again this year, which augments the long-running Bunbury Under-15's competition that provides a huge challenge and inspiration for that generation of cricketers.

All of this deserves recognition, which was officially forthcoming as David picked up a special award presented by the Professional Cricketers Association last September, to mark his services to the game. As the MC for the evening it gave me the chance and great pleasure to make the presentation myself.

But typically, that was not his only contribution to the evening ... Undoubtedly the most exciting and entertaining of the PCA's awards nights, it was topped by the performance of the Mark Butcher Bunbury Band, whose almost impromptu gig had them all rocking and rolling in the aisles and boxes of the Albert Hall.

If 'Butch' ever feels that the challenge of taking on the likes of Allan Donald has paled at all then he will be very much at home with guitar and microphone. His back-up band included Mark Illott on guitar alongside Wayne Morton; Graeme Fowler on drums; with Robin Smith and Phil Tufnell on auxiliary percussion, i.e. triangle! Also present? Just Bill Wyman, Paul Carrack, Roy Harper, Steve Harley, Ray Cooper, John Altman, to name but a few. That line-up will never appear on stage together again and the two thousand or so guests certainly showed their appreciation on the night.

Yes, it was Biffo who got them all together, and a big thank you is due to him for that on top of all his usual efforts. David, it's been a fantastic effort all round from you and it's not over by a long chalk (Chalkie!). This is only the beginning. I know you will take the Bunburys onwards and upwards and I salute you for it.

(October 2001)

The Year 2000 and Beyond

DAVID GRAVENEY
(Chairman of England's Selectors)

20 Bunbury Festivals, 2 Junior World Cups, England U15's vs. South Africa U15's. All tournaments require total commitment from a small band of tireless individuals to achieve success and in this regard no one individual could have contributed more than David English. It remains one of the highlights of 2000 to witness the aforementioned Mr English being honoured by the Professional Cricketers Association for his contribution to cricket in this country. (Even if he does make me travel the odd mile or two to help him out.)

The Bunbury Festival begins the road to the full England team. Long may David and his passion keep this wonderful week going.

Brother Kalli

ALVIN KALRICHARAN
(West Indies)

Another year of playing for the Bunburys X1 is over and I enjoyed every minute of it – camaraderie, fun and joy in doing good things for unfortunate people. Well, where do I start about 'Captain Uncertain'.

What's going to happen next? The Team is never complete with 30 people in a side.

Playing at Dunnington for Colin Graves, our sponsor, against the Bunbury X1 ... They batted first and scored 200 plus, which seemed at the time an easy target – but when we walked out to bat, there was not a patch of green on the field – all covered by men in whites, 40 on the field, the whites of *Emmerdale Farm* and the cows.

I had a call from Captain Unpredictable to play at Uxbridge. I apologised – explained that it was not possible to play. He pleaded and begged, crying on the phone that he was one short. Turned up at the ground. There were people all over the cricket field! Twenty-four fielders – 'Captain Uncertain', what a great man – a close friend – I am looking forward to another season '2000'.

Magic Moments

BILL WYMAN

Bill tells us of some of his defining cricket moments when he was growing up and some Bunbury highs and lows

Cricket became my love from the day, at age twelve, during a schoolhouse team match, our team were bowled out for 11. I proudly carried my bat for 2 not out. Unfortunately it impressed others less than it impressed me, and needless to say I was never chosen to play for the school team.

As a young teen I spent a few summers playing cricket in the local parks with school friends, and took on the job of scoring for the Lloyds Bank cricket teams in Beckenham. I would also occasionally go to Lord's or to the Oval to watch the Test matches. At Lord's in 1952 I saw Godfrey Evans score 98 before lunch against India – completing his century when play resumed. Next day I saw Mankad hit 184 in reply.

I also followed cricket on my grandmother's new TV set, with its 6-inch TV screen. God knows how we saw the ball. Compton was my hero – Brylcream was not! My fave Australians were Neil Harvey and Keith Miller, and I was fortunate a few years ago to have an entertaining lunch with Keith in London, where he relived wonderful cricketing moments with me.

In the mid-1950s National Service reared its ugly head, and I joined the RAF and was posted to northern Germany. Cricket was not a game you played on a cold wind-swept military base.

My next attempts at cricket came unexpectedly from being a father. I was invited (enticed) to play for two years for the Fathers vs the Sons at Onwell Park School, Ipswich, Suffolk. I was pleased to find that I could still bowl a reasonable amateur leg-break and googlie, and still score a few runs – even with a bat that was shaved down to 2 inches wide – presumably to balance the talents of the teams. It didn't! We lost!

In 1986 I was approached by Eric Clapton (the music business' answer to Wally Hammond) to join his charity team. I accepted with some reservations, but no regrets, and from that day on I played about a dozen or so games each season for ten years – first with Eric and then with David English and his Bunburys.

Suddenly I found myself batting with the likes of Robin Smith, Allan Lamb, Ian Botham, Brian Lara, Alec Stewart, David Gower, Graeme Hick and everyone I'd previously admired from afar.

Almost all our games of that first season were played in pouring rain and we won them all. Whenever the sun came out – we lost! We started doing rain-dances if we were losing.

The summers went by and the cricket became an obsession. And then there were those rare moments:

- Fielding in the slips in the rain with Dennis Lillee, who was gobsmacked to see Eric and I smoking during play – Eric in yellow oilskins, looking like he'd just stepped off a Norwegian whaling boat – letting every ball that came near him pass by for 4 runs – assuring us that his fingers were his first priority.
- Nick Cook running a full 50 yards along the boundary, and then diving full-length to take an absolutely stunning catch that I'll never forget.
- Batting with David English against Imran Khan at Edgbaston, scoring 46 in 2 overs (English 41, Wyman 5). Gary Mason fielding

on the boundary and dropping 5 skied catches one over – Eric having his finger dislocated in the slips by a ball he couldn't avoid – then getting stung by a wasp on the other hand as he was leaving the field for treatment.

- Wicket keeper Roger Forrester laughing about Eric's misfortunes – then being struck on the forehead by the very next ball joining Eric in the 'Hospital Tent'.
- Bowling Graeme Hick with my 'wrong 'un', but enjoying his friendship ever since.
- Doing the same to Michael Holding – who got his revenge – and some!
- Being hit in the gully by a square cut and having to go to the local hospital to have injections for a lump as big as an eff on my shin. The nurse was great though.
- Catching ex-England captain Brian Close one-handed in the gully, with my cigarette in the other hand, and being jumped on by wicket keeper Ian Wright, as if I'd just scored for England.
- Catching a second victim two-handed over my head a few moments later – this time the cigarette was in my mouth.
- Having my thumb impacted by Nick Cook's fast bowling at Stocks, just 3 weeks before joining the Stones for the Steve Wheel's tour of America in 1989.
- And finally, taking my hat trick at the Oval – televised by Sky Sports. At which moment, my wife Suzanne was taking our first daughter Katie for a walk around the pavilion, and missed it! Being informed on her return that 'Bill had done a hat-trick', she thought (being American – and not too 'up' with cricket jargon) that I'd been entertaining the team with magic tricks!

I realised that from that day on, everything I did on the cricket pitch would be downhill, so I was wise enough to retire gracefully, with the treasured short moment of fame! Oh! To have played cricket for a career.

PS: David English is the funniest man I've ever met. He MCs my Rhythm Kings gigs and has given me the chance to play cricket with the world's finest. He may be a loon but he's the best I've ever met.

A Night to Remember

RAY COOPER

I could ramble on, page after page, eulogizing about the feelings and emotions that encompass me when I walk up those hallowed steps to the 'Artists Entrance' of the Royal Albert Hall.

The Hall has been the home for so many years to great events, meetings, dialogues, music, sport; in fact probably every form of performance, every emotion has been vibrantly allowed to flourish under the Hall's magnanimous cupola.

The occasion that had me once again scaling the stairs to the Artists door was a wonderful invitation by Mr David English to pay 'homage' to cricket, a truly great sport. This was an opportunity to say 'thank you' to the players, heroes of the sport, by way of playing music and entertaining them. It was also a great excuse to enjoy as much foot tapping as possible. Sport and music have much in common, the ability to create and enjoy a party is certainly one level at which the two worlds collide gloriously: we were going to create the bacchanalian cricket event of the century!

My first memory of what great 'road' companions the English cricket team could be was in Australia 1986 – Gower, Botham, Gatting, etc. I was on tour with Elton John when cricket and music collided! Many things have been said and written about both tours, but I just remember being overwhelmed by the capacity my sporting heroes had to enjoy themselves both on and off the pitch!

The Albert Hall occasion brought back wonderful memories. I saw faces, both musical and sporting, that I hadn't seen for many years; I had the opportunity to entertain and thank my sporting heroes for all that they had given me over the years. I was able to help raise money for the children of the world who will continue to flourish and grow with sport and music as a part of their lives.

So 'thank you' David English, the Bunbury's Cricket Club, Gower, Botham and so many more for allowing me once again to 'tread the boards' at the Albert, my home from home, to make a public nuisance and spectacle of myself, not a pleasant sight but hopefully an entertaining one!

Thank you for an evening of great music, a chance to glance stage right for one of Bill Wyman's enigmatically reassuring smiles, the chance for a little workout, a little sweat, great comradeship and a lot of foot tapping, dancing and embracing. As I disappeared into the wet night, there was more than a touch of nostalgia in the air. If only the rest of life was like this!

Music and sport are the food of life. Play on and on and on and on!!!

Tufters at the Albert Hall

PHIL TUFNELL
(Middlesex CCC and England)

Well what a top laugh that was, the best time I've had in years; I thought I performed all right once I got over my nerves.

No I'm not talking about a cricket match or tour I've been on, I'm talking about my debut performance on triangle at the Albert Hall no less, with the world-famous Mark Butcher Band. Once again Dave and the Bunburys stopped the show, and we even got an encore. I wish they had encores when I was batting and that they kept calling me back or do I!

I'd personally like to thank the Bunburys for playing a Phil Tufnell xi during my benefit year; and Stephen Tompkinson for a sparkling display with the bat that day.

I look forward to seeing everyone in the future and am sure there will be great years for Bunbury cricket and everything else the Bunburys do. Once again thanks for letting me get up on stage and having the chance to play with a great band and a great bunch of lads. I can only hope I gave something to the performance.

Tuffers

PS: Dave if you need a triangle player for your next gig you need to go through my music agent!!

A Rockstar at Last

MARK BUTCHER

I must admit that when David English first mentioned the idea of the All Star Band, I went along with it never really expecting it to bear fruition. I mean, the thought of fronting a band containing a host of rock's legends at the Albert Hall was surely a fantasy too far-fetched to come true? I have since learned that you doubt Mr English at your peril.

Two months later David called me and started to reel off the stars' names who'd agreed wholeheartedly to be part of the band. It was definitely for real, and my hitherto blasé attitude was replaced by nervous rumblings in the pit of my stomach. I was to be bandleader, I was to pick the songs for the set list and I hadn't played 'live' with a band for nearly four years. Fair to say I was petrified.

September the 8th, Nomis Studios, Kensington, 12.00 p.m. It was official. The date, the time, the place for the Mark Butcher Band's one and only rehearsal. The one thing that was not completely certain was the band's actual line-up; and the only person who had confirmed to me his presence was none other than Wayne Morton, ex-England physio and sometime strummer of acoustic guitar.

Professional cricketers are always last to pitch up at benefit games whilst the amateur goes through his kit bag in nervous expectation. Thus, Wayne and I were easily the first to arrive at the studio, anxiously awaiting the arrival of the proper musicians. Fair to say, David had surpassed himself. Providing the foundation for the band was none other than Bill Wyman on bass and his partner-in-rhythm Terry Taylor on guitar. Percussion duties were sensationally taken care of by ex-Eric Clapton band members Henry Spinetti (drums) and Ray 'I'll hit anything that makes a noise' Cooper – who'd, incidentally, left his smouldering house to join us – on anything that made a noise. John Etheridge, Sting's guitarist, Tim Cansfield from the Bee Gees band and Martin Taylor, the world's greatest jazz player, completed our battery of guitar players; and finally, Hollywood legend John Altman interrupted his schedule to arrange the numbers, tinkle the ivories and blast the odd saxophone solo. David and John had also sourced backing vocals from The Drifters, just in case!

I remember an amazing feeling of exhilaration as the songs started to come together. The guys were incredible to play with, instinctively knowing which direction to take any given time. They also put me at ease very quickly, perhaps sensing how apprehensive I was about performing alongside them. Five hours later, with the outline of the set pretty much taken care of, I drove home feeling as though things couldn't get much better, Surrey had just won the championship and I'd just become an honorary rock star!

At approximately 11 a.m. on 29 September I got my first view of the Albert Hall from the stage where I'd be performing later that night. It was too late to back out now, the boxes and tables were all being prepared and the sound and light engineers had started their pre-gig routines. I was shown to dressing room No. 6 where I left my guitar and dinner suit, then made my way back out into London as I had a previous engagement to attend for my sponsors, OCS. As I crossed Pall Mall, a red Ferrari pulled over and parked just in front of me and who should step out but none other than Eric Clapton himself. I attempted a cool acknowledgement, which probably appeared to him like the actions of a drooling imbecile, and carried on walking. Surely this was a good omen, seeing my hero in person on the same day that I was to play at one of his favourite venues. It all sounds highly unlikely, but I assure you it's true.

- 3 p.m. The band is ready and available for a much-needed sound-check and rehearsal. My nerves have reached critical mass because

David has asked a few more people along to join us. The band had expanded massively and new unrehearsed numbers are appearing on the set list. Paul Carrack, Steve Harley, Roy Harper and Phil Cool are set to join us on stage, so we could use an hour or so running through the new tunes.

- 5 p.m. Still no soundcheck, still no rehearsal. Even Bill Wyman is becoming a little edgy.

- 6 p.m. We finally get on stage but are told we must be off in thirty minutes, as the guests will be arriving for the PCA dinner. Tempers are a little frayed and the sound engineer cops a bit of flack. We managed to run through Paul Carrack's 'How Long' and Steve Harley's 'Make Me Smile', but the rest have to be left to memory and a bit of luck!

- 10.30 p.m. The whole ensemble is waiting in the wings whilst David English, resplendent in white tuxedo, introduces the band one by one. As he calls the guys onto the stage I realise how many people are there. The cheers that greet them onstage are very loud and very close. Phil Tufnell was invited into the band at the last minute to play the triangle, and I remember firmly having to tell him that I wasn't interested in where he was going to come in with his instrument as I had more important things to worry about. Finally, Dave called my name and I strolled out under the lights. A quick four count and we were off with 'I Shot the Sheriff', my dream had come true, a rock star at last!

The Ultimate Accolade

WASIM AKRAM
(Pakistan)

I have opened the bowling with some of the greatest fast bowlers in the history of the game, including Waqar Younis and Shoab Akhtar. It is quite true that fast bowlers hunt best in pairs. Imagine my surprise when making my debut for the Bunburys I proceeded to bowl maiden after maiden, but my fearsome strike partner and Captain got smashed all over the ground including a couple of balls which are still in orbit!

Nonetheless, to compensate I was given the ultimate accolade, a slip cordon of seventeen players. It was truly a memorable debut for me at Alconbury. Quite apart from the fun on the field I know of no other team which would have had an audience consisting of a former Prime Minister, John Major; one of the all-time great umpires in Dickie Bird; the Indian Test Captain Azharuddin; as well as a host of other television celebrities and former cricket stars including Brian Close and David Steele. I hope to carry on representing the Bunburys for many years to come. My only request to David is, can you please go back to coming on as a third change.

What a Laugh!

FRASER HINES

My mobile phone went. 'Fraze,' the voice said, 'Skipper here, what are you doing?' 'I'm driving my horse box picking up two of my yearlings,' I said.

'Let me give you the list of games this season,' said Skipper.

'David, I'm driving a horse box – I've no pen.'

'We've got Kalli playing, Viv Richards' half of the Worcestershire side. "Judge" Smith.' And so it went on.

You could be halfway up Everest and David would be enthusing about the new season. And the enthusiasm rubs off on us. The Bunburys are an enthusiastic lot. And all encouragement we thesps get from the old pros is amazing. Or is it? Are they the real ex-pros or had David looked in the back pages of 'The Stage' and hired look-a-likes? They're too nice and helpful and for me playing with Kalli – Robbo – Hicky – Walshy and Leslie Grantham – Leslie? Oh well you can't win them all. Well here's to a new season with Russell keeping wicket, Tuffers laughing and us all drinking to the girls that come to encourage us in every game.

The David 'Teddy' Thomas Benefit Match at Chesham CC Sunday, 15 August 1999 David Thomas XI V Bunburys XXI

MICKEY STEWART
(Ex-England Manager)

I first knew David English more than twenty-five years ago when he was a handsome blond, finely groomed athlete and no mug as an elegant left-handed bat – believe all that and you will believe anything! Therefore, at his request, it was a pleasure to agree to make this contribution to his book.

But I was aware from past experiences that it would probably involve a period of regular telephone communication with David, something like half a dozen calls averaging a quarter of an hour each call. The content of each call will include two minutes of discussion of the job in hand and thirteen minutes of the latest jokes from the English extensive repertoire – and by the way, the David English 'Watershed' time is 9 o'clock, a.m. not p.m.

The subject of this piece is the benefit match for the former Surrey player David 'Teddy' Thomas, staged at Chesham CC between 'Teddy's' team and David English's Bunbury XXI!

A few years ago David Thomas was diagnosed with

Multiple Sclerosis and with the passing of time it has gradually taken a stronger grip on him which has meant his being chair-bound for the larger part of each day. Typically, Teddy has continued to fight hard and is still active in his business of corporate hospitality and travel.

Surrey County Cricket Club have often supported Teddy's benefit activities and therefore at his request I readily agreed to help him gather his side together to play against David English's Bunbury XXI! It was no great task, for beginning with the peers of his Surrey days I received an immediate positive response from Alan Butcher, Keith Medleycott, Monte Lynch and David Smith. Geoff Howarth had already agreed to captain the side and three of the current Surrey team – Adam Hollioake, Mark Butcher and Alec Stewart – travelled from Taunton, where they had suffered a disappointing Nat West semi-final defeat, to play the Northants contingent of Kevin Curran, Rob Bailey, David Capel and young Graeme Swann. It was some day for Graeme, for it had been announced in the morning that he was in the full England squad for the Test match at the Oval against New Zealand.

The Bunbury XI was made up of the usual star-studded cross section of people from the world of sport and show business with 'himself', David English, as captain of course. Geoff Miller, the former Derbyshire, Essex and England cricketer, and myself donned the umpire's coats to complete the line-up.

It was lovely to see all these people support 'Teddy', some having travelled many miles to do so, and everyone enjoyed the fun. Mind you, we umpires had to keep the field, for their captain liked a comment or discussion after nearly every ball and had this been a county game he would definitely have suffered a very heavy fine for an abysmal overrate!!!

Despite David English's delaying tactics, the 'Teddy' Thomas XI were putting together a very healthy total, but with only a couple or so overs to bat, captain Geoff

Howarth was still waiting in the pavilion with his pads on. Something had to be done to get him to the crease. So when star footballer Ian Wright hit Kevin Curran on the pads and appealed for lbw, despite the fact that it wouldn't have hit another set of stumps down the leg side, I raised the dreaded finger making Kevin the sacrificial lamb!

In addition to getting Geoff Howarth in to bat, my decision was also influenced by the possibility of a couple of free tickets to see West Ham play, but sadly within a couple of weeks Wrighty had gone on loan to Notts. Forest, so no tickets to see Ian play for the Hammers. The match ended in the Bunburys having to taste defeat with their captain delivering yet another reprimand in the dressing room!

The day was a great success for 'Teddy' Thomas and rewarding for the host of stars who had supported him in the event. It wouldn't have happened but for all the efforts of Chesham CC, all the supporters and 'himself', David English, he's 'tom drawer'.

All the best,

Mickey Stewart

The Bunbury Skipper

DEVON MALCOLM
(Derby CCC and England)

Throughout the history of the game of cricket there have been some outstanding captains. Some have been known for their ability to read the game, like Mike Brearley; others for the way that they have led their sides by example, like Viv Richards. But surely the most devious captain in the history of the game must be David English.

If he thinks he has got a fast bowler who is going to take the edge of the bat and provide a catch to a slip fielder then the David English School of Captaincy makes sure that you've got nineteen slips! If a batsman is looking well set how do you distract him? The answer is you put Samantha Fox on to bowl. If you think the opposition looks mean and fit then the answer is to start chatting to them before the game, making sure their wine glasses are constantly refilled. It is this most unusual and entertaining reading of the game by David and the Bunburys that has made turning out for them a pleasure.

I highly recommend that anybody who thinks that cricket is a dull and slow game spend an afternoon watching or playing with the Bunburys. I certainly intend to spend many more summers playing for them. And David, it is not having nineteen slips that counts – it is whether or not they catch the ball!

What do Dominic Cork, Darren Gough, Philip Defreitas, Angus Fraser and Samantha Fox have in common? Answer: they have all opened the bowling with me.

The only difference is, when I play with the boys, I take the new ball. When I turned out for the Bunburys at Oundle School, Sam took it. That remains the only time in my career I have opened the bowling and not taken the new ball.

And do you know what? Sam bowled better than me. Every ball was on a length.

I love playing for the Bunburys because it gives me a chance to meet my heroes. After Sam, Ian Wright is the best non-cricketer I have played with. He is so keen, just like he is when he played for Arsenal. He gives the ball a mighty whack and is brilliant in the field.

Afterwards, everybody has a drink and a chat. It is the one event I try to make space for in my diary. After Derby and England, the Bunburys are my favourite team.

Regards,

Devon Malcolm

Supremo David

CHRIS SMITH
(Hants CCC and England)

*During my professional cricketing days, I had heard much of
the Bunburys and longed for a call from 'Supremo David' in
respect of an appearance . . . Sadly one was never
forthcoming and it took eight full years following my
retirement for my quite considerable spin bowling and
fielding to be finally recognised.*

*My debut was as part of the famous Bunbury 7.
Supremo David tried to assure the assembled ageing athletes
that normally 27 turned up . . . I can only assume that news
of my inclusion had filtered out.*

*Playing against the might of the Kevan James Benefit XI,
which included sloggers like Robin Smith (I mean big hitters),
would have been a difficult task for 11 fit men . . . but for 7
ageing sporting geniuses it was a little more difficult.*

*The opening bowling partnership of Joe Cuby and Huw
Williams extracted good pace and movement from a benign
wicket but with the opposition reaching 100 without loss in 8
overs, I concluded finally that we had been a little out of luck.*

*The famous 7 soldiered on manfully and in very
demanding circumstances we were constantly mesmerised
and motivated by the 'Skipper's' quite wonderful and
emotional team talks.*

*I felt that the target of slightly less than 400 in
approximately 35 overs was a demanding one, particularly
in the light of 5 first-class bowlers all eager to get at us.*

*The 'Skipper', Joe Cuby, and our photographer David
Betteridge set a great example to the remaining 4 batsmen,
and having all contributed manfully to the daunting task I*

*was finally at the crease requiring 16 runs off the last over
... an over being bowled by my younger brother Robin.*

*Sadly, what would have been one of the most
extraordinary victories of all time was scuppered due to my
inability to ease the 'younger Smith' over the boundary for a
second successive occasion.*

*Soldiering on so manfully with 7 dedicated athletes
taught us all valuable lessons ... I have little doubt that we
shall all find the game of cricket significantly easier with a
normal complement.*

All the best,

Chris Smith

Proud to Be a Bunbury

MARK RAMPRAKASH
(Middlesex, Surrey CCC and England)

I am only too pleased to put down on paper the sincere gratitude I owe David English and the Bunbury cricket team. I remember all those summers ago watching Test cricket on TV as an innocent 7-year-old; seeing my hero, Viv Richards, scoring runs with dazzling stroke play, such style and confidence; then going back out onto a rough concrete driveway and trying to emulate the sheer joy of batting I had just witnessed.

In later years I was lucky enough to play on opposing teams against the best batsman ever to walk the planet. However, imagine my excitement when I turned up at a little cricket ground in Northampton and I am down to play on the same side as him. Not only does he nonchalantly take a running catch on the boundary but he is down to bat at number 3 and I'm opening. Now this is no slight on Mike Gatting, but for me to bat with Viv he's got to go.

Unfortunately, or fortunately depending on your point of view, Gatt is taken out of the equation, lbw in the 1st over to Paul Taylor. The *great* man cruises to the wicket in his unmistakable style . . . *he's* in control. Taylor comes in and lets go a full in swinging delivery. Viv, who is so still at the crease, comes forward and plays a graceful push drive through mid-off that races for four to the longest boundary. Of course I meet midpitch with I.V.A. Richards, sharing big grins and high fives!

The Bunbury cricket days are great for all the family to enjoy but I never lose sight that ultimately it all happens for good causes. How does David English do it? He is a remarkable man who puts so much time and energy into fundraising every year, a *real* gent. Thanks David for giving me the opportunity of saying I'm proud to be part of the Bunbury's.

Drop the Dead Donkey

DICKIE BIRD, MBE

I always enjoy umpiring the Bunbury Celebrity Cricket Team matches. They are always very enjoyable games, with plenty of fun, and they raise lots of money for charity and provide a tremendous amount of support and help for schools alike, which has produced cricketers who have gone on to play for England.

The Bunbury Cricket Team is led by David English, one of the greatest captains in the history of the game. David does a tremendous amount of work for charity and schools cricket.

I spent a wonderful and very enjoyable day on Friday, 16 July 1999 at Alconbury where I umpired Norma Major's XI v Bunbury XI for Mencap. It was a great day and the match ended in a tie. I think the scores were 350 to each team.

*It was there that I saw the great captain David English
come into action. With Norma Major's X1 on 250 for no
wicket, after the opening batsman had seen off Wasim
Akram of Pakistan and Paul Taylor of Northants and
England, David decided to bring that great Donkey Drop
bowler on, Joe Cuby, and he played tricks with Donkey
Drops, that went higher than a space ship.* He put Charlie
Palmer, the old Leicestershire cricketer, to shame; he once
bowled Surrey out at Leicestershire with Donkey Drops.
Joe turned the game, with balls that dropped onto the off
stump.

*With that, David removed him from the attack, to give
the batting side a chance. Then, with my advice, the great
captain English brought Lloyd Honeyghan into the attack,
and removed him from the attack after one over.* 'Poor
soul', he had only gone for 26.

*I was very impressed with the fielding that day. Graham
Kelly fielded magnificently at mid-on, where they were
running threes to him, and it was not his fault the ball kept
going through his legs.*

*The captain asked Rod Farrant to take his sweater after
two balls because he thought he was throwing the ball.*

*It was nice to see Brian Close and David Steele still
playing. Steele has not changed much; he asked me if I could
lend him something.* He did not buy me a drink. *They could
not get Brian out, he retired,* old age.

*John Kettley said it would rain because I was umpiring.
I told him the sun would shine, and it did. He did not last
long when he was batting, Joe did him with a Donkey Drop.*

*I thought it was a tremendous piece of captaincy by
David English to keep the batting team down to 350 for 1
wicket. Well done David.*

*It was very sad when the day came to an end, but it was
a wonderful day enjoyed by everyone. It was so nice to see
all the celebrities there . . . from all walks of life. Well done
to them all for giving up their time to help a tremendous*

cause. I think we made a bob or two for Mencap. Well done lads.

I very much enjoyed my day. It was good to be out there in the middle once again with all those stars and to be part of the Bunbury Celebrity Cricket Club.

One of the funniest parts of the day was when Joe bowled his first ball, which was hit for four, and I shouted, 'take him off,' to a tremendous moan and laughter from the crowd. It was a day I will always cherish and remember.

Best wishes,

Dickie Bird

'Love from Emmerdale'

CHRIS CHITTELL

When first encountering David English and the Bunburys my thoughts were they had a high opinion of themselves. Ten years on and they still have a high opinion of themselves and quite rightly too. Anyone who will give up their only free day of the week to accrue money for various charitable causes deserves praise indeed. Ah! you might say. Come on, it's a jolly, get over to the venue night before, get ratted, get lucky, stay Sunday night, home in the morning. Well, that night is for some of the England side – Hush my tongue. But most of these guys are a bit long in the tooth for all that. Now hang on, that does not constitute being old. Wives and families are dragged to the four corners of our cricketing world. Giving the impression of contentness would be an understatement.

To wit, one Sunday in October 1999, twenty-four players of all shapes and sizes descended upon a little place not far from York – all there to support the Bunburys and

*more so their captain. A great credit to you David English!
That is enough. It goes against the grain to be
complimentary to anyone other than myself, even more so
when he who must be obeyed forces me to bowl. Not a
pretty sight to say the least. Nevertheless, it is a joy to play
with these guys, as it is to play against them.*

*Good cricket. Good humour. Great vibes. Long may
they reign?*

All the best.

Smudger Remembers

DAVID SMITH
(Surrey CCC and England)

'Hello Smudger, it's Mickey here.' A call from the manager Mickey
Stewart asking me to play in a game for David Thomas, an ex-Surrey
colleague who sadly suffers from MS.

The game was to be against the Bunburys. I'd last played for
the Bunburys at the Oval in the VE day game and hadn't heard
from David English since. I presumed that I hadn't performed well
enough and that he had been looking at younger players in the
interim.

On meeting at the ground at Chesham I was greeted by the sight
of at least twelve International cricketers and then Dave English.

'Dave Boy, it's great to see you, come and have a drink.' I
thought, nothing's changed.

When I meet Dave we're always recounting Harrogate some
years ago when Dave, Ray Barker from Surrey and I were out for a
drink. On leaving the wine bar we were confronted by a policewoman who asked us to be a little quieter.

Dave seemed to think that the policewoman was a hoax and
proceeded to play around with her. I think it was whilst telling one

of his now famous jokes that she produced her warrant card and we sobered up very quickly.

The Bunburys are great fun to play with and do so much fine work. Long may they continue!

Thanks Dave and Joe.

Show us your growler.

Dedicated to a Worthy Cause

STUART LAMPITT
(Worcestershire CCC)

When David asked me to put an article together for his book, first I thought what a privilege to be asked to contribute to such a worthy cause, and then my thoughts turned to the tremendous amount of time and dedication 'the Loon' puts in for the organisation – as this year happens also to be my own Benefit Year at Worcestershire CCC and there will be a constant battle to organise teams, especially one as upmarket as this! Congratulations Loon.

I first met 'the Loon' way back in the 'halcyon days' of Worcestershire cricket, in the late eighties/early nineties, when the boundary boards were reverberating to the sound of another Botham home run, and the huge crowds were being entertained royally by cricketers of the highest order.

I must admit that as a teenage youngster trying to make his way into the first-class cricket arena, watching people such as Botham, Dilley, Hick, Moody and Radford at their best plying their trade in the sacred turf, and then walking off to be greeted by Eric Clapton, Elton John and the rest of Beefy's entourage, was a little daunting at first, but in 1989 my chance came and fortunately, as they say, the rest is history.

The lessons learned and the confidence instilled by mixing, watching and competing with these players was second to none. I regard myself as being very fortunate to have been a part of Worcestershire cricket, not only through those successful times but also in later years. New Road is, and always will be, one of the most picturesque grounds to both play and watch cricket. We are really spoiled at Worcestershire. It has been a pleasure to arrive at the ground and look out of the home team dressing rooms and view the surrounding beauty for so long. Motivation has never been a problem!

One of the first memories I have of meeting 'the Loon' was during the famous Ian Botham East Coast Walk. Mark Scott (now Youth Development Officer at Worcestershire CCC) and myself had decided to join the walk for two days. 'The Loon' happened to be Beefy's travelling companion, keeping him entertained throughout the constant day-to-day hardship of walking (near-jogging at Beefy's pace!) the length of the East Coast.

Beefy, however, made the mistake of giving 'the Loon' the job of drumming up interest, keeping everybody entertained and informing the little villages in the north-east of the country that Ian Botham was about to walk through town. That's OK but when you put a *loudspeaker* in the hands of a nutter, all hell breaks loose!

These little villages certainly got a wake-up call. How somebody can talk constantly through a loudspeaker all day and every day is unbelievable. 'Loon', you certainly kept yourself, Mark Scott and the rest of the troop entertained on our little saunter from Middlesborough to Whitby, so much so, that at the end of the day it was the aching jaw and ribs from laughing so much that were in need of treatment, not the feet! During the walk you also did a wonderful job for Leukaemia Research; as you are doing for various charities and concerns, with the Bunburys, especially for English cricket.

As always, it is a pleasure to contribute towards the Bunburys as you highlight, amongst other worthy causes, an area of English cricket that is vitally important: Youth Development. I've certainly had, and continue to have, the fortune of enjoying a successful and happy career at Worcestershire, thanks to a lot of people who helped me and gave me opportunities in the past.

At the moment I am also part of the Youth Development Team at Worcestershire CCC, and see, day-to-day, the importance of providing opportunity for our kids to play and enjoy the game. We certainly need to go back to grass roots and attract more youngsters into the game and provide more encouragement for them to compete. Over the years, the Bunburys have certainly helped in no small way, with cricket festivals and the fantastic ground-breaking Youth World Cup, 'the Costcutter Under-15 World Challenge'.

Loon, long may your input and good work go on, and I look forward to our next encounter on the turf!

Never a Dull Moment

JONATHAN WILLS
(Willsy ITN *London Tonight*)

Of course everyone has heard of the Bunburys! The millions raised for youth cricket . . . their colourful leader . . . the impressive array of talent that turns out for the cause all over the country. So when the call came for me to make my debut, the answer was of course yes. But was it to be a normal cricket match – most definitely . . . NO!

For a start there was what I believed must have been the traditional Bunbury welcoming ritual. The normal introductions were followed by the handing-out of the Bunbury shirt (a prized possession in cricket circles) and of course a bar of Coal Tar soap . . . yes as in yellow and with a distinctive smell. What was a new Bunbury to do with such an item? Clearly one did not want to offend on such an important debut but this part had not been explained at all! Fortunately at this point David English was telling a story which, involving a number of high-class celebrities and much hand waving by the teller, had grabbed everyone's attention giving me the perfect opportunity to hide the soap in my cricket bag.

After that the rest of the game at the delightful Wisborough Green went off without a hitch. Well almost. Determined to make a good impression I set off to save a boundary off the skipper's highly impressive medium pace (I'll take the first over next season skip!) and with the ball about to cross the line there was nothing for it but to bring out the obligatory dive. What I failed to see in my blinkered state of concentration was the park bench in front with a couple and a dog sitting on it.

Clearly the couple thought that it was all part of the Bunbury entertainment as I slid towards them . . . under them . . . and out the other side to emerge dusty but with the ball and to their somewhat bemused and polite applause! The rest of the debut went off without hitch . . . I bowled in tandem with Phil Tufnell . . . doesn't everyone! And for the remainder of the season the distinctive scent of Coal Tar was never far away from my kit but I had been well and truly bitten by the Bunbury bug!

For those taking part in the Costcutter Under-15 World Challenge, congratulations on selection for your respective countries. Without doubt it will be a competition to remember and with the flair and enthusiasm of David English at the helm I am sure it will be as memorable as the senior equivalent.

The only advice I would give to all those taking part is to truly enjoy the wonderful Bunbury Festival. In my role as sports presenter of *London Tonight* I am all too aware of the problems facing English cricket and how depressed both players and spectators are. For many, the fun has gone out of the game and now it is up to the next generation to show that not only can England win again but that they can do it with a smile on their faces.

Liam's Choice

LIAM BOTHAM
(Hampshire CCC and England U-15s)

I well remember the Bunbury Festival of 1992 when I represented the North at Charterhouse. I then went on to play for the HMC XI against ESCA, very much hoping to be chosen for the England side to play against a South African touring side in a series of one-day and three-day Test matches.

With a combination of skill, a little luck and a following wind I achieved this ambition and embarked, I thought, on my chosen path, towards a cricketing career.

Five years later I found that the path had a fork and that the signpost pointing to the right had 'Rugby' written on it – not the town, the game! I was finding that it was becoming impossible to play both sports at a high level and realised that the time had come to make a decision. I hope I never again have to make such a difficult one. Eventually I chose the path that forked to the right.

I shall greatly miss my Hampshire teammates and will experience a sense of something lost when the new cricket season starts. However, I intend to play as much as possible, not least with the Bunbury XI alongside the founder of that prestigious team.

When professional county cricket left me hardly any time to continue my association with the Bunburys I greatly missed the repartee enjoyed in that slip cordon of Duncan, Botham, English and Keeble (Robert, Liam, David and John respectively). I wish I could share it with you but much of it is unrepeatable! I look forward to picking up the threads of these educational conversations again, though I fear that in view of advancing years and failing eyesight our captain may have to find a less demanding fielding position.

Cricket is a great game. I shall never cease to be involved in it at some level until I am too old to hold a bat. I have learned a lot from it and I don't mean just how to play it. It is a good way to meet new friends and to have great times both on and off the field. I have already found that the only way to succeed is to work hard at your chosen sport whatever it may turn out to be.

Who was it that once said, 'The only place where success comes before work is in a dictionary'?

Bunbury School's Magic

JACK SIMMONS
(President of Lancashire CCC)

It is a pleasure to say a few words in the Bunbury's brochure. It can't be stressed enough how important under-age and schoolboys cricket is, even to our National game. It is the foundation for it.

Many, many years ago I had the good fortune of competing in Under-15s schoolboy cricket in Lancashire. This culminated in representing my County, on the great Old Trafford ground. It was absolutely fabulous and gave me the motivation to try and make County cricket as a professional. This I did, and after 22 years as a first-class player for Lancashire, I still did not want to finish or retire. All good things come to an end though, but it is still a privilege and great honour to continue in cricket as Chairman of Lancashire County Cricket Club.

Every youngster needs help, guidance, sponsorship and a little luck to arrive on the scene at the right time. This is why every youngster who competes in the Bunbury's English Schools Cricket Festival will be seen by the right people and will have every chance of progress to the England Schoolboys side, and maybe much further, to a dream, similar to mine.

We all owe a great deal of gratitude to David English and everyone connected to the Bunbury's Cricket Organisation, for giving this chance to so many.

David English

Bunburying

MATTHEW ENGEL
(Editor of *Wisden Almanack*)

*Bunburying has many different moods. Sometimes it can
mean helping old cricketers as well as young ones.*

*Winston Davis is 40 (which isn't old unless you happen
to be about 14) and in the 1980s was one of the world's best
and fastest bowlers. He played only 15 Test matches because
he came from the Caribbean island of St Vincent and in that
era the West Indies had more top-class fast bowlers than
some countries (England, for instance) get in the average
half-century.*

*He was good enough to capture the World Cup record
bowling analysis (seven for 51 against Australia), break a
few fingers and make a lot of friends, both at the
international level and with Glamorgan and
Northamptonshire. He was always a religious man, and in
November 1997 he was back on St Vincent helping to build
a church when he fell from a tree he was trying to cut down.*

*It was only an eight-foot fall; normally you would feel
sorry for yourself if you broke an ankle. But, by terrible
fluke, Winston was left a tetraplegic, meaning he was
completely paralysed in both his arms and legs.*

*It took him a year to get out of hospital. But his
response to this terrible adversity was amazing: 'I don't ask
"Why me?" A quarter of a million people in Britain have
disabilities. Why not me?' Unfortunately, cricket, which
gives benefits to the able-bodied almost as a matter of
routine, had no provision for someone like this who had
retired from the game.*

Readers of the Guardian *and also* Wisden Cricket

Monthly *responded with outstanding generosity when they heard about his plight. This enabled Winston to buy a specially adapted vehicle so he could get about. Then enter the Bunburys. I moaned to David English that I would like to run a benefit game somewhere but I was completely hopeless and no one would help and blah-blah-blah.*

Twenty minutes later he was back on the phone: 'Attention, hands out of pockets . . . The Bunbury's will be playing a Winston Davis XI at Finedon in Northamptonshire on May 23; Canada Life will be sponsoring; Viv Richards and Allan Lamb will be playing, you will be doing this; so-and-so will be doing that; and it won't rain, I've fixed it . . . All clear? At ease.'

And so it all happened. It was a fantastic day. Everyone at Finedon worked their socks off. Loads of great players turned out on the field. Viv (Sir Vivian now to be exact) creamed a few through the covers and took a catch that proved you don't lose the knack; Norman Cowans (ex-Middlesex and England) took an even better catch; Rory Bremner did a wonderfully funny commentary; half the England team came along to say Hi to Winston even though they had just been walloped by South Africa the day before; and Samantha Fox promised to auction her bra – but somehow we never quite got round to that.

And about £25,000 was raised to try and help ensure that Winston can live the rest of his life in dignity and as much comfort as possible. That's Bunburying.

Anyone who wishes to provide any further help for Winston, or even just write him a letter, please contact me at The Oaks, Newton St Margaret's, Hertfordshire HR2 0QN (Donations to 'The Winston Davis Fund'.)

Best Wishes.

I'll Bat at Number 11

KEVIN PIETERSEN
(Hants CCC and England)

The Bunbury Cricket Club is something you hear about long before you see one of their games.

The name of the club reaches far and wide, and when you see the names that have pulled on the shirt, it was an honour for me to be approached to play. Those who know David English also know that there was not much of a discussion involved. It was more like I was told rather than asked (I have since found out that David's other name is 'Loon'!). When he said he might be able to find a spot for me at number 11, and that I would have to turn up for a net, I knew this was no standard club side!

There are an awful lot of charity organisations these days, all with great causes. The Bunbury's club has raised over £9 million for various charities and organisations and helped to develop the game at grass roots level, so it is a fantastic cause to be involved with. Considering the amount of time we get off during the summer, you can see how important this is to players and celebrities who support this club.

So I look forward to my Bunbury trial at some point during the summer, and hope that the Loon can see fit to find me a spot at number 11. Having heard about his running between the wickets, I might just offer my services to do the scoring!

Keep up all the great work.

(March 2005)

High Jinks in Budapest

MARK CHILTON
(Lancs CCC)

It has been a few years since I first came across David
English at Charterhouse School in 1992. I was representing
the North of England in the Bunbury Festival and remember
the experience quite vividly. The team had some great games
against the other regions and I had many laughs along the
way. The week holds fond memories for me and it is an
honour to be part of the many players who have gone on
from that festival to enjoy successful first-class careers. I
think our team alone included Andrew Flintoff, Gareth
Batty and Matthew Hoggard.

The Bunbury Festival is a great opportunity for quality
young cricketers to get together and compete against each
other. It was certainly crucial in my development both as a
cricketer and as a person. It also gave me the belief that I
was good enough to play at that level and after that festival
my cricket really began to take shape and become something
I was determined to be involved in for a long time.

Unfortunately my meetings with David have not been as
frequent as I would like since then, so it was great to share a
few drinks recently in Budapest whilst celebrating Freddie's
stag party. It was clear from the party that David's
enthusiasm for life has not diminished at all, I am sure I
caught a glimpse of him hurling a chicken leg down the table
to some unsuspecting diner as we all rolled back the years
and had a great big food fight! It is great to be around
someone who shows such a passion for everything he does
and it rubs off on all those around him, even encouraging
myself and Mal Loye to have a competition to see who

could hit the great ex-Man. Utd right back, Viv Anderson,
with a handful of peanuts!

I would like to take this opportunity to wish all the
players at this year's Bunbury all the best; I hope you all
have an enjoyable week.

'Chilt' (March 2005)

To Win my Bunbury Cap

STEVE HARMISON
(Durham CCC and England)

It's good to be back from England's tour to South Africa.
The last year has been good for me and the England team.
However, after a disappointing three months personally I'm
now looking ahead to the Ashes.

I have played 30 tests and 20 ODI's and with over 100
first-class games for Durham the Bunbury's cap seems to be
the toughest cap to get but I will get there in the near future.

Best wishes David for the Bunbury Festival ahead and
good luck to all who take part. Hopefully by the end of the
season I will have won my Bunbury cap and England will
have won the Ashes.

Cheers!

Stephen Harmison

(September 2004)

Two Great Bunbury Festivals

BEN HARMISON
(Durham CCC)

*The two Bunbury Festivals I played in were very enjoyable
and helped a great deal when it came to touring with
England U-19's (Bangladesh World Cup, India 2005).*

*I played at Taunton 2000 and Winchester where my
team mates were Tom Smith and David Griffiths. Also in
the team was Mark Lawson, whom I roomed with in India
for far too long!!*

*India was a great education of cricket and a good but
tough place to tour.*

*Thanks David for the two weeks I enjoyed with the
Bunburys and good luck to all involved in this year's
festival.*

Best wishes,

Ben Harmison

Boot Hill

GRAHAM THORPE
(Surrey CCC and England)

What a great winter the boys had in SA.

*Our first was down there in 40-odd years and some
great performances by the boys too.*

Everyone did something special when we needed it and

that's what got us the victory, which we know gives so much pleasure to people who follow the game.

I see a big change in the English game. The biggest being that short leg is now occupied by the senior player in the team! Hussain has got to take a lot of the blame for that one surely!

'Boot Hill.' The final resting place for the senior pro! I feel honoured though. Look at the heroes who went before me – Hussain, Atherton, Gooch, Gatting – what were they thinking when they volunteered!!

Still, I have to say if it wasn't for Micky Vaughan ordering me to get in there that 100th Test catch may never have come along (every cloud . . .).

Dave, it's fun under the lid, everyone should try it one day. They say you have to be a little mad to do it. I think I know who would be good there too!! D— E—.

From England No. 1 short leg! To England No. 1 Top man Loon!

Best wishes,

Thorpey

Dear David,

Thank you for all your great help. We have really enjoyed playing for the Bunbury's this year and greatly appreciate your time and effort, which makes this great team possible. We love your jokes both on and off the field and can't wait to play next year. We hope you have a very good Christmas and keep well.

> *You are the captain and your name is skip,*
> *You do what you want so you field at slip,*
> *You like to joke and muck around,*
> *In the changing room and on the ground.*
> *You make us feel like Bunburys in every game,*

And treat every player exactly the same,
We've got some great memories of playing with you,
So all we can say David is
THANK YOU.

From
Arjun (Arji), Vishal (Vishi) and Froggy (aged 17, 16 and 16)

This season playing for the Bunburys was by far the most
enjoyable cricket of my summer. I had loads of fun both on
and off the field. I loved the atmosphere in the changing
room and best of all I made lots of new friends. The most
amazing thing I found playing for the Bunburys was that
even before the game I was playing in had finished, I was
already looking forward to the next game.

I have learned so much from David English about what
it takes to be a true Bunbury. CHEERS skip.

Thanks to all of my fellow Bunburys with whom I share
such great memories. I really look forward to meeting
everyone next season.

Arjun Patel (17)

I have truly enjoyed playing for the Bunbury's this summer.
I very much enjoyed spending time and meeting other people
within the Bunbury's team and also the opposition teams.
Playing with the Bunbury's has enabled me to gain more
confidence in my performances.

David English has inspired me to become a true
Bunbury player and has inspired me to continue playing
with the team. I look forward to the next Bunbury season
and meeting up with my friends within the Bunbury team.

Thanks David English and the rest of the Bunbury team
for all the effort and making me feel welcome in the team.

Vishal Patel (16)

I am proud to confirm that we will continue to raise vital funds for the disadvantaged whilst showcasing the talents of our famous players in our fun-filled Bunbury Days for all the families throughout the world . . . And remember . . .

> *A Bunbury stands for freedom, stands for fun,*
> *Stands for ever being young;*
> *So do a good turn unto others,*
> *Never turn from your quest,*
> *For you are a Bunbury*
> *And a Bunbury does his best.*

Dr David English, MBE

PART THREE

Final Thoughts

Mother and Lover

I'm flippin' through your photo albums and understanding the years that have ticked by in your face . . . Just sitting on the couch, sinking snug, listening to Barry Gibb.

The Sneakers lying barefoot in the hall as the kiddies drift off to dreamland and I am left to look at these pictures which express the sign of your times, baby's first step, looking up at her mum for love and support, caught, in a moment of helpless emotion and fragrant memory . . .

And all the time the mighty sea crashes against this boiling land, cooling us down so we can sleep and look forward to another day when I can hold your hand and together move forward to paint our picture of a worthwhile tomorrow.

The sound of the sea rushing through my head, bathing my brain with its deafening presence and the wind blowing in from the Cape whistles through the beach huts of St James, empty shells of summer dreams.

Today, we ate mussels from an earthenware pot, washed them down with Chardonnay from Stellenbosch and all the time I was consumed by you and your beautiful face and the fleeting glance of a child.

Cape Town 2003

The Tree of Life

I stand here as lonely as a tree,
Naked on the hill for all to see.
Branches, like fingers
Against a troubled sky.
Memories that linger,
The Red Balloon,
The wind on high.

Sounds of the children
Carry on the summer breeze,
To other meadows
Circled by trees.
Lovers carve their initials
Under a Hunters' moon,
Sad September arrives
Time to go, so soon.

I used to know another tree,
Just over there,
Not unlike me.
I watched its seasons come and go,
I watched it breathing to and fro.
We almost touched, its branches and mine
But now it's gone . . .

The sap that weeps
And tears apart,
To testify the tree of life
Its broken heart.
The leaves that fall
And kiss the ground,
Those tears of mine
That turn to brown.

I look down and see
The children play
But they don't see
And I can't say.
It's sad September,
And time to go
Gone are my friends
On the wings to fly
And the roots to grow.

I stand here as lonely as a tree,
One so many
Just like me.
And soon like them
I shall not be
The tree of life
No more.

Zimbabwe

Wide of girth, after birth
the bag ladies sashay past the jacarandas
with their babes in tow
and buses bursting at the seams
roar on to Harare
to disperse the dreams
of the young boys selling peas
and metal work effigies
of hippos in threes.

Hard nose the highway
that belies the fears;
let the good conquer evil
and roll back the years.

Pray for this land,
guide and protect them
with a gentle hand.

Lead them to safety
from the rulers that rule
with their meanness and greed
the insanity of a fool.

Rekindle the spirit that
still flickers strong in the
hearts and minds of the
elders for so long.

For yours is the wisdom and
goodness God planned
to bring peace and happiness
back to this land.

More lines from Zimbabwe

Two little water babies
swimming in the pool
filled with the joys
of an afternoon delight
two little blondies
exhuming pleasure
rich in promise
blissful treasure.

As the days of summer slip by with
the fleeting glimpse of the swallow that
soars northwards to warmer climes
high on the winds from Africa
the breeze in the trees
the warm whisper through the branches
bends the leopard's ear
and rallies the lion from endless sleep.

The cool breath kisses this parched earth
and with it brings the birth
of another chance to succeed
together or apart
to face tomorrow with the
same beating heart.

David English

Our Family

The winds in the wires
the termite spires
the dusty trail 'neath a hunters' moon
where children link hands and
walk barefoot with gran
and super slim Bob and sexy young Rob
and a thousand dogs to
the sounds of a September song
the trees with stark fingers
stand in rings of fire
the workers don't linger
but return home on bicycles
from the day's toil of hours
amongst the flowers
and all this time I shuffle
along content in the knowledge
that our family is strong.

Make My Day

And the maid by day
disappears to her home
with food in her hands
and love in her heart
to feed her little boy
a bundle of fun
who runs stiffly with an exuberant smile
to his loving mum
and stares with a steady gaze
to feel the strength of his mother
through the September haze
'make my day'
maidei
make us laugh and smile
and teach us what it is to be an African.
To do the simple things well
to be loyal and true
patient and trim in an apron
without shoe
to protect and shield
the children by night
as they sleep under the silver moon
eyes closed tight
to dream of the swimming pool
and racing cars
and cuddles with mum
and grandmamas.

The wind that whistles
is the breath of a child
that sweeps through the city
from the land of the wild.

David English

How I miss my children
their little hands
the tears that fall
from a heart that weeps
when their daddy calls
how many sleeps
till I see you dad?

The garden lies empty and still
the cries of the children
have died in the setting sun
which stands as a red disc in the sky;
gone are the memories of our summer dreams
the joyous expectancy of a tousled face
the depth of feeling that abounds this place
in our small corner of Africa.

Midday sun and the dogs have searched
for the shadows to stretch out and
recharge from their constant patrol.
The weaver birds flutter busily above their nests
watched by the kingfisher atop his pole
and the yellow hammer twitters from the telephone line
just the sounds of silence and the
incessant rasp of the crickets in time and here I am in England
torn apart to grieve for my children
with a heavy heart.

Monkey Town

Food *amongst the flowers*
Gazing out to sea for hours and hours
Having time to think and revaluate
And get the picture back in perspective
To prioritise and focus on the main objective to feel the
    young hearts beating in the room

And the wonderful reassuring sounds of the teacups tinkling
    with mum
Who stands there blonde and soft
A crumpled joy of skin and bones
And ever increasing tum.

I'm taking the caterpillar train to Monkey Town
I'm going to slip through the surf when no one's around
I'll trek to the mountains for their wisdom
And I'll sit by the magic pond to ponder on the past that has
    slipped through our fingers
Like the fine yellow sand
And we'll eat food amongst the flowers
Isn't life grand.

David English

Last Game of the Summer

The last Beatles song has been played,
The monkey has ground to a halt
The bouncy castle has lost its puff
and the Mayors XI have had enough.
So it's off to the Cricketers
For a Guinness or three.
See you next year at Bun Bury!